RESEARCH IN URBAN ECONOMICS

Volume 4 • 1984

THE CHANGING ECONOMIC AND FISCAL STRUCTURE

RESEARCH IN URBAN ECONOMICS

A Research Annual

THE CHANGING ECONOMIC AND
FISCAL STRUCTURE

Guest Editor: **ROBERT D. EBEL**
Executive Director
State of Minnesota Tax
Study Commission

Series Editor: **J. VERNON HENDERSON**
Department of Economics
Brown University

VOLUME 4 • 1984

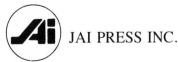 JAI PRESS INC.

Greenwich, Connecticut   *London, England*

CONTENTS

LIST OF CONTRIBUTORS   vii

EDITOR'S INTRODUCTION
Robert D. Ebel   xi

STRUCTURAL CHANGES IN ADVANCED
ECONOMIES AND THEIR IMPACT ON CITIES
IN THE 1980s
Bertrand Renaud   1

URBAN ECONOMIC AND DEMOGRAPHIC
CHANGE: RECENT SHIFTS AND
FUTURE PROSPECTS
Kathryn P. Nelson   25

DEMOGRAPHIC CHANGE AND URBAN FINANCE:
THE OUTLOOK FOR THE 1980s
Philip L. Clay   51

THE INFLUENCE OF COMMUNICATIONS AND
DATA PROCESSING TECHNOLOGY ON
URBAN FORM
Benjamin Chinitz   67

UPPER INCOME RESIDENTIAL REVIVAL IN THE CITY:
SOME LESSONS FROM THE 1960s AND 1970s
FOR THE 1980s
Clifford R. Kern   79

DISAMENITIES, LOCAL TAXATION, AND THE
INTRAMETROPOLITAN LOCATION OF
HOUSEHOLDS AND FIRMS
Michael J. Wasylenko   97

CREATING NEW JOBS FOR OLDER CITIES:
THE ROLE OF THE PUBLIC SECTOR
*George A. Reigeluth,, Susan J. MacCracken and
David L. Birch*   117

TOWARD A MORE PRODUCTIVE MUNICIPAL
GOVERNMENT
Werner Z. Hirsch 133

CHANGING FEDERAL-LOCAL RELATIONS IN A
PERIOD OF FISCAL AUSTERITY
Albert J. Davis and Nonna A. Noto 147

THE STRUCTURAL CHARACTER OF FEDERAL AID:
AN EXAMINATION OF FISCAL IMPACT
Robert M. Stein 167

AMERICA'S INTERGOVERNMENTAL SYSTEM:
AN EXPANDED ROLE FOR THE STATES?
Henry A. Coleman and Colin L. Wood 187

LOCAL GOVERNMENT REVENUE: TAX RELIANCE,
REVENUE DIVERSIFICATION, AND
METROPOLITAN FINANCE
Ronald C. Fisher and Janet E. Kohlhase 205

THE POST MUNICIPAL CITY
Anthony H. Pascal 229

URBAN GOVERNMENT EXPENDITURES
IN THE 1980s
David L. Puryear and John P. Ross 243

HOUSE PRICES AND LOCAL GOVERNMENT
ACTIVITY
Michael J. Lea and Michael S. Johnson 257

FEDERAL GRANTS TO LOCAL GOVERNMENTS
AND CHANGES IN THE PROPERTY TAX
*Robert M. Buckley, Lily Ann Marden and
John C. Simonson* 273

MANAGING PROGRAM TRANSITION:
TAKING HOUSING VOUCHERS SERIOUSLY
AS A NATIONAL PROGRAM
John M. Quigley 289

INDEX 307

LIST OF CONTRIBUTORS

David L. Birch

Program on Neighborhood and
Regional Change, Massachusetts
Institute of Technology

Robert M. Buckley

Chief Economist
U.S. Department of Housing and
Urban Development

Benjamin Chinitz

College of Management Science
University of Lowell

Philip L. Clay

Joint Center for Urban Studies
Massachusetts Institute of
Technology and Harvard University

Henry A. Coleman

Office of the Chief Economist
U.S. General Accounting Office

Albert J. Davis

U.S. Advisory Commission on
Intergovernmental Relations

Ronald C. Fisher

Department of Economics
Michigan State University

Werner Z. Hirsch

Department of Economics
University of California,
Los Angeles

Michael S. Johnson

Department of Economics and
Finance
University of New Orleans

Clifford R. Kern

Department of Economics
State University of New York,
Binghamton

Janet E. Kohlhase

Department of Economics
University of Houston

Michael J. Lea

Federal Home Loan Mortgage
    Corporation
Washington, D.C.

Susan J. MacCracken

Program on Neighborhood and
    Regional Change,
Massachusetts Institute of
Technology

Lily Ann Marden

Department of Economics
University of Massachusetts

Kathryn P. Nelson

Office of Economic Affairs
U.S. Department of Housing and
    Urban Development

Nonna A. Noto

Congressional Research Service
Library of Congress

Anthony H. Pascal

The Rand Corporation
Santa Monica, California

David L. Puryear

Public Policy Program
Johns Hopkins University

John M. Quigley

Graduate School of Public Affairs
University of California, Berkeley

George A. Reigeluth

Arthur D. Little, Inc.
Cambridge, Massachusetts

Bertrand Renaud

Urban Development Department
The World Bank

John P. Ross

Office of Urban and Community
Studies, U.S. Department of Housing
    and Urban Development

John C. Simonson

Department of Economics
University of Wisconsin,
Platteville

Robert M. Stein

Department of Political Science
Rice University

Michael J. Wasylenko

The Maxwell School and
   Department of Economics
Syracuse University and
   Pennsylvania State University

Colin L. Wood

Scottish Development Department
Edinburgh, Scotland

EDITOR'S INTRODUCTION

In April 1983, the University of the District of Columbia (UDC) and the U.S. Department of Housing and Urban Development (HUD) brought together a number of scholars from throughout the nation to discuss the future of urban policy; there was much to build on. The post-World War II emergence of a strong national government, which was accelerated in the 1960s by the Great Society and the "New Federalism" of the Nixon Administration, had led to the creation of an urban policy that was incremental, Washington based, and premised on the view that the dominant problem for most developed nations was urban growth and the inevitable creation of large cities. In the U.S., for example, the 1968 HUD Annual Report focused on the significant population growth occurring in urban America and stressed the need for HUD to "plan for the kind of development this growth requires."

During the 1970s, however, it became evident that major and powerful exogenous forces were changing the urban environment. Demographic and economic structural trends were converging that gave strong reasons to not only question the growth as inevitable, but also the homogeneous character of national urban policies. Indeed, by the late 1970s and early 1980s, even as a topic urban policy declined in its importance, it became clear that not only would debates over industrial and trade policy prevail over the urban, but also that the national governments were pulling back on their urban policy involvement. By 1982, both a socialist President Mitterrand and a conservative President Reagan had announced policies to decentralize and limit national government involvement in urban affairs.

The UDC-HUD conference was designed to take a look at this "new urban economics" with specific reference to the implications of the changing economic and demographic structure for financing public services. The result is a set of well integrated chapters that are framed within the context of a growing pressure for a more efficient allocation of resources (public and private) and a recognition that with an increased diversity in urban America, greater attention needs to be given to people rather than place oriented policies. It is a book that looks to the decade ahead both in terms of what is the "urban problem" and what are the key policy research questions that are yet to be addressed.

The publication of this volume is the result of the efforts of several people. The list includes Jerome Paige at UDC (a superb job of organization), Heather Aveilhe and Katherine O'Leary at the HUD Office of Research Utilization, and Arlene Perazzini who helped it all come together at JAI Press.

Robert D. Ebel
St. Paul, Minnesota
Guest Editor

STRUCTURAL CHANGES IN ADVANCED ECONOMIES AND THEIR IMPACT ON CITIES IN THE 1980s

Bertrand Renaud

I. INTRODUCTION

Major structural changes are currently taking place in advanced economies. These changes have demographic, economic, and social dimensions which combined greatly reduce the margin of maneuver for government policies. What is that margin in the urban context? The objective of this paper is to examine the impact of structural changes in advanced economies on their cities and the implications of these structural changes for urban policies in the 1980s.

The central theme of the present analysis is that the cities of most industrial countries are presently exposed to the stresses of two major converging but distinct structural changes. The first is endogenous to the urban sector and coincides with the end of urbanization as it has been known to date in these countries, where populations are now fully urbanized and rural-urban migration has slowed to a trickle. The other is apparent to all: since the late 1960s and the

Research in Urban Economics, Volume 4, Pages 1-23.
Copyright © 1984 JAI Press Inc.
ISBN: 0-89232-423-6.

1

first oil crisis, Western economies have entered a phase of slow growth, accompanied by major structural adjustments, particularly in the manufacturing sector.

The economic base of cities is central to policy formulation as it determines private demands and public resources. Much emphasis should be placed on the ongoing economic restructuring of advanced countries, on its impact on the location of economic activities and the effect on the economic base of cities. Then the scope of policies open for consideration by various levels of government can be discussed.

This analysis does not argue—against the evidence—that all advanced economies are facing the same situation. Rather, it is against diversity that the dynamic effects of structural changes must be evaluated, and the validity of the analysis appraised. Because, more than others, demographic trends can be anticipated in the short to medium term, they are discussed first. This is followed by discussion of the changing international division of labor and the industrial restructuring of national economies. It is then possible to evaluate the impact of demographic and economic changes on cities. The problems that are raised and the scope and nature of government actions are discussed in the last section.

II. URBAN DEMOGRAPHIC STRUCTURAL CHANGE

A. Nature of the Demographic Structural Change

The first of the two important structural changes affecting urban policies in the 1980s is essentially demographic in character. During the last 20 years the demographic structure of industrial societies has undergone major changes: there has been a rapid decline in birth rates following the postwar demographic explosion, populations are now aging significantly, and the massive postwar urbanization has exhausted its potential.

The urban impact of demographic changes can be anticipated more easily than most others in the short to medium term. We already know the number of children who will be entering the active labor force in the next 20 years and are likely to form new households—they are already born. More delicate to appraise correctly are the socioeconomic factors influencing behavior and changing birth rates, household formation, and migration patterns.

First, trends in birth rates, death rates, fertility, and migration patterns can be examined in their relation to the age structure of the population, the growth of the active population, and the changes in the size and number of households. Then, the implications of such changes for urban development can be explored.

B. Demographic Trends in Advanced Economies

1. Size of Population

Between 1950 and 1980 the total population of the 24 countries with advanced economies has increased by 36% from 580 million to 793 million. During the

1980s the expected total growth is only 6% with the population rising very slowly to about 844 million by 1990.[1] In addition, there will be variable growth rates across countries. A few will account for most of the growth, while others will have very stable populations and several are even expected to regress. Austria, Germany, Switzerland, Sweden, and the United Kingdom are expected to have declining populations. Others, like France, Belgium, and Norway, will barely grow. On the other hand, Japan, the United States, and several Mediterranean countries will continue to expand.

Three factors account for population change: birth rate, death rate, and migration. Population trends in advanced economies are dominated by fertility rates because mortality rates are very low: crude death rates are all very close to the group weighted average of 9 per thousand. On the other hand, a most striking situation prevails at the moment: in most of the member countries total fertility rates have fallen so low that the replacement of generations is not guaranteed. As noted earlier this situation has prevailed long enough already in some countries to lead to actual decline.

A minimum of 2.11 children per woman is required to maintain a stable population. At present only eight countries meet that level. This by itself has serious implications for long-term urban development. The current age structure dictates growth or decline, depending on whether the population is young or old.

A variety of socioeconomic and cultural factors account for this situation: the rapid diffusion of family planning methods bringing the actual number of children closer to the desired family size, the economic crisis and the increase of unemployment, and the increasing level of education among women and their entry in the labor force. In addition to the marriage age which has increased, trends toward cohabitation associated with lower marriage and increasing divorce rates have been significant factors. Since 1965 divorce rates have been rising in all countries except Greece, Turkey, and Yugoslavia.

Migration has played and will continue to play an important role in these countries, and migration patterns are major components of the urban demographic structural changes that are taking place at present. In the 1980s the international and internal components of migration will play a role different from that of the past 20 years.

2. International Migration

A major change has taken place in international migration. Following World War II, many governments, especially in Europe, encouraged international migration from countries with high fertility levels to those with low fertility levels which had experienced significant losses during the war. Twenty years of postwar economic expansion was sustained in an important way by foreign workers. The economic crisis since 1973 has abruptly ended this intense international migration which governments now actively discourage. But the permanent settlement of migrant workers continues to attract direct family members and other dependent relatives. The magnitude of the populations involved constitutes an important source of social problems concentrated in large cities.

3. Internal Migration

The change in internal migration patterns is at the core of the present urban structural change, and will be so in the future, particularly because natural growth of the national population will be small, and at times negative, in the 1980s.

Between 1950 and 1970 rural-urban migration played an important role in the expansion of the urban sector, the growth rate of the urban population being approximately twice that of the total population. But by now the role of internal migration in urban growth is very small and the reservoir of rural migrants has been depleted. Between 1960 and 1970 the urban population increased by approximately 24% while the total population increased only 11%. During the 1970s the depletion of potential rural migration was already evident and the urban population increased by 11%. During the 1980s the urban population of countries of advanced economies is projected to increase by 8%, equal to the projected increase of the total population. Four-fifths of this increase will come in the Mediterranean countries, North America, and Japan.

The stabilizing effects of rural migration on the growth of most cities will be absent in many countries, and demographic urban growth will often take on the appearance of a zero-sum game. Growth in one city will have to be provided more and more at the expense of another city. Accompanying these emerging mobility patterns, a new phenomenon is occurring: for the first time the largest metropolitan regions such as Paris, Vienna, Brussels, Milan, and New York are losing their powers of attraction. In a very empirical way the residents of these large urban centers are providing the answer to the question of whether diseconomies of scale are associated with larger urban size. Through their revealed preference, by "voting with their feet," urban residents are showing that such diseconomies do exist. In many European countries the cities benefitting from migration are now the cities of about 200,000 people or above, where most of the service jobs are now being created. It is generally agreed that high congestion, pollution, and other problems of metropolitan centers are playing an important role in creating these very different migration patterns.

The family life cycle, too, plays an important role. Between the ages of 20 and 29, migrants are influenced by study needs, training possibilities, and employment opportunities which are concentrated in the service sectors of medium to large cities. Between the ages of 30 and 50, mobility is reduced, but the new location patterns of employment favor small and medium cities. After the age of 50, mobility increases again, but is more independent of labor markets or other economic considerations. Thanks to the retirement systems built over the postwar period, retired people move to warm coastal regions of their country whenever possible (eastern Australia, southeastern United States, southern England, etc.).

Because employment location and migration are closely associated, another change of great policy importance is the redistribution of population between the center and the periphery of large urban areas. The trend toward declining central city populations has accelerated during the 1970s in some advanced countries, particularly the United States. In other countries the prevailing situation has been stagnating or slowing down in the centers with continued expansion in the rest of the metropolitan areas.

4. Changing Demographic Structure

In addition to the regional and urban implications of changing mobility patterns, three important trends affect the urban economy: (1) the graying of the countries through the changing age structure; (2) the changing composition of the active population; and (3) the rapid increase in the number of households and their changing nature.

The aging is general. In 1950 people over 65 made up 7.6% of the population; in 1975 their share was 10.5%; even under favorable assumptions this share is expected to increase further to 12.4% by the year 2000. Moreover, 38.5% of this age group will consist of people 75 years old or more, i.e., a remarkable 4.8% of the population of the industrial countries will be over 75.

The active population will have three characteristics. First, labor force participation rates for females are expected to increase during the 1980s; for instance, they could reach 51.6% in France, 64.9% in Denmark, and 60.8% in the United States by the end of the decade. Second, growth of active population will decelerate over the next 20 years, but the need for higher rates of job creation will remain high in the 1980s; the active population is expected to grow by 50 million between 1975 and 2000 (a 17.5% gain) and the total population by 80 million (only a 12% gain). Third, during the 1980s the active labor force will grow younger because of continuing entry of the baby-boom generation into the market, increased labor force participation by females in the younger age groups, and lower participation rates among the older age groups.

Changes in the number of households and in their composition are crucial factors affecting the adequacy of the housing stock in terms of number of units, size, and location. During the last 10 years the growth rate of the number of households has been consistently higher than overall population growth rates because of the rapid decline in household sizes. In particular there has been a very significant increase in both single-parent households and single-individual households. In several countries these new types of households make up 20% of the total. For instance, in the United Kingdom from 1950 to 1977, population growth was 0.47% per year, the growth rate of the total number of households was 0.90% per year, and the growth rate of single-parent and single-individual households was a very high 3.41% per year.

During the current decade a slowdown in the growth rate of the total number of households is expected, resulting from the convergence of several forces: low immigration; a slowdown in the nuclearization of households because high unemployment rates will induce young people, particularly young female workers, to stay with their parents; and the almost complete disappearance of large families, which renders a further decline in household size unlikely. At the other end of the family life cycle, one should expect an increase in the number of elderly households.

C. Incidence of Urban Demographic Structural Change on Urban Development

The incidence of the ongoing urban demographic structural change is not very difficult to trace qualitatively, even if rigorous quantitive projections are difficult to make. The implications for the 1980s can be listed as follows:

- The reduced volume of potential and actual internal migration wil accentuate the differences between cities. As noted, this internal migration is strongly influenced by the family life cycle. Young migrants are attracted by employment opportunities; the retired are attracted by amenities and a lower cost of living, and the social protection developed over the last 20 years has given them more freedom of choice. This favors small- and medium-sized cities.
- Cities with a comparatively weak economic base will have more out-migrants than in-migrants. Two things will happen: they will lose residents and their remaining population will age more rapidly because of the selectivity of out-migration. Depressed local real estate markets will contribute to lock in older residents who have invested all their savings in housing and are threatened with substantial capital losses.
- Cities with a strong economic base will attract young migrants. Population will increase more rapidly because of the demographic multiplier (young migrants have children). They will become younger.
- Diverging trends will develop in the level and composition of demand for local services between growing and declining cities. A slowdown of population growth will lead to a deceleration in investment associated with negative multiplier effects. In the residential construction sector this demographic effect is combined with slow economic growth, inflation, stagnant real incomes, and very high interest rates at the moment. This has a very marked effect on local employment and on the structure of the construction industry. Growing cities will not be caught in the same spiral, however, as commercial investment wil play a particularly positive role.

- International migration could conceivably compensate for the vanishing rural-urban migration, and in a few areas it does (in a legal or illegal way). But its contribution will be small for two reasons: first, most countries, particularly European countries, have not welcomed international migration since 1974. (Others like Japan never have.) Second, international migrants have tended to concentrate in specific regions and urban centers, typically areas of old-line industries where problems are most serious.
- The changing household structure requires significant readjustment in the composition of the housing stock. Given current economic conditions, there will be more improvement and modification of the existing structures rather than the building of new structures.
- Suburban development is particularly affected by changing patterns of housing investment. Because of land use regulations or just natural scarcity, land costs are very high. In addition, construction costs have also risen very rapidly and financial costs are at their highest historical level. Smaller, less affluent households will find it more and more difficult to satisfy their desire for detached individual housing units. The impact of the smaller, younger households on the private rental housing market will be very pronounced. Another factor affecting the rate of suburban development within the large urban areas will be the changing location distribution of new employment, particularly in the now dominant service sector.

III. ECONOMIC STRUCTURAL CHANGES

A. Structural Changes Require New Urban Policies

The future of cities of advanced economies cannot be understood and policies cannot be designed and implemented without an examination of the economic structural changes currently taking place. The preceding section stressed that intercity and interregional population movements will be the prime factors explaining the growth or stagnation of a city. These population movements are predominantly determined by employment opportunities and income levels. The economic base determines private sector demands and an important part of the public resources needed to meet them. The economic structural changes pervading advanced economies are on everyone's mind. They are presently characterized by the transition from an extended period of rapid and sustained growth during the 1950s and 1960s to the present period of slow and uncertain growth. The view presented here is that the rapidly changing international division of labor, major technological changes, and the dramatic impact of energy cost increases are presently generating centrifugal forces creating increasing segmentation among the various sectors of the economy. This increasing segmentation is making the macroeconomic management of the economy particularly difficult, because a given policy instrument can have totally opposite effects on two different sectors.

The urban structural change caused by the end of urban-rural migration and very slow population growth creates already a very heterogenous urban policy environment by producing urban population growth in one place and decline in another. This urban heterogeneity is greatly intensified by the economic restructuring of the advanced economies and will determine the types of urban policies needed in the 1980s together with their mode of operation. The selectivity of the impact of these two structural changes will make concerted actions between the public and the private sector more difficult.

B. The Changing International Division of Labor

The world economy is going through an economic crisis. The large and growing number of unemployed people in advanced countries is bringing back grim memories of the 1930s crisis. However, the 1929 crisis was essentially financial whereas the present crisis is industrial and structural in nature. It is tied to the emergence of a world market over the last 30 years. The two oil crises have simply made this emergence clearer and quickened the pace of change. This world market is transforming the relations between developing and developed countries and among developed countries as well. The new international division of labor is making itself deeply felt within each country. The urban economy is only part of this change.

Between the end of the postwar reconstruction of Europe (1953) and the first oil crisis of 1973, the level of international trade increased dramatically. It grew twice as fast as the domestic output of the advanced countries, which itself was growing at an historically very high rate. This led to an increasing division of labor, each country becoming increasingly specialized in producing the goods to which it was best suited.

The surge of trade by itself created growth differentials among industries in each national economy. Although this rapid increase in trade produced some dislocation, the benefits of fast growth in specific industries were widely shared by all sectors of the economy. The changes imposed by the growth of each new industry on the others was limited because all industries benefitted from the cost reductions that came with the investment in these new activities.

Three major events have reinforced each other in the 1970s to create a new economic policy environment: the slowdown in economic growth, the structural change in the demand for manufactured goods and, last, the shifts in the terms of trade with the oil-producing countries. These changes have interacted. The economic slowdown induced by changes in the demand for manufacturing goods have been accentuated by the oil shock of 1973 and 1979. Both internal problems and structural changes in world demand have increased further.

The growth of output in the newly industrialized countries is not the main cause of the weakening of industrial activities in Western economies at present. Nonetheless, it has been a significant factor in precipitating the decline of certain industries and firms located in specific urban regions. The role of centrally planned economies in the world markets remains small, less than 5% after exclusion of trade within that group of countries. The Polish experience with an export-led growth strategy may discourage further efforts in that direction in Eastern European countries.

Because of the concentration of heavy industries in selected regions and cities of advanced countries, it is worth mentioning that the industrial crisis preceded the energy crisis. The record shows very clearly that world demand for manufacturing products began slowing down at the end of the 1960s before the 1973 oil crisis. The 1969 turning point is particularly noticeable for the steel and metallurgical industries as well as electromechanical industries—which represent 40% of total industrial activities and constitute a major source of demand for the metallurgial industries.

The 1980s will continue to see a trend toward reorganization of industrial activities on a world scale, with the restructuring and relocation of many manufacturing activities. During this period of restructuring, advanced economies seem to be hit by centrifugal forces and industrial sectors pulled apart. There are widening differences in the growth of output, employment, investment, and profits among industries. Because of the increasing segmentation of these industries at the moment, global evaluations of economic trends are not particularly helpful.

The increasing differentiation among sectors of the same economy is due to the fact that recent investment in the economy has not led to cost reductions. This investment was in energy resources that followed the quadrupling of energy prices in 1973 and the additional tripling in 1979. Between 1973 and 1980 the rate of energy investment in advanced countries was at least twice as large as the overall rate of investment.

Higher energy investment did not reduce the real cost of the product to the other industries. At best it prevented the cost of other industries from rising as fast as they would otherwise have risen; energy prices rose faster than in any other sector. The result was an increasingly segmented economy as the expanding energy investment put direct and indirect pressures on other industries.

The impact has been particularly devastating on the industries which had already begun declining before the first oil crisis of 1973 and were most exposed to the shifting international division of labor. Old-time manufacturing sectors were particularly hard hit either because their industries have a high input of energy relative to other resources (for example steel) or because their final products use a lot of energy directly (automobiles) or indirectly (tires).

As a rule, soaring energy costs have enhanced the growth rates of industries and products that use little energy or conserve it. They lowered the growth rates of those that used a lot of energy in their production process or supply energy-intensive products.

The indirect impact of the energy crisis has been that high levels of energy investment are competing successfully for capital and are crowding other industries out of the financial markets in a period of slow growth and scarce capital. Since energy-related industries are far more profitable than most other activities, their borrowing capacity is much stronger. Another drag on nonenergy industries has been the high proportion of all their outlays (10-15%) which has been going to mostly energy-related "nonproductive" types of investment.

Looking beyond the present energy-related problems many analyses say that the profound changes that we are witnessing are the beginning of a third industrial revolution in the advanced economies. The first industrial revolution which started everything was based on coal, the steam engine, railroads, and textiles. The second industrial revolution was based on petroleum products, chemicals, the automobile, and electromechanical industries. The ongoing revolution is based on new energies, electronics, information industries, and bioengineering. The first two revolutions, especially the first, strongly favored urban concentration, which the third one does not. According to this interpretation one could also think that the 1980s are not the beginning of a period of permanently slow growth but rather constitute a transition toward new forms of growth. During that period different countries and different cities will adjust differently according to their choices of policies and their ability to implement them.

C. Centrifugal Forces Within Advance Economies: Trends in Five Major Sectors

A detailed account, industry by industry, to understand the ongoing industrial restructuring is neither feasible nor necessary. A possible framework to describe the increasing segmentation of the structure of the advanced economy is to consider five broad sectors: (1) energy; (2) traditional or old-time manufacturing; (3) high technology; (4) services; and (5) agriculture.

Energy industries (1) will not follow similar paths in all countries. Countries with both natural resources and an advanced technology like the United States, will have an energy industry that will resist recession. The very large requirements of this sector will continue to squeeze the financial resources available to other industries. Countries such as France which do not have natural resources but a high technology may continue their investment in nuclear energy. Other countries also lacking natural resources and more divided on the future of nuclear energy will develop defensive strategies to expand the output of this crucial resource through a mix of conventional and nonconventional sources.

Basic manufacturing industries (2) have been the core of the advanced economies. Automobile, steel, machinery, textiles, appliances, shipbuilding, and transportation equipment are now running into serious international competition from both developed and developing countries. The competitive portion of these industries can be maintained only on the basis of more successful management and investment strategies. Further restructuring is still ahead within each nation.

The large mature industries (autos, building products, chemicals, containers, food processing, metal, rubber, steel, textiles, etc.) have very low returns on capital together with overcapacity, much of which is uneconomic and obsolete. Their survival will depend on their shrinking down to an efficient competitive core. Competition within these no-growth sectors will be particularly severe, often brutal.

Of course, these industries will not disappear. But, by rapidly shifting capital from expansion to concentrated efforts on productivity gains, these sectors will have fewer firms and fewer plants in order to become more efficient and more profitable—a basic requirement for recovering a larger domestic market share. In all sectors, firms will concentrate all their efforts on their profitable operations.

More competitiveness and higher productivity will be achieved by the elimination of weak competitors and the—sometimes massive—shutdown of obsolete plants. For instance in the United States, 23 tire plants have closed since 1973 and in the steel industry a closing down of 11% of capacity since 1977 has raised productivity by 50%.

If consolidation is the price to be paid by firms for success in the global competition for mature industries for the 1980s the most important price for survival will be paid by labor. Only to a limited extent will consolidation mean that the labor force displaced by the failed competition is picked up by the survivors. More often the price of survival in autos, textiles, steel, will be technological change which makes substantial unemployment a sure thing. To what extent and under what conditions this labor force can adjust to and retrain for new activities is one of the major problems of the 1980s.

High technology industries (3) playing a role opposite to that of the energy industries, are creating new market opportunities with each new investment and new product. Capital expansion is not only beneficial to the sector but to other industries as well. While centered around semiconductors this sector encompasses a wide variety of industries: computers/communications equipment, scientific instruments, rockets and aerospace industries, optical instruments, medical instruments, office equipment, etc. At present, even though the capital intensity of this sector is rising, it is expected that in the leading countries (mostly the United States and Japan) these activities will continue to have a high growth potential. This sector will tend to behave more independently from the rest of the economy than the others sectors, the constraint being of course that their customer industries should be able to finance their own growth in order to purchase the output of the high technology sector.

One fundamental force operating in favor of *services (4)* is the explosive increase in energy prices. These price increases have been and are still changing the methods of producing goods and services. These economies are moving more and more toward labor-intensive production and away from production that uses large amounts of capital and energy. Since capital equipment requires large amounts of energy to operate, any increase in energy will also increase the operating cost of capital: as producers use less energy in response to rising prices they also cut back on the use of capital. Consumers also are substituting labor- and energy-saving capital for high priced energy. The ongoing restructuring will eventually be in favor of increasing employment, much of it in the services industries.

To appraise more accurately the role of the services sector in the 1980s it is necessary to move away from the traditional classification of industries by Clark (1940) into three sectors: primary industries (agriculture, forestry, fisheries, mining), secondary industries (manufacturing, construction, utilities) and tertiary industries (trade, transport, communications, finance, and services). It is better to distinguish between services which are primarily intermediate inputs to production from services for final consumption. In addition, one recent classification has proposed to consider the institutional setting within which services are provided, i.e., private, public, or nonprofit. Without attempting to achieve functionally perfect classification, we can distinguish six service groups (Noyelle, 1981):

a. *The distributive services* (transportation, communications, utilities, and wholesaling) which are intermediaries from producers to mostly intermediate buyers;
b. *Corporate services* (finance, insurance, business services, legal services, etc);
c. *Nonprofit services* (health, education);
d. *Retail services*;
e. *Mainly consumer services* (hotels, personal services, repair services, travel and recreation);
f. *Government services.*

From the viewpoint of trade, productivity, and technology, the services sector will be playing a major role in the 1980s. Manufacturing firms operating in no-growth industries will not disappear nor necessarily become unprofitable. The successful survivors will often concentrate on advanced technical goods which will include an important component of intermediate services. These firms will have to learn that the services that accompany their product are often as important as quality and price. On the other hand, the sectors that will yield to the international division of labor will be those producing "standardized goods," which are either low capital intensive consumer goods (leather goods, textiles, light mechanical industries, etc.) or the more ordinary industrial goods, either of strategic significance to developing countries or based on available local resources (steel and metallurgy, paper, fertilizers, etc.). On the international market many do not perceive the rapidly growing volume of services exports in the activities of advanced countries and their importance to balance of payments.[2]

Goods-producing businesses will incorporate improvements in services productivity in their operations. Within each of the six categories of services outlined above, i.e., whether they are distributive, corporate, nonprofit, retail, or consumer services, significant gains in productivity can be expected from the substitution of capital for labor. This probably implies that services employment, while growing faster than other types of employment, will grow at a slower rate than in 1970s. Specific subsector projections are needed to detail the impact of the computer on these increasingly differentiated services activities.

However, two types of industries are likely to behave differently from the general trend—nonprofit services (health, education) and government services. Because of the cutback in central and local government budgets, employment in these two sectors will not rise rapidly if at all. We should expect intensified competition in these sectors that are typically very fragmented, eventually leading to significant increases in productivity. Government policies moving in the direction of deregulation and of lesser government activities are likely to help the growth and productivity of private services involving government.

To complete this picture of segmented advanced economies made up of sectors behaving quite differently from each other, a few words should be said also of *agriculture (5)* even though it is a sector less crucial to urban affairs than all the others. At this moment, it is feared that agriculture will replace energy as a major source of inflation in the 1980s. On a global basis it is expected that farm output will not keep up with the rapid rise in the growth of demand. Simplifying, because weather factors have been and will remain important, the growth rate of output was faster than that of demand in the 1960s, about even with the growth of demand in the 1970s, and is likely to fall behind in the 1980s. On the demand side the three dominant forces are the world population growth, the rising standard of living of developing countries, and the changing diets with increasing meat calorie intakes. On the supply side rapid increases in the costs of fuel and fertilizers together with the sharp increases in the cost of capital are preventing farmers from increasing capacity and improving productivity. For these reasons it is anticipated that, instead of declining as it did during the last 30 years, the real price of farm products will increase during the 1980s. In short, agriculture could be a source of inflation and inflation is not favorable to the economic health of countries and their cities.

D. New Limits of Economic Management

The divergent paths followed by the various sectors, together with their increasing competition for scarce capital resources, will make the successful management of national economies much more difficult than in the past. Traditional

macroeconomic policy instruments do not yield predictable or controllable results. In a real sense national governments do not have to manage one economy
but several: a deep slump in a sector can coexist with great resilience and growth
in others. Problems of efficiency and equity are becoming very acute. The
management of the mixed economies of the advanced countries must cut its path
between two equally unfeasible alternatives—giving entirely free play to the
changing international division of labor at a very high social and political cost
on one side and on the other refusing to adjust to the ongoing structural changes
(in more vivid language "refusing to submit blindly to the international division
of labor") by raising all kinds of barriers to changes. Such barriers would slow
the economy down, delay changes but not prevent them while raising the costs
of adjustment even higher several years down the road.

Urban policies at the national level are dependent on the ability to manage
economic change. At the local level they must adapt to the regional and urban
consequences of structural change.

IV. URBAN AND REGIONAL CONSEQUENCES OF THE TWO STRUCTURAL CHANGES

A. Increasing Urban and Regional Differentiation

The impact of the simultaneous occurrence of industrial restructuring and of the
end of urbanization through rural-urban migration in advanced countries is profound. They are exposed to the risks of both regional and social fragmentation.
Among their cities important differences have emerged and are continuing to
unfold in terms of capital investment, employment creation, population, and
income levels. Important differences exist between countries that are reorganizing
their economy around the industries that appear most promising on a broad front
and the other countries whose speed of adjustment seems to be less rapid.[3]

The obvious question is how the cities of the countries which happen to
combine a stagnant or declining national population with a slow speed of industrial adjustment will fare in the 1980s. There is no ready answer as these
countries will still have choices regarding the policies which they wish to follow.
There exists a broad range of alternatives from allowing full play to the ongoing
dislocations in the expectation of a rapid transition to a more positive environment
to deliberate effort to slow the transition with the possibility of a protracted
evolution toward a more satisfactory economic urban environment.

Tracing the regional and urban impact of the industrial restructuring is not
difficult on the basis of the four nonagricultural sectors discussed earlier. The
situation is particularly striking in the United States where old manufacturing
activities are concentrated in the Northeast and the Midwest while energy resources as well as high technology industries are found in the South and West.
But sharp regional differences exist also in other countries (France—the North

and Lorraine; Germany—the Ruhr area; the United Kingdom—Merseyside and Midlands; Italy—Turin; Belgium—the Walloon region; etc.). A long process of capital, employment, and population transfer is underway. Reinforced by recent recession, this massive transfer of resources has gathered momentum.

As noted earlier, the large, mature industries (autos, chemicals, textiles, steel, rubber, etc.) are burdened with high levels of overcapacity (20% to 30%) in uneconomic and often obsolete plants. Slow growth of demand also means that, for lack of internally generated funds, those industries are also burdened with large debts.

Swollen debts, shrunken profits (after adjusting for inflation), and reduced reliance on internally generated funds have created a serious liquidity crisis in old-line manufacturing activities where liquidity positions have fallen to a level never experienced over the last 20 years. Cash and short-term investments as a percentage of current liabilities have fallen.

Other measures of short-term liquidity as well as ratios of long-term debt to equity, internal funds to capital expenditures and interest coverage show a similar deep deterioration. Such a situation explains the accelerated rate of closure of plants and other facilities in recent years of very slow growth of demand combined with extremely high interest rates. In their effort to modernize, firms are experiencing a continuing gap between cash flow and capital expenditures. The present situation of economic recession combined with high interest rates now threatens the very existence of quite a few firms.

The closing of a very large number of antiquated facilities is resulting in a downturn of past regional trends and a deepening of problems. For instance, in the 1960s growth in U.S. manufacturing in the South was three times that in the North, but in the 1970s factory jobs in the Northeast and the Midwest were dropping while increasing 25% in the South and West. The year 1974 is a benchmark, for the first time the South holding more industrial jobs than the Northeast. Concurrently, during the last decade construction employment increased by less than 3% in the Northeast and Midwest while growing by 55% in the South and West. If the fast-growing services sector provided some relief it did not slow down these regional trends; while it doubled in the Northeast and Midwest it tripled in the already favored regions of the South and West.

This continuing regional shift is now strengthened by the self-feeding process of industrial decline or rather decay. An old or obsolete captial stock means plants poor productivity from aging machines. Low productivity combined with high labor costs associated with good wages (until now) led to low profitability, ending in a regrouping of capital resources and plant closures. Fewer jobs mean in a first step that those who are retiring are not replaced; this is followed by layoffs requiring migration of the work force. Declining businesses and shrinking populations mean a shrinking tax base with the further result that higher taxes become required from those remaining in the states and cities of the regions, just to maintain existing levels of services. A major regional-urban problem is that in the absence of appropriate measures, the deteriorating infrastructure and rising tax rates of the traditional urban centers may lead the survivors to move to more promising areas of the countries (such as the "mini-steel" plants in Florida).

B. The New Economic Context

From this rapid review of the economic structural changes that are taking place several conclusions can be drawn.

First, because of the diverging trends of various major sectors of the economy, broad-based macroeconomic policies are likely to have perverse results both on a sectoral and on a regional and urban basis. They could cause inflation in the healthier areas without producing much result in the troubled areas.

Second, reliance on unfettered market forces during this decade of major structural adjustment would impose costs so severe on selected sections of the labor force and selected regions and cities that such a strategy would not be tenable very long.

On the other hand "refusing to submit to the blind forces of the international division of labor" would simply mean blocking change for a given period of time while raising the ultimate cost of adjustment at the end, with even more massive disruptions because of the increased gaps between industries and social groups.

Because social justice is one of the main justifications for the existence of government, government cannot help but be involved in reducing the burden of those who pay the heaviest prices for structural adjustment, while at the same time enhancing the vitality and power of the national economy.

On the industrial front, countries will have to facilitate the regrouping of the old manufacturing sectors, each according to its national traditions and concepts of industrial policy.

On the labor front, governments will be confronted with an increasingly bifurcated market with either two-professional households working in the service and high technology sectors enjoying high income or one-earner or single-person households with uncertain employment prospects. High priority will have to be given to labor market adjustment policies: even though governments are faced with fiscal retrenchment they have to develop retraining policies, special retirement schemes, and other methods of reinserting the work force of old manufacturing industries in the new growth sectors.

V. THE SCOPE FOR URBAN POLICIES

A. Past Policies

The policy implications of the two ongoing structural changes are more easily understood if they are contrasted with the conditions that prevailed previously.

Until the early 1970s, urban growth had the following characteristics: national population increase; continuing transfers of population from the countryside associated with the development of services employment, a differential increase of larger cities and the formation of city regions; an increasing demand for space per capita; and, finally, a long-term concentration of population into the more favored regions.

Being confronted with these urban trends, governments developed policies in an incremental way and responded to problems as they emerged. Only limited attention was paid to the context within which urban issues should be debated and policies evaluated. Rapid urban growth in most advanced countries led to an increase in the scope of objectives, in the range of population to be served, and in the number and variety of instruments to be tried. A significant shift took place from a early and almost exclusive consideration of physical planning problems to a more comprehensive focus on the socioeconomic problems of cities. There was an increased emphasis on income redistribution in an urban context accompanied by the concern for economic efficiency in solving problems. The rapid growth of urban programs frequently led to serious problems of co-ordination and sometimes of bureaucratic congestion.

During this period policy objectives at the *metropolitan level* were often to seek a better balance between home and workplace; to improve transport conditions to reduce lost time and fatigue; to offer a variety of housing, especially to the disadvantaged; to develop public services close to residential areas; to improve existing services; to improve access to the natural environment; to redistribute economic activities to the periphery; to maintain industrial activities within the metropolitan region. At the *regional level*, frequent objectives were: to create new employment and service centers; to create new towns; to implement large transport investment programs.

In order to achieve such aims, new procedures were frequently used such as: influencing employment location through permit systems (for industry and services); coordinating public expenditures among regions; creating new institutions such as the public/private corporation (French *sociétés d'économie mixte*); developing new land use planning and control powers and related new land use instruments (such as the French "operational planning zones" or the German "regional" planning system); and creating new financial institutions to facilitate local government financing of private housing investment.

Because of urban growth, local governments faced new problems. There was a marked tendency for urban areas to outgrow their government limits. They faced inadequate authority to coordinate actions over areas related to problems. They had inadequate power to act and inadequate resources for action. Increasing intervention by local governments was often accompanied by policies supported by national governments; amalgamation of government units or creation of ad hoc associations of governments; creation of new local tax bases as well as modernization of existing ones; increasing reliance on transfers from higher levels of governments; rapid expansion of services financed on a pay-as-you-go basis, through borrowing, taxes, or transfers.

Also characteristic of the earlier urban policy era was the frequent stress on decentralization of economic activities and population as a means of solving congestion and environmental problems of the largest cities, based on expectation of continuing high rates of urban growth. Technical interest in the design of new facilities and new urban technologies often overtook the understanding of the effective demand for services by various urban groups. This supply side, designer-dominated provision of services was later better understood and partially corrected. Rapid urban growth and increasing mobility led to greater spatial segregation of urban activities, a spontaneous pattern of change reinforced by views of urban designers (as typified by the 1933 Athens charter). These spontaneous trends toward spatial segregation were also reinforced by economic incentives in favor of new urban investments against maintenance of existing facilities. Such incentives have been well analyzed in the case of housing but are present elsewhere.

Because of the coexistence of urban growth and rapid economic growth, there was a frequent emphasis on large-scale expensive urban projects of long duration requiring large central government participation (i.e., subsidies) such as new towns and major infrastructure systems for transportation. This emphasis on new expensive systems was accompanied in some countries by very harmful "deferred maintenance policies" in existing urban areas. During that period an increasing understanding of the urban implications of the rapid expansion of the private automobile in existing cities led eventually to a move back toward better public transit and private transport.

In the housing sector many countries made the transition from facing absolute shortage of housing (quantitative policies) to providing for better housing (qualitative policies). There was also a misunderstanding of sources of urban decline in large central cities as mostly a physical problem of deteriorating infrastructure and housing which could be solved through large-scale urban renewal projects. With demographic structural change the problem is now shifting to the mismatch between the structure of the existing housing stock and changing household needs.

During the previous period the relative balance in public-private cooperation shifted steadily toward dependence of urban investment on central government subsidies. It was the result of increasing assumption of long-term investment risks by the public sector and the growing uncertainty of long-term commitments by the private sector.

During that period when urban policies were most important to advanced countries because of the size and intensity of urban change, their specificity remained ambiguous. Maximalists felt that urban policies were all the policies that dealt with the problems of urban residents including employment and welfare. More restrictive and specific analysts emphasized sectoral policies of major significance to cities such as housing, urban transport, and local finances, paying great attention to the problems of the internal organization of cities and its impact on the quality of urban life.

The analysis of demographic and economic structural changes in the 1980s presented earlier gives strong reasons to believe that in practically all countries the more specific and more limited concept of urban policy will prevail, the most obvious reason being that with the "end of urbanization" practically the entire population of many countries is urban is character. Therefore, under the maximalist definition all government policies have become urban policies. This can become an unnecessary source of confusion in decision making and at the limit could lead to government paralysis. In fact, it is most unlikely that urban policy objectives will take precedence over those of, say, industrial policies or trade policies in the 1980s.

The specificity of urban policies has been most thoroughly questioned in federal countries such as Australia, Canada, and the United States where the differentiation between the coordination of policies and their execution is most sharply defined by level of government. It is in those countries that the distinction was made first between explicit urban policies, i.e., those of urban agencies, and implicit urban policies, i.e., those that do not have urban objectives but have a strong and differentiated impact on cities. This is, indeed, a very important distinction. The earlier analysis of current industrial restructuring showed that explicit urban policies to assist a city or a region could be greatly weakened or negated by the forces set in motion by implicit urban policies embedded in industrial or marcoeconomic policies. Seen in that light many urban policies could become remedial policies, but other and more sectoral actions are probably more suitable at present.

Because it has so far proven most difficult to net out the urban impacts of implicit urban policies in order to propose specific actions, it becomes even more crucial to define the scope of the explicit urban policies. It is quite important to identify the extent to which policies addressed directly to the problems of cities are both needed and effective.

B. Scope and Characteristics of New Urban Policies

The scope of new urban policies must be defined against four major urban issues:

- How to improve the economic base of cities, because so many of them are now confronted with major problems of reconversion from an old manufacturing base to services and high technology activities
- How to improve their social environment, because industrial restructuring is leading to very sharp income inequalities and explosive conditions in many large cities

- How to improve urban services in response to changing size and composition of resident populations, while confronting major maintenance needs
- Given the growing heterogeneity of local conditions among cities, to examine to what extent urban policies be carried out effectively from the central government level or decentralized to lower levels of government

From the preceding analysis of the urban and industrial changes that are taking place during this decade, it is clear that new urban policies will have to be more flexible and more diversified. Urban projects will have to be smaller in scale and resource preserving. Cooperation between the public and the private sector and central and local governments, as well as horizontally between local governments, will have to become a virtue out of necessity.

Because of the nationwide impact of industrial restructuring which affects social groups selectively the relative balance between social (people-oriented) policies and urban (place-oriented) policies focusing on helping local government and business is shifting in favor of the former. However, among the advanced economies, there is no unanimity in favor of reducing the central government's role in urban affairs. Wholesale migration and the merging urban zero-sum game could leave substantial amounts of expensive infrastructure underutilized. The deep—if possibly transitional—social problems of the people left behind are seen as a focus for national solidarity and not exclusively a local responsibility.

A tentative profile of the new urban policies for the 1980s in the advanced economies can be attempted regarding style of governance, the strengthening of the local economic base, and the residential sector and local government resources.

- In the political domain a strengthening of local governance will be an important factor in making a relatively safe journey through the decade. Rapidity of adjustment by tailoring policies and resources to local conditions will demand greater cohesiveness between the various institutions which shape the life of cities. Central governments, local governments, business associations, and labor unions as well as neighborhood associations will have to find better ways of working together. In an environment of fiscal austerity there will have to be a shift of emphasis away from resource-dissipating adversary relations toward cooperative actions and shared interventions.
- Regarding infrastructure investment and the needs of the business sector, there will be a clear trend toward mixed land use to meet the composite needs of a rapidly changing economy. Smaller-scale projects will aim to satisfy jointly the needs for office space, warehousing and distribution, and workshops and smaller processing facilities. From the earlier segregation of activities that was leading to major socioeconomic costs (low-income housing estates, very large manufacturing zones) there will be an attempt to closer integration of various urban activities.

- To maintain activities and employment in downtown areas every advantage will be taken of renewal and revitalization operations. New business districts will tend to stress the kind of rental arrangements and services most suited to smaller- and medium-scale firms. Greater attention will be paid to the interaction between large firms and their subsidiaries. The strong revival of interest in small- and medium-size establishments (independent or not) will continue because of their greater flexibility and adaptability.
- Regarding housing and neighborhood needs, more modest and better integrated policies will be needed including recovery of deteriorating housing stock and expansion of neighborhood upgrading and revitalization. There should be a much clearer orientation toward smaller-scale housing projects and a critical evaluation of detached housing which may or may not impose high marginal costs of services depending on location.
- There are considerable differences among countries in the way local government resources are raised. Possibilities for further diversification exist among the five traditional sources of revenues (taxes, user charges, borrowing, intergovernmental transfers, and local enterprises). There will be renewed emphasis on cost-effective institutional arrangements where local governments set priorities and select among policy alternatives but rely on private firms under public control for the actual delivery of services. User charges, because they establish a transparent link between the actual use of a service by residents and the collection of resources, will be favored. New taxes may also be introduced, particularly on undesirable behavior such as pollution.

ACKNOWLEDGMENTS

This paper discusses the new context for urban policies in the 24 OECD countries during the present decade. It is based on the experience of the author when he was Head of Urban Affairs Division of the Organization for Economic Cooperation and Development (OECD) in Paris in 1980 and 1981. The author is solely responsible for the views presented here; in no way can they be taken to represent the views of the OECD or those of the World Bank.

NOTES

1. See *Demographic Trends*, OECD 1950-1990, Organization for Economic Cooperation and Development, Paris, 1979.

2. Among these services are: accounting, advertising, banking, construction and engineering, franchising, health services, insurance, motion pictures, shipping, tourism and transport.

3. See *Changes in Industrial Structure in the European Economies Since the Oil Crisis 1972-1978*, Directorate General for Economic and Financial Affairs, Commission for European Communities, Brussels, 1979.

BIBLIOGRAPHY

The following documents have been consulted even though they may not always be reflected or referred to directly in the text.

Demographic Trends

1. Demographic trends in the OECD member countries: Implications for Social Policies in the 1980's, (Background Note by the Secretariat), 3 October 1980, OEC, SME/CPSBN/80.22 (19 pages, including additional references).
2. L. Shettle, *Implications des evolutions recentes en matiere de demographie sur le development urbain dans les pays membres de L'OCDE* (note interne, 17 fevrier 1981, 21 p.).
3. Peter Hall, *Trends in European Urban Systems*, Conference on Security and Cooperation in europe (CSCE), Hamburg, March 1980.
4. Peter Morrison, *Demographic Structure and Implications of Recent Non-metropolitan Growth*, Rand Corporation, September 1976, WN-9627-EDA
5. *Long-Term Futures of the Urban Environment*, 4 April 1980, UP (80)11, final unrestricted, OECD

Economic Trends

1. EEC- *Changes in Industrial Structure in the European Economies sine The oil Crisis, 1973-1978, Europe - its Capacity to Change in Question!* Directorate-General for Economic and Financial Affairs, Commission of the European Community, Special issue, 1979
2. *Annual Report* to the OECD Council by the St. Committee (note by the Secretary-General), c(81)82, 1st June 1981 (9 pages)
3. T.V. Noyelle, *Services Activities: Their role in National Economies and their Contribution to the Economic Base of Cities. Prospect for the 1980's*, Columbia University, Paper for the Urban Affairs Division, March 15, 1981
4. *Current Development in U.S. International Service Industries*, U.S. Department of Commerce, International Trade Administration, March 1980. (131 p.)
5. Recent International Direct Investment Trends, OECD Council c(81)23, 21 May 1981, 104 p.
6. *Adjustment Positif et Politiques Regionales: Principales Questions*, OECD, CPE/PAP(80)1, 12 March 1980, (18 p.)
7. *Politiques Regionales dans le Contexte de l'Adjustment Positif*, OECD, IND/WP6(80)2, fevier 1980, (21 p.)
8. *Working Party on Future Industrial Structures, 8th Meeting, March 1981*, Examination of Draft Report, (approximately 350 pages.
9. *Report on Some Structural Aspects of Growth*, Commission of the European Communities, 22 June 1978, Brussels, COM(78) 255 final 28 pages.
10. *Specialisation et adaptation face a la crise*, (Etats Unis, japan, Allemagne, France, Royaume Uni), Gerad Lafay et Michel Fouquin (ed) *Revue de CEPIT*, No. 1, 1980, Paris, Documentatin Francaise.
11. Yves Berthelot, Gerard Tardy, *Le Defi Economique du Tiers-Monde*, Documentation Francaise 1979.
12. Norman Glickman, *International Trad, Capital Mobility and Economic Growth: Some Implications for American Cities and Regions in the 1980s*, Paper for the President's Commission for a National Agenda for the 1980s, June 1980. (105 pages.)
13. Henry Coleman, *et. al. Business Cycles and Cities: Past Experience, Prospects and Policy Alternatives*, HUD, PR&R, Division of Economic Development and Public Finance, February 1981, p. 65.

14. Norman Glickman, *The Changing International Economic Order and Urban and Regional Development in OECD Countries*, Report to the Urban Affairs Divn., OECD, 17 Nov. 1980, p. 63.

Impact of Structural Changes

1. Bluestone and Harrison, *Capital and Communities: the Causes and Consequences of Private Investment*, the Progressive Alliance, Washington, D.C., April 1980, (p. 334 and annexes).

2. *The Welfare State in Crisis*, OECD, Paris 1981, (274 pages).

3. Ville de Roubaix, *L'impact des transformations de l'appareil industriel sur les zones urbaines, le cas francais du Nord/Pas-de Calais*, Secretariat au developement, 25 Mars 1981, p. 17.

4. R.J. Johnson, *The Spatial Impact of Fiscal Changes in Britan, Regional Policy in Reverse?* Environment and Planning, Series A, 1979, Vol. 11, pp. 1439-1444.

5. Lesley Punter, *The Inner City and Local Government in Western Europe*, CALUS repot, London, February 1981, p. 123.

6. K. Young, C. Mason, E. Mills, *Urban Government and Economic* Change, SSRC Inner City Working Paper, Report No. 11, London 1980 (100 pages).

7. J.A. Schofield, "Urban Size and Unemployment in Canada," *Canadian Journal of Economics*, 1980, pp. 490-499.

8. B.C. Moore, J. Rhodes and P. Tyler, *Interaction of Regional and Urban Policy in the U.K.*, preliminary paper for the U.K. PPG on urban/Regional Coordination Ad Hoc Group, 1981 p. 943.

9. *Urban America in the Eighties*, U.S. President's Commission for a National Agenda for the 1980's, Washington, D.C., 1980 (112 pages).

URBAN ECONOMIC AND DEMOGRAPHIC CHANGE:

RECENT SHIFTS AND FUTURE PROSPECTS

Kathryn P. Nelson

I. INTRODUCTION

As both population and economic activity have dispersed across the United States since the late nineteenth century, regional economies have become more similar in terms of development levels and well-being (ACIR, 1980). Within the United States, many summary indicators suggest that differences among regions and divisions continued to diminish in the 1970s. Because population growth was higher in less dense places, Census divisions became more alike in density and in degree of urbanization. As the national industrial mix shifted from manufacturing toward services, regional employment structures became more similar to one another and to the nation. Perhaps most important, regional disparities in per capita income continued to narrow, especially when adjusted for differences in cost of living (see Table 1).

The crucial question, of course, is whether these trends represent an approach

Research in Urban Economics, Volume 4, pages 25-49.
Copyright © 1984 JAI Press Inc.
All rights or reproduction in any form reserved.
ISBN: 0-89232-423-6

toward equilibrium or whether they will "overshoot" to a new configuration of regional or intraregional disparities. The extent of interregional and interstate disparities in needs and resources is especially crucial as we reexamine the optimal allocation of responsibilities and resources between public and private sectors and among levels of government.

The summary of regional and intraregional shifts in population and employment in this paper is intended to provide a helpful overview of the economic and demographic context in which governments and other actors will have to make decisions in the 1980s. It focuses on the changing location and composition of jobs and people within central cities, suburbs, and nonmetropolitan areas of the several regions in the 1970s to provide a basis for projecting the geographical implications of ongoing industrial and demographic shifts. We intend to: (a) review interregional and intraregional shifts in the location of employment between 1969 and 1978, focusing on the effects of two recent business cycles; (b) survey changes in population and household composition in different types of jurisdictions in the 1970s, and compare past trends in migration with preferences about future moves and residential location in the 1980s; and (c) summarize the apparent implications of these trends and differentials for changes in regions and types of jurisdictions in the 1980s, and for the public finance and urban development issues they will face.

Table 1. Per Capita Income Levels by Region in Relation to the U.S. Average 1950 to 1980

				1975		
Region	1950	1960	1970	Actual	Adjusted[a]	1980
United States	$1,496	$2,222	$3,966	$5,902	$5,902	$9,458
New England	107	110	108	103	89	105
Mideast	117	116	113	109	100	106
Great Lakes	111	108	104	104	102	103
Plains	95	93	95	98	99	97
Southeast	68	73	82	86	93	86
Southwest	87	87	89	93	99	98
Rocky Mountain	97	94	91	94	98	95
Far West	119	118	111	111	106	112

Note:
[a] Crudely adjusted by ACIR for cost-of-living differences.
Sources: ACIR. (1980) *Regional Growth: Historic Perspective*. Table A-2 Washington, D.C.: ACIR, June.
    U.S. Bureau of Economic Analysis. (1981) *Survey of Current Business* (April).

II. REGIONAL AND INTERREGIONAL SHIFTS IN EMPLOYMENT

Jobs have been decentralizing from the industrial belt and out from central cities for many decades (Mills, 1972). Decentralization continued in the 1970s in all

Census divisions (see Table 2). The Country Business Patterns (CBP) data used cover most industries, but not government, and have the advantage of constant geography over time. A disadvantage is lack of data on central *cities*; in Table 2, based on 1970 SMSA definitions, "core" counties contain a central business district (CBD), only defined in central cities with population above 100,000, while "other central" are all others having a central city. Although these definitions underrepresent suburban employment, the data clearly record shifts of national employment away from the three northeastern divisions and out from central counties in all divisions. Core counties in the South Central, Mountain, and Pacific divisions gained share of national employment, but their relative share of their division's employment declined.

Because manufacturing grew only 6% between 1967-1978 while tertiary industries grew more than six times as quickly, manufacturing's share of national employment fell from 36 to 30%, while the share for trade, finance, and service industries ("tertiary" industries) increased from 50 to 57%. Manufacturing's share of employment fell in all divisions, although it still ranged from 35% of CBP employment in the East North Central division to 16% in the Mountain division. National changes in industrial composition were mirrored in both core and nonmetropolitan counties: in each, manufacturing declined 6 percentage points while the tertiary group gained 7 points. Suburban counties experienced a larger shift: their share of employment in manufacturing dropped 10 points while services grew 9 points. Thus, by 1978, suburban industrial structure had become more similar to that of central counties, but core counties retained the highest concentration of tertiary employment (60%) and the lowest of manufacturing (25%). The share of employment in services was least in nonmetropolitan counties, but even there it had reached 50%. Nonmetropolitan areas were still most dependent on manufacturing, which accounted for one-third of employment.

But for future planning and prediction, the question is not the fact of employment decentralization, but the rate and the determinants of change. Resolution of such questions has been hindered by poor data, by differences among industries in the extent and rate of decentralization, and by the poorly understood impacts of business cycles (Harrison, 1974). To deal with these issues, and to isolate regional and intraregional shifts, an extended shift-share technique was used to control for the national business cycle and for industrial composition (Nelson and Patrick, 1982). Two downturns and recovery periods were studied over two recent business cycles: 1969-1972 and 1974-1978.

In terms of shifts *between* regions, the yearly percentage rates of change shown in Table 3 for each division identify the Middle Atlantic division as having by far the largest interregional losses, with its relative losses to other divisions being much greater during periods of recovery. Although the rate of interregional loss did not accelerate between the two recovery periods, in 1975-1978 more of the losses were due to shifts in trade and services. The interregional position of the New England and East North Central divisions, on the other hand, improved

Table 2. Percentage Distribution of National CBP Employment[a] in 1969 and 1978 by Metropolitan Status of County and Census Division

| | Metropolitan Status of County in 1970 | | | | | | | | | | Change |
| | Core[b] | | Other central | | Suburban | | Nonmetropolitan | | Total | | 1969-1978 |
Census Division	1969	1978	1969	1978	1969	1978	1969	1978	1969	1978	
New England	3.7	3.1	0.2	0.2	2.2	2.2	0.7	0.8	6.8	6.2	−0.6
Middle Atlantic	11.9	8.7	2.6	2.1	3.9	3.9	2.7	2.5	21.1	17.3	−3.8
East North Central	12.3	10.4	2.6	2.7	2.5	2.8	4.2	4.2	21.6	20.2	−1.4
West North Central	3.5	3.1	0.7	0.7	0.7	1.0	2.5	2.9	7.4	7.7	+0.3
South Atlantic	5.1	4.7	2.3	2.8	1.6	2.2	5.1	5.5	14.1	15.2	+1.1
East South Central	2.1	2.2	0.5	0.5	0.2	0.3	2.5	2.7	5.3	5.7	+0.4
West South Central	5.0	5.8	0.9	1.2	0.3	0.4	2.2	2.4	8.4	9.8	+1.4
Mountain	1.4	1.8	0.5	0.8	0.2	0.5	1.1	1.5	3.2	4.5	+1.3
Pacific	9.0	9.5	1.4	1.8	0.6	0.7	1.1	1.4	12.1	13.4	+1.3
Total	54.0	49.3	11.7	12.8	12.2	14.0	22.1	23.9	100.0	100.0	
CBP employment in millions[c]									55.7	69.8	+14.1

Notes:

[a] The major industry not covered by CBP is government, which constituted 20.7% of the employment covered by BEA in 1970 and 19.6% in 1978. In 1978 government shares of regional employment were near the national average in most Census divisions, except for lows of 16.1% in East North Central and 16.6% in New England, and highs of 24.3% in Mountain and 24.6% in South Atlantic.

[b] "Core" counties are defined as those counties in which the Central Business Districts of central cities are located, and thus include only the central counties of Standard Metropolitan Statistical Areas (SMSAs) with a central city whose population was above 100,000 in 1970.

[c] Base: civilian employment, as measured in *County Business Patterns.*

Source: U.S. Bureau of the Census, *County Business Patterns* (1969 and 1978), calculated from data on magnetic tape.

Table 3. Interregional Shifts of Employment[a] for Core Counties, by Census Division, 1969-1978

Census Division	Total Employment				Manufacturing		Retail Trade		Services	
	1969-71	1971-2	1974-5	1975-8	1971-2	1975-8	1971-2	1975-8	1971-2	1975-8
New England	-1.0	-1.0	-1.7	-0.8	-1.2	-0.4	-0.4	-2.0	-0.8	0.5
Middle Atlantic	-1.0	-3.2	-0.2	-3.0	-3.6	-2.7	-3.1	-3.2	-2.5	-3.2
East N. Central	-0.8	-1.1	-0.8	-0.4	-0.9	-0.2	-1.3	-0.6	-0.9	-0.6
West N. Central	-0.7	0.1	2.2	0.3	1.1	0.2	-0.7	-0.1	0.4	0.5
South Atlantic	1.8	3.0	-1.6	—	2.3	0.8	2.2	—	3.2	-0.3
East S. Central	1.5	2.4	-0.3	0.9	4.5	1.0	2.7	1.3	0.1	0.2
West S. Central	1.3	1.1	3.0	1.9	1.4	2.1	1.3	2.2	0.3	2.1
Mountain	3.4	5.6	1.4	3.6	4.9	2.7	5.9	3.5	3.2	3.2
Pacific	-0.8	1.1	1.2	2.3	2.4	1.6	0.6	2.2	0.7	2.6

Note:
[a] Expressed as an annualized percent of initial employment.
Source: Calculated from tables in K.P. Nelson and C.H. Patrick, "The Impact of Business Cycle on Decentralization of Employment," 1982.

between the two cycles, with lower rates of interregional loss during the more recent business cycle.

Turning to the "growing" regions, shifts into the East South Central division slowed over the decade, while for the South Atlantic division, the formerly large interregional gains became losses during the last recession and then completely halted. The slowdown in these divisions was concentrated in tertiary industries, as they continued to gain manufacturing employment. Interregional shifts into the West South Central, West North Central, and Pacific divisions increased, with the acceleration spurred more by services than by manufacturing, particularly in the Pacific division. Thus services, in addition to becoming more dominant in the economy, also appear to be leading the interregional shifts in employment.

Intraregionally, jobs were shifting out from core counties in *all* divisions (see Table 4). Intraregional shifts out from core counties were highest and increasing over time in the South Atlantic division. Contrary to some earlier results (James, 1975), decentralization *from* central cities seems to have been accelerated by the business cycle, with faster rates of relative core county loss during recovery periods. This distinction between downturn and upturn was especially marked in the vulnerable Middle Atlantic and East North Central divisions, and in the faltering South Atlantic division. The faster rates of decentralization during recovery were concentrated in the "secondary" industries of construction, manufacturing, and transportation and public utilities. Among tertiary industries, the yearly rate of decentralization was close to the national average of 1% in both recession and recovery. Consistent with Birch's (1979) studies of births and deaths among firms, the relationship between recovery and decentralization seems to result not from higher rates of establishment closings in central cities during recessions (as had earlier been hypothesized), but instead from faster growth during recovery outside central counties in both number of establishments and in employees per establishment. For policymakers, this distinction emphasizes the importance for job growth of aiding new industries and facilitating expansion in existing industries.

Although decentralization proceeded throughout the two cycles, the counties that were *gaining* jobs changed markedly. In the recent cycle, *suburban* counties gained more employment from intraregional shifts than did nonmetropolitan counties in all divisions other than the New England and Pacific divisions. This pattern was in marked contrast to the early 1970s, when nonmetropolitan counties were growing faster than suburban counties, both absolutely and relatively, in all divisions except the Mountain and West South Central. The slowdown in nonmetropolitan growth was most drastic during the 1974-75 downturn in the less dense central divisions of the country, and corresponds to a post-1975 slowing of nonmetropolitan population growth noted by John Long (1981). It may well result from the upward spiral in gasoline prices and transportation costs that began in 1973, and it suggests a particular vulnerability of nonmetropolitan

Table 4. Intraregional Shifts of Employment[a] among Central, Suburban, and Nonmetropolitan Counties, by Census Division, 1969-1978

Census Division	Core Counties				Suburban		Nonmetropolitan	
	1969-71	1971-72	1974-75	1975-78	1974-75	1975-78	1974-75	1975-78
New England	-0.7	-0.7	-1.0	-1.1	1.1	0.5	1.0	2.3
Middle Atlantic	-0.9	-1.4	-0.8	-1.2	1.8	1.8	1.3	1.7
East N. Central	-0.4	-1.6	-0.6	-1.1	1.4	2.4	0.2	1.0
West N. Central	-1.2	-1.4	-1.6	-1.8	1.8	4.1	0.6	0.6
South Atlantic	-1.0	-1.7	-1.3	-2.6	3.5	2.0	1.0	1.5
East S. Central	-0.5	-1.0	–	-0.9	-0.7	2.9	-0.5	0.7
West S. Central	-0.1	-0.5	0.8	-0.2	-0.8	2.0	-1.5	0.2
Mountain	0.6	0.4	-2.4	-0.9	2.2	2.3	2.6	-0.3
Pacific	-0.5	-0.7	-0.6	-0.8	0.3	0.3	2.0	3.3

Note:

[a] Shifts of employment within census divisions, controlling for industrial mix, expressed as an annualized percent of initial employment.

Source: Calculated from tables in K.P. Nelson and C.H. Patrick, "The Impact of Business Cycles on Decentralization of Employment," 1982.

employment to recession. Thus, higher energy costs may have shifted relative advantage from nonmetropolitan to suburban, though not back to central, counties.

Nevertheless, other research with CBP data for this period by Long and DeAre (1982) shows substantial gains in manufacturing and other employment—other than mining or recreation—in nonadjacent nonmetropolitan counties through 1978. Thus, the shifts in employment to nonmetropolitan areas that occurred during the 1960s and 1970s appear to have laid an economic base for future population growth.

Changes in Characteristics of Resident Population

County-level employment data demonstrate the similarity of the process of decentralization across regions and its persistence over the past decade. Complete analysis of the impact of employment changes on cities and their financial base, or on the residents of cities, suburbs, and nonmetropolitan areas in different regions and states, must await 1980 Census results.

Although regional or local data are not yet available, sample data from the Current Population Survey (see Table 5) suggest that such decentralization has most severely affected the central cities of the largest (1 million plus) SMSAs, which are predominantly located in the North and West. There the number of employed residents dropped more quickly than did either adults or total population. In each other type of location the number of employed residents grew more quickly than the adult population. Residents of central cities were particularly hurt by the decentralization of manufacturing, with the number of employed residents dropping 17% in the largest cities and 6% in smaller central cities. Residents of large cities gained jobs only in professional and business-related services, industries shown by the shift-share study to be moving west. Even in these industries, moreover, the growth rates for large cities and smaller cities were lower than for all other locations.

In terms of occupation, the highest losses for large central city residents occurred in the better-paid blue-collar occupations of operatives and craft-workers. Large cities also lost sales and clerical occupations, while the fastest growth rates for both cities and other locations were in the lower-paying service occupations. City residents did gain professional and managerial jobs, but at lower growth rates than in other types of residence.

As the access of city residents to jobs apparently declined, suburbs of smaller SMSAs had the highest growth in employed residents, with service industries and occupations obviously the growth leader. Nonmetropolitan residents gained more of the manufacturing, craft, and operative jobs than did the other jurisdictions.

III. POPULATION GROWTH, AND CHANGES IN INCOME, BY REGION AND TYPE OF RESIDENCE

Census data on population growth by region and size of place between 1970 and 1980 (see Table 6) demonstrate how pervasive the trend toward deconcentration

Table 5. Percent Change in Population, Employment and Households by Metropolitan or Nonmetropolitan Residence, 1970-1977

Type of Residence

| | U.S. Total | All SMSAs | Metropolitan Areas of | | | | Nonmetropolitan Areas |
| | | | more than 1 million | | less than 1 million | | |
			city	suburbs	city	suburbs	
Population							
Total	6.4	4.4	-7.1	11.7	-1.6	12.5	10.7
Adult (16+)	15.2	13.5	1.8	23.0	6.4	24.1	18.9
Industry of employment							
Total	17.2	14.2	-6.5	25.7	7.7	28.2	24.4
Manufacturing	3.4	-1.6	-17.2	6.4	-6.5	6.4	15.0
Retail trade	23.2	21.3	-3.7	33.2	15.6	38.7	27.9
Prof. services	35.1	32.0	11.2	45.4	17.2	56.0	43.1
Bus. services[a]	30.5	27.8	3.4	43.4	22.6	49.5	42.4
Major Occupation							
Professional[b]	31.5	28.8	9.7	37.3	18.3	46.2	39.6
Sales or clerical	12.1	9.0	-14.6	20.4	4.8	29.8	23.2
Craft worker	7.6	3.2	-15.6	11.0	-2.1	13.2	17.5
Operatives	1.5	1.0	-20.6	8.0	-6.9	–	12.9
Service worker	44.2	41.2	21.2	56.1	28.3	66.4	51.5

33

Table 5. (cont.) Percent Change in Population, Employment and Households by Metropolitan or Nonmetropolitan Residence, 1970-1977

			Type of Residence				
			Metropolitan Areas of				
			more than 1 million		less than 1 million		
	U.S. Total	All SMSAs	city	suburbs	city	suburbs	Nonmetropolitan Areas
Years of School (age 25+)							
Total	12.6	10.2	-4.0	18.3	5.1	20.4	16.8
HS Graduate	29.6	24.0	6.0	27.8	21.5	39.6	42.9
College 1-3	40.0	40.1	26.8	45.6	30.2	56.0	40.0
College 4+	60.8	58.6	44.3	64.0	44.1	80.2	68.5
Households							
Total	16.9	15.0	1.6	22.3	12.3	24.8	21.1
Hus/wife families	8.6	5.0	-12.0	12.5	-2.5	17.6	16.1
Male head family	-9.9	-3.0	-15.6	19.4	-14.1	–	-23.3
Female head family	33.9	35.0	22.9	47.5	34.0	44.8	31.3
Male individual	51.6	51.5	27.0	76.8	60.4	66.9	52.0
Female individual	35.7	34.5	16.9	46.4	38.5	53.4	38.7

Notes:
a Includes finance, insurance and real estate, and business and repair services.
b Includes technical, managerial and administrative workers.
Source: U.S. Bureau of the Census (1978). "Social and Economic Characteristics of the Metropolitan and Nonmetropolitan Population: 1977 and 1970." *Current Population Reports*: Special Studies, Series P-23, No. 75.

has been. In almost every case, *smaller* places in each region had higher rates of population growth than did *larger* places, and nonmetropolitan places grew more quickly than those in SMSAs. In all four regions, the fastest growth rates were experienced in locations outside places. In the West and Northeast, adjacent nonmetropolitan counties grew more quickly than did suburban areas (roughly paralleling the employment shifts to nonmetropolitan areas in these regions), but in the North Central and Southern regions the fastest growing counties were suburban. The largest losers by far were large cities in the Northeast and North Central regions. There both categories of large cities with population above 100,000 had rates of loss greater than 10% over the decade.

The impact of population losses during the decade, however, was cushioned

Table 6. Annual Rate of Population Change Per 1,000 Average Population From 1970 to 1980 By Size of Incorporated Places in 1970, Metropolitan/Nonmetropolitan Status, and Region

	U.S.	North-east	North Central	South	West
Total	10.8	.2	3.9	18.1	21.4
Outside Places 2,500+	19.3	11.5	13.6	24.5	27.6
2,500-24,999	13.3	−4.6	10.0	18.1	31.0
25,000-99,999	6.3	−5.8	−1.3	12.1	19.4
100,000-999,999	0.3	−13.4	−10.7	5.4	12.2
1,000,000+	−6.9	−11.7	−14.8	25.5	5.4
Metro,[1] Central County	7.4	−4.0	−1.9	16.2	19.0
Outside Places 2,500+	19.4	10.0	12.1	29.4	24.5
2,500-24,999	20.3	−4.7	13.2	31.8	38.6
25,000-99,999	7.1	−5.2	−1.6	12.3	19.7
100,000-999,999	0.4	−13.8	−10.9	5.5	12.2
1,000,000+	−7.0	−11.7	−14.8	24.5	5.4
Metro,[1] Fringe County	16.2	3.3	15.1	28.1	27.5
Outside Places 2,500+	21.4	8.9	23.5	30.0	35.9
2,500-24,999	12.6	−5.5	15.9	24.2	31.1
25,000+	3.2	−8.0	−1.6	19.4	22.6
Nonmetro[1] 3%+ Commuting to Metro	15.3	13.0	8.8	17.7	34.1
Outside Places 2,500+	19.2	19.6	12.2	20.7	38.0
2,500-24,999	7.7	−2.6	3.2	10.4	28.7
25,000+	2.9	−8.5	.3	7.2	24.9
Nonmetro[1] <3% Commuting to Metro	13.2	9.4	5.2	13.9	24.5
Outside Places 2,500+	16.2	14.6	6.8	17.4	27.8
2,500-24,999	8.6	−4.0	3.8	7.8	20.2
25,000+	6.2	.3	−.9	6.2	17.4

Note:
[1] Metropolitan areas as defined January 1, 1980.

Source: Long, John. (1981) *Population Deconcentration in the United States.* CDS-81-5, Special Demographic Analyses. Washington, D.C.: U.S. Bureau of the Census.

by high rates of household formation, which maintained demand for both housing and public services in most local markets. During the 1970s, the 27% increase in households far outstripped the 11% growth in population. The disparity was in large part due to the maturing baby boom: the rate of increase in *age*-specific rates of household formation slowed between the 1960s and the 1970s and was noticeably lower in the second half of the 1970s.

The combination of high rates of household formation and a large cohort of young adults was particularly beneficial for central cities. Rates of migration into central cities have traditionally been highest for young adults. In spite of population losses in large central cities, the number of households increased there as well as in the nation, although there were dramatic shifts in household composition. Both large and smaller central cities lost husband-wife families while gaining families with female heads and primary individuals. Indeed, Annual Housing Survey data suggest that primary individuals between 20 and 34 were the only type of household to increase numerically in large northeastern cities in the 1970s.

In spite of the ample publicity given to gentrification, changes in median income by region and type of place suggest that growth in households occurred predominantly among poor households, often with female heads, in large northeastern cities (see Table 7). There, population decline has been accompanied by a drastic worsening of the relative income of the population and by a widening of income disparities between these central cities and their suburbs. In 1980, the median income in large northeastern central cities was lower than that in any other location in the nation, including the historically poorest, nonmetropolitan South. Accounting for cost-of-living differences would only widen the disparity.

Moreover, poverty has become increasingly concentrated in central cities since 1969 (see Table 8). Although geographic detail is lacking, northern central cities have probably captured most of the increase. Between 1969 and 1974, while the rate of poverty decreased in the nation and in most locations, it rose only in the central cities of large SMSAs, and in the Northeast. Between 1974 and 1980, poverty also increased more sharply in central cities than in the nation, as the national poverty rate increased 2 percentage points. Past employment decentralization and job losses for central city residents suggest that present increases in poverty will also be disproportionately concentrated in northern central cities.

Although the proportion of blacks in poverty remained near one-third throughout the decade, the relative incidence of black poverty shifted dramatically toward northern central cities, in large part because of the increasing concentration of black female-headed households there. Reductions in poverty rates in the South and in nonmetropolitan areas were balanced by increases in the Northeast and North Central regions, and in central cities. In each region, the concentration of blacks within central cities increased over the decade in spite of net out-migration from central cities. Rates of net out-migration from central cities remain much higher for whites than for blacks and black out-migration also is selective

Table 7. Median Family Income or Household Income in Relation to National Median by Type of Residence and Region, 1969, 1976, 1977 and 1980

| | Median Family Income | | | | Median Household Income | | | | | | | | | |
| | North & West | | South | | Northeast | | North Central | | South | | West | | US | |
Type of Residence	1969	1976	1969	1976	1977	1980	1977	1980	1977	1980	1977	1980	1977	1980
Total Metropolitan	112	108	96	101	105	103	115	115	103	101	107	112	108	108
Metro 1 million +														
Central City	103	91	91	92	78	76	86	83	93	84	95	105	87	86
Suburbs	125	122	118	120	128	125	140	138	129	128	120	127	129	130
Metro <1 million														
Central City	103	98	87	90	82	83	94	96	89	89	93	92	90	90
Suburbs	111	108	93	100	118	117	123	123	103	103	107	106	113	112
Nonmetropolitan	90	93	69	77	106	101	90	85	79	81	91	92	87	87
Total	107	104	83	90	105	103	105	103	91	92	103	107	100	100

Sources: U.S. Bureau of Census (1978). "Social and Economic Characteristics of the Metro and Nonmetro Population, 1977 and 1970," *Current Population Reports*, Series P-23, No. 75.

U.S. Bureau of the Census (1978). "Money Income of Households in the United States: 1977." *Current Population Reports: Consumer Income*, Series P-60, No. 117.

U.S. Bureau of the Census (1982) "Money Income of Households, Families and Persons in the United States: 1980" *Current Population Reports: Consumer Income*, Series P-60, No. 132.

Table 8.   Percentage of Persons Below the Poverty Level by Region, Type of Residence and Race Between 1969 and 1980

	Total Rate of Poverty			Black Rate of Poverty		
	(Percent)			(Percent)		
	1969	1974	1980	1969	1974	1980
Total Persons	12.1%	11.2%	13.0%	32.2%	30.3%	32.5%
Metropolitan	9.5	9.7	11.9	24.5	26.7	30.1
Central City	12.7	13.7	17.2	24.3	28.3	32.3
Suburban Balance	6.8	6.7	8.2	25.4	21.3	24.3
Non-metropolitan	17.9	14.2	15.4	54.3	41.1	40.6
Northeast	8.6	8.8	11.1	22.5	25.4	30.7
North Central	9.6	8.8	11.4	22.7	26.3	33.3
South	17.9	15.4	16.5	40.8	34.9	35.1
West	10.4	10.1	11.4	19.9	22.1	19.0

Sources: U.S. Bureau of the Census. (1980) "Characteristics of the Population Below the Poverty Level: 1978." *Current Population Reports*, Series P-60, No. 124.
U.S. Bureau of the Census. (1981) "Money Income and Poverty Status of Families and Persons in the United States: 1980." *Current Population Reports*, Series P-60, No. 127.

by income. The result is further income and racial disparities between central cities and their suburbs.

IV. MIGRATION TRENDS AND DIFFERENTIALS

Although back-to-the-countryside and back-to-the-city reversals in migration patterns received much publicity during the 1970s, recent trends and future preferences in migration point to further regional and intraregional deconcentration and disparities in spite of these mild equilibrating tendencies. As Table 9 shows, net out-migration of whites from cities continues at high levels in all regions, while migration into nonmetropolitan counties appears to be an offshoot of population growth in the South and West. The selective nature of these migration streams combined with continuing shifts from Frostbelt to Sunbelt presages further economic and social disparities between cities and suburbs, particular in the North.

According to CPS estimates, migration into central cities increased during the 1970s, both numerically and as a proportion of the original city population (see Table 9). Because of this, rates of net out-migration of whites from cities declined slightly in all regions other than the West, in spite of offsetting increases in total white out-migration. Blacks joined whites as net out-migrants from cities in all regions, although black rates of net out-migration were less than half those of whites.

Closer analysis of the increase in migration to cities (Nelson, 1982) reveals that it resulted more from compositional and cohort effects than from greater

Table 9. Rates of In and Out Migration for Cities, Suburbs, and Nonmetropolitan Areas, by Race and Region

	Northeast		North Central		South		West	
	1970-75	1975-80	1970-75	1975-80	1970-75	1975-80	1970-75	1975-80
Central Cities								
Whites								
In	5.6	7.4	11.8	13.8	15.4	16.0	23.9	23.7
Out	−18.3	−19.3	−28.9	−29.3	−32.0	−29.4	−31.4	−31.7
Net	−12.6	−12.0	−17.1	−15.5	−16.6	−13.4	−7.5	−8.0
Blacks								
In	5.3	2.7	6.8	7.0	9.5	8.9	13.4	16.6
Out	−9.4	−8.9	−9.7	−8.8	−9.5	−11.7	−16.0	−18.4
Net	−4.0	−6.2	−3.0	−1.8	−0−	−2.8	−2.5	−1.8
Suburbs								
Whites								
In	11.8	10.7	18.8	17.0	35.8	30.1	26.4	25.9
Out	−10.8	−9.8	−13.1	−12.9	−15.7	−16.3	−16.8	−17.5
Net	1.0	+0.9	5.7	4.1	20.1	13.8	9.6	8.4
Blacks								
In	18.7	14.0	25.0	22.5	26.9	35.9	58.6	36.3
Out	−12.5	−9.2	−16.5	−18.7	−15.5	−13.9	−19.3	−23.5
Net	6.2	4.8	8.5	3.7	11.4	22.0	39.3	12.7
Nonmetropolitan Areas								
Whites								
In	11.8	11.1	10.6	11.3	16.5	14.9	21.5	21.7
Out	−11.1	−11.9	−10.1	−11.9	−10.5	−9.6	−15.4	−15.8
Net	0.7	−0.8	0.5	−0.6	6.0	5.3	6.1	5.9
Blacks								
In	23.7	21.1	16.1	10.6	6.0	6.1	14.8	28.2
Out	−16.7	−26.7	−11.8	−16.4	−9.4	−7.5	−21.1	−45.3
Net	7.0	−5.6	4.3	−5.8	−3.4	−1.5	−6.3	−17.1

Source: U.S. Bureau of the Census (1980) "Geographic Mobility: March 1975-1980." *Current Population Reports*, Series P-20, No. 368, and unpublished tabulations from the 1975 Current Population Survey.

preference for cities. For most age groups, the increase reflected similar or lower rates of migration to cities on a growing base of noncity residents rather than increases in age-specific in-migration rates. Furthermore, although cities were aided by shifts in household composition toward household types with greater preferences for city living, over the decade *out*-migration from cities increased among each household type.

The only national evidence of gentrification, in terms of greater preference for cities among higher status groups, occurred among city residents. Rates of out-migration from central cities dropped among young adults, and whites of all education levels above grammar school left cities at lower rates.

The most marked drop in white out-migration rates occurred among college graduates and those in professional or managerial occupations. Both changes are consistent with the national growth in professional occupations and industries in large central cities, and with gentrification. However, these minor changes did not reverse the prevalent pattern of net out-migration from central cities among all groups, along with selectively higher net rates of out-migration among higher status whites and blacks.

In terms of households income, the decreased out-migration among professionals was reflected in a drop in out-migration of 6 percentage points among husband-wife families in the highest income category (over $30,000 in 1979). However, the slight decreases in out-migration were concentrated in husband-wife families in the lowest income categories (below $6,000 in 1979). There were no increases in in-migration rates in any income category. The effect of net out-migration from cities combined with the higher income of movers to suburbs implies that by the end of the 1970s central cities had "lost" some $60 billion in annual income of residents because of movement between cities and suburbs during the decade.

A. Net Migration into Nonmetropolitan Areas

The migration rates in Table 9 also suggest that movement into nonmetropolitan areas is rather tenuous. By the second half of the decade, out-migrants from nonmetropolitan areas—both white and black—exceeded in-migrants in both the Northeast and North Central regions. White rates of net migration into nonmetropolitan areas had also declined in the South and West. Overall, movement between metropolitan and nonmetropolitan areas does not appear to be very selective by status characteristics. Distinct differences by age remain, with the 20-24 age group still migrating into SMSAs on net throughout the decade, and the 25-29 age group joining them in 1975-1980. But rates of net migration into nonmetropolitan areas were approximately similar—and average—for each education or income subgroup. Thus, it does not appear that differential migration will increase status differences between metropolitan and nonmetropolitan areas as it has done between cities and suburbs. Indeed, in view of past poverty and low income in nonmetropolitan areas, one could hope that more income resources were moving in to finance the new population growth.

B. Interregional Migration

Between the 1960s and the 1970s, net migration continued into the West and accelerated into the South but became more negative for the Middle Atlantic and East North Central divisions (see Table 10). In terms of actual flows of migrants, in both 1970-1975 and 1975-1980 interregional migrants to the South and West greatly outnumbered reverse flows to northern regions. During each half of the 1970s, the Northeast and North Central regions lost 2-3% of their initial population because of internal migration, while the South and West each gained almost 3%.

The selectivity of migration heightened its regional impacts. Despite the high propensity of elderly retires to move to the Sunbelt, over 60% of the net gain in population due to migrants in the South and West were persons under 45, a net influx of young adults which will further increase regional disparities in fertility rates. Within the labor force, in-migration to the South and West was higher among professional, sales, and service workers than for either craft and operatives or unemployed workers, a differential consistent with the faster growth rates in service industries there. Northern regions had higher rates of out-migration among employed workers than for unemployed workers. Thus, as migrants respond to employment opportunities and amenities in the Sunbelt, they improve both the potential market and the quality of the labor force, and further increase the attractiveness of the region for future economic growth.

C. Future Regional Preferences

Comparison of interregional migration flows in 1965-1970 with flows in the 1970s shows that net migration out of the Northeast and North Central regions doubled between the two time periods, while net migration into the South almost tripled (from 660,000 to 1.83 million). In spite of the general stability of interregional migration during the 1970s, such past volatility implies that the 1970 patterns of migration will not necessarily continue in the 1980s. But in response to a 1979 question asking where households heads would prefer to live in five years, about 15.4% of the heads indicated that they preferred to move and were "likely" or "very likely" to act on this preference. According to Larry Long (1982), "these figures. . .imply a future rate of migration that is not too far out of line with past observed rates of intercounty migration in the U.S."

As Table 11 shows, the proportion of household heads who feel that they are likely to move among regions between 1979 and 1984—i.e., 6.5%—is almost exactly the same as the fraction of households actually moving between regions in each five-year period during the 1970s. But *if* these expressions of preference are a valid indicator of future migration, the effects of interregional migration

Table 10. Average Annual Rates of Components of Population Change Per 1,000 Population for Regions and Divisions for 1960 to 1970 and 1970 to 1980

Regions and Divisions	Population Change		Net Migration		Natural Increase	
	1960 to 1970	1970 to 1980	1960 to 1970	1970 to 1980	1960 to 1970	1970 to 1980
United States	12.5	10.9	1.7	4.6	10.9	6.3
Northeast	9.4	0.2	.7	-3.9	8.6	4.1
New England	12.0	4.2	2.7	0.2	9.2	4.0
Middle Atlantic	8.5	-1.2	.1	-5.2	8.4	4.0
North Central	9.2	4.0	-1.4	-2.6	10.6	6.6
East North Central	10.6	3.5	-.4	-3.4	11.0	6.3
West North Central	5.9	5.2	-3.8	-0.7	9.7	5.9
South	13.3	18.2	1.3	11.5	12.1	6.7
South Atlantic (excluding Florida)	12.8	13.0	.3	6.1	12.5	6.9
Florida	31.3	36.1	22.7	33.6	8.7	2.5
East South Central	6.1	13.6	-5.6	6.6	11.7	7.0
West South Central	13.1	20.6	.2	12.4	12.9	8.2
West	21.6	21.5	9.2	13.7	12.4	7.8
Mountain	18.9	31.6	4.3	21.4	14.6	10.2
Pacific	22.4	18.1	10.7	11.1	11.7	7.0

Source: Long, John. (1981) *Population Deconcentration in the United States.* CDS-81-5, Special Demographic Analyses. Washington, D.C.: U.S. Bureau of the Census.

will be quite different in the next five years. The responses imply a further acceleration in net out-migration from the North Central region as the result of less in-migration and more out-migration, and more out-migration from the Northeast as well. The results also predict a slowing of in-migration into the South and faster growth in the West. More of these likely future migrants intend to move to the West, while fewer western residents plan to leave.

Table 11. Past and "Future" Rates of Interregional Migration of Households, by Region, 1970-75, 1975-80, and 1979-84[a]

	U.S.	North-east	North Central	South	West
1970-75					
U.S. Total	6.4%				
In		+2.8	+3.9	+6.8	+7.2
Out		−6.3	−6.1	−4.1	−4.8
Net		−3.4	−2.2	+2.7	+2.3
1975-80					
U.S. Total	6.3%				
In		+2.9	+4.6	+7.9	+10.4
Out		−7.6	−7.3	−4.7	−6.3
Net		−4.7	−2.7	+3.2	+4.1
1979-84[a]					
U.S. Total	6.5%				
In		+2.0	+1.7	+6.7	+11.3
Out		−8.6	−9.9	−3.8	−4.2
Net		−6.7	−8.2	+2.9	+7.1

Note:

[a] 1979-84 "rates" of interregional migration assume that preferred moves are actually made by all respondents to the 1979 AHS who consider a move to be "likely" or "very likely."

Source: U.S. Bureau of the Census (1981). "Geographic Mobility: March 1975-1980." *Current Population Reports*, Series P-20, No. 368, and unpublished tabulations from the 1975 Current Population Survey and the 1979 Annual Housing Survey.

D. Future Preferences by Size of Place

The questions on likely migration also asked the desired type of destination. The results suggest that movement from large central cities and SMSAs to small places will continue or accelerate. "Rural" was clearly the preferred destination, since it was selected by 30% of all likely movers. Conversely, residents of the suburbs and cities of the largest SMSAs reported the highest rates of likely out-migration in all regions except the Northeast, while residents of nonmetropolitan rural areas had the lowest preferences for leaving.

In addition, differentials by income in likely migration presage further worsening of the income resources of central cities and of differentials between cities and their suburbs (see Table 12). Differences by income in likely out-migration rates are greatest among residents of central cities of large SMSAs, particularly in the South and Northeast. Higher income residents of southern large cities report themselves fully twice as likely to move as lower income residents, suggesting that income disparitities between cities and suburbs may increase in the South. In large cities in the Northeast and North Central regions, higher income residents also consider themselves 50% more likely to leave than do lower income residents. In no other type of residence are the differentials by income in plans to move so great.

PROSPECTS FOR THE FUTURE

Extrapolation from the redistribution trends summarized here must be tempered by recognition of the effects of ongoing evolution in industrial structure and demographic composition. As tertiary industries become more important but also more capital intensive, recent growth based on gains in manufacturing may slow, and tertiary and quarternary employment may shift toward regions and locations (and countries) that can provide the best combination of new capital and skilled labor. The aging composition of the population implies that the high rate of household formation experienced during the 1970s will fall, and total mobility is also likely to drop because of aging. In addition, economic considerations, such as the present recession and fall in housing production, point to still lower levels of household formation. The slower rate of growth in incomes resulting from the recession also will restrict the ability of households to act on preferences, or perhaps to migrate at all.

Nevertheless, the basic differentials in employment growth among regions revealed by the shift-share analysis, especially those in the expanding tertiary sector, are generally consistent with the preferences for future residence expressed in 1979. Both the interregional shifts that control for industrial composition and migration preferences suggest a drastic slowing of recent growth in the South Atlantic division, particularly if manufacturing employment continues to decline nationally. Conversely, both migration preferences and shifts among tertiary industries point to continued strong growth in the West, particularly the Mountain division. The pre-auto-industry-depression results suggest that employment conditions were improving in the East North Central division through 1978, but the current depression added to preexisting high preferences for out-migration presage serious losses in population, jobs, and revenue there. Both the economic and net migration results point to continued heavy losses from the Middle Atlantic region, as even its relative losses in the faster-growing service industries are accelerating while its labor costs remain relatively high.

Intraregionally, the relative decentralization of employment and population from central cities appears likely to continue. At present, employment decentralization rates are lowest in the less urbanized Mountain and South Central

Table 12. Percent Distribution of Preferred Residence in 1984 and Likelihood of Moving, by Region, Type of Residence and Income in 1979

Type of Residence and relation to local median income in 1979	Northeast				North Central			
	Prefer Same Place	Want to Move Unlikely	Want to Move Likely	Different Region Likely	Prefer Same Place	Want to Move Unlikely	Want to Move Likely	Different Region Likely
Central City of SMSA 1 million plus								
<80% median income	67.9	19.7	12.4	9.0	69.0	15.8	15.2	10.0
80% median income +	64.6	18.1	17.3	11.6	65.9	14.2	19.9	11.7
Suburb of SMSA 1 million plus								
<80% median income	68.9	15.3	15.8	7.2	66.9	14.1	19.0	10.9
80% median income +	70.5	12.5	17.0	9.5	61.4	15.3	23.3	13.2
All other SMSAs								
<80% median income	70.0	13.1	16.9	8.7	68.3	14.0	17.7	10.8
80% median income +	71.3	12.8	15.9	7.4	69.7	12.2	18.3	11.0
Nonmetropolitan urban								
<80% median income	67.8	14.7	17.5	8.9	72.2	11.3	16.5	10.2
80% median income +	69.4	12.5	18.1	9.2	76.6	9.4	14.0	8.3
Nonmetropolitan rural								
<80% median income	79.8	9.2	11.0	5.0	82.4	7.1	10.5	4.9
80% median income +	79.8	7.8	12.4	6.2	79.9	7.1	13.0	5.9
Regional total	70.4	14.0	15.6	8.5	70.7	12.2	17.1	9.9

45

Table 12 (cont.) Percent Distribution of Preferred Residence in 1984 and Likelihood of Moving, by Region, Type of Residence and Income in 1979

Type of Residence and relation to local median income in 1979	South				West			
	Prefer Same Place	Want to Move		Different Region Likely	Prefer Same Place	Want to Move		Different Region Likely
		Unlikely	Likely			Unlikely	Likely	
Central City of SMSA 1 million plus								
<80% median income	80.9	8.7	10.4	4.4	67.6	14.0	18.4	5.1
80% median income +	69.2	10.7	20.1	7.5	64.5	14.0	21.5	4.7
Suburb of SMSA 1 million plus								
<80% median income	69.5	13.0	17.5	7.0	64.6	13.2	22.2	4.2
80% median income +	65.8	13.9	20.3	6.0	63.2	13.4	23.4	4.1
All other SMSAs								
<80% median income	79.6	8.2	12.2	4.6	66.9	13.0	20.1	4.7
80% median income +	77.7	8.3	14.0	4.0	72.6	9.3	18.1	3.4
Nonmetropolitan urban								
<80% median income	82.2	7.3	10.5	2.9	70.3	10.5	19.2	5.6
80% median income +	80.5	8.4	11.1	2.5	72.6	8.8	18.6	3.9
Nonmetropolitan rural								
<80% median income	88.2	4.6	7.2	1.9	79.7	7.5	12.8	2.5
80% median income +	85.9	5.5	8.6	2.0	78.2	6.2	15.6	3.4
Regional Total	79.5	8.2	12.3	3.8	68.4	11.7	19.9	4.1

Source: Special tabulations from 1979 National Annual Housing Survey, Office of Economic Affairs, HUD, 1982

46

divisions, but employment is decentralizing in all major industries in all divisions. Evidence that rates of decentralization accelerate during recoveries suggests that the rate of recovery from the present recession and the relative incentives given to new investment vs. reuse and rehabilitation of existing facilities may be particularly important for future employment in central cities.

Suburbanization of population from central cities is also occurring in all regions, even though western and southern cities have been gaining interregional migrants. The scant evidence of increased migration to central cities among whites appears unlikely to reverse the prevailing pattern of out-migration rates that increase with status, and preferences suggest that selective outmigration will continue in all regions but the West.

In terms of my original question about equilibrium or new disparities, I conclude that the apparent narrowing of regional differences in the 1970s hides real tendencies leading to future disparities in income and resources within and among regions. Furthermore, these problems could be worsened if the nation's past commitment to reallocating resources among regions, jurisdictions, and persons is reduced.

This conclusion arises from the most striking implication of these trends: that the present problems of the largest cities in the Northeast and North Central regions are likely to get even *worse*, as employment—even that in services and other tertiary industries—continues to decentralize, as past population decline is exacerbated by future declines in the number of households, and as selective out-migration further worsens the income distribution. The increasing concentration of poor, female-headed, and often black households in these cities suggests that service needs will continue to increase, while revenue and appropriate employment opportunities for residents will further decline. The higher income levels in northern suburbs suggest that resources to address the needs of central cities may be available on a state or regional basis, if political and jurisdictional obstacles to providing such assistance can be overcome. However, high preferences of suburban residents for moving, particularly to the South and West, combined with the prospect of lower population and employment growth in northern suburbs, suggest that there are important built-in limits to such an approach. Pursuing metropolitan- or state-level income redistribution policies without federal aid could further exacerbate regional differences by accelerating out-migration from northern suburbs.

Large cities in the West do not seem to have as many problems as those in the North at present since median income levels are rising and out-migration preferences are less selective by income. However, they are experiencing decentralization of both employment and population. In the South, the combination of lessened regional growth, accelerated decentralization of employment, and faster out-migration of higher income population may pose real problems for cities in the decade ahead.

If high levels of out-migration from large cities continue, small towns and rural areas will be increasingly faced with problems of managing population growth and financing the needed infrastructure. The expansion of employment in nonmetropolitan areas suggests that more revenues may be available to support this growth, particularly in the Northeast and West, but such aggregate data do not ensure a proper match of needs and resources at the local level. Furthermore, the business cycle results raise questions about the fragility of the new economic base in nonmetropolitan areas. In any case, there will undoubtedly be needs for improving management techniques in smaller jurisdictions.

Finally, the diversity of suburbs makes it hardest to say anything definitive about suburbs from the amalgam of statistics used here. In the aggregate, suburbs remain the most prosperous areas in all parts of the country, with the highest levels of median income and lowest rates of poverty. The shift-share analysis furthermore identifies suburbs as the most attractive location for employment growth in the late 1970s, with particularly high rates of growth in the expanding tertiary sector. But individual suburban jurisdictions range from old large Yonkers to small affluent enclaves, and other data (McCarthy, 1982) suggest that older suburbs are themselves coming to resemble older central cities, with increasing concentrations of population with service needs. Lacking revenue transfers from other levels of government, small older suburbs may have fewer resources than central cities, where people and investors at least retain commitment to cultural attractions and CBDs. If the high propensity to migrate among the present suburban population were combined with older infrastructure and housing in small jurisdictions with few financial resources, relatively quick transitions to suburban pockets of poverty could result. Such speculations highlight the need for more detailed analysis of Census data to determine how conditions and trends in particular areas vary from the general patterns of redistribution reviewed here.

REFERENCES

Advisory Commission on Intergovernmental Relations (1980). *Regional Growth: Historic Perspective*. R-74 Washington, D.C.: ACIR.

Birch, David L. (1979). *The Job Generation Process*. Cambridge: MIT Press.

Harrison, Bennett (1974). *Urban Economic Development: Suburbanization, Minority Opportunity and the Condition of the Central City*. Washington: The Urban Institute.

Long, John (1981). *Population Deconcentration in the United States*. Washington, D.C.: U.S. Bureau of the Census.

Long, Larry (1982). "Residential Preferences: Some Clues to U.S. Migration Between 1979 and 1984." (mimeo).

Long, Larry and Diana DeAre (1982). "The Economic Base of Recent Population Growth in Nonmetropoltan Settings." Paper presented at Association of American Geographers, April.

Jackson, Gregory, George Masnick, Roger Bolton, Susan Bartlett and John Pitkin (1981). *Regional Diversity: Growth in the U.S. 1960-1990*. Boston: Auburn House.

McCarthy, Kevin (1982). *Metropolitan Suburbs: Profile and Prospects*. WS-1298-1-HUD Santa Monica: Rand.

Mills, Edwin (1972). *Urban Economics*. Glenview, Ill: Scott, Foresman & Company.

Nelson, Kathryn and Clifford Patrick (1982). "The Impact of Business Cycles on Decentralization of Employment." (mimeo).

Nelson, Kathryn (1982). "Migration and Central Cities during the 1970s." (mimeo).

U.S. Bureau of the Census (1978). "Social and Economic Characteristics of the Metropolitan and Nonmetropolitan Population: 1977 and 1970." *Current Population Reports*, Series P-23, No. 75.

U.S. Bureau of the Census (1980). "Characteristics of the Population Below the Poverty Level: 1978." *Current Population Reports*, Series P-60, No. 124.

U.S. Bureau of the Census (1981). "Geographic Mobility: March 1975-1980." *Current Population Reports*, Series P-20, No. 368.

U.S. Bureau of the Census (1982). "Money Income of Households, Families and Persons in the United States: 1980."*Current Population Reports*, Series P-60, No. 132.

DEMOGRAPHIC CHANGE AND URBAN FINANCE:
THE OUTLOOK FOR THE 1980s

Philip L. Clay

I. INTRODUCTION

The beginning of a decade is always an occasion for looking forward to what the next years will bring. With respect to the outlook for central cities, two concerns are nearly always near the top of the agenda. The first relates to future population and the second to fiscal outlook—the ability of local communities to support the service needs of their citizens through available revenues.

This paper explores the relationship between recent demographic and public finance trends and the outlook on these issues for cities between now and the year 2000. The size and composition of the population are important issues in the outlook for cities because they provide a basis for understanding the relationship between the needs and demands of the cities' population, on one hand, and their ability to amass and then redistribute fiscal resources on the other.

The present concern for demographic and fiscal outlook comes at a time when

Research in Urban Economics, Volume 4, pages 51-65.
Copyright © 1984 JAI Press Inc.
All rights or reproduction in any form reserved.
ISBN: 0-89232-423-6

the role and capacity of government at the different levels are undergoing more systematic scrutiny than any time since the 1930s. Several questions have emerged. Who will be the constituency of local governments in the year 2000? What are the varieties of demands local governments face? What will be the resources available to local government for meeting these demands, and how will both the needs and resources change as a function of demographic shifts?

Most popular analysis in demography relates to the size of the population, yet size is not the only dimension of the population, and not the most important one. Age structure, racial and income mix, household formation rate, household size and type, fertility and migration patterns are all far more significant for policy and for projection than population magnitude alone. This range of issues affects, indeed drives, economic activity, which in turn creates private jobs on the one hand and the revenue base for the public sector on the other.

Likewise population is a driving force affecting government since its characteristics determine many of the major factors in public finance. The composition of the population reflects, for example, how many people are producers and how many consumers.[1] A population with a large dependent sector (i.e., children and elderly) makes a different contribution to service demand and to resources than one with a lower level of dependency. Since the dependent sector of the population generates little wealth or income, an increase in their share of the population regardless of changes in the size of total population usually requires greater public expenditures. The composition of the population also affects the priorities for service that are reflected in voting.

Looking at the nation as a whole, these matters seem less important compared to various macro factors such as international economic trends, interest rates, unemployment, etc. Yet locally, demographic trends are critical, in some cases more critical than the macro factors. This concern about the role of demography raises the question of whether cities are heading toward a demographic future that is dramatically different from what we have experienced in recent decades. We will suggest that the answer is yes and that the implications for public finance are significant and ominous.

A. Demographic Trends

Data released from the 1980 Census thus far give us some interesting glimpses of demographic changes in recent years and provide, as well, a basis for looking into the future.[2] First, the Census indicates a growing diversity in the pattern of regional growth. In the simplest terms there is a major shift in the population both in terms of migration and rates of growth between the Frostbelt (northeast, north central, and New England states) on the one hand, and the Sunbelt (western and southern states) on the other.

Frostbelt states are experiencing outmigration and moving toward a population which is older. Moreover, several central cities in the northern part of the country continue to experience population decline, many on the order of the 10% experienced between 1970 and 1980. This is summarized in Table 1. This decline continues a trend that goes back to the 1950s.

Further decline is expected in these northeastern and north central cities. The decline will result both from declining (even negative) rates of natural increase and from increased outmigration. The combined effect of these rates will be an additional decrease and aging in the population of several major cities, and entire states.

The Sunbelt, on the other hand, is experiencing rapid growth (see Table 1). Cities such as Dallas and Phoenix are finding their population rapidly growing both by inmigration and by higher rates of natural increase.[3] The relative youth of the population ensures that growth will continue over the years even if migration declines. Growth in the Sunbelt contributes to a substantial demand for infrastructure improvement and private residential development, as well as the demand for public services. However, growth also means new workers who increase the income base. A major public finance and demographic question for these communities is how to manage growth so as to control fiscal impact.[4]

There are also some important compositional changes in the population of cities. For example, many of the older cities are experiencing decline in the number of households as well as total population, though the decline in number of households is often less dramatic. Between 1970 and 1980, only Boston, among large eastern cities, was able to stabilize or increase its number of households (see Table 1). Among other cities with comparable total population losses,

Table 1. Change in Population and Households in Central Cities 1970-1980

	Percent Change in Population 1970-1980	Percent Change in Number of Households 1970-1980
Atlanta	− 14.1	+ 0.1
Baltimore	− 13.1	− 2.7
Boston	− 12.2	+ 0.4
Chicago	− 10.8	− 3.9
Denver	− 4.5	+ 14.2
Detroit	− 20.6	− 12.9
Los Angeles	+ 5.5	+ 10.5
New Orleans	− 6.2	+ 7.8
New York	− 10.4	− 1.7
Philadelphia	− 13.4	− 3.5
Phoenix	+ 30.9	+ 53.2
Pittsburgh	− 18.5	− 6.7
St. Louis	− 27.2	− 17.4
San Francisco	− 5.2	+ 1.3
Seattle	− 7.0	+ 6.5
Washington, DC	− 15.8	− 3.7

Source: Calculated from U.S. Census of Population, 1970, 1980.

the decline in number of households ranges from less than 5% in Baltimore, Washington, Chicago, New York, and Philadelphia to more than 5% in St. Louis, Detroit, and Pittsburgh.

The difference between rates of change in total population and number of households reflects a general trend, stronger in some places than others, toward smaller households and a greater incidence of one- and two-person households. The median size of the American household declined from more than 5.0 persons per household after World War II to a present level of about 2.7. This house-holding behavior is a consequence of a number of trends—later marriage, higher rates of divorce, the elderly living longer and independently, changing lifestyles, etc. The maturing of the baby-boom generation and these smaller households held up demand for housing during the 1970s even as population declined. The pressure, especially the maturation of the baby boom, will continue through most of the 1980s. However, the rate of growth in the number of households will drop off significantly as we move into the 1990s. At that time, the decline in the level of demand for central city housing may be quite steep.

A related recent trend is the growing incidence of nonfamily households. In 1970, one- or two-person households were 47% of households. In 1980, they were to 57%. These smaller households are composed of a varied mixture: young single persons, divorced persons, young couples without children, and the elderly.

The lower incidence of families in cities portends a much more differentiated constituency for urban services, and perhaps a different set of concerns on the revenue side as well. The decline in a number of families, for example, might lead to declining support for elementary and secondary public education which is the largest single local expenditure and one that to date has increased even as total central city enrollments have tumbled. The trends we have outlined suggest that enrollments will continue to decline. Families left in the city will increasingly be the "truly needy." The smaller nonfamily households will have interests and needs which are different than what families have had. They may even opt for privatization of formerly public services in the belief they are better (and more cheaply) served by paying directly for what they use.

Another trend of some importance is the shifting racial composition of cities. The outmovement of whites, combined with the growth (mainly by natural increase) in the minority population (which occurs at a much faster rate because minorities are younger than whites) has led to a dramatic increase (see Table 2) in the share of the central city population that is black. While blacks represent only 11% of the national population, they represent almost 25% of the central city population, which is in turn concentrated in a few regions and in the oldest and largest cities. Latinos further augment in minority share.

Because of the changing age structure we already pointed to, the percentage of minorities in cities is expected to grow dramatically in the years ahead; additional cities will move from predominantly white to majority black. Given that blacks have lower income than whites (and assuming no change in this

Table 2. Percent Black of Total Central City Population in
Selected Cities, and Change 1970-1980

	Percent Black 1980	Percent Black 1970	Percent Change 1970-1980
Atlanta	61.9	51.3	10.6
Baltimore	54.8	43.9	10.9
Boston	22.4	16.3	6.1
Chicago	39.8	33.3	6.5
Denver	12.1	9.1	3.0
Detroit	63.1	43.7	19.4
Los Angeles	16.8	17.8	−1.0
New Orleans	54.3	45.0	9.3
New York	25.2	18.4	6.8
Philadelphia	37.5	33.8	3.7
Phoenix	4.9	4.8	0.1
St. Louis	45.5	40.9	4.6
San Francisco	12.7	13.4	−0.7
Seattle	9.4	7.3	2.1
Washington, DC	70.2	69.7	0.5

Source: U.S. Bureau of the Census, Census of Population, 1970, 1980.

regard), the population shift portends a dramatic shift in the urban income distribution and revenue-generating capacity. Cities will have a larger proportion of the poor and of those on fixed income and transfer payments. This will surely mean a widening gap between the fortunes of central cities and their suburbs— a gap already evident in income data through 1977. It also means a widening gap between the fiscal needs and fiscal capacities of cities.[5]

Central cities have long played an important role as the center of manufacturing. Manufacturing jobs were concentrated for a long time in the Frostbelt cities. These jobs have increasingly shifted to the Sunbelt. Many of the workers left the city as well, leaving behind facilities that had to be serviced but which contributed little if anything to the revenue or income base.

The reduced role of manufacturing in cities was only partially compensated for by growth of office and service jobs. Many of the cities that experienced substantial population decline and manufacturing job loss also experienced dramatic growth in office jobs that attracted both suburban and urban workers. Neither the income of their well-paid (increasingly suburban) workers nor the information or services are typically part of the local tax base.[6] In addition, to attract office jobs, cities have offered tax concessions to developers, which often result in shifting (and increasing) taxes on residents.

The limited gain in revenue that this transition entails is one issue. The more important issue, however, is an increasing mismatch between the skills required for the type of central city jobs that are growing and the job skills of its resident population. The downtown development which has been widespread in recent years may create increased viability for the downtown core of cities without increasing economic opportunity for its residents.[7] Low-skilled, often unemployed, workers are unable to pay taxes sufficient to support services they need and demand. Moreover, as businesses invest in capital (i.e., computers, word processors, communication technology) and substitute highly trained professional and technical workers from suburbia, little contribution is made to creating personal income of city residents that could be taxed to support the public sector. Taxing business directly has its practical limits given the competition for business location among cities and regions.

The trends discussed above are not isolated nor are they likely to be short-lived or of limited impact. They originate deep in the demographic and economic dynamics of urban areas and reflect, in most cases, the continuation of trends that have been in place for years. It is unlikely that there will be a major increase in fertility, movement back to the city from the suburbs, a reversal of southward migration, or a return of low-skill but well-paid manufacturing jobs to the city. Indeed, many of the trends are subject to further acceleration to the detriment of central cities, so that the impact may be even more serious than we now estimate.

B. Trends and Public Finance

Other papers presented in this volume detail the major trends in expenditures, taxation, and other aspects of public finance.[8] First, per capita income, per capita expenditures, and taxes in cities have all increased dramatically in recent years. However, the gap between cities and suburbs on these measures has increased as well. This is particularly the case in northeastern and north central cities. Part of this increase in expenditures is accounted for by an increase in the range of services offered.

The local effort that central cities make toward meeting their service needs as reflected in taxes per $1,000 of income has increased dramatically and is substantially higher in cities than in suburbs, and in northern and eastern cities than in southern and western ones, yet the greater revenue effort on the part of cities has not closed or even narrowed the gap between revenues and expenditures.

An increase in state and federal aid has made up for the difference. Cities have been effective in Washington and in the capitals of several states in getting aid formulas that favor urban areas, or, more accurately, favor population groups concentrated in cities. Up to now (that is, before 1980), this has assured cities a pot of supplementary revenue which, while growing absolutely, declined in real terms since the mid-1970s. That source of support is now under serious review in Washington, and states too are resisting expanding aid to central cities. The amount and allocation process are major issues in the debate.

II. THE ROLE OF DEMOGRAPHIC CHANGE IN PUBLIC FINANCE

In this section of the paper we want to explore the three issues where demographics and finance interact critically to affect the future development of cities: housing and residential investment, the tax base, and intergovernmental transfer.[9]

A. Housing and Residential Investment

Increased *value* and *size* of the real property tax base are the bases for tax revenues.[10] A city whose property tax base is stable must raise the tax rate or find alternative revenue to meet the growing cost of services. A city with an expanding tax base can try to manage the growth of its expenditures to match the growth of its tax base; the data show that the tax base in most large cities has grown much more slowly in real terms than expenditures have, with the result that total revenue expanded only as a consequence of higher effective tax rates and/or aid from state and federal sources.[11]

Assuming there are real (political or other) limits on the taxes that can be levied locally (and voters seem to be insisting on some limits), a key question is, what prospects are there for real residential investment expansion?

Declining population, which most large cities experienced, at first glance suggests declining housing demand. Yet as we noted earlier, demand was sustained (and in selected areas increased) during the 1970s as the number of households declined much less rapidly than population, as household size declined, and as household formation occurred at a higher rate. Relatively little growth occurred in new private residential construction in central cities, resulting in little real increase in the tax base. A great deal is made of residential reinvestment activity (''gentrification'') but, while it has some local significance in some city neighborhoods, it represents only a small percent of the total stock; it is still dwarfed by the larger volume of disinvestment activity in the central cities.[12]

The outlook for household growth and, therefore, demand for residential development through the year 2000 is not very encouraging. While the maturation of the baby boom will help sustain housing demand through much of the 1980s, even as total central city population declines, the decline in the rate of household growth in the 1990s will almost surely occur as the population ages and the youthful base for household formation shrinks. Moreover, as already noted for the 1970s, the percentage of the population composed of minority, elderly, or poor households will increase. Barring improvement in these groups' economic status, their growth as a share of central city population represents a shaky basis on which to expand private residential reinvestment even if potential demand is strong. The incomes of the growing portion of the population will be insufficient to support private development or even high quality maintenance of the stock.

In the absence of subsidy, this means disinvestment as an erosion of the real value of the property tax base. The real question, though, is whether the residential property tax can be a reasonable basis for shouldering the burden of services which this population configuration will demand. The evidence to be presented by other authors in this volume suggests increasingly that it cannot be.

B. The Tax Base

In pursuing its fiscal goals cities will face a conflict between social goals and fiscal goals. Fiscal goals could be achieved by: (1) limiting the tax breaks to various groups, including tax breaks to the elderly; (2) increasing the sales or income tax; and (3) reducing various exemptions and incentives. Cities could, in addition, identify revenue sources that transfer the burden to nonresident users, and thereby divest themselves of certain expenditures through user fees, or they could seek to have costs assumed by the state or regional government.

Progress in these areas in the present environment may be difficult, if not impossible. Taking any of these actions runs up against advantaged interests in the city and outside it that seek to preserve present arrangements. While the example set by California—with Proposition 13—and Massachusetts—with Proposition 2½—has not been widely emulated by other states, clearly the public mood is to create no new taxes, and perhaps to decrease existing ones. Overall tax reform may bring fairness, but the income of central city residents places effective limits on any expansion in the revenue base of central cities.[13]

The problems we are alluding to here with respect to big cities will also apply to older suburbs and to medium-sized cities. In combination, the various urban communities may be able to build the powerful constituency needed for state tax reform that big cities to this point have been unable to build alone. From the state's point of view, defining reform to include cities of various sizes may be more acceptable than proposing to "bail out" big cities only. Giving local communities additional taxing power may be preferable to the state's replacing lost local revenue with state funds. Even so, additional taxing power has its limits and represents a reform largely useful in achieving equity (for example, by taxing services to tourists or commuters) rather than bringing a large increment in revenue.

C. Intergovernmental Aid

In the last 20 years state aid to local communities—often distributed by formulas which take into account demographic factors—has increased dramatically.[14] The formulas range from allocations based on revenue generated by the local jurisdiction to formulas based on the needs of various population groups who live in the local jurisdiction. Other formulas reflect the ability of local communities to pay for the service themselves relative to the needs they have.

Some states have multiple formulas (to reflect the multiple revenue sources or program purposes).

Shifting population trends will result in changes in the amount of aid cities stand to gain. Given the current generation of state-aid formulas and the demographics noted earlier, the typical impacts cities can expect include: (1) a decrease in aid which is based on the total population; (2) a decrease in aid based on central city share of state (or regional) population; and (3) decreasing aid based on the number of children (unless the formula is weighted heavily on the number of poor children). Older suburbs and nonmetropolitan areas will get a greater share of aid in a given state as they obtain a greater share of population. While the number of poor in cities may increase and concentrations of poverty may be more numerous now, strictly population-based formulas will put older cities at a disadvantage.[15]

A similar phenomenon may apply at the federal level given the regional shifts in population and the significant differential in growth rate of different age groups. School enrollment in Frostbelt cities is declining, while in Sunbelt cities it continues to grow. The combination of growth in these areas and the recognition that bilingual education, for example, is not just a New York issue should mandate shifts in federal assistance for this program away from the East, to the South and West. Similar shifts would apply to other programs.

A further concern in the redistribution of resources between levels of government is the increase in the number of nonfamily households—households which may not create a demand for certain family-related services such as education or welfare, but who nevertheless have a continuing need for more general public services and who will no doubt demand the maintenance or improvement of public services, even at the expense of social services. They expect the city to provide libraries and recreation, environmental services, public transit; and they will expect even higher standards of police, fire, and sanitation services because of ever-rising expectations about quality of urban life. What this adds up to is a continuing demand for services with enhanced quality. The number of households may decline, the number of persons may decline even more, but the amount of physical stock that the city has to service and the range of services the city provides (many of them with fixed costs) will continue to keep demands for revenue high.

III. POLICY IMPLICATIONS

Observations to this point suggest dramatic changes in public finance as a consequence of demographic change. In this final section we will explore three areas of policy which seem to be relevant to the discussion.

A. Local Management and Analysis

The years ahead will be marked by a new questioning of the role of government, fiscal austerity, and growing pressure to more effficiently allocate resources. We will not attempt in this space to deal with the specifics of management reforms that will be required. Rather, we will suggest some issues we think should guide local officials in taking account of the demographic trends identified.

We need first to identify service needs and demands for the new population configuration that will unfold in the years to come. The initial step in this area is to delineate significant population changes and significant new issues with respect to their demands and needs. The population will include four groups. First, traditional groups which are increasingly aging and organized in smaller, nonfamily households. Regardless of age, this type of household unit will be an increasing share of the whole population.

Second, the city will include families, a growing proportion of whom are minority (or in the case of Sunbelt cities, those who are recent migrants to the region). Unless there is a shift in the income disparity between races, this group will be increasingly a net consumer of public services and of family services. Their share of the population will increase as well.

The third group includes middle-class residents, some of whom are making commitments in the city reflected in gentrification and reinvestment in older neighborhoods. Their expectation is that their private reinvestment will be reinforced by public action.

The fourth group is the business, civic, and institutional "citizens" who look to the city as the site of their economic, institutional, and civic activity and who make demands on the system in support of their institutions and business activities. They have received numerous fiscal concessions in recent years and will continue to expect local government to be a partner in urban development.

The contribution of each of these groups to city resources and their claims upon them are substantially in conflict. Poor families expect redistribution. Middleclass households want tax relief and more limited government. Business wants a partnership that directs resources to them and burdens away from them. Homeowners want business to pay a bigger share of the burden. One way of getting out of this dilemma is to differentiate what the city (or government generally) can contribute directly and indirectly, what is expected from the private sector, and what can be expected from residents themselves. Over the years the number of activities in which government has been involved has increased, and for good reason, but as we face tougher times as well as new realities, each of these areas of government intervention must be reexamined in light of what we have learned from recent experience and in terms of what resources are available. Given fiscal austerity there will be strong pressure to increase the contribution of the private sector in planning, initiating and supporting major development initiatives and the volunteer sector in providing certain services which in recent years would have been financed by government transfer programs. While some change in this direction is possible and desirable, realignment would not add significantly more resources and would likely not address all legitimate needs.

A second area for local planning and assessment has to do with fiscal reform. There are at least four conceptions of what fiscal reform is. For some observers, fiscal reform means tax reduction. For others, it is redistribution of the tax burden to decrease the inequity of current schemes. For still others, fiscal reform has to do with how to squeeze additional revenue out of the various revenue bases with greater efficiency. Finally, fiscal reform means more careful connection between government function, revenue source, and tax administration. These conceptions are not entirely mutually exclusive and therefore part of the task of local government has to do with dealing with the legitimate claims of proponents for each of these conceptions. All of these conceptions get back to the question of who pays and who benefits; both of these determinations more than ever are based on a changing cast of characters and rapid movement on the part of various interest groups to influence the inevitable reconfiguration.

A third area has to do with participation in local government. Given the changing constituency, the alternative conceptions of what government can and should do, and how it should be paid for, there is a need to make sure that the various groups have their voice heard in local decision making. This is important for political reasons but it is also important because it is a first step in creating the confidence that will be critical to increasing the private sector role and to encouraging self-help.

In many older cities increasing participation will mean changing the established forms of decision making. For example, it could lead to district representation as opposed to at-large elections, or it could mean a greater role for partnerships among the private, public, and volunteer sectors.

B. Managing Population Impacts

Cities can do relatively little to shape the structure of their population. The dynamics are set, barring dramatic changes in migration, fertility, household formations, etc. People migrate largely for economic reasons and economic opportunity is determined mostly by regional and even national and international, rather than local, trends. For the most part, opportunities in the receiving areas and not the lack of opportunity in cities drive the migration loss cities have experienced. Nevertheless, there are many ways cities can influence population impacts.

First, local tax and regulatory policies affect residential and other investment activities as well as the maintenance of the existing physical resources. New development can be encouraged or discouraged by taxes and regulation. Cities can manage the disposition of their property in ways to increase the tax base and encourage reinvestment or to generate further disinvestment. All of these influence to some degree which residents are in which areas, how much value is added, and how attractive the areas are for further development. While such development cannot reverse decline for the city, it can make a major difference for small areas. A number of gilded small areas can mean a great deal for the city's total image.

The attitude a city has toward development over a period of time critically shapes its attractiveness to various groups both in terms of quality-of-life issues and in terms of economic opportunity. This attractiveness is translated into value and revenue. Attracting jobs might change fortunes of residents or bring in new ones. Some development attracts conventions and tourists who could fill the tax coffers with sales taxes, etc. While the rising tide will not automatically lift all boats, its does create resources that vastly improve the ability of cities to help the poor.

Cities can foster local self-help through policies which strengthen neighborhoods, encourage private investment, and promote the participation and cooperation of the private sector and residents. The involvement generated by these efforts might partially reduce the outmigration of nonpoor families from some neighborhoods. As populations decline, instability and disinvestment will surface in some housing submarkets. These problems can be dealt with through various policies of regulation and land management which on the one hand accept that there will be losses of obsolescent structures but encourage the improved utilization of housing, land, and capital facilities in remaining areas of the city.

Rather than taking an approach of either helping places (i.e., capital improvement, revitalization, economic development) *or* helping people (i.e., social services, job training, direct housing assistance, etc.), a more enlightened local urban policy accepts that different areas of the city at different times require one or both strategies. Either approach adopted citywide will be both ineffective and unfair. For example, when a significant portion of the housing stock in a given neighborhood declines and there is no reasonable prospect for reinvestment, strategies to help people move make sense. Using public resources for isolated rehabilitation makes little sense given that all our experience suggests that such rehabilitation needs to be done in an area where a combination of strengthening the social fabric and reinvestment will be available.

C. Dealing with Social Forces

Changing demographics and the related consequences for public finance potentially unleash several social forces within urban communities. The variety and extent of these will vary, but two appear to be certain candidates for extensive impact. The first is what may broadly be called a generational conflict. As the population ages, and especially if generational differences parallel other differences such as race or income, the potential for conflict increases. In older cities this will be manifested in a collision of interests of what is mainly an older white population and a younger minority population. These groups, as we have discussed in sections above, differ in income, social status, political power, and in the incidence of children and families in their populations. The demand for services, especially education, guarantees that there will be some conflict over the priority for various services and the attitude toward tax and spending. Education is a particularly significant one in this regard because a number of cities where populations and enrollments have declined have a high and growing minority percentage. Educational expenditures per capita have increased as well. When the tax burden is relatively high, education becomes an obvious candidate for cuts from the point of view of older voters who have no kids in school, while it remains a key service to be greatly enhanced from the point of view of the minority of voters with children. In any case, political issues which come up in this kind of environment and on issues which reflect the social character of the city, the conflict will be settled not on fiscal or management issues alone but will reflect demographic politics.

In newer cities, the generational conflict often has a different twist. Accommodating migrants from other regions and even other countries is the issue of conflict. These migrants bring additional demands and perhaps different expectations about what government is to provide and how it is to be paid for. As has occurred in many Sunbelt cities, migrants may be the major catalyst for reform and for political action to reflect their interest. When in-migrants reach a critical number or when they join politically with others, veritable revolutions in the local political order can result.

A second social force that seems increasingly pervasive is the issue of displacement. The demographic dynamics we have described involve some rearrangement of households. This rearrangement is often associated with reinvestment. Displacement is often one of the side effects of this process. The poor near the core of the city, for example, might be displaced by the gentry who restore housing in these older areas. Condominium conversion frequently displaces renters. Other residents might be moved in order to assemble large parcels of land for commercial or office development.[16] Prices and rents in unimproved areas might be affected by nearby or anticipated development. Because reinvestment expands the tax base and increases the attractiveness of an even larger area than the area of direct impact, development should be and is strongly encouraged, even subsidized. Yet many of those displaced in this process have limited options. This may not seem obvious if the city's population is shrinking, yet the point is that a boarded up apartment is not a resource until it is rehabilitated and it will not be rehabilitated if the return on investment continues to be inadequate to justify rehabilitation.[17] An essential aspect to promoting development will have to be dealing with the side effects of development such as displacement. If displacement is not dealt with, then conflict around it will substantially discourage some development that ought to take place.

IV. CONCLUSION

The outlook for American cities plays out demographic dynamics set in motion after World War II. The fiscal pressure on cities has been around for a while, but has been made more immediate by the changing views of government and the extended economic downturn. By bringing to bear our knowledge about demographic and fiscal interactions, our cities will be better able to emerge from the 1980s in a stronger position. But let us not be fooled by promises of sweeping reform. There is unlikely to be a reversal in the declining fortunes of older cities. It is the demographics and economics, not the ideology, that will determine the extent to which we can minimize and localize the decay.

NOTES

1.   In this connection, a producer is someone who has earnings which are taxed to support local government. Consumers of government services are those largely outside the labor force. The largest proportion are children and elderly persons. The significant policy issue related to dependency is the extent to which the dependent population is swelled by adults who are outside the mainstream ("the underclass"). A working hypothesis is that this group is growing as a proportion of the urban core population. See Auletta (1982).

2.   For a discussion of past trends and projections on population and other matters, see Jackson (1981).

3.   The reader will note that a substantial part of the growth in Sunbelt central cities is the result of annexation and that in the older neighborhoods of these cities, the population is declining just as is the case in cities outside the South.

4.   For a detailed discussion of the development fees and the changing role and influence they have in housing development, see Hack and Ginoza (1982).

5.   For a discussion of central city poverty trends, see Department of Housing and Urban Development (1981) and Sternlieb (1980).

6.   In a few cities, this has been accomplished through taxes on hotel occupancy, airport taxes, taxes on professional, business and personal services, fire service fees, and by classification of property based on use.

7.   For a detailed discussion of this phenomenon applied to the Boston area, see *Future Boston* (1982).

8.   See the papers in this volume by Puryear and Ross.

9.   See paper in this volume by Nelson.

10.   See Peterson (1976).

11.   See Peterson and Muller (1980).

12.   There are no good data on the magnitude of this phenomenon, but HUD has estimated that there is far more disinvestment than there is reinvestment. See generally, Department of Housing and Urban Development (1979).

13.   See in this volume the paper by Pincus.

14. State to local aid increased from $35.0 billion to $60 billion between 1971/72 to 1976/77. See ACIR (1980). Also see in this volume, paper by Stein.

15. Evidence of this is reflected in the 1977 changes in the CDBG formula which was changed to include age of central city housing as an element. It was a way to offset the loss the Frostbelt cities would have experienced based on a formula that focused on demographic and poverty figures alone because most of the older housing is in Frostbelt central cities.

16. For an excellent discussion of the sources and dynamics of displacement as well as examples and auggestions for relief, see Hartman (1981).

17. For a detailed discussion of the investment future of rental housing see Sternlieb (1981).

REFERENCES

Advisory Committee on Intergovernmental Relations (1980). *Recent Trends in Federal and State Aid to Local Government*. Washington, D.C.: ACIR.

Department of Housing and Urban Development (1979). *Final Report on Housing Displacement*. Washington, D.C.: DHUD.

Hack, Gary and Ginoza, Otis (1982). "Public-Private Responsibilities in Housing Site Development". (draft). Cambridge: MIT-Harvard Joint Center for Urban Studies.

Hartman, Chester (1981). *Displacement: How To Fight It*. San Francisco: National Housing Law Project.

Jackson, Gregory (1981). *Regional Diversity*. Boston: Auburn House Publishing Company.

MIT-Harvard Joint Center for Urban Studies (1982). *Future Boston*. Cambridge, Mass.: Joint Center for Urban Studies.

Nelson, Kathryn (1982). "Population and Employment Shifts in the United States." (this volume).

Peterson, George (1976). "Finance" in William Gorham and Nathan Glazer (eds.) *The Urban Predicament*. Washington, D.C.: The Urban Institute.

Peterson, George and Muller, Thomas (1980). "The Economic and Fiscal Accompaniments of Population Change," in Brian Berry and Lester Silverman (eds.), *Population Redistribution and Public Policy*. Washington, D.C. National Academy of Sciences.

Pincus, John (1982). "Troubles in Suburbia: Urbanization, Exclusion, and Metropolitan Decline." (this volume).

Puryear, David and Ross, John (1982). "Urban Government Expenditures in the 1980s." (this volume).

Stein, Robert (1982). "The Changing Character of American Federalism: Structure of Federal Aid." (in this volume).

Sternlieb, George (1980). *America's Housing*. New Brunswick, N.J.: Rutgers University Press.

Sternlieb, George (1981). *The Future of Rental Housing*. New Brunswick: Center for Urban Policy Research.

THE INFLUENCE OF COMMUNICATIONS AND DATA PROCESSING TECHNOLOGY ON URBAN FORM

Benjamin Chinitz

I. INTRODUCTION

This is an era of rapid technological change in communications and data processing (CDP). New products and services are creating new enterprises and transforming old ones. Consumers, whether enterprises or households, are not just substituting these new products and services for old products and services but they are changing their life-styles—how they organize themselves, how they manage themselves, how they get things done.

An important question for the future of cities which we would like to address in this paper is whether these life-style changes lead to or include changes in industrial location as between downtown and suburbs in the urban area. The locational implications of the CDP revolution are particularly important in assessing the outlook for economic growth in the great urban centers of our nation whose vitality has been challenged in recent decades by equally dramatic forces

Research in Urban Economics, Volume 4, pages 67-77.
Copyright © 1984 JAI Press Inc.
All rights or reproduction in any form reserved.
ISBN: 0-89232-423-6

like the growth in automobile ownership, technological changes in production and distribution, the racial transformation of the urban population, and the escalation of costs in the provision of public services and the support of indigent residents. Will the CDP revolution cause further erosion of the urban economic base?

To get from the dizzy heights of CDP technology to the prosaic issues of locational choice and urban change, we need to define the CDP revolution in ways which are relevant for our purposes. But before we do that, we shall articulate the theory by which we expect the CDP revolution to impact locational choice.

Urban economists have tried to account for intrametropolitan locational choices of enterprises in terms of three sets of variables: (1) its social and institutional attributes; (2) variables related to accessibility—how readily a given site can be "connected" to other relevant sites by transportation and communication; (3) variables describing the unit making the location choice—the inputs to the production process, the location of the market, and the nature of the product or service.

Models and theories which incorporate these three sets of variables have had "some" success in "predicting" patterns of location which conform to existing patterns. The success is limited by the deletion of important variables, the misspecification of variables, the rigidity of the statistical technique, but probably most of all by the extreme difficulty of capturing the force of inertia in such models or in any kind of theoretical frameworks.

Nevertheless, as we look to the future with a focus on locational change, we are bound to find the structure of these models helpful in organizing our speculations. They identify the sources of dynamics in convenient categories. We expect locational change to be triggered by changes in these three variable sets: the characteristics of alternative sites, accessibility, and the industrial mix of the economy. To the extent that communication substitutes for transportation we have to consider whether the impact on accessibility calculations is important enough to affect the relative attractiveness of different sites for both households and enterprises of different kinds. But the impact of these technological developments transcends the issue of substitution for transportation to include the possible implications for site selection of the sheer growth of information processing and communication as an activity of the enterprise.

An analogy to transportation will help to clarify the last point. When air transport became an important reality, locations had to be reevaluated in terms of their access to actual or potential airports. When you introduce a new form of communication—say, cable TV—you have to ask whether the location you otherwise prefer is at a disadvantage with respect to this new communications medium.

Finally, there is potential for locational change arising out of a change in the industrial mix, i.e., what we do for a living. Among the forces which have had a positive impact on urban centers since World War II has been the growth of service industries which—relative to manufacturing—have had a stronger attachment to core locations and have therefore served to sustain the economic base of cities even while the suburbs displayed more rapid relative growth industry by industry. This is the much heralded "mix" effect in the literature of urban and regional economics. Thus, aside from its impact on the relative attractiveness of alternative locations, the communications revolution is relevant in terms of its impact, if any, on the industrial composition of the economy.

Again, an analogy may be helpful to bring home the point. The introduction of television in the late 1940s and early 1950s created a new activity—the production of programming for broadcast on TV—which had to be located somewhere, and Manhattan has certainly been the beneficiary of that particular aspect of the communications revolution of three decades ago.

II. CDP: TECHNOLOGY AND APPLICATIONS

The current burgeoning of new products and services in CDP is founded on a number of major technological developments which are briefly summarized here. *Microwave transmission* has made possible high capacity, low-cost, nationwide interconnection of local telephone exchange systems, as well as special purpose intercity networks. *Digital communications* technology greatly reduces the cost of data communications and also facilitates more efficient handling of basic telephone communications. *Solid state electronics* has reduced the size, cost, and power consumption of electronic equipment. These reductions have made it possible to distribute highly sophisticated electronic products and systems throughout a vast market with thousands of applications. *Communications satellites* relay vast amounts of information between widely separated locations on the earth's surface and make it possible to bypass a substantial part of the existing telephone network. *Fiber-optic systems* provide for transmission through an inch-wide cable of thousands of conversations and hundreds of video channels. *Cellular radio* promises to accelerate the growth of radio telephones. *Two-way* coaxial cable communications is currently being explored for a variety of educational and commercial uses.[1]

I make no pretense of understanding the technical side of CDP nor am I in a position to catalogue all the developments which are relevant to our discussion. But these products and services are illustrative: cable TV, the personal computer, teleconferencing, electronic mail.

Cable TV, when in full bloom, will shrink distances between places as dramatically as the telephone did a century ago. One author refers to the new era as the "Wired City."[2] Many television programs plus hundreds of voice and data services can be carried to homes on a wire. The cost of transmission is small. The variety of services is large. They include entertainment, education, and other public services. Cable TV, like the telephone, will substitute communication for transportation as an input for both producers and consumers but will at the same time expand the scope of possible interactions among economic units.

The personal computer is evolving as a tool for both data processing and communication and for households as well as enterprises. Like an ordinary computer terminal it facilitates contact with a large computer at great distances but it also erodes the cost advantage of large computers for small-scale data processing exercises. One dramatic prospect is "telecommuting," using the telephone and the personal computer to interact with the office.[3]

Teleconferencing is an application which mainly affects accessibility between urban areas but which may also have implications for locational choice within urban areas. This excerpt from a recent newspaper story captures the flavor of this new technology:

> The teleconference, a video meeting, is on the rise. Key executives use it as a management tool to reduce travel expenses and increase productivity. Nationally, companies are using teleconferences for many purposes. The American Library Assn. is planning a satellite teleconference beamed to 54 sites; Shearson/American Express of New York recently gave a teleconference seminar in new interest rates; 22,000 brokers from New England to Hawaii attended. And the US Chamber of Commerce will use teleconferences for lobbying and for sharing information.[4]

Electronic mail is correspondence that people transmit and receive over computer lines. The correspondence can be one-word messages or 10-page letters; it can be mail that is interoffice, intraoffice, office to household, or, ultimately, delivered by the postal service. The message can be sent to 100 different addresses per mailing or it can be destined for only one.[5]

These applications of CDP technology, and others, affect accessibility, taken one at a time. Their cumulative impact is multiplied when they are employed in combination. The interaction between developments in communications and developments in data processing is so intense that the borders between these two exciting technological fields are now hard to define. Instead, we must contemplate a future in which the processing and communication of information will be fully integrated.

The issue for us is, given these dramatic new capabilities and their ubiquitous adoption, what bearing, if any, do they have on location decisions? Assume, for the moment, that all locations will have equal access to these technologies—an assumption we will relax later—why should they alter the balance of forces affecting the competition between downtown and more remote locations in the urban area?

III. CITY AND SUBURB: A BALANCE SHEET

Elsewhere[6] I have developed the balance sheet—the pros and cons—of high density downtown locations. The entries are familiar and not original. The inherent cons are congestion and high rents. Other liabilities which tend to be associated with downtown locations are high wages and high taxes, and, in some places, dirt and crime. The fundamental pro is the savings in transportation and communications costs coupled with the less tangible but nevertheless real benefits of face-to-face contact and the random but productive contacts which are more likely to occur on busy city streets and in downtown restaurants than in low-slung suburban office buildings with spacious lawns and plenty of parking space.

Other assets, less compelling, are the residual advantages which downtown locations enjoy as transport nodes for both intraurban and interurban movements. Needless to say, the transportation revolution of the first half of this century has greatly eroded this advantage but in the very largest cities the metropolitan labor force is still more accessible to downtown than to any other location in the region.

The fact that downtowns have not altogether vanished—in fact, some are thriving—suggests to me that for some enterprises (and households) the pros still outweigh the cons in their locational calculations. Others will argue differently, namely, that inertia, combined with subsidies, has delayed the ultimate unravelling of high density patterns which have become technologically and economically obsolete. For them, the CDP revolution is not essential to define the new equilibrium (although, presumably they will not look a gift horse in the mouth).

My own view is influenced by the fact of heavy unsubsidized private investment in the downtowns of many of our cities, the rapid transformation of the economy in ways which favor the downtown,[7] and the sense that inertia is not devoid of economic rationality. Thus, it is urgent to speculate as to how the CDP revolution will further disturb the delicate equilibrium of forces shaping patterns of urban growth.

IV. COMMUNICATION IMPROVEMENTS: A DOUBLE-EDGED SWORD

Other authors[8] have already noted the contradictory impacts of transportation improvements. On the one hand, the motive to concentrate in order to economize on transportation costs is weakened, thus encouraging the dispersal of activities to take advantage of cheaper land and labor, the amenities of low density development, superior natural environments, and to accommodate new production and transportation technologies which require a lot of space for maximum efficiency.

But there is another side to the coin. When concentration is motivated by scale economies in production or by the superior characteristics of a particular site that have nothing to do with transportation, the reduction of transportation costs extends the radius of the market that can be economically served from that site. The concentration of manufacturing in the Northeast and Midwest during the latter part of the nineteenth century and the early decades of the twentieth century was encouraged by the development of the railroad, as was the concentration of agricultural production in the West and the South. Growth of cities during that period was likewise facilitated, rather than impeded, by improvements in transportation.

In modern times, the introduction of air travel, and particularly jet air travel, has had these contradictory impacts. Blouses designed and cut in the garment district of Manhattan can be flown to Puerto Rico to be sown because the availability of cheap labor in Puerto Rico now becomes relevant to the producer's location choices. But the market for Manhattan's exotic and esoteric activities which thrive on the scale and diversity of Manhattan is also extended by air travel, thus intensifying rather than diminishing their concentration in Manhattan.

A similar logic pertains to communication improvements. The telephone facilitates communication over great(er) distances. If we congregate at a particular site to facilitate communication but would otherwise prefer to be dispersed, the telephone facilitates dispersal. But if we congregate to exploit economies of scale, the telephone facilitates further concentration.

An example within the world of CDP will bring us closer to "home." The computer terminal which is connected by phone to the large computer where vast amounts of data and a great variety of computer programs are stored makes it possible for geographically dispersed users to avail themselves at great distances of the economies of scale of the large computer. This is a force for dispersal. But as long as those economies of scale remain relevant from a cost point of view, the market area for that main frame is enlarged. It can serve customers over a wider radius.

Enter the personal computer. To the extent that it improves access, it enhances concentration. To the extent that it erodes economies of scale, it enhances dispersal.

Before we attempt to appraise the balance of these forces making for concentration and dispersal, we have to take account of yet another dimension which is often neglected in the literature. We said earlier that an inherent constraint on central business district (CBD) growth is congestion. Technological developments and capital investments which facilitate interaction within the CBD and reduce congestion favor the CBD by expanding its holding capacity. The introduction of elevators certainly had that kind of effect. The telephone greatly expanded the holding capacity of the CBD because it substituted phone conversations for face-to-face meetings which would otherwise generate a lot of personal movement within the CBD. Absent the elevator and the telephone, the constraint of congestion would be operative at much lower volumes of activity.

Similarly the new CDP technologies, by facilitating communication *within* the CBD will expand its capacity. Electronic mail is perhaps the best example of this kind of development, particularly when viewed as an extension of the telephone, rather than as a substitute for postal service, although the latter is not totally irrelevant to the argument.

The scenario which emerges therefore is of a CBD with a greater holding capacity for activities which have other compelling reasons to locate there but the urgency to locate there for reasons of easy communication is reduced. What is the net impact?

Here is a suggestive conclusion from an expert in the consulting practice of industrial location:

> I believe that the more successful corporations increasingly will consider decoupling of modules within their existing organization. The approaching reality of a low-cost, national digital information network will facilitate the structuring of their new office configurations. The rapid and reliable transmission of data and documents will sharply reduce past requirements for geographic proximity.[9]

"Decoupling" is a good term which captures the potential negative impact of CDP on downtown employment. If the parts of an operation can be separated because they can be linked via communication, then those parts which have no other reason to be downtown can be located where rents are cheaper, wages are lower, etc. But will the "elite" component stay downtown and will it grow in response to the increased capacity to control subordinate activities at a greater distance?

Probably, yes. Average income will be higher, thus favoring proximity to the amenities of downtowns. Average intensity of contact with peers in other organizations will be greater, given their level of responsibility. Average cost in terms of space and the diseconomies of congestion will be lower.

But decoupling is also a double-edged sword. The company which had a large labor force downtown will decouple and relocate part of its staff elsewhere. The company which had a large labor force in the suburbs may, as a by-product of its decoupling, locate its elite downtown. Whether the gains will exceed the losses is doubtful, given the relative proportions of elite and nonelite. But if there is a net loss of employment, the income effect could be very positive and very supportive of continued vitality in downtown areas.

The proposed scenario should be quite familiar. At a more refined level of detail, it is the logical extension of the process which has operated at the grosser level for some time, namely, the outward movement of manufacturing and other goods-handling employment and the growth of office employment. For the former, the cons of downtown locations became oppressive, and the pros less compelling. For the latter, the reverse was true.

Another writer reaches a similar but stronger conclusion when he adds the productivity factor. He acknowledges that CDP technology will, for example, decentralize those banking functions which can be fully automated. But the market for banking services which cannot be fully automated, like financial and tax consulting, will be expanded. Automation will reduce banking employment in the suburbs but not downtown.[10]

Implicit in an optimistic forecast for the urban core is the assumption that the potential for substituting electronic communication for face-to-face communication is greater within organizations than between organizations. As an amateur organization theorist I would support that assumption with the generalization that communication within an organization mainly serves the goal of control, while communication between organizations is more oriented toward negotiation. The flavor of the distinction is reflected in studies showing that, after relocation, an organization's pattern of communication will change substantially and that considerable contact with organizations near the old site will be required.

V. SITE VARIATIONS

So far we have explored the locational implications of CDP on the assumption that alternative locations do not differ in terms of access to CDP services. One author who has addressed the subject of this paper head-on affirms that assumption as his starting point:

> Since telecommunication services—the telephone, telegraph, telex and data-communication services—are available everywhere in advanced countries at tariffs which are relatively independent of location, telecommunications is not now an important factor in decisions concerning office location. Even though advanced services are usually offered first in major cities (especially in North America, where competition between telecommunication carriers results in specialist services being offered on a limited geographical basis), it is not expected that many organizations will choose an office site in order to obtain access to services in the same way that they now do for access to transportation.[11]

While there is a slight suggestion that major cities might have a temporary advantage, the operating conclusion is that access to communications services will not be a significant location factor. In other words, my earlier introductory analogy to airports is invalidated.

Surprisingly, this very question is the focus of concern for others interested in the impact of CDP on urban centers.

> The next two decades will see the introduction and broad use of a new form of infrastructure that has important development implications for urban economies. A city's telecommunications infrastructure will become as critical an influence in business location and expansion decisions as its roads and water treatment capacity have been in the past. Yet much of this potential growth threatens to bypass our cities if the restrictive regulatory policies of federal, state and local governments are not amended.[12]

The thrust of the argument is that unwarranted regulation which grants monopoly powers to the chosen provider of cable television will inhibit the full development of the potential of CDP in cities and the result will be less service and higher prices than might prevail in a free communications market.

While I would not quarrel with the conclusion that regulation is likely to be distortive, it is not clear to me how "this potential growth threatens to bypass our cities.'' It is not obvious why ''other'' places will not be subject to the same problems, given that the cable franchising process seems to operate in the same manner throughout the nation.

If there is a basis for concern it would seem to be that cities which might otherwise enjoy superior communications services because of the size of their markets will fail to realize that potential because of ill-conceived regulatory policies. But the main point to recognize is that potential for comparative advantage. Urban economists have long recognized this tendency for cities to be ahead in the technological race precisely because the size and density of their markets permit ever-increasing specialization and the widest scope for experimentation.

Thus, I would be inclined to reject the conclusions and the concerns expressed by the authors quoted above and argue instead that from the perspective of access to the latest and most efficient communications services, the city, and particularly its CBD, is likely to be a more attractive location, ceteris paribus. I would also expect this factor to reinforce the positive impacts of improved communication discussed in the previous section.

VI. CONSEQUENCES OF A CHANGING MIX

We made the point earlier that aggregate location patterns are strongly influenced by industrial structure, i.e., the distribution of employment by industry. At any given state of technology, the location patterns of specific industries will differ. For example, the city and its CBD will generally have a smaller share of the metropolitan area's total employment in manufacturing and a larger share of the area's employment in such service sectors as banking and finance, and corporate headquarters, even while both shares may be declining over time. Thus, if there is a shift in the composition of employment toward industries for which the city boasts a larger share of the area's total, that shift helps to sustain the city's economic base. In broad terms, the relative growth in recent decades of the services sector of the national economy, particularly as such service activities are performed in office buildings, has had precisely that kind of positive impact on cities.[13]

The CDP revolution is relevant in this regard, as well, for several reasons. First, there is the direct impact on industrial structure caused by the growth of the producers and providers of CDP products and services. The locational choices of such producers and providers will have some impact on the overall geographic distribution of employment. Generally speaking, we would expect the growth of manufacturing enterprises associated with CDP to favor the suburbs, while the growth of service providers would favor the city. (Xerox machines vs. copy centers.) Unfortunately, we do not yet possess the data which would permit us to quantify these disparate effects.

But, perhaps, more significant is the impact of CDP on labor productivity throughout the industrial structure and within segments of the same organization which are decoupled per our earlier discussion. When the measure of an industry is *employment*, as opposed to *output*, we can experience significant mix changes not only from changes in demand patterns but also because of differential rates of productivity growth among industries. The classic historic case, of course, is agriculture, where phenomenal increases in labor productivity eroded the demand for labor and caused rapid economic decline in rural areas.

From this perspective, will CDP have an urban or a suburban bias? This question compels us to speculate further on what happens inside the enterprises which use CDP products and services. Each new advance in CDP is "absorbed" one of two ways. One is to use it as a substitute for doing exactly what you were doing before more efficiently. Personal computers substitute for calculators and for some of the labor which worked those calculators. Similarly, the use of electronic mail may reduce the use of telephones and the labor previously required to man a busier switchboard. Teleconferencing may reduce the travel budget with ambiguous effects on labor requirements. Cable TV may reduce labor requirements in department stores by substituting phone orders for counter orders. As the inventory control process is automated, there could be further reductions in labor requirements.

The substitution effect would be adverse to the city. Given the industrial profile of the city vs. the suburbs, I would expect greater opportunities for labor-saving applications of CDP to occur in the city. Fortunately (for the city), it is the rare CDP innovation that is restricted in its application as a substitute for other devices to accomplish the same set of tasks with less labor (or less of other factors). More typically, CDP advances result in dramatic expansions of the functions which they facilitate, namely, the acquisition and dissemination of information. Companies spend more time and money on both. How these incremental expenditures get translated into greater profitability is not an easy question to answer. But this has been the history of most technological advances in both transportation and communication. Airplanes did not just substitute for train or auto travel. They encouraged a lot more travel. Xerox did not just substitute for mimeograph machine, it encouraged a lot more copying. The telephone did not just substitute for mail, telegrams, or personal visits. It encouraged a lot more communication. And the computer. . .

When these functions expand, what contracts, and what happens to the distribution of employment by industry? So far, advances in CDP have correlated well with the growth of employment in service sectors and in the service components of manufacturing operations. These trends, as noted repeatedly, help to sustain the economic base of cities.

VII. SUMMARY AND CONCLUSIONS

The evolution, growth, and spread of new technologies in data processing and communications will undoubtedly have profound effects on the organization and location of enterprises in many sectors of the economy. As we contemplate the impact on urban areas we anticipate cross currents of concentration and dispersal but we do not predict, as some are disposed to, that the net effect will be prejudicial to the urban core in competition with outlying areas. The core is favored by early access to the new technologies, by improved internal communications which reduce congestion within the core, and by the further growth of service employment which has sustained the core economy in recent decades. These positive aspects of CDP are likely to offset the negative effects of dispersal facilitated by easy communication.

NOTES

1. Robert O'Connell, Andrew Silton, and Roger Vaughan, "Telecommunications: The New Urban Infrastructure," Commentary, Spring 1982, National Council on Urban Economic Development.

2. Harold J. Barnett, "Resistance to the Wired City," Spatial, Regional and Population Economics, Gordon and Breach, 1972.

3. Evan Peele, "How to Make Tele-Commuting Work," *Personal Computing*, May, 1982.

4. Eleanor Siegel, "Business As Usual, And Without All That Flying," *The Boston Globe*, December 27, 1981.

5. Jeffrey Rothfeder, "Electronic Mail Delivers The Executive Message," *Personal Computing*, June, 1982.

6. Benjamin Chinitz, "Economy of the Central City," The Urban Economy, Norton, 1976.

7. J. Thomas Black, "The Changing Economic Role of Central Cities and Suburbs," The Prospective City, M. I. T. Press, 1980.

8. John R. Meyer and José A. Gómez-Ibáñez, *Autos, Transit and Cities*, A Twentieth Century Fund Report, Harvard University Press, 1981.

9. Keith Wheelock, "The New Dimensions of Office and Personnel Location," Fantus Management Report, 1981.

10. Boris S. Pushkarev, "The Future of Manhattan," New York City's Changing Economic Base, New York, Pica Press, 1981.

11. Roger Pye: Office Location: The Role of Communications and Technology in P. W. Daniels Spatial Patterns of Office Growth and Location.

12. See reference in note 1, above.

13. See references in notes 6 and 7, above.

UPPER INCOME RESIDENTIAL REVIVAL IN THE CITY:

SOME LESSONS FROM THE 1960s AND 1970s FOR THE 1980s

Clifford R. Kern

People often snicker when they first hear of it. A renaissance in New York City? The rich moving in and the poor moving out? The mind boggles at the very notion. After all, what about the graffiti, the abandoned buildings, the chronic fiscal crisis? Hard as it is to believe, however, New York and other cities in the American Northeast are beginning to enjoy a revival as they undergo a gradual process known by the curious name of "gentrification"— a term coined by the displaced English poor and subsequently adopted by urban experts to describe the movements of social classes in and around London. . . . Indeed the evidence of the late 70's suggests that the New York of the 80's and 90's will no longer be a magnet for the poor and the homeless, but a city primarily for the ambitious and educated—an urban elite.

Blake Fleetwood,
"The New Elite and an Urban Renaissance,"
New York Times Magazine
(January 14, 1979):16ff.

Research in Urban Economics, Volume 4, pages 79-96.
Copyright © 1984 JAI Press Inc.
All rights or reproduction in any form reserved.
ISBN: 0-89232-423-6

I. UPPER INCOME DEMAND FOR URBAN LIVING

In recent years, rebirth of upper income demand for urban living has been widely celebrated in the popular press as a welcome change from the litany of decay that has dominated the postwar history of American cities. Benefits cited by enthusiasts include:

- Downtown activities—some provided by profit-making firms, such as restaurants and movie houses; others by nonprofit organizations, such as symphony orchestras; and still others by local government agencies, such as museums and libraries—that owe their diversity and often their very existence to the size, density, and affluence of the urban market and to the expenditures, philanthropy, and government support that it contributes.[1] These activities serve not only city residents but workers with jobs in the city and occasional visitors as well.
- New residential options in cities that have recently lacked the amenities and activities required for attractive urban living.
- Savings in resources that stem from reuse of existing housing, rather than new residential development, and absence of the road construction, sewer and utility line extension, and automobile travel implied by suburbanization.[2]
- Contributions to municipal revenues. Although increased tax receipts are not net benefits to society but transfers to the city from taxpayers or from taxing jurisdictions where upper income residents might otherwise have lived, they can be reckoned as benefits on equity grounds if the city's budget is strained by provision of services to the poor.[3]

Enthusiasm for a return of the rich to the city has been based largely on the experience of isolated neighborhoods.[4] Important questions remain unanswered:

- Are many cities, or only a few, among the likely beneficiaries?
- Are the numbers of people and numbers of neighborhoods involved sufficient to reverse upper income dispersal to the suburbs?
- Can growth of upper income demand for urban living be expected to persist in the future?

In the remainder of this paper, potential sources of growth in upper income demand for central sites are derived from a general discussion of residential choice. Alternative hypotheses are assessed with data from New York and other cities, and inferences that address these questions are drawn.

II. RESIDENTIAL CHOICE

For more than a decade, economists have used a simple model of urban residential behavior to examine household location in metropolitan areas. The model highlights commuting from home to work as a principal determinant of residential choice. All other things being equal, workers prefer to minimize the cost of journeys-to-work by living near their jobs. Competition for sites convenient to employment drives their prices higher than those of remote locations. The importance of the central workplace means that land prices rise higher there than elsewhere in the metropolitan region and decline steadily as distance from the center increases. In choosing where to live, workers sacrifice convenience to the center in return for low cost land. Because the highest income households demand the most residential land, they obtain the greatest savings from low land prices and face the strongest incentives to suburbanize, even when suburbanization means long work trips to central jobs. Once upper income communities have become established in the suburbs, their neighborhood attributes and tax/public service packages offer further incentives to suburbanize, especially for households with incomes high enough so that commuting costs are not a major burden.

At least two countervailing incentives have been identified in the literature. First, journeys-to-work require time as well as money—time that could otherwise be devoted to work or leisure. The higher the commuter's wage per hour worked, or the greater his income relative to leisure time, the greater the compensation required for time spent commuting. Even when demand for land implies substantial savings at low cost suburban sites and when suburbs offer far more amenities than the city, incentives to suburbanize may be insufficient to offset the loss of work or leisure imposed by lengthy work trips.

Second, in addition to employment, there may be goods and services that can be acquired only in the center or are made available there in much greater variety than elsewhere in the metropolitan region. Cultural, social, and entertainment opportunities are prominent examples: concerts, theater, movies, cabarets, bars, and restaurants. So are consumer goods for specialized markets. To buy centrally supplied goods and services requires nonwork travel to the center, and each such trip increases the cost of living in the suburbs. When purchases from and travel to the center increase with income, strong incentives to reduce trip length are created.

The nature of incentives favoring residence in the city and those fostering dispersal to the suburbs suggests several demographic attributes likely to distinguish upper income city dwellers from their suburban counterparts:[5]

1. *Childless households*—For individuals and couples who have not made the commitment to home and family implied by the decision to raise children, the value of social and entertainment opportunities in the city should be high and remain high even with frequent use. On the other

hand, reductions in residential density are apt to provide small and rapidly declining increments to satisfaction for childless households. Exterior space where children can play safely without supervision is of obvious value where children are present but irrelevant when children are absent from the household. Neighborhood characteristics and public services (such as schools) may also be less important for childless households than for those with children.

2. *Unmarried adults*—Opportunities for meeting and entertainment in the center should be particularly attractive for unmarried adults, even when they are heads of families with children.

3. *Education*—Besides the skills it develops, higher education seeks to enhance understanding and appreciation of a wide variety of cultural experiences that are most frequently found in the city center. It should therefore increase the pleasure they provide and sustain it during repeated attendance that would quickly bore the uninitiated.

III. UPPER INCOME RESIDENTIAL DEMAND IN THE CITY: SOURCES OF GROWTH

This discussion of residential behavior suggests two potential sources of growth in upper income demand for central sites: rapid growth among household types for whom incentives to live in the city have always been strong and weakened incentives to suburbanize for all household types. Each is discussed in turn.

A. Demographic Change

Table 1 documents rapid recent growth among childless adults and single parents, while the number of married couples with children grew hardly at all. These patterns reflect several demographic trends. First, the babies of the postwar baby boom have grown up, greatly enlarging the number of young adults who have yet to marry or to start their families. Second, there have been widespread changes in styles of living throughout the population—decisions to remain single, to delay marriage, to divorce, and to postpone or forego children. Third, increased life expectancy has increased the numbers of couples whose children have grown and of elderly surviving spouses.[6] Even if the relative attractiveness of city and suburban living has not changed in favor of the cities, the rapidly growing segments of the population have been those with the strongest incentives to live in the city when income is high.

Table 1. Married Couples and Single Adults in the United States,
by Age, 1960 and 1975[a]
(000)

	1960	1975	Net Change
20-34 Years			
Married couples, childless	1,955	4,252	+2,297
Married couples, children	11,164	12,461	+1,297
Single, childless	6,856	13,906	+7,050
Single, children	1,062	2,542	+1,480
35-59 Years			
Married couples, childless	10,588	12,811	+2,223
Married couples, children	10,474	9,911	-563
Single, childless	7,971	8,499	+528
Single, children	1,334	2,038	+704
60 Years and over			
Married couples, childless	5,059	7,402	+2,343
Married couples, children	144	139	-5
Single, childless	9,298	12,549	+3,251
Single, children	147	141	-6

Note: [a]Age of each married couple is determined by age of the wife; "single" persons are those who have never married and those currently widowed, separated, or divorced; "children" means that children under 15 are currently in the household.

Source: J. Pitkin and G. Masnick, "Analysis and Projection of Housing Consumption by Birth Cohorts: 1960-2000," research report prepared for U.S. Department of Housing and Urban Development, Grant H-2842RG, August, 1979, Attachment 1.

B. Changes in Residential Behavior

Most popular accounts of urban residential revival appeal to differences in residential behavior between upper income households today and their counterparts in the heyday of postwar suburbanization.[7] Unlike their parents, who grew up in the city and moved to the suburbs, today's upper income adults were often raised in suburbia. Therefore, it is argued, they are less likely than their parents to romanticize the virtues and more likely to recognize the defects of suburban life. At the same time, it is alleged that suburban virtues themselves are less compelling than they used to be. Increased density, congestion and pollution, rising crime rates, and dissatisfaction with school quality in the suburbs have all worked to narrow the differences between suburban and urban living. The burdens of commuting from city jobs to suburban homes may also have risen over the years, owing to increased traffic congestion and higher fuel prices. Finally, greatly increased costs for suburban land and for new residential construction have made suburban homes increasingly expensive. In parts of the city, by contrast, well-constructed older housing, left behind by previous generations of migrants to the suburbs, is available for renovation at comparatively low cost.

Together, these forces may substantially weaken incentives for suburban living and explain upper income revival in urban neighborhoods.

IV. EVIDENCE FROM NEW YORK CITY

Although urban residential revival has only recently been widely acknowledged, upper income population growth had already begun by the 1960s in some parts of some cities. The Census enumerations of 1960 and 1970 can therefore provide much more systematic and comprehensive information on its early years than the anecdotal accounts that have served as evidence heretofore. Although 1980 Census data released as this discussion is written are insufficient to support an equally thorough study of more recent years, comparison of the 1970 Census with subsequent data from the Annual Housing Survey provides some insight into what has happened in the 1970s.

Tables 2 and 3, which sketch the spatial distribution of families and of unrelated individuals, by income class, in the New York Metropolitan Region (SMSA), yield useful insights into both the size of upper income demand for city living and its evolution during the 1960s. Geographically, the region has been divided into four parts. The city center has been defined as that part of Manhattan lying south of 110th Street, an area about 8 miles long and 2 1/2 miles wide that encompasses the central business district (CBD) and immediately surrounding neighborhoods. Parts of the Bronx, Brooklyn, and Manhattan that surround the center and lie within 8 miles of the heart of the CBD have been grouped together to represent old, densely developed inner-city sites just beyond the center itself. The rest of the city, labeled the outer boroughs in the tables, consists largely of areas where distance from the center and limited public transportation have led to recent, low density development more like the suburbs than the urban core. Nassau, Rockland, Suffolk, and Westchester counties are the suburbs as defined by the Census.[8]

Both families and unrelated individuals have been grouped into three income classes. For 1970, family income classes have been defined so that $0-6,999 represents low income; $7,000-14,999 is moderate income; and $15,000 and more marks the upper income class. For unrelated individuals, the levels of income that divide the classes are one-third lower. Comparisons between 1960 and 1970 are included in these tables to identify gains and losses of residents, by income class, in different parts of the metropolitan region. Therefore, 1960 income classes must be defined so that an area where both the number of residents and their socioeconomic status had remained unchanged over the decade would have shown no gains or losses in any income class. Because a resident with unchanged socioeconomic status would normally have received increased nominal income over time, owing both to inflation and to economic growth, 1960 classes encompassing the same nominal income ranges as those for 1970 are clearly inappropriate, since classes so defined would register changes in numbers

Table 2. Number of Families, 1960 and 1970, by Location and Level of Income, New York SMSA

	1960		1970		1960 to 1970	
	Number	Fraction of SMSA	Number	Fraction of SMSA	Absolute Change	Percentage Change
City Center[a]						
Low[a]	102,399	13.3%	74.357	9.2%	− 28,042	− 27.4%
Moderate	83,485	6.9%	73,688	5.7%	− 9,797	− 11.7%
Upper	77,073	9.4%	81,508	9.4%	+ 4,435	+ 5.8%
Rest of Inner City						
Low	257,215	33.5%	267,635	32.9%	+ 10,420	+ 4.1%
Moderate	263,380	21.6%	219,893	17.0%	− 43,487	− 16.5%
Upper	96,395	11.8%	68,182	7.9%	− 28,213	− 29.3%
Outer Boroughs						
Low	291,511	38.0%	338,934	41.7%	+ 47,423	+ 16.3%
Moderate	561,946	46.1%	599,012	46.5%	+ 37,066	+ 6.6%
Upper	346,428	42.2%	335,734	38.7%	− 10,694	− 3.1%
Suburbs						
Low	116,861	15.2%	131,485	16.2%	+ 14,624	+ 12.5%
Moderate	310,109	25.4%	397,069	30.8%	+ 86,960	+ 28.0%
Upper	300,801	36.7%	382,928	44.1%	+ 82,127	+ 27.3%

Note: [a] For definitions, see text.

Sources: U.S. Bureau of the Census, *U.S. Census of Population: 1960, General Social and Economic Characteristics, Final Report PC(1)-34C* (Washington: Government Printing Office, 1962), Table 76; U.S. Bureau of the Census, *Census of Population: 1970, General Social and Economic Characteristics, Final Report PC(1)-C34* (Washington: Government Printing Office, 1972), Table 89; unpublished tabulations of 1960 and 1970 Census enumerations, by health area neighborhoods, prepared for the Department of City Planning, City of New York.

where no socioeconomic change had taken place. A resident with unchanged socioeconomic status would, however, probably have remained in the same relative position in the metropolitan income distribution. Therefore, both for families and for unrelated individuals, the 1970 income classes defined above have been translated into percentiles of the 1970 metropolitan distribution, and corresponding 1960 classes have been selected to mark off identical percentiles of the 1960 distribution.

The distinction in Tables 2 and 3 between unrelated individuals and families allows the residential decisions of unmarried, childless adults to be isolated from those of other households. Unfortunately, the definition of families encompasses several household types, principally married couples with children, childless couples, and single-parent families with children. Although different residential behavior can be expected for each of these types, the data for families are probably dominated by decisions of husband-wife families with children. Not only is this group a larger fraction of all families than any other, but current locations of

Table 3.   Number of Unrelated Individuals, 1960 and 1970, by Location and
Level of Income, New York SMSA

	1960		1970		1960 to 1970	
	Number	*Fraction of SMSA*	*Number*	*Fraction of SMSA*	*Absolute Change*	*Percentage Change*
City Center[a]						
Low[a]	135,193	25.3%	136,958	20.7%	+ 1,765	+ 1.3%
Moderate	97,734	32.9%	115,420	31.3%	+17,686	+18.1%
Upper	59,603	46.6%	77,691	49.0%	+18,088	+30.3%
Rest of Inner City						
Low	152,117	28.5%	158,724	24.0%	+ 6,607	+ 4.3%
Moderate	76,433	25.7%	73,328	19.9%	− 3,105	− 4.1%
Upper	17,103	13.4%	15,429	9.7%	− 1,674	− 9.8%
Outer Boroughs						
Low	158,401	29.7%	243,980	36.9%	+85,579	+54.0%
Moderate	85,929	28.9%	126,426	34.3%	+40,497	+47.1%
Upper	31,636	24.8%	38,610	24.4%	+ 6,974	+22.0%
Suburbs						
Low	87,886	16.5%	122,026	18.4%	+34,140	+38.8%
Moderate	36,982	12.4%	53,309	14.5%	+16,327	+44.1%
Upper	19,444	15.2%	26,793	16.9%	+ 7,349	+37.8%

Note: [a] For definitions, see text.
Sources: U.S. Bureau of the Census, *U.S. Census of Population: 1960, Detailed Characteristics, Final Report
PC(1)-34D* (Washington: Government Printing Office, 1962), Table 142; U.S. Bureau of the Census,
Census of Population: 1970, General Social and Economic Characteristics, Final Report PC(1)-C34
(Washington: Government Printing Office, 1972), Table 89; unpublished tabulations of 1960 and 1970
Census enumerations, by health area neighborhoods, prepared for the Department of City Planning, City
of New York.

older childless couples and single-parent families often reflect past decisions of
married couples with children, from which they have evolved.

If the description of residential choice in Section II is accurate, unrelated
invididuals should be more closely clustered around the center than families of
equivalent income. As income rises, individuals should be drawn more closely
to the center while families are dispersed toward the suburbs. These predicitions
are borne out in the tables. In 1970, for example, nearly half the high income
individuals in the metropolitan region lived in the center, compared with less
than 10% of upper income families. The center's share of metropolitan residents
rose with income for individuals and fell for families, except for families
in the highest income class. Even this exception is consistent with the preferences
suggested above. If education yields incentives to live near the center and to

live nearer as income rises, at very high levels of education these incentives may dominate incentives to suburbanize, even for families. Since levels of education and income are highly correlated, such behavior will be most apparent at the highest income levels.

Net changes in population during the 1960s are summarized in the last two columns of the tables. Growth in the upper income population of the inner city was confined to the most central neighborhoods, where it was substantial in both absolute and percentage terms, and was concentrated among individuals. Growth among individuals, which exceeded 18,000 residents, stemmed far more from an increase in their number throughout the metropolitan region than from an increased attraction to central neighborhoods. Any movement back to the city would have appeared in the data as a greater fraction choosing central sites and a smaller proportion living in the suburbs. The fraction of upper income individuals living in the center did rise over the decade from 46.6% to 49% of the total number in the metropolitan region, but even if the fraction had remained at its 1960 level, the number in the center would still have grown by almost 14,500, accounting for 80% of the growth that was actually observed.

More generally, for upper income families, the share of metropolitan residents remained constant in the center during the 1960s, fell sharply in the rest of the inner city, and grew rapidly in the suburbs. The center's share of individuals with high incomes grew modestly, but at the expense of adjacent neighborhoods, not the suburbs, which also enjoyed a modest growth in share. Rather than reversal of upper income suburbanization, the data reveal a city center that was holding its own while upper income dispersal persisted in the rest of the metropolitan region.[9]

V. THE 1970s

In New York during the 1960s, there was no rush of upper income residents into inner-city areas they had previously shunned. Growth in their numbers took place where they were already well represented. This growth, moreover, stemmed less from a growing propensity to live in the center, among either families or unrelated individuals, than from rapid metropolitan growth among upper income individuals, who had been strongly attracted to the center even at the beginning of the decade. Some potential sources of change in residential behavior, especially the increased price of fuel, were not present until the 1970s, however. More recent data are required to test whether conclusions drawn from the evidence of the 1960s are valid for more recent years.

Data for 1976 are available from the Annual Housing Survey. Conventions followed in collecting and reporting these data require some changes in definitions. Definitions of the city center, the rest of the inner city, and the outer boroughs, which were based on Census tracts for the discussion of the 1960s, must be replaced by less precise definitions based on counties, with the center represented by all of Manhattan, the rest of the inner city by all of Brooklyn and the Bronx, and the outer boroughs by Queens and Staten Island. In addition, instead of families and unrelated individuals, the Annual Housing Survey reports information for households, defined to comprise all residents of a dwelling unit. Households have been subdivided into five types: one person, under 62 years old; two people, both under 62; one person, 62 years or older; two people, at least one of whom is 62 or over; and three or more people. Unlike the geographic definitions, which are less precise than before, this detailed disaggregation of households may better reveal differences in behavior patterns than the distinction between families and individuals. Comparisons with 1970 have been made possible by a special tabulation of the 1970 Census done for the U. S. Department of Housing and Urban Development with geographic and demographic definitions that match those of the Annual Housing Survey.

Table 4 shows how the number of upper income households of each type changed between 1970 and 1976 in different parts of the metropolitan region. To be consistent with earlier analyses, upper income in 1970 has been defined as $10,000 or more for one-person households and as $15,000 or more for households that are larger; for 1976, income definitions have been chosen so that upper income refers to the same fraction of the metropolitan income distribution for each household type in both years. The pattern of change shown in Table 4 is remarkably different from the pattern of the 1960s. Briefly summarized, in the 1970s the center lost both numbers and share of upper income residents in all household types. In adjacent parts of the inner city, both numbers and share fell sharply for larger households but stablized for two-person households, both young and elderly, and increased for households of one person.

The weakness in the center can be tied directly to weakness in the Manhattan economy. Between 1970 and 1976, white collar jobs (in corporate headquarters, finance, insurance, real estate, law, education, and business and professional services) declined by more than 11% after having grown by about 50% in the previous decade.[10] Because downtown jobs complement nonwork activities as incentives for central residence, job loss can be expected to cause weakness in residential demand.

One might be tempted to ascribe the new-found stability in inner-city neighborhoods adjacent to the center to a movement back to the city that had not yet taken root in the 1960s. Annual Housing Survey data on migration, shown in Table 5, offer no support for this view, however. During the year prior to the survey, virtually no upper income residents of any kind moved to Brooklyn or the Bronx from either the suburbs or from outside the metropolitan region. Comparing the city as a whole with the suburbs, movement from city to suburb far overshadowed suburb to city migration except for young one-person households, who presumably left their parents' homes and who moved exclusively to Manhattan, where they could always have been expected to go. Stability of small households with high incomes in Brooklyn and the Bronx probably reflected,

Table 4. Upper Income Households, 1970 and 1976, by Location within the New York SMSA

	1970 Number	1970 Fraction of SMSA	1976 Number	1976 Fraction of SMSA	1970-1976 Absolute Change	1970-1976 Percentage Change
1 Person, under 62						
Manhattan	52,800	54%	51,800	47%	− 1,000	− 2%
Bronx, Brooklyn	16,500	17%	20,300	19%	+ 3,800	+ 23%
Queens, Staten Island	13,600	14%	15,700	14%	+ 2,100	+ 15%
Suburbs	14,100	15%	21,900	20%	+ 7,800	+ 55%
2 Person, under 62						
Manhattan	40,400	23%	34,900	19%	− 5,500	− 14%
Bronx, Brooklyn	38,400	22%	39,700	21%	+ 1,300	+ 3%
Queens, Staten Island	42,000	24%	34,700	19%	− 7,300	− 17%
Suburbs	55,800	32%	77,400	41%	+ 21,600	+ 39%
1 Person, 62 and over						
Manhattan	13,400	46%	12,700	40%	− 700	− 5%
Bronx, Brooklyn	5,300	18%	6,900	22%	+ 1,600	+ 30%
Queens, Staten Island	4,200	14%	5,600	18%	+ 1,400	+ 33%
Suburbs	6,500	22%	6,500	21%	000	0%
2 Person, 62 and over						
Manhattan	19,800	26%	9,700	14%	− 10,100	− 51%
Bronx, Brooklyn	17,900	24%	16,700	23%	− 1,200	− 7%
Queens, Staten Island	14,800	20%	16,300	23%	+ 1,500	+ 10%
Suburbs	23,300	31%	28,400	40%	+ 5,100	+ 22%
3 + Person						
Manhattan	51,500	8%	24,800	4%	− 26,700	− 52%
Bronx, Brooklyn	142,200	22%	101,200	17%	− 41,000	− 29%
Queens, Staten Island	139,100	22%	124,200	21%	− 14,900	− 11%
Suburbs	306,700	48%	331,100	57%	+ 24,400	+ 8%

Sources: Unpublished tabulations of the 1970 Census and of the 1976 Annual Housing Survey, New York SMSA.

Table 5. Origins and Destinations of Upper Income Household Heads
Who Moved within the Year Preceding the Survey

Destinations	*Origins*		
	New York City	*Suburbs*	*Outside SMSA*
	Young, 1 Person		
Manhattan	8,300	1,000	2,200
Bronx, Brooklyn	1,400	0	0
Queens, Staten Island	3,800	0	0
NYC—Total	13,500	1,000	2,200
Suburbs	300	3,000	500
	Young, 2 Person		
Manhattan	3,800	500	1,000
Bronx, Brooklyn	5,600	500	0
Queens, Staten Island	6,000	0	0
NYC—Total	15,400	1,000	1,000
Suburbs	4,100	9,000	1,200
	Elderly, 1 Person		
Manhattan	500	0	0
Bronx, Brooklyn	0	0	0
Queens, Staten Island	0	0	0
NYC—Total	500	0	0
Suburbs	0	200	0
	Elderly, 2 person		
Manhattan	500	0	0
Bronx, Brooklyn	1,400	0	0
Queens, Staten Island	0	0	0
NYC—Total	1,900	0	0
Suburbs	1,100	0	0
	3 + Person		
Manhattan	2,800	0	500
Bronx, Brooklyn	8,000	0	0
Queens, Staten Island	5,800	500	0
NYC—Total	16,600	500	500
Suburbs	8,100	12,800	1,500

Source: Unpublished tabulation from the 1976 Annual Housing Survey, New York SMSA.

for younger households, a spillover of demand from upper income Manhattan,
which had caused renovation of brownstones to flourish in adjacent Brooklyn
neighborhoods in the early 1970s, before the Manhattan economy had weakened
so severely. For the elderly, it must have stemmed from the aging of an upper
income population that had first moved in many years before.

Evidence for New York from both the 1960s and the 1970s suggests that
revival of upper income demand for urban sites is a product of rapid growth

among demographic groups who have traditionally been found in the city, rather than any change in residential behavior favoring urban living. This demand has been concentrated in the most central parts of the city, those closest to jobs and to the nonwork opportunities that make the city an attractive place to live. On the evidence of the mid-1970s, it is quite vulnerable to weakness in the white-collar economy of the CBD.

VI. OTHER CITIES

This discussion of incentives for upper income residence in the center has emphasized the attractiveness of social, cultural, and entertainment activities. But it is at least theoretically plausible that the value of time, rather than nonwork attractions, is principally responsible for upper income demand for central sites. For highly paid workers with jobs in the center and demographic attributes that limit demand for residential land, the benefits of suburbanization may be insufficient to justify the allocation of valuable time to lengthy work trips. The choice of central residence may have little or nothing to do with the presence or absence of nonwork opportunities.

Data recently gathered by Postlethwaite and reported in Table 6 make possible a crude but suggestive examination of this proposition. The first line in the table lists the number of professional and managerial workers with jobs in the CBD in each of five large cities during 1970. Line 2 shows the number of professional and managerial workers living within 2 1/2 miles of the CBD for the same cities in the same year. These measures are crude both because workers called professional and managerial include moderate as well as high income earners and because a measure of jobs in the CBD neglects centrally located jobs in immediately adjacent areas. Despite the crude data, Table 6 reveals striking differences in the resident/employment ratio among cities. It is roughly twice as high in Boston, Philadelphia, and San Francisco as in Detroit or St. Louis.

Data on nonwork attractions in the center are nearly nonexistent. About the only available measure is the number of restaurants, shown in line 4 of Table 6. There is a strong correspondence between the resident/employment ratio and the number of restaurants in the center. This correspondence is consistent with an important role for nonwork attractions in stimulating upper income demand for central residence, either by attracting to central jobs disproportionate numbers with weak incentives to commute to the suburbs, by strengthening incentives for centrally employed workers to live in the center, or even by attracting central residents with jobs in other parts of the metropolitan area.[11]

VII. LESSONS FROM THE 1960s AND THE 1970s

Patterns of upper income residence in the 1960s and the early 1970s suggest an important message both for policymaking and for setting the agenda of research

Table 6. Professional and Managerial Employment in the CBD, Professional and Managerial Residents within 2½ Miles of the CBD, and Number of Restaurants in the CBD and in Major Retail Centers within 2½ Miles of the CBD

	Boston	Philadelphia	San Francisco	Detroit	St. Louis
Professional and Managerial Employment (CBD, 1970)	24,431	34,200	52,395	21,262	8,439
Professional and Managerial Residents (2½ Mile Radius around CBD, 1970)	19,292	20,803	29,721	6,784	3,194
Resident/Employment Ratio (Line 1/Line 2)	.80	.61	.57	.32	.38
Eating Places (CBD and Major Retail Centers within 2½ Miles of CBD, 1972)	276	356	489	145	79

Sources: A.J. Postlethwaite, "The Return of Upper-Income Persons to the City Center: Fact or Fantasy," unpublished senior honors thesis, Harvard University, Cambridge, Massachusetts, April, 1977, Tables 3-7, 4-1; U.S. Bureau of the Census, *Census of Retail Trade, 1972, Major Retail Centers: California RC-C-5, Massachusetts RC-C-22, Michigan RC-C-23, Missouri RC-C-26, Pennsylvania RC-C-39* (Washington: Government Printing Office, 1975), Table 1.

questions to be addressed with newer data. The message is one of caution. Urban residential revival may be neither as pervasive today nor as persistent tomorrow as has often been alleged. In particular:

1. To the extent that upper income demand for central residence is dependent on the uniqueness and diversity of the goods and activities provided in the center, the strength of residential revival will vary markedly among cities. As Sternlieb has pointed out, many, perhaps most, American cities now have few downtown activities that cannot be duplicated and even excelled in their suburbs.[12] Creating downtown centers of the arts and entertainment in cities that currently lack them may be impossible, even though demographic change has generated latent demand sufficient to support them. The problem arises from the interrelationship between residential decisions and nonwork attractions. Without attractions, only a small central population of upper income residents is likely. But, as Rothenberg has pointed out, a large one is required to support diversity and uniqueness. Until an adequate market is apparent, private business will shun the center; but until attractive activities are provided, an adequate market will not develop.

2. Large-scale coordinated development, planned and sponsored by government and civic organizations, typically lacks the attributes required to foster upper income residential demand. Typical features of a large-scale project include parks, a convention center, an auditorium for concerts or theater, a sports arena, office buildings, a hotel, and limited retail space. But these are really insufficient to provide a vital mix of downtown activities. What is lacking, and what certainly equals and probably exceeds the importance of the lavish facilities in planned developments, is an exhilarating profusion of small-scale enterprise: both ethnic restaurants and haute cuisine; foreign films, first-run movies, and revivals of classics from the past; ice cream parlors and coffee houses; experimental jazz and chamber music; and lots of stores in which to browse. As a result, significant residential revival may require an existing array of downtown activities on which to build.

3. In New York City, which is rich in downtown activities, significant growth of upper income residential demand seems to have been limited to the most central neighborhoods and dependent on the strength of the white-collar economy of the CBD. Downtown growth of upper income residents cannot be relied upon to offset decline in other parts of the city, so as to yield net gains for the city as a whole. Even in the 1960s, when the downtown economy was strong and residential rebirth was vigorous, growth of upper income families and individuals in the center fell short of losses elsewhere. In the mid-1970s, as economic strength gave way to weakness in the CBD, the number of households with high incomes fell sharply in the center, augmenting, rather than offsetting, declining numbers in the rest of the city.

4. Upper income demand for urban living may be currently inflated by unusually large numbers of 20-34 year olds, for whom single, childless living

arrangements are common, reflecting the coming of age of the children of the baby boom. As the population ages, the next cohort to enter this age group will be substantially smaller than the current one, as is evident from the demographic forecast shown in Table 7. An important source of urban residential revival will disappear unless the current generation of young adults retain their present life-style as they move into what has traditionally been the prime age group for raising a family. Current forecasts (see Table 8) suggest that many will, so that the number of single adults, families headed by single adults, and childless couples will continue to grow rapidly even as the size of the 20-34 age group levels off and begins to decline. Such forecasts, however, are necessarily un-certain, and if they are wrong, the new-found prosperity of central neighborhoods

Table 7. U.S. Adult Population, by Age, 1970 and Projections to 2000 (000)

Age	1970	1980	1990	2000
20-34	41,278	57,611	60,157	51,794
35-59	56,281	59,508	71,568	90,414
60 and over	28,683	34,729	40,304	42,324

Source: J. Pitkin and G. Masnick, "Analysis and Projection of Housing Consumption by Birth Cohorts: 1960-2000," research report prepared for U.S. Department of Housing and Urban Development, Grant H-2842RG, August, 1979, Appendix to Section III.

Table 8. Married Couples and Single Adults in the United States, by Age, 1970 and Projections to 2000[a] (000)

	1970	1980	1990	2000
20-34 Years				
Married couples, childless	2,902	3,710	3,417	3,015
Married couples, children	11,628	13,076	12,504	10,293
Single, childless	10,011	18,406	22,944	21,547
Single, children	1,889	3,563	4,310	3,640
35-59 Years				
Married couples, childless	11,835	11,881	12,890	17,241
Married couples, children	10,361	10,825	13,021	14,346
Single, childless	8,411	9,912	13,794	19,446
Single, children	1,879	2,409	3,358	3,923

Note: [a] See note (a), Table 3.

Source: J. Pitkin and G. Masnick, "Analysis and Projection of Housing Consumption by Birth Cohorts: 1960-2000," research report prepared for U.S. Department of Housing and Urban Development, Grant H-2842RG, August, 1979, Attachments 1 and 2.

could be as ephemeral as the boom in elementary, high school, and college enrollments that also stemmed from the baby boom and evaporated in its aftermath.

These substantive inferences are necessarily tentative given their reliance on data for one city and the absence of information for more recent years. Besides these tentative findings, this paper has illustrated methods for measuring residential gains and losses by income class and location within a metropolitan region and for distinguishing demographic change from changes in residential behavior. The generality of the substantive conclusions can be tested by applying these methods to data for other cities and, as available, more recent years.

ACKNOWLEDGMENTS

Thanks are due to the editor of this volume, Robert Ebel; to discussants at the Conference on Economic Development and Public Finance, Katharine Bradbury and Douglas Diamond; and to my colleague Larry Lichtenstein for suggestions that have substantially improved the content and exposition of this paper.

NOTES

1. See Jerome Rothenberg, *Economic Evaluation of Urban Renewal* (Washington: Brookings, 1967): 71.

2. Reuse of existing structures for upper income residential development need not impose overcrowding or other extensive hardship on lower income residents displaced by the process. In most large cities, their housing needs can be accommodated in surplus dwellings that would otherwise be abandoned. This line of reasoning does not imply that no hardships will be borne by the displaced. Ties to the old neighborhood will be disrupted; moving costs must be borne; and new accommodations may be inferior to the old in either dwelling or neighborhood attributes. But the hardship should be far less than in tighter housing markets.

3. The contribution to municipal revenues is potentially substantial. In New York City, for example, the CBD and immediately surrounding neighborhoods contained 12.9% of the city's 1970 population but accounted for more than a quarter of the city's residential property assessments. Comparable contributions to other tax collections can reasonably be assumed. The assessment figures are for the fiscal year 1973/74 and are from Emanuel Tobier, *Aspects of the New York City Property Market* (New York: Citizens Housing and Planning Council, 1975).

4. A representative sample of such accounts is discussed in Howard J. Sumka, "Displacement in Revitalizing Neighborhoods: A Review and Research Strategy," *Occasional Papers in Housing and Community Affairs* 2 (1978): 134-167.

5. These relationships are demonstrated formally in Clifford R. Kern, "Upper-Income Renaissance in the City: Its Sources and Implications for the City's Future," *Journal of Urban Economics* 9 (January, 1981): 106-124, from which the following several paragraphs have been taken with only slight alteration.

6. A good discussion of recent demographic change may be found in William Alonso, "The Population Factor and Urban Structure," in Arthur P. Solomon (ed.), *The Prospective City* (Cambridge, Mass.: The MIT Press, 1980): 32-51.

7. An example is the Fleetwood article quoted at the beginning of this paper.

8. This rough partition of the metropolitan area, selected to be both intrinsically meaningful and consistent with a reasonable data collection effort, conforms only roughly to the descriptions presented in the text. The large geographic subdivisions guarantee substantial heterogeneity within each area, especially in the outer boroughs, which include some neighborhoods that are decidedly inner city in nature, although most are distinctly suburban.

9. An econometric model showing that attractive housing available for renovation, often cited as a strong incentive for rebirth of upper income residence in the city, made at most a peripheral contribution to this trend in the 1960s appears in Clifford R. Kern, "Upper-Income Residential Revival in the City: Some Lessons from the 1960s for the 1980s," State University of New York at Binghamton, Department of Economics, Working Paper 79-5, which is available from the author.

10. These rates of growth and decline have been estimated from data in U. S. Bureau of the Census, *County Business Patterns, 1976, CBP-76-34* (Washington: Government Printing Office, 1978), Table 2, and earlier volumes of the same data source from 1970, 1964, and 1959. More recent data from this source show the weakness of the mid-1970s to have been temporary, with all of Manhattan's loss of white-collar jobs having been restored by 1980.

11. A correlation between numbers of upper income residents and numbers of nonwork activities in the center is consistent with but not proof of the importance of the activities in attracting the residents. This correlation would also arise if upper income residents were attracted to the center for other reasons, and their presence then created a market for the activities that would not otherwise exist. The correlation cannot identify the direction of causation. Still, it is difficult to identify any such other reasons for the differences in resident/employment ratios presented in Table 6.

12. George Sternlieb, "The City as Sandbox," *The Public Interest* 25 (Fall, 1971): 14-21.

DISAMENITIES, LOCAL TAXATION, AND THE INTRAMETROPOLITAN LOCATION OF HOUSEHOLDS AND FIRMS

Michael J. Wasylenko

I. INTRODUCTION

The New Federalism may have important effects on the intraurban location of households and employment. Most of the present discussion of the New Federalism focuses on the fiscal squeeze that has been imposed on large cities, and the increase in state and local taxation that has occurred in response to the first round of cuts in federal grants-in-aid.

While these first round fiscal effects are important, the resulting increase in local taxation may induce population and employment shifts within metropolitan areas. Changes in fiscal federalism are likely to exacerbate the fiscal inequities that exist within metropolitan areas, and especially between the central cities and their suburban jurisdictions. Central cities are likely to lose more federal aid than suburban jurisdictions because the structure of many grants-in-aids presently favors central cities. Thus, if fiscal variables affect location decisions,

Research in Urban Economics, Volume 4, pages 97-116.
Copyright © 1984 JAI Press Inc.
All rights or reproduction in any form reserved.
ISBN: 0-89232-423-6

central cities requiring larger tax increases to maintain existing public services will lose population.[1]

This paper reviews the research on the factors affecting intraurban population and employment location to assess the relative importance of local fiscal variables on location decisions. Since the working assumption of this paper is that grants-in-aid cuts will result in relatively higher taxes for central cities (and the older suburbs) than for the newer suburbs, the focus of the literature review will be on central vs. dispersed location patterns and land use.

The next portion of the paper reviews the evidence on factors affecting intraurban population movement, while the intraurban location decision of firms is discussed in a subsequent section. A final section draws some conclusions about how population and employment location decisions interact and about the potential influence of the New Federalism on urban structure.

II. INTRAURBAN LOCATION OF HOUSEHOLDS

A. Rent-Gradient Models

Traditional models of intraurban household location eschew fiscal influences and emphasize the mononuclear city in which households equate the marginal saving on residential land consumption and the marginal cost (including time) of commuting to the city center to determine an optimal residential location (Muth, 1969; Alonso, 1964; Beckmann, 1969; Mills, 1972). Within this basic framework higher income households locate farther from the city center if the income elasticity of demand for land is positive and if the marginal costs of commuting are invariant with respect to income. Higher income households will consume more land and therefore save more total land rent by moving farther from the city center than lower income households.

Both Alonso (1964) and Muth (1969) emphasize the importance of the assumption about the invariance of marginal commuting costs with respect to income. Unit time costs are larger for higher income families implying that, while the marginal saving on total land rent may increase with income, the marginal cost of commuting also increases with income. Thus, with a fixed rent gradient, whether higher income households move farther from the city center than lower income households depends on the magnitude of the income elasticity of land consumption compared to the magnitude of the income elasticity of the marginal total (including time) cost of commuting. If the income elasticity of marginal time cost is larger (smaller) than the income elasticity of land consumption, these models predict that higher income households will choose residential locations closer (farther) to (from) the city center.

B. Some Empirical Evidence on the Rent-Gradient Model

In the United States, the fact is that higher income households have on average more decentralized residential locations than lower income households. If the monocentered models of urban structure are correct, the implication is that the income elasticity of demand for land is larger than the income elasticity of marginal commuting costs. Wheaton (1977) tests this implication of the monocentered model.

Using Alonso's (1964) bid-rent function, Wheaton specifies a constant elasticity of substitution utility function in land, housing characteristics, financial cost, travel time cost to work, and other goods. He places the CES utility function in the Alonso bid-rent framework and, using micro data on households from the San Francisco Bay area, he estimates the parameters of the utility function and the corresponding slopes of the bid-rent curves. He estimates separate bid-rent and utility function parameters for different sociodemographic groups and income classes, allowing for different preferences among the groups and classes.

From the parameters of the utility function, the amount of land consumed and the value of commuting time are calculated for various income groups, which in turn can be used to calculate the income elasticities of land consumption, of the value of travel time, and of total (time plus financial) commuting costs. The estimated income elasticity of the demand for land is about 0.25 while that of the value of travel *time* is between 2.5 and 7.5. However, when both time and money costs of commuting are considered, the income elasticity of total travel costs is about the same as land or 0.25.

An income elasticity of demand for land that is larger (smaller) than the income elasticity of the marginal cost for travel implies higher income groups will have less (more) steeply sloped bid-rent curves and will (not) outbid lower income groups for land in decentralized locations. The estimates of the land and total transportation cost elasticities being the same imply that the slopes of the bid-rent curves do not vary significantly across income groups.[2]

Based on these results the decentralized location of higher income households does not appear to result from a high income elasticity of demand for land relative to travel cost.[3] Wheaton suggests that fiscal incentives resulting from municipal government fragmentation and differences in other amenities may be important reasons why higher income households locate in the suburbs.

Using a different approach than Wheaton and data for Chicago suburbs, Diamond examines the income elasticity of the marginal valuation of access to the central city as well as that of other amenities including distance to the nearest commuter rail station, access to Lake Michigan, public safety or lack of crime, air quality, and topography. Diamond finds that the income elasticity of the marginal evaluation of public safety is 2.36, that of access to the central business district (CBD) is 2.11, and that of access to Lake Michigan is 0.72. The income elasticities of the marginal valuations for access to rail lines, air quality, and topography are not statistically significant.

In contrast to Wheaton's neutral marginal valuations across income classes or bid-rent curves between land price and distance that have the same slope across income classes, Diamond reports that marginal valuations for access to the center are directly related to income. Moreover, his estimates of an income elasticity of 2.11 indicates that, other things equal, higher income groups will outbid lower income groups for land closer to the city. Public safety has a larger income elasticity (2.36) than access to the CBD, and higher income households value safety much more highly than lower income groups. According to these findings access to the CBD should draw families back toward the central city. Presence of crime, low air quality, and low levels of other fiscal amenities explain the decentralized population pattern now observed in urban areas.

C. Direct Tests of the Influence of Amenities on Urban Location

Tiebout was the first to theorize that households examine local fiscal advantages in choosing residential locations. Oates (1969) and others have tested Tiebout's proposition using the jurisdiction's property value as a left-hand-side variable and its public expenditures and tax rate as right-hand-side variables. Oates's basic argument is that favorable net fiscal residuals attract households, raising housing and land demand and their respective prices. Thus, property values are expected to have a positive correlation with local expenditure and negative correlation with the local tax rate. Oates finds evidence consistent with Tiebout's hypothesis while Pollakowski (1973) and others using different data obtain results with mixed support for Tiebout's proposition.

Hamilton (1976) argues, however, that any set of coefficients on expenditure and taxes may be consistent with Tiebout's hypothesis. The capitalization of fiscal advantages into property values results from either disequilibrium in the market for residences in fiscal havens or a substained advantage in production functions for producing public services or for revenue raising, such as a larger industrial tax base.

If, for example, there was a supply shortage of jurisdictions with low expenditures on public services and low taxes, then to be consistent with Tiebout's hypothesis the sign of the coefficient relating property value to public expenditures should be negative. On the other hand, if the system of jurisdictions is in long-run equilibrium there may be no correlation between property value and fiscal variables. Such empirical results cannot necessarily be construed as rejection of Tiebout's hypothesis and of the importance of fiscal variables in location choice.

More direct tests of the influence of fiscal factors and other amenities on household location use population distributions between city and suburbs rather than property values as left-hand-side variables. Bradford and Kelejian (1973) examine the importance of fiscal variables in the location choice of lower, middle, and higher income groups. Specifically, the proportion of households in each income class in each urbanized area that resides in the central city is hypothesized to be related to locational amenities and housing market conditions in the central city compared to the suburbs. Bradford and Kelejian test these hypotheses using data from the 87 most populous urbanized areas in 1960.

They find that a middle-class family is more likely to reside in the suburbs the higher the percentage of central city families who are poor, the higher the median family income in the urbanized area (a measure of the rent gradient or higher demand for land), and the more unfavorable the central city fiscal residual for middle income families. Poor families are more likely to live in the suburbs the greater the proportion of suburban housing that is old, the lower the proportion of central city housing that is old, and the lower the central city fiscal surplus for poor families.

Frey (1979) analyzes the factors that affect the decision of white central city residents to move anywhere in the SMSA (standard metropolitan statistical area) and their propensity to move specifically to the suburbs and performs this analysis using data on intraurban household movement in 39 SMSAs between 1965 and 1970. The decision to move is measured as the number of white central city residents who move within the SMSA between 1965 and 1970 as proportion of the total number of white central city residents. The propensity of central city movers to locate in the suburbs is measured as the number of white central city movers who locate in the suburbs as a proportion of the total number of white central city movers. Note that multiplying these two dependent variables yields the proportion of total white central city residents who migrated to the suburbs between 1965 and 1970.

He regresses the first two dependent variables on 10 independent variables measuring population structure and racial factors in the city, the ratios of suburban to city taxes and educational spending, the city crime rate and the amount of recent employment decentralization. Frey finds that newer housing development in the suburbs, higher central city taxes relative to those in the suburbs, less central city education expenditure relative to that in the suburbs, higher city crime rates and recent employment decentralization have some influence on overall mobility of city residents. But all of these factors have a much stronger influence on the propensity of city movers to locate in the suburbs.

Frey then combines the results of these two regressions using path analysis to determine what factors influence the proportion of central city residents who move to the suburbs. Frey finds that both higher taxes and lower education expenditures in the city relative to the suburbs influence white migration to the suburbs. Using beta coefficients, Frey also finds that more recently developed suburbs, the percent of the city residents that are black, and the degree of recent employment decentralization have as much or more influence on white movement to the suburbs as the fiscal variables.

Grubb (1982) updates Bradford and Kelejian's study using 1970 data for 106 SMSAs and expands the number of right-hand-side variables in the model to include employment decentralization and explicit measures of education and noneducation expenditures and of central city tax rates. All of the variables are measured as the ratio of central city to SMSA values. Grubb also analyzes separately the decentralization of white and nonwhite households.

Grubb finds white households are more suburbanized in SMSAs that have a higher ratio of central city to SMSA expenditure on noneducation, a higher relative central city effective tax rate, a higher ratio of central city to SMSA property tax base (reflecting higher cost of capital land values), a more decentralized service employment, and a less decentralized wholesale trade and retail trade employment. Upper income white households are more decentralized when the ratio of violent crime in the central city relative to the suburbs is higher, when the ratio of central city to SMSA noneducation expenditure and effective tax rates are higher, when the ratio of central city to SMSA property values is higher, and when retail trade employment is more decentralized.

Nonwhite households are more decentralized when there is a higher central city to SMSA ratio of violent crime and when central city property values are relatively high. Upper income nonwhite households are more decentralized when the central city to SMSA ratio of violent crime is higher and when wholesale trade employment is more centralized. Fiscal variables appear to have no effect on the overall decentralization of nonwhite households nor on the decentralization of upper income nonwhite households.

Overall Grubb finds that high central city crime rates and effective tax rates influence the decentralization of white households. Moreover, upper income white households are more likely to remain in a central city of an SMSA where retail trade or shopping is less decentralized. However, he also finds that white households decentralize when land prices are less expensive in the SMSA. One cannot draw conclusions about whether upper income white households are less responsive to lower land prices than lower income households, and Grubb's findings may be consistent with Diamond's on the income elasticity of the marginal value of access to the CBD. Crime is also an important determinant of nonwhite household decentralization, and higher property price in the central city is a statistically significant determinant of overall nonwhite decentralization but does not affect the decentralization of upper income nonwhites. Fiscal variables are not statistically significant determinants of nonwhite household decentralization.

Reschovsky (1979) examines the movement of households between 160 suburban census tracts within the Minneapolis-St. Paul metropolitan area. In the 1970 to 1971 period 45,000 households moved within the metropolitan area. He tests whether households move among the area's census tracts in response to fiscal variables, other location amenities, and socioeconomic status of the location, and he includes distance to downtown Minneapolis as a right-hand-side variable to capture rent-gradient or population density effects. He runs six separate migration regressions; the sample is stratified by housing tenure and by low, middle, and higher income groups.

Reschovsky uses three fiscal variables on the right-hand-side of the equation: local effective tax rates, per capita local expenditures, and public school quality. The effective tax rate coefficient has the expected negative sign in all six of the regressions and the coefficient is statistically significant in three of the six regressions: low income renters, low income owners, and middle income renters. Per capita municipal expenditure has the expected positive coefficient in all six regressions and the coefficient is statistically significant in the low and middle income renter equations. The results for the school quality variable were mixed. The coefficient on school quality has the expected positive sign for low income and middle income renters and for higher income homeowners, and for the latter two cases the coefficients are statistically significant. For low and middle income homeowners and for high income renters the coefficients for school quality are negative and for the latter two cases the coefficients are statistically significant.

While the negative coefficients for school quality are unexpected, Reschovsky points out that higher income renters may not have children and may view high quality schools as costly in terms of higher future taxes which renters may believe will be reflected in future rent increases. This is reminiscent of Hamilton's point that public goods are not necessarily valued the same by all households, and unexpected signs on coefficients of fiscal variables do not necessarily imply that household location choice is perversely responsive or nonresponsive to fiscal variables.

Bradbury, Downs, and Small (1982) have made the most comprehensive study of urban decentralization to date.[4] They test a number of theories about the reasons for urban decentralization. To test the theories, they use a set of cross-section regressions performed on 121 SMSAs for the period 1970-1975. They also estimate similar regressions on a subsample of 87 SMSAs for the period 1960-1970.[5] Two dependent variables are used to measure population and employment decentralization or suburbanization: percentage change in central city population relative to percentage change in SMSA population and the percentage change in central city employment relative to percentage change in SMSA employment.

The population suburbanization variable is regressed on variables that reflect disamenity avoidance theories such as poor quality schools and race; tax avoidance theories; positive attraction theories, such as low-density living and economic opportunity; economic evolution theories, such as mismatches between business location and unemployed labor and incubation of firms prior to employment growth; biased policy theories, for example, homeownership subsidies and the location of new housing construction; and demographic trends, such as the age structure of the population and selective out-migration. Under disamenity, they find that suburbanization is lower when city school districts extend beyond the central city boundaries. This may imply that one of the advantages of suburbanization is leaving central city (or lower quality) schools; and when avoiding central city schools is more difficult, suburbanization is lower. Also, they find that a high concentration of blacks within the central city fosters suburbanization. This finding is consistent with Frey's but it is opposite to Bradford and Kelejian's, who find that the initial distribution of low income households between city and suburbs affects middle income household suburbanization, but that racial composition of the central city does not affect middle income suburbanization.

On tax avoidance, Bradbury, Downs, and Small find that a greater number of local governments in an SMSA leads to more suburbanization. This result is consistent with Tiebout's hypothesis in that the existence of more local jurisdictions allows a wider range of choice among alternative tax and public services packages. They also find that a larger disparity between city and suburban per capita taxes influences suburbanization between 1970 and 1975; however, data to test this hypothesis for the 1960-1970 period is not available. Their findings on taxes support the view that higher central city taxes increase suburbanization for the 1970-1975 period.

For positive attraction theories, a high proportion of old central city housing led to more suburbanization. They also find that population suburbanization results in part from employment suburbanization for the 1960-1970 period, but the influence of employment suburbanization could not be tested for the 1970-1975 period.[6]

D. Summary of Population Decentralization Literature

There is growing evidence that fiscal advantage and urban externalities exert greater influence on household intrametropolitan location decisions than the income elasticity of land and the tradeoff between land consumption and transportation costs. Wheaton finds in the San Francisco Bay area virtually no difference between the income elasticity of demand for land and the income elasticity of the marginal cost of transportation to the city center. This result suggests that a large income elasticity of demand for land is not a principal motivation behind the decentralization of middle and upper income households. Diamond's results suggest that the marginal valuation of access to the CBD is highly income elastic and that in the absence of disamenities higher income households would outbid lower income households for the land closer to the central city.

Oates, Bradford and Kelejian, Frey, Grubb, Reschovsky, and Bradbury, Downs, and Small all find statistical support for the hypothesis that favorable public service and tax packages influence suburbanization. The findings on the role of urban disamenities and racial prejudice in the flight from the central city to the suburbs are less conclusive, but a higher proportion of older housing and less employment opportunity in the central city are generally associated with suburbanization. The results on racial prejudice against blacks as a reason for suburbanization are mixed, but the findings of Frey and Bradbury, Downs, and Small suggest that racial prejudice cannot be ruled out as a reason for suburbanization.

An important issue is whether urban areas would be less decentralized if there were little (or no) variation in public service or in tax rates throughout the region. The empirical work reported here suggests that urban areas would be less decentralized with less variation in local government expenditure and tax patterns. But urban decentralization in the United States has occurred since at least the early 1800s and, at that time, it occurred within city boundaries so that public services and local taxes, which were small by present standards, probably were not significantly different within the city boundaries. This early decentralization could have been caused by the income elasticity of demand for land relative to transportation cost, but also could have resulted from a desire to avoid urban disamenities, such as congestion, an aging housing stock in the center, and the factory noise that existed in the industrial core later in the 1800s.

III. INTRAURBAN LOCATION OF BUSINESS[7]

Net change in intraurban employment patterns results from business births, deaths, on-site expansions and contractions, and relocation. Because of difficulties in obtaining data on firm location, there are relatively few studies of the factors that affect intrametropolitan business locations and no existing study completely analyzes all five aspects of business location decision.

There are six factors that are generally hypothesized to affect business location choice. Traditional models of urban structure generally rely on a tradeoff between lower priced land at decentralized locations and the cost of transporting commodities to the city center to explain manufacturing business location. There is little doubt that truck transportation, instead of rail transport, allowed considerably more business location flexibility and had a significant impact on business location choice. Thus two factors which enter empirical models of business location choice are land rent or distance from the city center, and proximity of location sites to interstate highways or beltways to represent the accessibility of a location to transportation. Agglomeration economies, which are generally measured as the proportion of firms in the SMSA that are located at a particular site, and proximity to labor markets, measured as population density or number of employed residents within commuting distance of a location, are also important determinants of business location decisions. Firms may also choose intraurban locations based in part on fiscal variables, especially local taxes. And some firms producing primarily for local markets, such as retail trade and service firms, are expected to choose intraurban locations based on the size of the local market.

Most of the firm location research examines the decentralization of manufacturing. But a few studies expand this inquiry to include firms in other industries. Two principal research methods are used to analyze business location decisions:

questionnaire or interview surveys of firms that inquire into specific factors for the firm's location decision, and econometric studies relating firm locations to right-hand-side variables representing the six factors (land, rent, transportation, etc.) mentioned above. For purposes of this paper, attention is primarily devoted to whether local fiscal variables, particularly local taxes, affect employment decentralization.

The importance of local taxes rests on whether and the extent to which they vary across local jurisdictions. If local tax variations account for only a fraction of profits, then location decisions are more likely to be based on factors other than taxes.

When local taxes are found unimportant in locational decisions, it is often attributed to the fact that taxes are only a small portion of total costs. While local tax differentials are a small part of total costs, they may be a significant part of profits. For Boston, Hamer estimates that the effective property tax rate for manufacturing firms is about 5% in the city and 4% in suburban jurisdictions. Stigler calculates that manufacturing firms earn a 14% rate of return on invested capital. If capital bears the full burden of the property tax—as it would if it was not mobile between city and suburb—a 1% property tax differential in the Boston area implies profit levels are 7% higher in the suburban jurisdictions than in the city. Thus, taxes are an important part of firm profits, especially when other markets and cost factors are the same across jurisdictions.[8] Similar reasoning applies to nonmanufacturing locational decisions if product and factor markets are the same between two jurisdictions.

The decentralization of existing central city firms can be viewed as two decisions. Existing firms decide to leave the city; and given that they decide to leave, certain variables determine their ultimate destination within the metropolitan area. Most studies have considered only one of the two decisions. The first stage of the decision is generally analyzed using survey data obtained from questionnaires while the latter is analyzed using both survey data and econometric methods.

A. Survey Results

Hamer cites a questionnaire study of Boston SMSA firms, performed in 1969 by the Boston Economic Development and Industry Commission. The results indicate that firms are quite mobile. Nearly one-half of all suburban firms moved to their new sites between 1960 and 1969. The questionnaire asked firms considering moves and those not considering moves about the reasons for their decisions. The responses of city and suburban firms were analyzed separately. Two-fifths of the city and suburban firms considering moving cite space availability and cost; one-third of city firms cite labor-related factors. The questionnaire did not ask specifically about local taxes.

For Boston city firms that are not interested in moving, one-fourth cite high costs of moving their equipment and a desire to be close to existing clients as reasons for not moving. This is evidence that moving, adjustment, or transaction costs cause some locational inertia. Suburban firms cite favorable space- and labor-related factors as reasons for their location satisfaction.

Schmenner (1978) used questionnaire data to analyze the movers' decisions for firms in Cincinnati and New England. He concludes that mover firms are smaller (fewer employees) than nonmover firms; that space-related reasons, particularly the desire to expand the plant, are most frequently mentioned for moving; and that mover plants are more independent of local customers and suppliers than nonmover plants.

For tax rates, Schmenner finds in Cincinnati and New England that only about one-quarter to one-third of the relocating plants actually move to new locations which have lower property taxes. About 40-50% either move within the same tax jurisdiction or to locations in towns which have similar tax rates. Another one-fourth move to jurisdictions which have higher property tax rates.

Apilado (1973) interviewed Arizona firms receiving local government industrial aid bonds in an attempt to assess the role of industrial aid bonds in a firm's decision to branch, expand, or locate in a jurisdiction. Industrial aid bonds are used in 29 states and are the most substantial form of local government financial inducement. Apilado finds no evidence that the aid bonds provided incentives for the location or volume of firm investments.

B. Econometric Evidence

1. Demand

Moses and Williamson's (1967) study of intrametropolitan manufacturing locational decisions in Chicago is the first that empirically related firm expansions and relocations to a vector of cost variables. Using 582 transportation zones in the Chicago area, the authors analyzed a cross section of firm densities (number of firms in a zone divided by land area in a zone) for moving and expanding firms. For relocations, they find that fewer relocations occur in zones farther from the central city, and the percentage of land in manufacturing use in the zone has a positive effect on the number of firm relocations. The latter variable is likely to be a proxy for agglomeration economies, since more manufacturing land use implies more manufacturing employment and firms. The other variables in the model are not statistically significant.

For expansions, they find fewer expansions occur in zones farther from the central city, and also that the percentage of land in manufacturing use in the zone has a negative effect on firm expansions. The latter variable may proxy the space in the zone for on-site expansion.

They also studied expansions and relocations of firms in different subareas of the SMSA, and ran separate regressions in each subarea. The percentage of land in manufacturing use or agglomeration economies is directly related to the number of firm expansions and relocations in a zone. The variable distance from the central business district (CBD) is inversely related to firm movement expansion, but its coefficient is statistically significant in only four of the eight regressions. They use a dummy variable—equal to zero if the zone is in Chicago and equal to one otherwise—to proxy tax, zoning, and other fiscal differences between city and suburban zones. The coefficient of this tax variable is never statistically significant.

Schmenner's (1975) study examined three aspects of manufacturing firm location using establishment and employment data for jurisdictions within four metropolitan areas. Schmenner explained the existing pattern of establishment (employment) densities (number of establishments in a jurisdiction divided by land area of the jurisdiction), the net change in establishment (employment) densities, and the relocation densities of establishments (employment) moving from the central city. He analyzed two different periods, 1967-1969 and 1969-1971, and studied Cincinnati, Cleveland, Kansas City, and Minneapolis-St. Paul.

Schmenner examined the four SMSAs separately and then pooled the sample of four SMSAs (5); he used both establishment and employment as dependent variables (2) and used two time periods (2). Therefore, he estimated 20 (5 × 2 × 2) regressions for the analysis of existing density patterns, for the analysis of the net change in density, and for the analysis of relocation densities. As independent variables, Schmenner used three measures of fiscal differentials between the city and each of its respective suburban jurisdictions: property tax rate differential, personal income tax rate differential, and per-pupil education expenditures differential. Other independent variables included measures of rail and highway transportation facilities in a jurisdiction, distance to the central city, population density (a measure of labor supply), and existing establishment density in the jurisdiction as a measure of available agglomeration economies.

The results of the analysis (20 regressions) for the *existing* pattern of firm densities indicate that the coefficients of population density (16—which implies the relevant coefficient was statistically significant in 16 of the 20 regressions), railroad access (8), highway interchange (4), and the property tax differential (3) were statistically significant in a portion of the 20 regressions. Population density, a proxy for the distribution of the metropolitan labor force, most consistently predicts the existing density pattern of firms. The transportation variables are next in importance, while the property tax differential is only occasionally statistically significant. Specifically, the coefficient of the property tax variable is statistically significant and has the hypothesized sign for Cleveland in the 1969-1971 employment equation and for Minneapolis-St. Paul in both the 1967-1969 and the 1969-1971 employment equations.

The net change analysis met with less success. Population density (3), highway interchange (3), existing firm density (2), and railroad access (1) are statistically significant with the hypothesized sign in a small portion of the 20 regressions.

For the mover equations, the coefficients of population density (7), existing firm density (3), highway interchange (2), property tax rate differential (2), railroad access (1), educational expenses differential (1), and income tax rate differential (1) are statistically significant and have the hypothesized sign in a smaller portion of the 20 regressions. The coefficient of the property tax differential is statistically significant and has the hypothesized sign for Kansas City in the 1967-1969 establishment and employment equations. The coefficient of the income tax variable is statistically significant and has the hypothesized sign for the pooled establishment regression during the 1967-1969 period.

Schmenner's results indicate that the income tax variable is not a significant determinant of firm location, while property taxes may be significant especially in Kansas City, Minneapolis-St. Paul, and, perhaps, Cleveland. But the results for the property tax are not robust. The statistical significance of the property tax coefficient depends, but not consistently, on the period being analyzed, on whether establishment or employment measures of firm location are used, and on which aspect of location (i.e., existing pattern or net change or mover) is examined. In part, the unimportance of property tax rates for firm location may result from the similarity during the period of analysis of these rates in the cities and their suburbs. In all cases, the central city effective property tax rate is no greater than 2.0% while the suburban rates are not lower than 1.3%. Thus, for cases where there is a greater property tax differential between city and suburbs, property taxes may be more important.

Schmenner concludes that tax effects are second-level concerns in business location decisions. A low tax rate is no guarantee that industry will be attracted to the jurisdiction, nor is a high tax rate guaranteed to scare off new industry. Labor supply, as measured by population density, is the most consistent determinant of firm location.

Erickson and Wasylenko (1980) estimated a model of establishment location choice for movers from Milwaukee to its surrounding 56 suburbs. They estimated their model for seven different industries: construction, manufacturing, transportation, wholesale trade, retail trade, finance, and services. Their independent variables represent land markets, labor markets, transportation facilities, agglomeration economies, fiscal characteristics and, for some industries, consumer markets in each jurisdiction. Retail, finance, and service establishments are presumed to increase their profits by locating in areas with more consumer demand as well as with lower costs. Establishments in the other industries are assumed to locate on the basis of cost.

They find that moving firms in every industry choose suburban jurisdictions having a supply of labor within commuting distance of the jurisdiction and that are near other firms in the industry—presumably to capture agglomeration economies. Lower land prices (distance from CBD) are statistically significant for some industries, but the coefficients of the fiscal variables are not statistically significant for any industry.

Bradbury, Downs, and Small examined employment decentralization in 87 SMSAs for the 1960-1970 period. Suburbanization of total employment is responsive to population (labor force) and income changes within the metropolitan area. But an available pool of labor in the city, as measured by the central city unemployment rate, does not attract firms to the central city. In fact, the higher the city unemployment rate the greater is the suburbanization of firms, and the relationship is statistically significant. Although data on the spatial distribution of unskilled labor is not available to them, if one assumes that the higher central city unemployment rate is associated with greater concentrations of unskilled labor in the central city, employment growth is not attracted to unskilled labor areas within metropolitan areas. Data on tax levels are not available for the 1960 to 1970 period and the influence of taxes on employment suburbanization is not tested in this analysis.

Grubb also analyzes employment suburbanization in 1967 for manufacturing, services, retail trade, and wholesale trade. His principal conclusions are that high population density in central cities tends to drive employment to the suburbs, and that relative property tax rates do not influence employment decentralization.

2. Supply Side

All of the above studies analyze only the firm's demand for space in zones or localities. As Oakland also notes, these analyses omit the willingness of communities to supply industrial sites. In two separate studies, Fischel (1975) and Fox (1978) suggest that some local governments rationally exclude firms from locating within their boundaries or supply no industrial sites. They argue that residents of communities derive utility from environmental quality, public goods, and private goods. The presence of industry in a jurisdiction presumably results in larger increases in tax revenues than in expenditures, and permits more consumption of local public and private goods at the expense of environmental quality. Communities with stronger preferences for environmental quality will require higher tax revenues from firms or larger increases in private and public goods to accept losses in environmental quality.

Some communities with strong environmental preferences may want to increase their property tax rate on firms to adequately compensate for losses of environmental quality. But since the property tax rate must be applied uniformly to residential and nonresidential property, residents are constrained to trade increased public goods for losses in environmental quality and, as a result of higher taxes, losses in private consumption. If communities find either or both of these tradeoffs unacceptable, then they are likely to zone very little or no land for industrial use. A similar environmental quality argument can be made for commercial property, although most commercial property is likely to have less detrimental environmental effects than industrial property. Nonetheless, some suburban communities do zone out large shopping malls because of their environmental effects. The argument here (and in Oakland's study) is that including jurisdictions that zone out firms in an analysis of firm site choice may lead to biased estimation results, especially with respect to fiscal variables.

Empirical tests of the community supply of sites are not available, but Fischel provides indirect evidence. One of the prerequisites to Fischel's theory is that fiscal benefits exist for communities that admit industry and commerce. Using a sample of 54 communities in Bergen County, New Jersey, he concludes that there are some fiscal benefits to communities from commercial and industrial property. By his calculations, about 70% of all commercial and 52% of all industrial property tax payments benefit residents either by lowering residential taxes or increasing educational expenditures.

Since some fiscal benefits exist, Fischel then used a regression analysis to determine whether a lower amount of commercial and industrial property in a jurisdiction is associated with higher median family income in a jurisdiction, using proximity to New York City and land area of the community as control variables. He reasons that if environmental quality is a normal economic good then higher median income communities will choose more environmental quality and zone a lower percentage of land for industrial and commercial property than will lower income communities because in high income communities the fiscal benefits of industry are less likely to compensate adequately for their lower environmental quality.

His results indicate that higher income communities have relatively more commercial establishments, while industrial property is found in lower income communities. These results imply that lower income communities get the industrial firms, while higher income communities get commercial firms that probably cause less loss in environmental quality than industrial firms.

In separate studies, Fox (1981) and Wasylenko (1980) analyze demand for sites and incorporate the supply side into their models. A fully specified model of site choice would consist of demand and supply relations for industry sites using the tax rate or the price of land as the equilibrating variable, and other variables as shifters of the demand and supply curves. Since data on the supply of sites or zoning practices in each suburban jurisdiction are difficult to obtain, neither Fox nor Wasylenko is able to use a fully specified model for the supply of sites.

Fox regresses the amount of land in industrial use in each of Cleveland's suburban jurisdictions on land market, fiscal, and transportation access variables for these jurisdictions. Using 43 suburban jurisdictions as observations, he finds that the coefficients of fiscal and other variables are not statistically significant. To consider the supply side, he then omits from his sample 19 jurisdictions having no land in industrial use. He reasons that these jurisdictions completely zone out industry. When the same regression is run using the remaining 24 suburban jurisdictions as observations, the coefficient of each of the fiscal variables has the expected sign and each is statistically significant. This evidence supports Oakland's contention that the supply side should be an important consideration in models of firm location, and that demand analyses not accounting for jurisdictions zoning out industry may produce bias and misleading results for fiscal variables.

Following Fox, Wasylenko re-estimated the Erickson and Wasylenko model omitting jurisdictions that zoned out industrial or commercial firms. Using movers instead of total industrial land may give better estimates of the statistical parameters, since total industrial land use presents only an accurate picture of location incentives to the extent that industry is in its equilibrium location. Given the possibility of considerable inertia in the land market due to moving costs, examining movers would seem a better test of the importance of fiscal variables. Moreover, Fox's results may be biased, since he omits labor market variations among jurisdictions from his model.

Wasylenko estimates the model for six industrial categories; since transportation industry is zoned out of almost all jurisdictions, it is not analyzed. Using land use data, he reasons that 32 of the 56 suburbs zoned out manufacturing firms, 21 zoned out construction and wholesale trade firms, and 24 jurisdictions zoned out retail, finance, and service firms. The results for the subsample indicate that labor supply, agglomeration economies, and land market variables are again statistically significant determinants of location choice for all six industries. Moreover, the coefficient of the property tax variable has the expected sign and is statistically significant for manufacturing and wholesale trade firms. But the tax variables are not statistically significant for the other four industries. Wasylenko conjectures that manufacturing and wholesale trade establishments are more sensitive to property tax rates than are other industries, because firms in the other industries may follow consumer markets and place less emphasis on fiscal characteristics, while manufacturing and wholesale trade firms are more concerned with cost.

Charney has examined the destination decisions of relocating manufacturing firms in the Detroit metropolitan area between 1970 and 1975. The analysis includes 126 zip code areas, and as in the Fox and Wasylenko studies she omits zip code areas that attract no relocating firms. But she includes central city zip codes as well as suburban zip codes; the consideration of central city destinations as well as suburban destinations is an improvement over other relocation studies.

Six categories of firms are analyzed: all manufacturing, durable manufacturing, nondurable manufacturing, small, medium and large manufacturing firms. For all categories of manufacturing firms, she finds that destination zip codes are close to origin zip codes and destinations occur more frequently in zip codes with high employment densities. She also finds that the presence of low income and of high income households in zip codes deter relocations for all categories of manufacturing firms. The most interesting finding from the perspective of this review is that higher property tax rates discourage relocations of nondurable manufacturing and large manufacturing firms. The property tax coefficient is also statistically significant for the pooled regression of all manufacturing firms. Since Charney also omits zip codes with zero destinations, her results for the property tax are similar to the findings of both Fox and Wasylenko.

IV. SUMMARY OF FISCAL FACTORS AND URBAN DECENTRALIZATION

The classic urban economics literature assumes that the demand for land is income elastic, and thus people migrate to suburban areas to consume more land more cheaply in spite of the added transportation costs associated with suburban residence. Specifically, the utility gained from the additional land consumption in the suburbs compensates for the lost utility associated with additional commuting from the suburbs to the city center. To explain why families in higher income classes move to the suburbs, this literature assumes that the demand for land is more income elastic than is the income elasticity of the marginal cost of commuting. Thus, families in higher income groups consume more land and commute farther than their lower income counterparts.

Recent evidence rejects this classical thesis. Wheaton examines the land-transportation cost tradeoff explanation for population movement. His evidence indicates that the income elasticity of land is quite low compared to the disutility of extra commuting. Wheaton concludes that the demand for land does not explain the migration to the suburbs. Instead, he conjectures that people migrate from the central city to the suburbs due to favorable fiscal factors and other amenities such as educational quality in the suburbs. Diamond extends Wheaton's analysis and concludes that access to the CBD is highly income elastic. People move to the suburbs because of disamenities, and in the absence of these disamenities higher income households would locate closer to the CBD. Bradford and Kelejian conclude that families at or above middle income migrate to the suburbs, in part, because of an unfavorable central city fiscal residual. Frey, Grubb, Reschovsky, and Bradbury et al. all reach similar conclusions in their studies about the direct effect of unfavorable central city fiscal variables on population decentralization. Thus, from this literature review one may conclude that fiscal variables and urban disamenities directly influence the decentralization of households, especially white upper income households, from central cities.

There is also a growing body of evidence that fiscal variables have a significant influence on business location. Studies that incorporate the supply of industrial sites into locational choice analysis indicate that fiscal variables are statistically significant determinants for location of manufacturing and wholesale trade, i.e., industrial, establishments. The differentials are not the only statistically significant determinants of firm location. Proximity to a labor force and highways are often important determinants of firm destination.

Tax differentials may also have an indirect effect on industry location, through their effect on the movement of population or labor supply, which in turn affects industry movement. Only the study of Bradbury and associates explicitly esti-mated a more general equilibrium model of employment and population move-ment. They find some evidence of interaction between employment growth and population growth. Their results for the 1960-1970 period suggest that business or "employment follows population decentralization quite strongly, and popu-lation follows business less completely."

Using statistical causality tests, Steinnes (1977) also examined whether in-dustry follows people out of the central city or people follow industry or whether the relation between employment and population decentralization is simultane-ous. Steinnes found that service and manufacturing jobs follow people, but that people follow the retail industry out of the central city. Cooke's (1978) study extended Steinnes's work. He uses estimates of employment and population density gradient parameters as measures of decentralization and examined dif-ferent SMSAs. His results indicate that services follow retail, which in turn, follows manufacturing, which follows people. Industry follows a labor supply (or market) out of the central city. Thus, if people leave the central city in part due to fiscal factors, and industry is following people, then fiscal factors indirectly affect industry movement.

NOTES

1. This assumes that the public services financed by the federal grants are not completely eliminated and that jurisdictions do not reduce their expenditures by the full amount of the loss in the grants-in-aid. The determinants literature on grants-in-aid concludes that federal grants substitute in part for local government revenue. But the extent of substitution of federal grant money for locally raised revenue depends on the type of grant. If closed-end categorical grants are cut from the federal budget, local expenditures may decrease by the full amount of the grant-in-aid reduction (with locally raised revenue not affected by the reduction in aid), because these categorical grants tend to raise expenditure by the full amount of the grant. See Gramlich (1977) for a recent review of the local expenditure effects of grants-in-aid.

2. Wheaton finds that households with between one and three members and whose household heads are under 30 have the steepest bid-rent curves. This evidence is consistent with the casual observation that young and small households are largely responsible for city gentrification.

3. In a series of simulations, Wheaton changes the assumptions about travel cost. In some simulations, he decreases the money cost of travel and then decreases travel velocity or raises the time cost of travel. As might be expected, given the large income elasticity of the value of travel time, the bid-rent functions for higher income families become steeper than those for lower income families the more important travel time is relative to the money cost of travel.

4. In their study, SMSA or interregional growth patterns as well as intraregional growth patterns are examined. Only the results of the latter tests are reported here.

5. They study population and employment suburbanization and per capita income change in central cities for the 1960-1970 period, and only study population suburbanization and per capita income change in the central cities for the 1970-1975 period.

6. The jobs-follow-people issue is discussed in more detail in the next section of the paper after factors affecting business location decisions are reviewed.

7. The material in this section relies heavily on parts of my paper entitled "The Location of Firms: The Role of Taxes and Fiscal Incentives" (1981).
8. Oakland originally made this same point in his review of firm location.

REFERENCES

Alonso, W. (1964). *Location and Land Use*, Cambridge.

Apilado, V. P. (1973) "Public Administration of Financial Incentives in Industrial Plant Location: Industrial Aid Bonds." Papers in Public Administration 26, Arizona State University, Institute of Public Administration.

Beckmann, M. J. (1969). "On the Distribution of Urban Rent and Density." *Journal of Economic Theory*, 1: 60-67.

Bradbury, K., A. Downs, and K. Small (1982). *Urban Decline and the Future of American Cities*, Brookings, forthcoming.

Bradford, D. and H. Kelejian (1973). "An Econometric Model of the Flight to the Suburbs." *Journal of Political Economy* 81: 566-89.

Charney, A. H. (forthcoming) "Intraurban Manufacturing Location Decisions and Local Tax Differentials" *Journal of Urban Economics*.

Cooke, T. (1978). "Causality Reconsidered: A Note." *Journal of Urban Economics* 5: 538-542.

Diamond, D. B. (1980). "Income and Residential Location: Muth Revisited." *Urban Studies* 17: 1-12.

Erickson, R. and M. Wasylenko (1980). "Firm Relocation and Site Selection in Suburban Municipalities." *Journal of Urban Economics* 8: 69-85.

Fischel, W. (1975). "Fiscal and Environmental Considerations in the Location of Firms in Suburban Communities." In E. S. Mills and W. E. Oates (eds.), Fiscal Zoning and Land-Use Controls, Lexington, MA: D. C. Heath.

Fox, W. (1981). "Fiscal Differentials and Industrial Location: Some Empirical Evidence." *Urban Studies* 18: 105-112.

——— (1978). "Local Taxes and Industrial Location." *Public Finance Quarterly* 6: 93-114.

Frey, W. H. (1979). "Central City White Flight: Racial and Nonracial Causes." *American Sociological Review* 44: 425-448.

Gramlich, E. (1977). "Intergovernmental Grants: A Review of the Empirical Literature." In W. E. Oates (ed.), *The Political Economy of Fiscal Federalism*, Lexington Books: 219-240.

Grubb, W. N. (1982). "The Flight to the Suburbs of Population and Employment, 1960-1970." *Journal of Urban Economics* 11: 348-367.

Hamer, A. M. (1973). *Industrial Exodus from the Central City*, Lexington, MA: D. C. Heath.

Hamilton, B. W. (1976). "The Effects of Property Taxes and Local Public Spending on Property Values: A Theoretical Comment." *Journal of Political Economy* 84: 647-650.

Mills, E. S. (1972). *Studies in the Structure of Urban Economy*, Johns Hopkins.

Moses, L. and H. Williamson, Jr. (1967). "The Location of Economic Activity in Cities." *American Economic Review* 57: 211-222.

Muth, R. (1969). *Cities and Housing*, University of Chicago Press.

Oakland, W. H. (1978). "Local Taxes and Intraurban Industrial Location: A Survey." In G. Break (ed.), *Metropolitan Financing and Growth Management Policies*. Madison: University of Wisconsin Press.

Oates, W. E. (1969). "The Effects of Property Taxes and Local Public Spending on Property Values: An Empirical Study of Tax Capitalization and the Tiebout Hypothesis." *Journal of Political Economy* 77: 957-970.

Pollakowski, H. O. (1973). "The Effects of Property Taxes and Local Public Spending on Property Values: A Comment and Further Results." *Journal of Political Economy* 81: 994-1003.

Reschovsky, A. (1979). "Residential Choice and the Local Public Sector: An Alternative Test of the 'Tiebout Hypothesis.' " *Journal of Urban Economics* 6: 501-520.

Schmenner, R. W. (1978). "The Manufacturing Location Decision: Evidence From Cincinnati and New England." Report to the U. S. Department of Commerce, Economic Development Administration.

———— (1975). "City Taxes and Industry Location." Revision of his unpublished Ph.D. dissertation, Yale University (1973).

Steinnes, D. (1977). "Causality and Intraurban Location." *Journal of Urban Economics* 4: 69-79.

Stigler, G. (1963). *Capital and Rates of Return in Manufacturing Industries*, New York: National Bureau of Economic Research.

Wasylenko, M. (1980). "Evidence on Fiscal Differentials and Intrametropolitan Firm Location." *Land Economics* 56: 339-349.

———— (1981). "The Location of Firms: The Role of Taxes and Fiscal Incentives." In R. W. Bahl (ed.), *Urban Government Finance: Emerging Trends*, Vol. 20, Urban Affairs Annual Reviews, Sage: 155-190.

Wheaton, W. C. (1977). "Income and Urban Residence: An Analysis of Consumer Demand for Location." *American Economic Review* 67: 620-631.

CREATING NEW JOBS FOR OLDER CITIES:
THE ROLE OF THE PUBLIC SECTOR

George A. Reigeluth, Susan J. MacCracken
and David L. Birch

I. INTRODUCTION

This paper begins with a contextual discussion of how, over time, technological, economic, and other factors transform the economic functions of cities, the nature of the related urban problems, and the policy responses to these problems. On the basis of this discussion, the second section argues that of the two forces of change that comprise this transformation process (economic growth from births, expansions, and in-migrations of firms; decline from deaths, contractions, and out-migrations), policymakers should focus more of their attention on the causes, nature, and implications of the growth side of this process. This section also presents a more detailed look at the current transformation through which city economies are going. Given these trends, the last section focuses on what the public sector can do to help older, industrial cities improve their rates of employment gain, which are lagging behind other cities' rates, and are a large part

Research in Urban Economics, Volume 4, pages 117-132.
Copyright © 1984 JAI Pess Inc.
ISBN: 0-89232-423-6

of the reason for why these older cities are experiencing net employment loss. In particular, three public sector roles are discussed: (1) providing targeted up-front capital to help these cities remove the physical and other obstacles to development; (2) providing ways to reduce the unusually high operating costs which firms in these cities experience; and (3) helping the economic development officials in these cities improve their ability to identify firms that are most likely to want to set up branch facilities in their cities.

II. TRANSFORMATION OF URBAN ECONOMIES

Urban policy development and implementation have suffered because they have not proceeded from a complete understanding of the transformation process through which the economies of cities go. The dynamic nature of the economic development process in which the United States and other countries are involved has caused a series of transformations in the economic function and physical form of their cities. These changes, in turn, over time have altered the basic nature of the urban issues facing these countries. Finally, this change in the nature of urban problems has necessitated a constant adaptation of the role of national, state, and local governments in responding to these urban problems.

The first of these transformations, which came with the industrial revolution of the late eighteenth and early nineteenth centuries (first in England and later in America, the rest of Europe, and Japan), was caused in part by new methods of industrial and agricultural production. Prior to the industrial revolution, agricultural techniques required a large labor input per unit of output and industry was, by and large, decentralized, rural, and small scale. However, with the industrial revolution agricultural productivity increased dramatically, creating a surplus of labor. This labor was drawn to the growing industrial cities, where new industrial methods based on technologies such as the steam engine made large concentrations of workers both possible and necessary.

The different circumstances under which people lived and worked in these cities resulted, in large part, from the technological changes which accompanied and shaped the industrial revolution, and which radically changed the way in which economic activity was organized and carried out. These changes also significantly altered the economic function which urban centers performed within the emerging national economy and led, in turn, to alterations in the physical structures of cities. Whereas in the medieval era (ending in the latter half of the eighteenth century) cities acted primarily as administrative, political, financial, and cultural centers; in the capitalist era they came increasingly to carry out industrial, economic, and commercial activities as well.

The fact that industrial pursuits now took place in towns and cities, rather than in the country, was a consequence of the radically different manner in which they were being performed. The changes resulted, in part, from the increasing mechanization of production which, in turn, led to a greater division of labor that drew the craftsman out of his home and into the factory. Initially, rivers in relatively rural locations powered the factories; it was the introduction of steam power which made the urban location of factories both possible and necessary. The parallels of this chain of developments to more recent changes in urban structure are striking: just as new production techniques led in the beginning of the nineteenth century to the concentration of economic activity in urban areas so too has the development of horizontal production methods been partly responsible for the more recent decentralization of economic activity.

Other developments, such as basic improvements in communication and transportation technologies, made possible the establishment of the new system of international trade which the dynamics of the growing capitalist system required for its survival and perpetuation. With the enormous increase in productive capacity, the industrializing and urbanizing nations came to require from the rest of the world, unprecedented levels of two things: markets for the commodities being turned out by the new factories of the growing urban centers and raw materials for the expanding production systems. As a result of these basic needs, the international dimension of the capitalist system initially manifested itself in an imperialistic manner—the industrializing nations carved out trading empires for themselves in Africa, Asia, and South America.

The development of this system of international trade is one of the factors which explains the rapid growth of cities in the Western world, particularly during the latter part of the nineteenth century. Many of the raw materials used in the urban factories were supplied by this system, as were markets for the products. Rising trade resulted in an increasing demand for both the city's products and for the labor to produce them, as well as in an increasing flow of income into export-good-producing cities. Similarly, the fact that some developing countries have now begun to compete with older industrial centers in the production and export of manufactured goods is one factor behind the fall in demand for those cities' exports, and the resulting problems associated with it (e.g., declining productivity, plant closures, and rising unemployment).

The impact of rapid industrialization on the form and structure of nineteenth-century cities was far-reaching. Rapid urban growth and limited transportation options caused high density urban development which, without adequate sanitation facilities, created a public health crisis. It was in response to these adverse environmental impacts of this first urban transformation that public sector intervention, as we know it today, first took visible shape, in the form of municipalizations and extensions of gas, water, sewer, transportation, and housing facilities.

These late-nineteenth-century public initiatives—together with the invention of the internal combustion engine, rising incomes, and other changes beyond the control of public policy—led, in turn, to a second urban transformation, characterized by population and employment decentralization. As the rate of growth of manufacturing employment slowed in these cities, they began to develop competitive advantages in other economic activities—first in consumer, and then in producer, services. This second urban transformation from the high density, industrial city of the nineteenth century to the lower density, suburbanized city of the twentieth century gave rise to new urban problems, to which the public sector had to adapt. Most recently, the diffusion of population and employment within urban areas has been extended in the United States and several European countries to redistribution of economic activities away from metropolitan areas to small towns and rural areas. Many of the largest metropolitan areas are now experiencing absolute declines in population. This change from the trends of the last two centuries may thus represent the start of a third urban transformation.[1]

Each of these urban transformations has been precipitated by powerful factors (such as changing technologies, prices, incomes, and tastes) which have altered the basic economic functions and physical form of cities. These changes have, in turn, generated new urban problems which have prompted reactions and adaptations on the part of public officials and programs. This historical experience strongly suggests that those public policies that attempt to deal with these problems by altering or reversing the direction of a particular transformation, or the underlying factors causing it, are far less likely to succeed than are those policies that flow with the tide of the transformation and that focus on mitigating its adverse impacts.

For example, the nineteenth-century municipal reformers would have met with far less success at trying to deflect or slow down the tide of rural to urban migration than they experienced in addressing the public health problems which resulted from it. The limited success of most of the many later European population and employment dispersal policies supports this contention, as does our own experience with public policy attempts to slow down or reverse the more recent process of urban deconcentration and decline.

This brief overview of policy response to urban transformations begins to define the limits within which public policies can expect to be effective. The following sections attempt to be more specific about what public policies can do within these limits—starting first with a more complete understanding of the transformation process and moving next, on the basis of this understanding, to the development of realistic strategies and programs.

III. A MORE DETAILED LOOK AT THE CURRENT URBAN TRANSFORMATION

The first step in determining what public policies can realistically accomplish within the above limits is to develop a more complete understanding of the nature of the transformation through which urban economies are currently going. Only with this understanding can policy officials focus their attention on real, as opposed to perceived, aspects of urban development. Given the complexity and size of this question, this section makes no pretense of being exhaustive; rather, the intent here is to examine, in a progressively more focused fashion, recent findings about the nature of employment change in cities. Again, the emphasis is on the growth side of the picture on the grounds that: (1) most past work has dealt with the negative side of the ledger; and (2) more importantly, available evidence shows that it is variations in the rates at which urban economies create—not lose—jobs that explains most of the interurban variation in net employment change. The following discussion will examine this contention in greater detail.

The transformation in urban economies occurs through the following six components of private sector employment change: births and deaths, in-migrations and out-migrations, and expansions and contractions of firms. In looking at how these components explain variations in employment change from city to city, Table 1 shows that very little of this variation is explained by firms moving in and out of cities. To be specific, many firms move short distances each year, but virtually none move from one metropolitan or rural area to another. When a move does occur, it is widely publicized in the press. Without evidence to the contrary such publicity makes it easy to begin to pin all of an area's economic woes on the fleeing firm. Any hard look at the numbers, however, will show that fleeing firms take only a small number of jobs with them, and that for every firm that flees there tends to be another firm, with a similar number of jobs, moving in. The net effect of firm migration is thus negligible, for most places, relative to both the job base and other job flows.

In examining the other four components, Table 2 (which summarizes the annual combined gains and losses from Table 1) shows that most of the differences in net change across cities are explained by variations in the gain rates, and that job loss rates are relatively similar both across cities, and from city to suburb. That is to say, cities seem to lose jobs (through firm contractions and deaths) at roughly the same rates, but gain jobs (through firm births and expansions) at widely varying rates. The key to economic growth therefore lies not in the rate at which existing jobs are lost, but rather in the rate at which new jobs are created. For example, between 1972 and 1976, while New Haven's employment loss rate of 7.3% was roughly the same as Houston's loss rate of 8.1%, its rate of employment gain (5.6%) was only one-third of Houston's rate of 14.4%.

Together with the earlier argument about the limits within which policies can be effective, this evidence strongly suggests that, for the purposes of urban economic development policy, public officials should spend considerably more time increasing their understanding of the processes by which new firms are started and existing firms expanded and less of their attention on job retention.

That is not to say that public policy officials wil be able to help a city like New Haven do any more about improving its rate of job creation—either relative to itself over time, or vis-à-vis places like Houston—than they can with job retention. The factors explaining intertemporal and interspatial differences in job

Table 1. Percent Components of Employment Change for Central Cities and Suburbs in 10 Metropolitan Areas, 1972-1976

Cities

Region	Change	Births	Deaths	Expansion	Contraction	Inmigration	Outmigration
Hartford	-14.1	15.7	-17.5	6.4	-17.1	0.7	-2.6
New Haven	-6.9	13.1	-19.4	8.2	-7.1	0.9	-2.7
Baltimore	-6.7	16.0	-20.9	7.6	-7.3	0.6	-2.7
Boston	-5.4	21.5	-26.8	9.0	-9.1	2.9	-2.8
Worcester	-5.4	10.0	-13.4	8.4	-10.2	0.3	-0.4
Rochester	-1.5	12.6	-17.1	12.2	8.2	1.2	-2.2
Charlotte	7.2	32.7	-27.5	10.5	8.4	0.3	-0.4
Dayton	-6.5	18.9	-17.0	7.6	-15.3	0.7	-1.5
Greenville	-14.7	18.9	-26.9	4.6	-7.3	2.7	-6.6
Houston	25.2	40.1	-25.0	16.5	-6.9	0.8	-0.4
Totals	2.7	23.9	-22.4	10.7	-8.8	1.2	-1.8

Suburb

Region	Change	Births	Deaths	Expansion	Contraction	Inmigration	Outmigration
Hartford	11.0	27.0	-20.6	11.7	-8.6	4.1	-2.5
New Haven	0.9	16.5	-16.8	9.4	-7.5	1.9	-2.6
Baltimore	21.6	37.4	-22.0	10.6	-8.6	5.2	-1.0
Boston	6.9	21.9	-17.5	13.0	-10.9	1.4	-1.0
Worcester	11.4	21.6	-14.5	13.3	-8.6	1.1	-1.4
Rochester	10.1	21.7	-18.2	13.5	-8.2	2.4	-1.1
Charlotte	19.2	35.4	-25.5	9.5	-6.3	7.3	-1.3
Dayton	17.7	31.5	-17.8	10.4	-7.7	2.2	-0.9
Greenville	-2.7	17.8	-24.4	7.6	-4.0	0.8	-0.5
Houston	35.8	59.9	-27.8	12.1	-2.8	6.7	-12.3
Totals	9.9	24.7	-18.6	12.2	-9.5	2.3	-1.2

Source: D. L. Birch, "Job Creation in Cities" 1980.

Table 2. Aggregate Annual Gain and Loss Rate for Central Cities and Suburbs by Area, 1972-1976

Area	Loss Rate		Gain Rate	
	Central City	Suburbs	Central City	Suburbs
Hartford	9.3%	7.9%	5.7%	10.7%
New Haven	7.3	6.7	5.6	6.9
Baltimore	7.7	7.9	6.0	13.3
Boston	9.7	7.3	8.3	9.1
Worcester	6.0	6.1	4.7	9.0
Rochester	6.9	6.9	6.5	9.4
Charlotte	9.1	8.3	10.9	13.0
Dayton	8.4	6.6	6.8	11.0
Greenville	10.2	7.2	6.5	6.5
Houston	8.1	10.7	14.4	19.7

Source: D. L. Birch, "Job Creation in Cities," 1980.

creation may be just as difficult to influence with public policies as are the factors that account for job losses. But we will not know the answer to this question until we focus more of our attention on the positive side of the transformation process and, in doing so, improve our understanding of the forces which cause cities to gain jobs at different rates.

Again this is an understanding which can only be gained by looking inside the process of job creation. When we do so, we find that roughly half of the growth in employment is explained by births of new establishments, and the other half by expansions of existing firms. Of the jobs created by firm births, about 40% are due to the new firms of independent, free-standing entrepreneurs, and 60% come from the establishments of branches of existing companies. Of the jobs created through expansions, roughly 60% are generated by independent companies, with the remaining 40% coming from the expansions of existing branches of other companies. In combination then, independent entrepreneurs create about half of all job replacement required for a place to break even or grow.

As one might expect from this finding, much of the replacement job growth occurs in small firms. In fact, of all the net new jobs created between 1969 and 1976, two-thirds were created by firms with 20 or fewer employees, and about 80% were created by firms with 100 or fewer employees.

The other more well-known characteristic of the firms that are generating employment growth is that they are predominantly in the service sector. During the 1970s, 89% of the net new jobs in the United States occurred in the service sector while only 5% took place in manufacturing industries.

City economies reflect the same general intersectoral trends that are occurring at the national level. Data on employment change by sector between 1972 and 1976 for a sample of 10 cities reveals the following pattern: the slower a city's economy grows, the more it relies on firms in the service and trade sectors to provide new jobs, and the less it relies on firms in manufacturing and other production sectors (Table 3).

Table 3. Urban Employment Change by Sector (1972-1976)

	Distribution of Net Employment Change by Industry				
Type of City	Manufacturing	Other Producers	Trade	Service	Totals
Fast Growth	16.1	29.0	19.8	34.9	100
Moderate Growth	−56.3	31.5	15.2	110.1	100
Declining	−138.7	−42.2	15.0	64.9	−100

Source: D. L. Birch, "Job Creation in Cities," 1980.

Figure 1 summarizes what we have learned in our effort to sharpen our understanding of the transformations through which urban economies are going. Migrations explain very little of the employment change in cities. Of the other components of change, the two components that make up the gain rate (births and expansions) account for considerably more of the variation in employment change across cities than do the two components of which the loss rate is comprised (deaths and contractions). On the gain side, births and expansions account for roughly equal shares of the gain rate. Finally, most of the employment growth in cities is happening in small firms in the service sector; and the older and more slowly growing the city, the more likely this is to be the case.

For today's urban policy officials, the implications of the nature of the present transformation process require at least as dramatic an adaptation as did the consequences of the changes brought by the industrial revolution for the public officials of that day. In the latter case, with very little past experience to guide them, public officials had to fashion public policies to address problems such as the serious urban public health crisis which was one by-product of the rapid transformation of cities into manufacturing centers. Similarly today, the picture presented above suggests that public officials will have to adapt their orientation away from one focused primarily on providing direct assistance (such as loan guarantees, interest rate subsidies, grants, public works, etc.) to a few large, old manufacturing firms, to one that acknowledges and addresses the importance of the growth of small, service-oriented firms.

IV. PUBLIC RESPONSES TO THE CURRENT URBAN TRANSFORMATION

This paper has argued that an understanding of the causes, nature, and impacts of the growth occurring in our economy is as important for addressing our urban

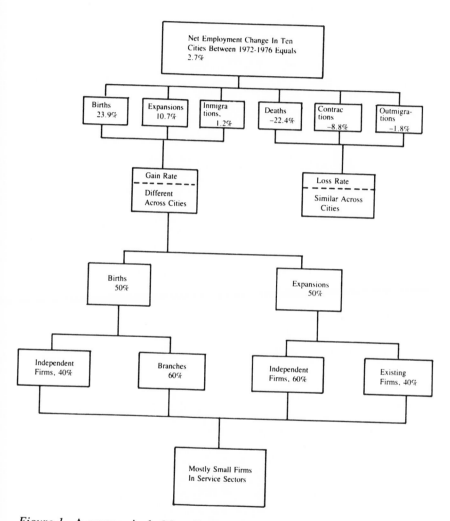

Figure 1. A progressively More Focused View of the Nature of the Current Urban Transformations.

125

and national economic problems as is a knowledge of the process of decline. Indeed, in focusing on the urban dimension of these changes the previous section has presented evidence that indicates that the key to understanding variations among cities in economic growth lies not in differences in the rates at which existing jobs are lost, but rather in variations in the rates at which new jobs are created. Therefore, for the purposes of developing workable and efficient urban development policies, it appears that our time and money would be better spent in an effort to develop an understanding of the factors which account for these variations in rates of job creation across cities. This knowledge can, in turn, form the basis of a new, more effective approach to development planning, by enabling us to determine what it is that the public sector can do to help cities improve their rates of private sector job creation.

Turning to the first of these tasks, the data presented above make clear the fact that those places exhibiting slow rates of job creation include many of our older, industrial cities. Built during the industrial revolution, these cities have physical, manpower, legal, and financial legacies which make them ill suited to the needs of the kinds of companies that are growing in today's economy. For example, many of the buildings presently existing in these cities are obsolete, inappropriate for the space requirements and new production methods of the types of hardware-based companies that offer significant growth potential for the urban core. Similarly—and perhaps even more importantly—the knowledge-based companies (which now typically account for an increasing share of the employment growth in an area) are unwilling or unable to use the buildings as they are.[2]

Further, the larger-scale physical attributes of these cities may provide a poor match to the locational demands of high growth firms. Existing firms of all types often find it difficult to expand because of the layout of buildings with respect to each other, because of the pattern of streets, and/or because of the inappropriate location and poor physical condition of much of the original infrastructure, such as water, gas, and sewerage systems. Companies may also find that their growth plans are not well served by century-old zoning ordinances, and other land use restrictions, that were instituted as solutions for the public health problems created by now-obsolescent technologies and out-of-date production methods.[3] In addition, firms that are growing often need labor skills that are different from those found in these old industrial cities.

Finally, growing firms must overcome financial obstacles if they want to grow in these locations. The above physical, legal, and manpower deterrents to growth translate into (1) higher up-front construction costs for the real estate development needed by growing companies; and (2) higher operating costs in the form of higher taxes, expenditures on insurance, safety, energy, and labor. As a result of these higher costs, and thus risks, together with the nature of the types of companies that are growing, established sources of capital (such as banks, insurance companies, and some other financial institutions) have been hesitant to finance these firms' start-up or expansion plans.

In sum, companies that want to grow in old, industrial cities must overcome a set of obstacles before they can do so. Given these deterrents, what is significant is the number of companies that continue to choose these cities as a place to grow. However, for most companies, these obstacles are too great to be overcome. Many companies may have good reasons for locating in these cities— because they could benefit from a specific facility, company, or resource that the city has to offer—but the types of obstacles presented above prevent them from taking advantage of particular attributes. As a result, growing companies choose other cities in which to grow, and the rates of job creation in old, industrial cities decline. By themselves, these companies are unable both to remove the obstacles and to carry out the new development needed to enable them to take advantage of certain attributes the cities offer.

As a result, if older cities are going to adapt, transform, and attract a share of the new growth that is occurring in the economy, they are going to need help from the public sector. This aid will be necessary: (1) to reduce the unusually high up-front capital costs associated with real estate development in older cities; (2) to lower the above-average operating costs incurred in doing business in these places; and (3) to match the special facilities of the cities with firms that really need them and thus increase the rate of job generation. Just as the public sector played an important role in facilitating the urban transformation of the nineteenth century by providing the capital, infrastructure, and environmental controls needed to address the public health crisis in cities of that day so too can today's public sector play an equally important role in facilitating the urban transformation of the twentieth century by removing the obstacles to private sector development.

To some extent the public sector is either already involved, or is considering becoming involved, in helping older cities to reduce the high up-front capital costs and ongoing operating costs associated with removal obstacles. The U.S. Department of Housing and Urban Development's (UDAG Urban Development Action Grant) Program has since 1977 been providing targeted financial assistance to economically distressed cities in the form of grants and subsidized loans for economic development projects involving private sector entities and capital which reportedly would not have gone ahead without the UDAG. In many instances, the cities and the firms involved in these projects have used UDAG funds to address the physical obstacles to development discussed earlier. One study of over 200 UDAG projects, for example, found that many of the UDAG funds have been used to defray high, up-front development costs such as land assembly and acquisition, demolition of certain structures, street and infrastructure provision, and rehabilitation costs.[4] Copley Place, the Baltimore Harbor project, and others are examples of such projects. Once in place these projects have provided space into which expanding firms have moved, and have encouraged additional development.[5]

The enterprise zone concept, as enacted in certain states and as framed in certain federal proposals, may also provide additional impetus to small firms' desire and ability to start-up or expand in these older cities, by reducing some of the high operating costs associated with doing business there.[6]

As these examples illustrate, public policies which act to remove obstacles to development and firm creation and expansion can begin to improve two important components (firm births and expansions) of the employment gain rate for older cities. But what of the component which remains? The foregoing analysis has shown that the third component—the establishment of new branches—accounts for roughly 30% of the gain rate in cities. To help cities improve this component of their gain rates, it is important to help them identify particular companies that are growing and that have a particular need for a certain facility or resource in a given city and that would, therefore, want to locate their next branch in that city. The key to the third component of economic growth thus lies in making a "match" between the city's unique set of resources and the firms which can exploit them, to their mutual advantage.

To date, the economic development efforts of cities have typically proceeded in a rather unsystematic, ad hoc, opportunistic fashion, with city officials using their development resources to call on a wide variety of firms or to respond to particular opportunities that happen to come along. Understandably, then, the returns to cities from these efforts (in terms of jobs created) have not been great relative to the resources expended for them. The efficiency of the efforts of cities to market and develop themselves has not been particularly high—not necessarily through any fault of their own, but because they have not had a feasible means of identifying and promoting their marketable resources. In our view urban economic development officials can improve the efficiency of their development efforts by identifying the individual companies that are in the greatest need of a series of specific physical facilities or resources their own city has to offer, and that thus have the highest probability to wanting to locate, expand, or set up a branch in their city.

The conceptual basis of this approach views a city as the sum of individual buildings, facilities, and resources, each of which has a particular utility for a certain group of firms. Rather than generating lists of "location determinants" for "economic sectors," this approach argues that a more disaggregated, micro view of cities is necessary if cities are to improve significantly the performance of their economic development efforts.

In some instances the specific facility may be a particular company. For example, many companies that produce high volumes of small, light-weight goods could benefit by locating their distribution plants where air freight companies are headquartered. Certain kinds of high technology companies will want to be in cities that have large numbers of specialized universities. Firms that make precision instruments, requiring very narrow tolerances, will choose locations in order to gain access to certain kinds of skilled labor, such as is found in Cleveland and other old, industrial cities. Firms that anneal ceramics will prefer a city with an abundant natural or synthetic gas supply. Firms that specialize in seismic analysis will want to be in a city that is near off-shore drilling operations (e.g., New Orleans), and so forth.

In each instance the key is to find those growing firms that can benefit, in a bottom line sense, from a particular facility that a city has to offer. Each specific facility generates its own list of firms that needs its resources. Based upon this observation, and in contrast to existing firm-attraction strategies—ones that try to promote the growth of an entire city by calling on a wide variety of companies—this strategy focuses on the city as a unique collection of special facilities, each of which is needed by a select group of firms. As such, this strategy can improve the efficiency of local officials' economic development activities in two ways, by providing them with: (1) a highly targeted list of firms that have a specific reason for locating in that city; and (2) a marketing rationale (i.e., the specific facility that a firm needs) for these officials to present to firms on the list as to why they should be attracted to a particular city.[7]

V. CONCLUSION

The foregoing discussion has argued that the roles that developed and developing countries play in the international economy, and that cities play in their respective national economies, are undergoing far-reaching changes. Indeed, in many ways the existing international economic order is being turned on its head. The developed countries, which used to export manufactured goods to each other, and to the developing countries in exchange for raw materials, are now seeing an increasing portion of their industrial activities performed by developing countries. As a result, the old industrial cities of the developed countries, which have historically been the locus for much of the world's manufacturing production, have experienced a steady decline in manufacturing and total employment.

Recently, we in the industrial countries have been somewhat preoccupied with the "negative" side of current economic transformation. We express understandable concern for the far-reaching social, economic, and national security implications of rising unemployment and falling productivity and competitiveness in many of our basic industries (such as steel, rubber, textiles, shipbuilding, and automobile manufacturing). As a result, we have attempted to arrest the decline of these sectors and of the urban economies in which these sectors initialy grew.

The historical experience with earlier transformations of this magnitude strongly suggests that it is difficult, if not impossible, for public policies (of the type acceptable to the citizens of most developed countries) to influence the powerful economic forces underlying these transformations. That is not to say that we should do nothing in response to the effects of the decline of certain sectors; but rather that we should be more explicit and precise about what we *want* to accomplish and to become, and be more realistic about what we *can* accomplish in our efforts to achieve these outcomes.

Obviously, we have a moral and social obligation to the hundreds of thousands of older, skilled workers who are now unemployed as a result of the structural transformation through which our economy is going. Nor can we lightly dismiss the national security implications of the declining prospects of many of our basic industries. But neither should we expect to be able to rebuild these old industries so that they will once more be as competitive in international markets as they used to be: too many powerful economic forces are working against that occurrence.

Realistically, the United States and other industrialized countries can expect to have smaller steel, auto, rubber, and textile industries in the future than they have had in the past. The locations in which those industries have historically been housed—the old industrial cities—have already begun to shrink, although how much smaller these industries and cities will ultimately become is not, at this point, clear. On the other hand, some manufacturing activities will be able to maintain their competitiveness, but may not be of the right type or size to address national security concerns.

The net strategic effect of this rescaling process is not obvious. What is more generally clear, though, is that our preoccupation with the decline of certain sectors and cities has prevented us from seeing the whole picture, and has in turn forced us to approach some admittedly knotty problems from a restricted (and thus, biased) perspective. More specifically, focusing on the decline side of cities' employment situations has prevented us from understanding that it is the growth, or replacement side, of this phenomenon which is the truly critical variable in determining a city's ability to foster and maintain sufficient levels of economic growth.

Thus, to help declining cities improve their employment situation we should spend considerably more time understanding the factors that retard their employment gain rates, and developing policies to address these factors. Our declining cities include many old, industrial cities which, as such, have significant physical, manpower, legal, and financial obstacles to firm creation and/or growth; obstacles which must be removed in order to ensure the continuing economic vitality of our older urban centers. The role of the public sector in this process will depend upon its ability to provide three things: (1) targeted capital subsidies (such as those provided by the UDAG Program) to reduce the unusually high up-front capital costs of real estate development in older cities; (2) programs (such as some Enterprise Zone proposals) to lower the above-average operating costs of doing business in these locations; and (3) a methodology for helping cities (or other areas) identify those resources and facilities of theirs which are relevant to the new economy, and for finding those firms that can capitalize upon these facilities, to the benefit of all.

The third suggestion represents a departure from—and, we believe, an improvement upon—past approaches in that it explicitly recognizes the importance of both the negative *and* positive sides of the transformation process through which cities are going. Further, this strategy has particular merit for older, industrial cities because it matches those features of their economies that are germane to the new world economy with those firms or sources of employment growth in the country that can benefit the most from the unique, yet unexploited, resources which these cities can provide. Finally, by viewing the city as the sum of its special facilities, this approach can increase the efficiency with which cities redevelop themselves, thereby improving their short-term employment gain rates while, at the same time, defining their long-term roles in the international economy of the future.

NOTES

1. For more on the international nature of these structural changes see another paper in this volume by Bertrand Renaud, "Structural Changes in OECD Economies and Their Impact on Cities in the 1980s."

2. This point should not be interpreted as a license to demolish historical structures or to unduly disrupt residential neighborhoods. Indeed, many of these structures can be and are being adapted from their former use to suit the needs of the new economy and are one of the attributes which make these cities attractive places within which to live and work.

3. This argument does not mean that we are advocating the wholesale repeal of environmental and land use regulations. Again, these regulations are a critical part of urban life. Technological improvements and other changes have, however, made it possible and necessary to adapt these regulations to the needs of the current economy.

4. George A. Reigeluth et al., "The UDAG Program: A Preliminary Evaluation" (1980).

5. In implementing the UDAG program, public officials should continue to be careful that funds are only provided to those projects that would not have been able to proceed without the UDAG assistance, and that the projects do not displace existing acitivities and firms. In fact, the type of analysis of components of change and of growth in cities presented in the previous section can help public officials ensure that their programs actually stimulate private investment, and thus avoid substitution of public for private capital. For example, knowledge about which sectors and companies are growing in a distressed city may be a useful indication of which private sector projects require public sector assistance to go ahead and which do not. If an application for assistance comes in for a project involving a growing company, it is more likely that market forces would have enabled such a project to go ahead without public assistance than is the case if the project involved a declining company. Public funding of such a project runs a greater risk of substituting for, rather than stimulating, private investment than would be the case with a project in a declining economic sector.

Of course, if demand for the growing company's product is such that market conditions in that company's sector are tight, than once in operation the project in question may displace less existing economic activity in that sector than would be the case with a project involving a declining company in a sector where market conditions are relatively loose. In this case, the public program may want to try and stimulate an amount of private investment in a growing company which is above and beyond the market-determined level. These examples over simplify a complicated set of local economic relationships, but serve to illustrate how a thorough knowledge of a city's growing sectors can help program administrators ensure that the projects they support actually stimulate private investment and produce long-term economic benefits for the locality.

6. To be effective, Enterprise Zones, like cities, will have to meet the needs of growing, job-creating companies. They must thus offer sufficient access to capital and trained people and provide

a sufficiently "civil environment" so that growing, knowledge-based businesses (in and outside of manufacturing) will find them attractive. This is no small order, and implies rather radical and innovative behavior on the part of state and local agencies as well as on the part of the federal government.

7. A group at the MIT Program on Neighborhood and Regional Change has developed a technique for implementing such a strategy. The basic idea behind this technique is to match the special characteristics of a given city with the specific productive demands of particular companies and then to select, through a filtering process, those relatively few companies that, because of a city's attributes, will have a compelling reason to choose it as a place in which to grow. City officials can then contact the firms on this list to ascertain their interest in setting up a branch office in the target city.

The first step in this process is to identify those special resources of a city that are of particular interest to certain kinds of firms, by virtue of the resources' (and thus the city's) ability to: lower a firm's production costs, increase access of the firm's products to markets, attract and retain certain types of labor, or to assist the firm in any number of other ways to become more profitable. The next step in this firm-identification technique is to determine the kinds of businesses that need a particular facility or resource that the city has to offer.

These two steps (identifying city's special resources and the types of firms that need them) are carried out in conjunction with various members of the community in question (for example, university, business, and city government representatives). This local expertise, with regard to the city's resources and the types of firms which they attract, is supplemented by an analysis of the kinds of firms (by size, industry, age, etc.) that have been growing in that city in recent years. This analysis uses data from Dun and Bradstreet, the Census, the Bureau of Labor Statistics (BLS), and BEA. The results of these efforts is a profile of businesses types which are most likely to grow in a particular city.

Being one of the promising types, while a necessary condition for being included on the final list of firms, is not a sufficient one however. The final step in this analysis is to develop an additional list of firm-specific filters. These other firm-specific screens might include such characteristics as the growth rate of the individual firm, branching activities of the firm, size and age of the firm, corporate affiliation, number of other branches in the region in which the city is located, and growth in cities like the city in question. Using Dun and Bradstreet data, this technique produces a final list of firms by passing a file of several million businesses through the combined filters. The firms that pass through all of the screens appear on the final list.

TOWARD A MORE PRODUCTIVE MUNICIPAL GOVERNMENT

Werner Z. Hirsch

I. INTRODUCTION

Municipal governments are facing a period of trial and tribulation in the 1980s. They will come under mounting pressure to be more efficient. The reasons are clear. All over the United States, citizens are vocally critical of what they consider to be flabby and inefficient municipal governments. Many states have joined the taxpapers' revolt which, in the late 1970s, gave birth to the revenue and taxation limitation movement. By June 1981, 29 states had enacted specific local property tax rates limits, 19 property tax levy limits, 14 overall property tax rates limits, 6 general expenditure limits, and another 6 limits on assessment increases; 5 states had general revenue limits. Additionally, 18 state governments had enacted state limits. California and Massachusetts voted in favor of particularly severe tax limits, and Arizona has as many as five such restrictions.

At the same time federal subsidies, to which local governments had become

Research in Urban Economics, Volume 4, pages 133-145.
Copyright © 1984 JAI Press Inc.
All rights of reproduction in any form reserved.
ISBN: 0-89232-423-6

accustomed, peaked in 1978. We agree with the conclusion of the Advisory Commission on Intergovernmental Relations that, "All indicators now point to a continued decline in federal aid flows over the next several years."[1] Thus, it is clear that municipal governments in the 1980s will feel the money pinch. Rather than mainly cutting back services, I would hope that most will seek to become more productive.

This paper will seek to offer an analytic framework within which strategies to meet the productivity challenge of the 1980s can be evaluated. Specifically, a shirking-monitoring framework will be presented. In applying this framework, some unique production and delivery problems faced by urban governments must be remembered. Urban governments operate under conditions of great interdependence; many of their actions have a host of serious indirect effects outside their own jurisdictions. Thus, externalities abound. The more numerous and consequential the externalities, the greater society's call for government intervention. Moreover, because service delivery is mandated by law, urban governments must serve locations private firms can shun. In other words, they may have to provide services, no matter how difficult the service conditions that must be overcome, and therefore no matter how great the transaction costs.

After presenting a shirking-monitoring framework, the paper will focus on four strategies that can be pursued toward increased municipal productivity. They reflect Adam Smith's venerable observation that: "Public services are never better performed than when their reward comes only in consequence of their being performed, and is proportional to the diligence employed in performing them."[2]

The following thesis underlies our examination: since at present rewards to municipal employees are only loosely tied to performance, the municipal labor force tends to work below capacity. Such behavior has been referred to as shirking, and it is not necessarily inefficient and socially undesirable. But today, municipal employees tend to trade off work and leisure in such a manner that the level of shirking is higher than the level which would be efficient. To bring shirking to the efficient level requires relatively high monitoring costs, parts of which are monetary and others of which are intangible. This paper will therefore examine a number of possible strategies to change the institutional setting within which municipal employees work, bargain, and receive rewards with the purpose of raising productivity.

One strategy focuses directly on the performance of workers. It will be argued that the better we can measure the performance of individual workers, the more readily we can tie their pay to their performance and thus stimulate efficiency. In the 1980s, rapid innovation in electronics and in information handling will offer great opportunities to monitor and measure the performance of workers. In the light of more widespread monitoring we can consider instruments to formalize the linking of rewards with performance. One such instrument is productivity bargaining, and it will be explored.

A second strategy addresses the performance of managers. Our objective is to induce municipal managers to use efficient production and distribution techniques and effectively monitor their work force.

There exist two further strategies which, however, work in an indirect manner to increase productivity. One relies on increased competition among service suppliers and, therefore, their employees, whether by contracting out or by disintegration. A further strategy involves changes in the legal environment in which municipal employees work. Good examples of laws that can bear on productivity increases are civil service provisions, residency requirement laws, and prevailing wage laws.

II. A SHIRKING-MONITORING FRAMEWORK

In 1966, Harvey Leibenstein pointed to a number of cases in which output increased with no observable change in inputs. He asserted that the change came about because inputs were more efficiently used and he called this phenomenon X-efficiency.[3] He went on to argue that gains from eliminating X-inefficiency are likely to exceed those from eliminating allocative inefficiency. Insofar as the labor input is concerned, X-inefficiency can be reduced by causing workers to exert themselves to a fuller extent, i.e., to "shirk" less. As Armen Alchian and Harold Demsetz have pointed out, workers trade off income for leisure (shirking) to achieve an efficient equilibrium. Some shirking is desirable, and the individual worker will choose an amount of shirking in line with incentives and constraints.[4]

Let us assume that a work day (k) can be completely divided between working hours (h) and shirking hours (s) and the worker is paid depending on the number of hours he works, i.e., his daily money income (I) is the wage rate per hour worked (w) times the number of hours worked per day. In this setting, extending a one-hour task to occupy two hours is considered to be equivalent to shirking one hour.

The single worker faces a budget constraint with slope of -w in Figure 1. His decision to shirk at a specified level reflects his trading off leisure and income. Let us turn to a team of n workers and assume for expositional simplicity that the product of the team is just the sum of the products of the members working separately, although each one is more productive than he would be working alone and that all workers are identical. We assume also that it is not possible to measure each individual worker's productivity. Each worker receives 1/n of the wages paid to the team. However, the wages paid are assumed to reflect the total number of hours worked by all team members. Each team member bears only a portion of the cost of his own shirking. An individual's wage has two parts—an essentially fixed component equal to his share of the pay for work done by others plus a variable component equal to his share of the pay for the hours he works.

The following example can illustrate some of the issues: Assume 10 workers

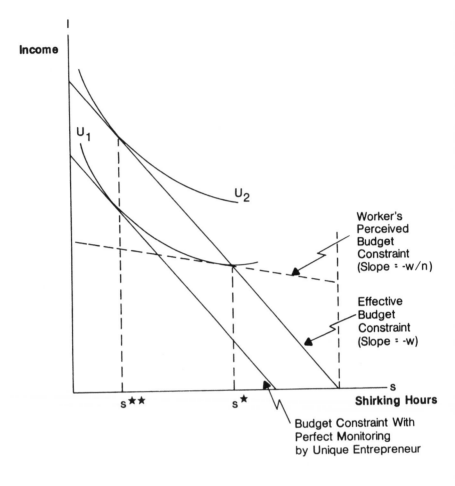

Figure 1

form a cooperative with the objective of producing 200 widgets per day. These widgets sell for $1 each, and the proceeds from the sales are distributed among the workers. Thus, if all workers do what is expected of them, each will take home $20 per day.

Now, suppose one worker values the time spent producing widgets at $.90 per widget. If he produces, say, only 18 widgets, he will enjoy $1.80 of leisure he would not have otherwise taken. However, the cooperative's output is only 198 widgets, so that each worker receives only $19.80 in the absence of monitoring. Thus, the shirker benefits fully from the $1.80 of leisure he took, but only bears $0.20 of the cost, the rest having been distributed among the other workers. Thus, the purpose of monitoring may be seen as incurring costs in order to either avoid shirking or else to make the shirker bear a fuller share of the costs he imposes.

Figure 1 shows both the perceived budget constraint for worker 1 and the effective (group) budget constraint. Worker 1 will maximize his utility by choosing to shirk s* hours, where his perceived budget constraint line is tangent to his highest indifference curve, i.e., U_1. If all team members could agree costlessly to shirk only a certain amount and agree to distribute team income according to total hours worked, and if enforcement were costless, they would pick an equilibrium where indifference curves were tangent to the effective budget constraint line, increasing each person's utility. All workers would then shirk less and receive more income, with worker 1 choosing s** rather than s*, and each would be on a higher indifference curve, i.e., U_2. The larger the team size, n, the less steep is the individual's perceived budget constraint line, moving points of tangency with the given indifference curve to the right and increasing the equilibrium number of hours shirked.

Monitoring workers includes measurement of productivity and apportionment of rewards of a contract. Under perfect monitoring, marginal factor rewards are equal to the factor's marginal productivity, and the slope of the team member's perceived budget constraint becomes identical with that of his effective budget constraint line. If each person were then paid the value of his marginal product per hour times hours worked, an equilibrium with s** hours would result (Figure 1).

We have assumed so far that, while the output of a team can be monitored perfectly, that of individual members cannot be monitored at all and, thus, that the average team productivity is attributed to each team member. A $1.00 change in productivity of an individual is associated with a $(1/n) change in his reward. Thus, the slope of his perceived budget constraint line will be 1/n times as steep as the effective constraint line, so that he will choose an equilibrium with s* hours shirked (Figure 1). Changes in the degree of effectiveness of the monitoring process can be reflected diagrammatically by changes in the slope of the worker's perceived budget constraint line. The more effective the monitoring of the individual, the more closely will rewards be associated with an individual's actual marginal productivity, i.e., the closer will be the slopes of the perceived and effective budget constraint lines. Monitoring of workers, thus, makes a large team appear to be a smaller team in terms of incentives to the individual worker. More monitoring of output leads to an increase in the slope of the perceived budget constraint line, making the worker behave as if he were in a smaller team than is actually the case.[5]

III. STRATEGIES DIRECTLY FOCUSING ON MUNICIPAL WORKERS

When we developed the shirking-monitoring framework, we made a point which deserves repeating—some shirking, i.e., having some leisure or slack during the working day, is beyond doubt efficient. This in turn will be anticipated in the wage actually paid. The crucial questions are what is the most appropriate shirking level and what are the incentives and constraints which we should impose so as to induce individual workers to move toward socially desirable levels. It is to the second question that we will apply our shirking-monitoring framework. We will focus on four strategies that can improve the performance of municipal labor. The first strategy counts on society's ability to better monitor and measure the output of workers, and to provide incentives and reward toward greater worker exertion and efficiency. Clearly, performance measures are more readily developed in some (largely blue-collar) municipal departments than in others. Where output can be directly measured, as for tax assessment, tax collection, janitorial services, etc., managerial evaluation is not overwhelmingly difficult. Rewards should then seek to reflect the value of the workers' marginal productivity. When workers are rewarded in line with their marginal productivity, the perceived budget constraint line in our shirking-monitoring framework becomes steeper and approaches the slope of the effective budget constraint line (see Figure 1).

In this connection recent great improvements in electronic and computer-based office machines have opened up unique opportunities. They promise to fuel a spurt in white-collar productivity, especially in municipal government, for two reasons. Not only will these rapidly breaking technological innovations reduce sharply the cost of monitoring and evaluating employees for a given job assignment, but they will also in general offer great opportunities for using more cost effective methods of performing one or perhaps even more than one task.

The following are examples of how far-reaching the effects of the electronic and computer-based information revolution can be: as computer terminals become less costly, municipal employees engaged in information services may in part work from their homes using computer terminals tied to government offices. Travel time and other work-related expenses could thus be eliminated or at least greatly reduced, and government could share in the gains. Or, the government could offer firemen the option to use part of the time they are on call at their fire station to work as electronic data processors. Thus, consoles could be placed in fire stations from which firemen could work, for example, for the office of the tax collector, purchasing agent, assessor and payroll agent. This arrangement could also have a long-term salutory side effect. Many cities are heavily burdened by generous retirement programs most of which are largely unfunded. For example, the Fire and Police Pension System of the City of Los Angeles in 1980 had a $2.4 billion gap between the system's assets and its projected liabilities, almost twice the city's budget! The city's 1980 contribution to the pension fund was $117 million, which is considerably larger than that year's property tax revenue. What has made pension obligations so onerous is their indexing. However, a number of cities with voter approval have scaled down cost of living adjustments. For example, the City of Los Angeles placed in 1981 a 3% limit on cost of living adjustments to the pensions of newly recruited officers. Thus, in our example, it is quite likely that as firemen become accomplished data processors and realize that private firms offer good wages for these skills, many will take early retirement and pursue their new occupation. As a result, the excruciating pension burden of cities should be eased.

Let us turn to the possibility of institutionalizing productivity improvement. Monitoring and performance evaluation can be put to more formal use if management and labor agree to productivity bargaining. In such an arrangement, specific wage and salary increases are based on an agreement by labor to meet certain performance standards. There is merit in labor and management joining forces in developing improved production and distribution methods. With the aid of joint labor-management productivity teams, it is often possible to improve methods for carrying out specified functions and then make sure that both share fairly in the fruits of productivity increases.[6] Labor benefits can take the form of increased wages, and management can gain reduced service costs. Joint efficiency teams could be assisted by a neutral party able to provide additional technical competence. Prior agreements would be reached to ensure the right of public employees to participate in developing and implementing proposals, and to provide a formula for distributing productivity gains. In many cases, no layoffs need result, and the reduced demand for workers could be handled by attrition.

IV. STRATEGIES FOCUSING ON MUNICIPAL MANAGERS

Management can enhance the productivity of municipal workers in two major ways—by selecting and implementing efficient production and distribution methods and by introducing the monitoring activities that are part of a manager's duty and output. Managers who engage in relatively little shirking make a major effort to carefully monitor their workers, which becomes more feasible in departments with more or less identifiable, quantifiable outputs.

In order to induce manages to exert themselves, we must design and effectively put to use appropriate incentives and reward schemes tied to up-to-date and powerful management evaluation systems.

While management salaries should be closely tied to performance, institutional factors make nonmonetary rewards particularly important for urban government managers. A major reason for this is the fact that salaries of elected officials are low in comparison with those in private industry and can seldom be exceeded by those of appointed managers.

What are promising incentives for municipal managers? Some relate to professionalization. Specifically, it is important for personnel in the management category to belong to professional organizations and actively participate in their activities. This allows managers to talk to other managers with similar problems and experiences and, more importantly, to compete with their peers throughout the country for professional recognition. Competition can take the form of seeking office in national or statewide professional organizations as well as presenting professional papers.

No less important can be public and media recognition. Thus, for example, local governments could annually select managers who have exhibited exceptional skill and attained unusual performance levels, to be recognized in public ceremonies.

Horizontal movement of management offers a second important approach. In the past, most management personnel in urban government have been promoted intradepartmentally—most school superintendents, fire chiefs, police chiefs, and park superintendents have come up through the ranks of the organization they serve. The assumption has been that only those who have been with an organization for a long time know enough about it to be able to manage it. Furthermore, it is often argued that prospects for advancement offer important incentives for people in a given department.

But there are great disadvantages to relying solely on vertical movement of management peresonnel. Managing in a given department at different levels perpetuates a static, and sometimes outdated, vision. Moreover, friendships are formed and obligations accumulated, all of which can interfere with making tough decisions. But perhaps the most serious shortcoming relates to the length of time that a person holds a given position. The number of management positions likely to open up in the next few years do not allow frequent moves. As a result, many managers who are allowed to go stale in their jobs thus have a (perverse) incentive to spend much of their time covering up mistakes they made early in their administration. For these reasons, it is useful to transfer management personnel not only upward, but also sideways. This is commonly done in the United Kingdom with its long tradition of appointing broadly educated persons to head up different departments at different times. Except in highly specialized professional areas, the emphasis is on managerial ability rather than knowledge of the subject matter. Thus, this scheme rests on the assumption that it is easier for persons with general managerial ability and experience to acquire knowledge of the area they are to administer, than for persons with great knowledge of a particular subject to acquire managerial ability. The emphasis on horizontal movement of management personnel has a number of implications. For example, in order to be able to have managers with an ability to manage in different departments, it is essential that management classifications be relatively broad and that, therefore, training of managers be general rather than highly specific.

V. INDIRECT STRATEGIES THAT CREATE COMPETITION

One of the widely discussed opportunities today involves steps to provide a more competitive environment for the delivery of urban government services. With this objective in mind, some form of contracting out or privatization is frequently considered. Government elicits bids for providng a service. The resulting competition can reduce monitoring costs, since reliance on the workings of the market reduces the need for monitoring. However, these benefits do not come without costs. In contracting out, the government loses the ability to monitor inputs, though in some instances monitoring inputs is the cheapest way to determine output. With trash collection, for example, output can be determined by direct observation; but with public health services, output measurement is difficult, if not impossible. Thus, contracting out for health services is likely to raise monitoring costs, while contracting out for trash services is likely to lower them. In terms of our framework of analysis, contracting out reduces the apparent size of the team by exposing workers to reduced job security and by providing information on the cost that other firms would incur to provide the same service. But contracting out can raise the apparent team size, when it is difficult to determine whether or not the agreed-upon output has actually been provided.

A recent empirical analysis of refuse collection in Minneapolis and 1,377 communities in 200 SMSAs confirms the argument offered above, i.e., that productivity increases result from privatization.[7] Specifically, the study of 200 SMSAs revealed that for cities of more than 50,000 population, private trash collection in the form of contract collection cost significantly less than municipal collection. The cost per household for municipal collection in these large cities was 29% greater than the corresponding costs of private (contract) collection, on the basis of refuse data in terms of tons, and 37% greater than the corresponding cost of private (contract) collection on the basis of refuse data in terms of cubic yards.[8]

Contracting out tends to run into strong opposition from labor leaders, particularly leaders of municipal unions who fear a decline in membership. In order to soften this opposition, urban governments can commit themselves to write into contracts with private firms that the latter give city employees right of first refusal at the wage at which the job will be filled. Beyond this assurance, city government might agree to provide jobs for all those who will be laid off because of privatization, though most likely at somewhat lower wages after a retraining effort. In assessing the advantages of contracting out, the costs of such assurances must be added to the price at which the private firm will deliver the service. At least government could place these laid off workers on a priority list.

A further approach reduces the existing extent of vertical integration of municipal government, a step that can have effects similar to heightened competition in that it increases the slope of the perceived budget constraint line. For example, government can separate planning and procurement of public services from their production and delivery.[9] Institutionally, this would mean altering the responsibilities of top officials in major municipal departments from producing outputs to procuring services produced by others. This rearrangement would increase competition within municipal government, which could be further increased if the variety of services to be procured by a single consuming agency were broadened to involve more than one producer. The producers could offer services that are seen as essentially different from the producer's viewpoint, but closely related from the consumer's viewpoint. If several such activities were placed under a single procurement agent, it could stimulate less shirking and more efficient resource use by shifting resources to that producer who most efficiently serves some relevant consumer demand. This strategy would also help reduce the incentives for agencies to spend all their funds in order to assure that budgets will not be cut in the next year due to insufficient "need."

VI. CHANGING THE LEGAL ENVIRONMENT

Over the years, municipal labor markets have been regulated by a variety of laws, some of which may have contributed to inefficiency. One law provides municipal workers with great job security and virtually automatic merit awards. I have in mind civil service provisions that have their origin in the turn of the century when a reform movement sought to protect public employees against excessive political influence.

Civil service provisions generally interfere with the imposition of penalties for shirking and, by specifying seniority raises and promotions, they prevent managers from granting rewards for productive behavior.[10] More emphasis on merit and less on seniority in determining promotions would lower monitoring costs by tying awards more closely to effort. Under a system based on seniority promotions, income is essentially independent of team or worker productivity. Any efforts to raise productivity must take into consideration the fact that workers are worse off both when they lose job security and when they are monitored more closely. Thus their compensation should rise somewhat if the workers are to be kept at the same level of utility. As long as the worker's perceived budget constraint is harmonized with his actual productivity, the increased productivity tends to outweigh the increased compensation needed to leave the worker at the same utility level.

Also procedures to implement discipline under civil service protection could be improved. A California manager is quoted to have said recently, "The merit system and collective bargaining law combine to make it almost impossible to fire anyone. . . . It may be easier to ignore him and have his share of the work done by someone else."[11] To remedy this state of affairs, which certainly was never contemplated by the reform movement that instituted civil service protection, three procedural steps could be taken. First, procedures could be streamlined so adverse action can be taken against municipal employees who perform poorly by forcing managers to show "substantial evidence" rather than the present commonly required "preponderance of evidence" to prove a case. Second, the unbelievably cumbersome appeals process could be streamlined. For example, in California an employee is entitled to an evidentiary hearing, which in case of an adverse decision can be followed by a rehearing, which in turn can then be appealed through the courts. A reasonable change would eliminate automatic hearings for employees appealing minor disciplinary actions. Third, disciplinary procedures for minor adverse actions could be made subject to collective bargaining.

Consideration should also be given to the possible repeal of prevailing wage laws, which became so common in the 1960s and 1970s. Prevailing wage laws, whether in the form of charter provisions or ordinances, mandate that government either pay or consider paying wages at least equal to those in private employment. Such laws can bias wage-setting procedures upward by setting the average wage as a floor, and in some cases by allowing the average increase in the private sector to be treated as the minimum increase for the public sector. An empirical study of a selected number of municipal labor markets tested the hypothesis that prevailing wage laws have a significant effect on municipal wages if compared to private firms.[12] The study covered 25 large U.S. cities over the 1978/79 period and 39 cities for 1970-1973. Using multiple-regression techniques, the presence of a prevailing wage law proved to have pushed wages up significantly.

Next we will turn to residency requirement laws which demand that, as a condition of employment, public employees reside in the city or county in which they work. Such laws have two effects which may offset each other. First, they restrict the pool of potential workers which, with an upward-sloping supply curve, should increase wages. This is a supply effect. A second effect, however, may bring productivity increases from workers' personal commitment to the welfare of the area in which they reside. This externality effect can be placed into a shirking-monitoring framework. Accordingly, municipal employees who serve the community in which they and their families live have strong incentives to exert themselves and work at a shirking level well below that which they would otherwise choose.

Clearly, this personal concern for the welfare of a municipality by its employees is likely to be more significant in small communities. In very large ones, no single public employee is likely to have a major effect on the quality, efficiency, and continuity of public service. But it is in exactly these small jurisdictions that the potentially positive effect of residency laws, i.e., lower shirking levels, is likely to be more than offset by the supply side effect. Specifically, in a small jurisdiction, by restricting employment to its residents, the supply of potential municipal workers is greatly curtailed. For any given demand, this will mean a shift of the supply function to the left and higher wage levels. However, the personal interest effect may result in a real wage fund offset as productivity rises. However, in large jurisdictions the supply effect is not as likely to be offset by increased productivity of the resident employee.

Finally, we will mention a potentially far-reaching legal development. The courts have recently taken a step that could reduce monitoring costs in the public sector sharply. In 1976, the United States District Court of Northern California ruled—and its decision has since been upheld on appeal—that postal employees are legally liable for failure to deliver the mail properly.[13] To the extent this ruling is precedent setting, it can provide new legal incentives which reduce monitoring costs. Of course, such changes also have their negative effects. If workers in a particular job can be sued for not performing their jobs properly, risk-averse but otherwise productive workers would exit this particular labor market. Consequently, there may be a reduced supply of workers and this result would drive up wages. The costs and benefits of such changes have to be weighed, but there seems to be no reason to assume that the current situation is optimal.

VII. SOME CONCLUDING THOUGHTS

Regardless of whether the strategies proposed here have merit, past experience would suggest that chances for their adoption are slim. Past failures to make changes have perhaps been caused not so much by the nature of the proposals for change than by a neglect of, or at least insufficient attention to, the process of implementation. Thus, I would like to suggest also some tactics that might be pursued to implement some of the proposed strategies.

Most change is painful and efforts to alter the governance and operation of municipal governments always run into strong opposition. The present serious financial crisis of many urban governments can, however, have a silver lining in that the prospect of great fiscal difficulties can offer city officials unique opportunities. The reduced job security will make income more dependent on worker or team productivity. For example, as soon as a municipal government realizes that it will face serious revenue shortfalls, whether because of the revenue limitation movement or federal retrenchment, or both, elected officials may want to reaffirm their total commitment to providing employees the kind of wages, fringe benefits, and working conditions that will attract and retain an able and committed labor force. Having committed themselves to decent remuneration, it becomes clear that for the sake of meeting this commitment at a time of fiscal retrenchment, a reduction in the work force will become a necessity. The city council may even spell out by how much it expects to reduce the work force during the next 2-3 years.

In view of these two statements, it now becomes possible to negotiate arrangements for contracting out services with municipal unions, since this arrangement for a reduction of the municipal labor force is less distasteful to the unions than outright dismissals. Moreover, in an environment in which labor and management have a common stake in making the limited public funds go the maximum distance, productivity bargaining is likely to be initiated and some modifications of civil service rules can be considered. Furthermore, in such an environment joint labor-management teams can be set up, as well as citywide productivity managers' committees and citizens' productivity advisory commissions. Whereas managers' committees should be composed of departmental managers, commissions should be composed of productivity experts from the private sector and academia as well as former government officials. They can work with departments, for example, to develop productivity improvement projects, assure use of engineered work standards, establish productivity improvement reporting systems to record progress, identify criteria for departments to use in selecting effective productivity improvement projects, and setting priorities for them as well as sponsor project management training for all productivity managers and others responsible for implementing projects.

ACKNOWLEDGMENTS

The paper has benefited from research on monitoring-shirking carried out jointly with Professor Anthony M. Rufolo and critical comments from Glen Elder and David Mengle.

NOTES

1. *Significant Features of the Fiscal Federalism*, 1980/81 edition. Washington, D.C.: Advisory Commission on Intergovernmental Relations, December 1981, M-132, 8.

2. Smith, Adam, *The Wealth of Nations*, New York: Random House, 678.

3. Leibenstein, Harvey (1966), "Allocative Efficiency Versus X-Efficiency," *American Economic Review* 56: 392-415.

4. Alchian, Armen and Harold Demsetz (1972), "Production, Information Costs, and Economic Organization," *American Economic Review* 62: 777-795.

5. For a more detailed exposition of the shirking-monitoring framework, see Hirsch, Werner Z. and Anthony M. Rufolo, "Shirking, Monitoring Costs and Municipal Labor Productivity," in *Economics of Municipal Labor Markets*. Hirsch, Werner Z. and Anthony M. Rufolo (eds). Los Angeles: Institute of Industrial Relations, 1983, 277-310.

6. The following is an example of the contributions a joint efficiency team might make: most fire departments staff companies uniformly around the clock, although there are great differences in the frequency of alarms and fires during the hours of the day. A study of the city of New York showed the demand during the early evening peak period is from 4 to 10 times greater than during the early morning hours: E.H. Blum, the RAND-New York City Fire Project, (Santa Monica, CA: RAND Corporation, 1968). More than 60% of all fires in New York City in the early 1960s occurred between 2 and 11 p.m. Thus a 2-10 p.m. shift could handle almost 60% of all fires, substantially more than the other two shifts combined. Management alone could not institute such a change to improve productivity, but in cooperation with labor new arrangements might be made.

7. Savas, E.S. (1977), "An Empirical Study of Competition in Municipal Service Delivery," *Public Administration Review* 37: 717-24, and "Policy Analysis for Local Government: Public Versus Private Refuse Collection," *Policy Analysis* 3: 1-26.

8. These results are statistically significant at a 0.01 level of significance.

9. For example, a large urban school district could be separated into a planning and procurement agency, and a number of agencies for which it might purchase various services. The planning and procurement agency could influence the public school system's behavior by, for instance, proposing to solicit service bids from public and private bodies.

10. In Chicago, major institutional revamping has recently taken place: civil service boards have been abolished, and hiring, firing, and promoting have been switched back to elected officials. Moreover, Chicago has streamlined procedures for disciplining, hiring, and promoting employees and brought them more in line with private industry. It increased the probationary period for newly

hired workers from 6 to 12 months, allowed the city to reduce the number of job classifications and revamped pay policies to reward performance (*Wall Street Journal*, September 22, 1975: 1 and 12).

11. California Assembly Office of Research, *Government Operations Review: Personnel* (Sacramento, March 1982: 103).

12. Hirsch, Werner Z. and Anthony M. Rufolo, "Effects of Prevailing Wage and Residence Laws on Municipal Government Wages," *Journal of Urban Economics* (forthcoming).

13. *Sportique Fashions v. William Sullivan*, United States District Court, Northern District of California, 1976. The trial court ruling was upheld by the 9th Circuit Court of Appeals on March 21, 1979 (docket #76-3264).

CHANGING FEDERAL-LOCAL RELATIONS IN A PERIOD OF FISCAL AUSTERITY

Albert J. Davis and Nonna A. Noto

I. A CHANGE IN FEDERAL STRATEGY TOWARD ECONOMIC DEVELOPMENT AND AID TO THE POOR

During the 1970s the United States still operated under the belief that prosperity—or strong real economic growth—was just around the corner. Even though in the late 1970s the economy came to suffer from low productivity, recession, and some unusual price shocks—the high cost of energy and interest rates in particular—the national economy was viewed as basically healthy over most of the decade. Consequently, special federal attention could be focused on those people, geographic places, and industry sectors that were not keeping pace with national growth trends. The special objects of this concern included poverty and minority population groups, old central cities, the "snowbelt" regions of the Northeast and Midwest, and certain basic manufacturing industries hard hit by

Research in Urban Economics, Volume 4, pages 147-165.
Copyright © 1984 JAI Press Inc.
All rights of reproduction in any form reserved.
ISBN: 0-89232-423-6

diminished demand and increased import competition—such as autos, steel, textiles, apparel, and shoes.

At the beginning of the 1980s, national concern turned toward the persistent lackluster performance of the economy as a whole. Instead of trying to revive old places and industry activities through targeted subsidy efforts, the economic development strategy of the Reagan administration has favored a broad-brush macroeconomic approach which, to borrow the cliche, is depending on a rising tide to lift all boats.

The approach emphasizes reducing government-imposed costs—through tax cuts, less regulation, and less federal interference in credit allocation and borrowing. It emphasizes expanding incentives to save, invest, and earn more. This approach puts more emphasis on investment in plant, equipment, and research and development, but less on housing and human capital. The approach implicitly encourages the movement of labor and capital resources out of industries and geographic locations which are failing and toward activities and areas of great profitability.

This attitude represents a big shift away from the emphasis on "saving the cities" that was popular in the 1960s and 1970s. Federal urban policies of that period reflected a strategy of trying to eliminate roadblocks to economic opportunity for the disadvantaged and distressed. Given the commitment, tactics were the issue. In search of the most effective approach, we argued over whether aid should go to people, places, or local governments; to "pockets of poverty" within well-off cities as well as to cities in overall distress; to physical capacity versus human development; or to income support versus education, job training, and social services for the poor.

For cities, there was the happy prospect that, whatever the approach selected, relief would flow in their direction. During the 1960s and 1970s, cities benefited not only from direct assistance to governments through revenue sharing but also indirectly from aid aimed at disadvantaged population groups or distressed geographic areas. City governments also served essentially as agents of the federal government for many population- and place-oriented programs. In the late 1970s, cities were drawn into the national effort to lift the economy at large through antirecession fiscal assistance, local public works programs, and public service jobs.

Urban policies of that era were encouraged by a perception that adverse conditions were only a temporary cyclical phenomenon or, if a structural problem, one that could be remedied by modest national investments in the fiscal health, economic development, or human capital of cities. But demographic and migration trends do not offer any indication that the decentralization of population away from the large cities will be reversed (see Kathryn P. Nelson, "Urban and Demographic Change," in this volume).

Instead, federal grant programs are now viewed increasingly as a form of permanent subsidy rather than a successful investment in economic adjustment.

Particularly in a period of slow overall economic growth, critics are now asking whether it is appropriate to siphon resources from the rest of the country to provide these continual subsidies to cities.

The shift in national economic development philosophy under the Reagan Administration has been accompanied by a change in the favored tools of financial assistance. There has been a move away from technical assistance, credit assistance, and public infrastructure grants that often were channeled through or influenced by local governments. Specific proposals have been made to cancel direct loan and loan guarantee programs that had staked their legitimacy on preserving and creating jobs in designated geographic areas. In particular, the general business development programs of the Economic Development Administration (EDA) and the Farmers Home Administration (FHA) have not received Administration support.[1]

The Reagan Administration's preference is instead for nationwide "supply-side" tax concessions that rely on the private sector as a conduit for growth. This is best illustrated by provisions of the Economic Recovery Tax Act of 1981 (ERTA), especially the Accelerated Cost Recovery System for depreciation and the investment tax credit.

What does such a shift in federal economic development strategy and policy instruments imply for the role of the cities? In general, reliance on the tax system—rather than on direct grants or credit allocation—as a method of distributing federal subsidies is likely to make it harder for the cities to compete for housing and employment activity. Exceptions would be the proposed Enterprise Zones approach, which would cut federal taxes selectively in distressed areas, and the Rehabilitation Tax Credit, which might be used extensively in cities with older structures. Far more important in dollar terms and breadth, however, are the federal income tax concessions that, by intention, are available to any qualifying individual or business in the country, regardless of location. Neither the large cities nor rural areas nor depressed regions are offered any competitive advantage.

In addition, local governments may face a diminished role as agents of federal economic development efforts. Federal aid is increasingly likely to go directly to private enterprises and to favor their private investment activities. Cities will have less bargaining power in the form of being able to offer federally subsidized infrastructure improvements or the technical advice and assistance that had been associated with the federal loan programs. Furthermore, there is likely to be less federal pressure on private firms to cooperate with areawide planning and economic development efforts.

A similar shift in both strategy and forms of assistance can be discerned in the Reagan proposals on aid to the poor. During the 1970s, aid was offered to poor individuals in the form of publicly provided services such as legal aid, job training, health clinics, and public housing, in addition to direct cash assistance. In the early 1980s, measures have been taken to reduce the extent of aid to the poor. This reduction involves both holding down the dollar growth in outlays and curbing the range of programs provided. Eligibility requirements for grants like Aid to Families with Dependent Children (AFDC) and direct federal programs like food stamps have been tightened. The cutbacks most severely affect those in the gray area between complete welfare dependency and self-sufficiency—that is, the working or intermittently poor. This philosophy has been expressed in terms of helping only the "truly needy." This new conservative national vision of a "safety net" for the "truly needy" seems intended only to catch individuals, not geographic places at large.

Potential reductions in assistance to their poor residents is not a matter of minor concern to cities. The indirect effect on city governments and urban economies of cuts in direct federal assistance to individuals could be as great as direct losses of federal funds to city governments. Anthony Downs estimated that while the proposed 1979 federal budget would provide $25 billion in "place-oriented" aid to central cities, another $66 billion would go to persons in central cities.[2]

In place of the public provision of services for the poor is a strategy of providing cash or cash substitutes in the form of vouchers directly to qualified persons. In the housing area in particular the Reagan administration favors a move away from construction subsidies toward housing vouchers. Central cities would lose some control over development and possibly some advantage they may have had in terms of geographic concentration of housing construction subsidies. Cutbacks in the CETA public employment program in exchange for more geographically generalized tax incentives for hiring welfare recipients has a similar effect in diluting concentration in cities.

The withdrawal of political and financial support for programmatic aid to the poor can be traced in part to opinions that some aid recipients could really fend for themselves. In addition, public programs that have been justified as helping the poor indirectly through improved local economies or government finances are being criticized as not being an efficient means of either helping the poor or producing an economic return on public dollars.

Doubts about programs for distressed places may have been fostered by a poor federal political record on ability to direct funds to areas with acute needs and to projects where benefits were likely to exceed costs. The politics of coalition building created programs with widespread eligibility and multiple purposes. These complex programs have become particularly vulnerable to charges of inefficiency. Considerable disillusionment also has set in with the idea that a program could be designed in Washington that was responsive to the diverse economic development needs of individual places.

II. FEDERAL BUDGET PRESSURES

Apart from shifts in philosophy or opinions on the merits of urban-oriented programs, federal aid to state and local governments has been caught in the squeeze between a reduction in federal revenue growth and an increase in pressures for federal expenditures in the other program areas. This squeeze was intensified by President Reagan's philosophical commitment to cutting federal taxes and cutting back the federal domestic role.

The origins of this retrenchment in intergovernmental assistance, however, predate the Reagan administration. It was evidenced in decisions made during the late 1970s to halt the decline in real defense spending and to try to contain the steadily increasing share of GNP taken by federal taxes. The Carter administration decided not to seek full-scale renewal of the expensive antirecession fiscal assistance or local public works programs, and not to continue to press for expensive welfare reform. As illustrated in the top panel of Figure 1, real per capita federal aid to state and local governments peaked in 1978, during the Carter administration.

Figure 2 illustrates how federal aid to states and localities has been, and is likely to continue to be, steadily squeezed by pressures to spend in uniquely federal areas of responsibility—especially defense, interest on the debt, and social security and medicare for the elderly.

The federal outlays projected on the basis of law and congressional policy at the end of 1981 provide some perspective on the magnitude of the budget squeeze even in the absence of later Reagan proposals. Grants to state and local governments, including those for individual benefit programs, were projected to decline from 17.4% of the FY78 budget to 10.5% for FY86. Social security (including medicare), defense, and interest on the national debt would account for about 70%. The projected FY86 deficit of $234 billion (22% in comparison to outlays) could not be eliminated even if the remainder of the budget, including grants, was cut by one-third and also one-third of the prospective FY86 tax relief enacted in 1981 was retracted.[3]

The Tax Equity and Fiscal Responsibility Act of 1982 (TEFRA), passed by the Congress in August 1982, would raise only about $52 billion in expected additional revenues for FY86.[4] This action retracts less than one-third of the prospective FY86 tax relief enacted in 1981 and falls far short of relieving the enormous pressure to cut the remainder of the budget if social security, defense, and interest are to be protected and the budget balanced. At the same time, the tax changes considerably exhaust the easy political possibilities for obtaining budget-balancing revenue from excise taxes, a rollback of business tax breaks, improved collection, and modest tightening of personal deductions.

In addition to having a smaller share of the budget, grants will be squeezed by the downward pressure of tax cuts on the entire budget. The federal tax cuts enacted in 1981 are not likely to be just a temporary damper on spending. They were a product not only of the "supply-side" theory of economic improvement, but probably also of the public desire for tax cuts that finally, after a number of years, worked its way from the state and local to the federal level.

The bottom panels of Figure 1 show, in terms of the per capita expenditures

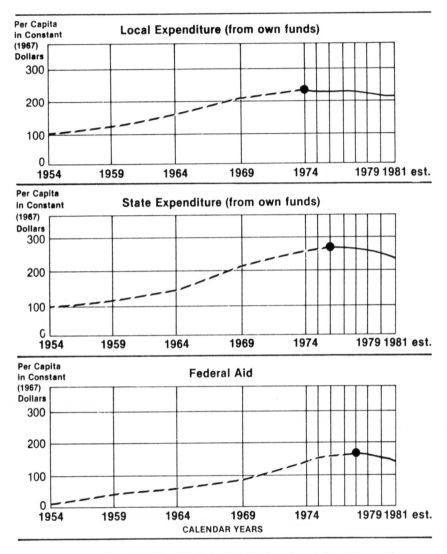

Figure 1. Declines in "Real" Federal Aid, Local and State Expenditures

● High points.

Source: Advisory Commission on Intergovernmental Relations, Significant Features of Fiscal Federalism, 1980–1981 Edition, Report M-132 (Washington, D.C.: ACIR, 1981), p. 9.

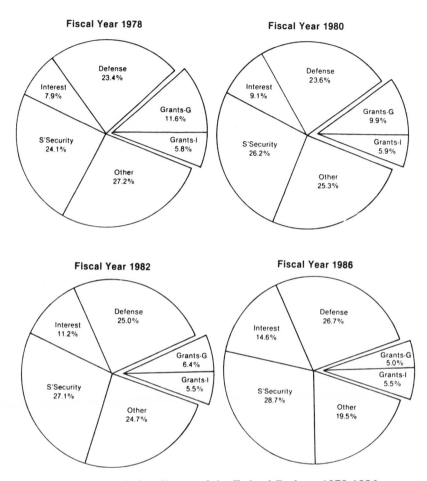

Fiscal Year 1978

Defense 23.4%
Interest 7.9%
Grants-G 11.6%
S'Security 24.1%
Grants-I 5.8%
Other 27.2%

Fiscal Year 1980

Defense 23.6%
Interest 9.1%
Grants-G 9.9%
S'Security 26.2%
Grants-I 5.9%
Other 25.3%

Fiscal Year 1982

Defense 25.0%
Interest 11.2%
Grants-G 6.4%
S'Security 27.1%
Grants-I 5.5%
Other 24.7%

Fiscal Year 1986

Defense 26.7%
Interest 14.6%
Grants-G 5.0%
S'Security 28.7%
Grants-I 5.5%
Other 19.5%

Figure 2. Relative Shares of the Federal Budget, 1978-1986
The Squeeze on Grants
(Projected According to Congressional Action Through End of 1981)

Abbreviations: "S'Security" — Social Security including Medicare
"Grants-I" — Grants to State or Local Governments Primarily for Direct Benefits to Individuals;
for example, Medicaid, Aid to Families with Dependent Children, Housing Subsidies.
"Grants-G" — Grants to State and Local Governments for More General or Governmental Purposes;
for example, General Revenue Sharing, Community Development Block Grants.

Sources: Budgets of the United States, and Congressional Budget Office. "Baseline Budget Projections for Fiscal Years 1983-1987,"
February 1982.

153

from own funds in constant (1972) dollars, that local expenditures peaked in 1974 and state expenditures peaked in 1976. This was considerably before the passage of Proposition 13 in California in 1977 launched a spate of state-local tax and expenditure limitation legislation—some version of which passed in at least 15 states after 1977. Having finally reached the national as well as local and state levels, pressure for keeping taxes down continues and is not likely to be eliminated by lack of immediate success for the Reagan supply-side tax policy. In addition, reduced economic growth sharply cut expected revenues in 1982, despite inflation.

In short, the tight fiscal conditions expected for the 1980s do not leave much room for largesse in federal responses to distressed areas and persons. Without substantial progress in controlling such "uncontrollables" as medical costs or a massive broadening of tax base, protection cannot be given simultaneously to intergovernmental grants and to social security, defense, and the tax rate cuts for individuals enacted in 1981.

III. LOCAL RELIANCE ON FEDERAL AID

Fueled by a rapid expansion in federal grants, municipal reliance on federal aid grew rapidly during the 1960s and 1970s. Federal aid to state and local governments rose over tenfold from FY60 to FY80, from $7 billion to $91 billion. The average annual increase was 13.7%. This rate of increase was more than twice that for inflation over the same period. As a percentage of total state-local expenditures, federal aid rose from 13.5% to 24.8%. From 1962 to 1980, direct federal aid (excluding amounts passed through by states) to municipalities rose from 5 to 23 cents per home-raised dollar, more than a 400% increase in the proportional reliance on federal aid.[5]

The numbers of grant programs increased just about as rapidly as did real dollar grant funding, growing from 132 in 1960 to 498 in 1978. More types of grantees qualified for direct federal aid—cities, counties, schools, other special districts, nonprofit organizations, and hybrids. Increasingly the states—through whom "pass-through" of federal grants to cities had been more typical—were bypassed by direct federal-local arrangements. The proportion of federal intergovernmental aid going directly to localities increased from only 9% in 1960 to 28% by 1978.[6]

Reliance on federal aid became especially pronounced for the largest cities. Measured relative to own-source revenues for the 47 largest cities in the United States, except for New York City, reliance on intergovernmental aid in 1957 was only 2% for federal aid and 18% for state aid. For city fiscal years ending in 1977-1978, however, federal aid alone was 39% in comparison to own-source dollars and state aid was 25%. By the late 1970s reliance on federal aid had become particularly high—more than 50% relative to own-source revenues in some central cities of the Northeast and Midwest such as Buffalo and Cleveland.[7]

The heavy reliance on grants shown by these fiscal data does suggest that cities would be vulnerable to sudden reductions in federal aid. This does not mean, however, that financial emergencies, bankruptcies, or even massive city tax increases would necessarily occur if federal aid is cut back.

City governments can, have, and will continue to cut back spending as federal aid is reduced.[8] Because federal grants have been used to enlist cities as agents of federal purpose, and because the subcontractor relationship is understood, cities are more easily able to terminate federal programs when that outside support is withdrawn. Up to a point, not yet known, cities will pass these cuts through to the individuals who otherwise would have benefited.

Despite recent evidence of improved ability to cope with pressures of fiscal austerity, cities are still likely to have a hard time dealing with the problems that federal aid programs were created to address. Some cities are beset with serious structural economic problems reflected in population and employment losses. They face both the deterioration of the tax base and the special public service demands imposed by a large and high concentration of poor people.

For many cities, these problems are not likely to be washed away by a rising tide of general economic recovery. Nevertheless, federal domestic retrenchment and a swing toward more conservative values may necessitate more restraint in setting urban agendas for the 1980s than had been required during the 1960s and 1970s.

IV. ALTERNATIVE RESPONSES TO FEDERAL BUDGET AUSTERITY

A. The New Federalism: Fewer Dollars, Fewer Requirements

The Reagan administration's accommodation to its high priorities on defense, tax cuts, and social security, and to the President's own philosophy of less government is to impose fewer requirements on what kinds of services state and local governments are expected to provide in conjunction with the receipt of a reduced amount of federal aid. For fiscal years 1981 and 1982, this took two forms: administrative relaxation of federal regulations like those concerning public transportation for the handicapped and education for non-English-speaking children, and proposals, partly accepted by Congress, to consolidate narrowly defined categorical grants into less restrictive block grants.

The Reagan "New Federalism" initiative, announced in January 1982, would extend over a 7-year period, from FY84 to FY91. During the first stage, covering FY84-87, 35 or more categorical and block grant program areas would be folded into a temporary trust fund arrangement. This involves approximately $30 billion (for FY84) worth of programs primarily in the areas of transportation, education, social services, health care, and community development, as well as general revenue sharing.

In the second stage, over the FY88-91 period, the trust fund would be phased out by simultaneously cutting grants from the trust fund and repealing the federal excise taxes financing the fund. By 1991, state and local governments would thus be left entirely on their own to decide whether they valued the previous federal programs enough to be willing to raise their own tax rates in order to finance them.

In addition to the trust fund, the original New Federalism proposal of January 1982 contained a "swap" component concerning a reorganization of welfare-type responsibilities. The states would pick up the responsibility to replace the federal food stamp program and the grant-financed AFDC program, while the national government would fully take over the medicaid program of health care for the poor. This swap was intended to have its own rough fiscal balance between costs imposed on and costs relieved from the states. Subsequently, at the insistence of the National Governors' Association, the White House dropped the proposal to defederalize food stamps and suggested a less than complete nationalization of the medicaid program.

The New Federalism approach, though it may never be enacted in a comprehensive way by Congress, does represent one attempt to organize a federal domestic spending retreat according to a clear principle. The principle is that citizens should speak on matters of domestic affairs with more diversity than they have in the past 20 years: policies should be decided and conducted on a local and regional basis rather than through an intergovernmental system designed to encourage a nationwide norm. Under New Federalism, the responsibility for problems of distressed people, places, and local governments would devolve from the federal to state governments. An overall scale-back in public spending could be anticipated because programs are expected to face a sterner fiscal test at the state level than they had at the federal level.

We envision at least three alternatives to the New Federalism type of response to the pressures to cut federal spending. We call these "challenging other constituencies," "disorderly retreat," and "setting priorities." All three differ from the Reagan plan in maintaining a federal commitment to and role in addressing the objectives of earlier federal grant programs, albeit on a smaller scale than during the 1970s.

B. Challenging Other Constituencies

One response to a threatened cut in federal grants to local governments is to reject it and fight back. Under this alternative, recipients of federal urban grants would challenge the claims of other constituencies on the federal budget. Congress and the public would hear arguments that the problems of urban areas and the people in them are as severe as those of national defense and social security, let alone smaller programs like federal pensions, agricultural payments, and veterans' benefits. There would also have to be a confrontation with the tax-cut constituency.

Events of 1981 and 1982 made such challenges seem unrealistic. In mid-1982 the Congress did not appear willing to accept the Reagan proposal to again slash grants. Nonetheless, the 1982 tax act, although dubbed "the largest tax increase in history," was not large enough to prevent continuing large deficits even with improvement in the economy. In 1983 Congress will again have to decide whether to cut back spending or to raise taxes if it wants to reduce the federal deficit.

Ironically, a moderate economic recovery, even if it did enhance tax revenues, would not necessarily present an opportunity to return to the more numerous and larger federal grant programs of the 1960s and 1970s. It might only confirm the claim that tax cuts were essential to a long-term economic recovery. On the contrary, a continued economic slide would be the condition likely to bring back support for grants, because it would lessen Congress's commitment to controlling federal deficits.

C. Disorderly Retreat

Under our second alternative of a disorderly retreat, urban assistance advocates accept the idea that federal aid cuts are inevitable but are unable to respond to the New Federalism with a coordinated counterproposal. One manifestation could be an across-the-board cut in budgets for all programs, thereby avoiding the task of evaluating and ranking individual programs. This has become known as the continuing-resolution approach to budget making.

A danger of a persistent continuing-resolution approach is that by default much less domestic spending control will be exerted over entitlement programs like social security than over programs subject to annual appropriation. Most grants to city governments are subject to annual appropriations.

Another manifestation of the disorderly retreat would be the strong sway that would be exerted by organized and powerful constituencies at the expense of meritorious programs with weak constituencies. Innovative social or training services, for example, could suffer in comparison to visible brick and mortar projects such as highways.

While perhaps making a financial retreat, Congress, in its desire to serve clienteles and advance its influence, may impose more requirements on state or local governments without providing grant funding. While such mandates might respond to the pleas of some groups in urban areas, they might be counterproductive for the areas as a whole due to high costs and limited benefits.

The disorderly retreat would also encourage a form of politics by sniper attack in which advocates of one urban program were forced to attack other federal urban programs. Or urban supporters may sacrifice one program only to regroup behind another that appears safer from attack. The favored bulwark for 1982 and 1983 appears to be public infrastructure. States, localities, interest groups, and financial institutions have already woven a network of support for federal action on the infrastructure front, perhaps as a substitute for other programs.

Finally, inability to organize an disorderly retreat could mean large and growing deficits if the political will cannot be mustered to either increase taxes or reduce expenditures.

D. Setting Priorities

A seemingly preferable alternative to disorderly retreat would be a coherent counterproposal to the New Federalism that copes with austerity by setting priorities among urban programs. The priorities approach is tough politically for urban advocates because it would involve the unpopular task of picking among programs and beneficiaries and retreating from the notion of universal entitlement. It calls for targeting the remaining aid dollars on those local programs which are of high national priority and which depend heavily on federal assistance for their survival.

The setting-priorities option would benefit from a willingness to conduct a serious reevaluation of urban programs and problems. In the years since many federal programs were established, new problems have arisen, old problems have been reordered as relative causes of concern, and old methods for dealing with problems have been challenged. In particular, the effectiveness of federal grants to city governments needs to be compared with that of assistance directly to individuals and businesses. Furthermore, the tax subsidy approach should be evaluated in contrast to grants, loans, and public services for its effectiveness in stimulating economic growth. A setting-priorities approach should be guided by a number of testing points for the merit of current and proposed programs.

IV. TESTING POINTS FOR A MORE AUSTERE FEDERAL URBAN POLICY

The fiscal constraints of the 1980s call for a critical appraisal of past federal aid programs. While the ultimate decision on which programs survive and which are eliminated will be a political one, urban analysts can suggest testing points to encourage a more selective setting of federal aid priorities. For this purpose, we reconsider six of the popular rationales for federal aid to local governments: (a) aid to the poor; (b) horizontal imbalance; (c) vertical imbalance; (d) spillover; (e) public investment; and (f) state and local governments as federal agents.

A. Aid to the Poor

Experts generally agree that any consensus on the proper extent of income redistribution or welfare support will be frustrated by assignment of that responsibility to any but the highest or national level of government. If, instead, local or state governments must raise their own tax levies in order to redistribute income, they run the risk of driving out residents and activities subject to the tax and of possibly attracting beneficiaries from other jurisdictions. These problems afflict many central cities.

Unfortunately, the expert advice in favor of federal financing does not come directly to grips with the lack of a national consensus on the appropriate welfare or income support policy. In the absence of full national financing, use of federal grants is justified as a compromise that accommodates the diverse political geography of welfare preferences. Embedded in this heavy reliance on grants is a compromise between those who want less income redistribution or more tolerance for diverse welfare methods and those who want more generosity or national uniformity.

Yet the present system simultaneously provokes charges of fiscal irresponsibility and failure to stimulate adequate benefit levels in some states. Our current income-support system relies heavily on grant programs with very high matching rates such as AFDC, medicaid, and the HUD section 8 housing programs. An alternative would be full federal financing for higher food stamp benefits traded against less generous cost matching for federal grants to states or localities for programs like housing, school lunches, or some kinds of medical services whose costs have been difficult to control.

Urban areas have a stake in an improved welfare system. Cities have a keen interest in adequate levels of support for poor people who are particularly concentrated in central cities. But they also should be interested in a welfare system that does not encourage unnecessary dependency. If the opportunity should arise for improvements in welfare arrangements, cities should be willing to consider a sacrifice of dollars of aid to their governments in exchange for more effectively delivered dollars of aid to individuals.

B. Horizontal Imbalance

The harm from wide gaps in tax base among similar jurisdictions—localities or states—takes two forms, one involving inequity and the other involving economic inefficiency. The conventional equity concern is exemplified by school finance reforms intended to prevent either stinted educations for students in tax-base-poor districts or amplified tax rates for the taxpayers in such districts. The efficiency concern is that economic activity may shift toward areas that are able to offer a more attractive fiscal climate, more by accident or exclusionary design than by superior economic location.

The horizontal imbalance case for state or federal intervention should not be overstated, however. Capitalization into market prices can somewhat offset fiscal disparities (i.e., land prices are likely to be higher in areas with low tax rates). Fiscal conditions may not be excessively severe for all types of localities. Setting priorities in the category of horizontal imbalance would require identifying the particular kinds of places most seriously affected and adjusting allocation formulas to target assistance on them.

The relevance of disparities in tax base is widely appreciated and is acknowledged in the federal general revenue sharing formula. Recognition of public service need disparities was more likely to take the form of narrow-purpose grants for particular public services rather than unconditional fiscal assistance. A by-product of the conditional-grant method of infusing funds during the 1960s and 1970s may have been a lessening of the service and tax disparities between central cities and their suburbs. This, in turn, may have slightly slowed the outflow of economic activity from the central cities. However, such methods of assisting cities also encouraged cities to spend—primarily in an effort to secure the federal matching funds—on services that otherwise would have been considered more carefully.

In the 1980s, consideration should be given to a more general formulation of the needs-disparity problem. Local governments, as governments, may warrant compensation on the grounds of horizontal imbalance because they are obligated to provide standard public services to a group that does not pay much in the way of taxes. In addition, these governments must deal with problems associated with a large concentration of poverty and minority population, such as drugs, crime, high unemployment especially among teenagers, and low-achieving students. Perhaps with the service-surrogate form of urban assistance being challenged, cities will be able to be more selective and more forthright about requesting assistance simply on the basis of the fiscal disadvantage they face because of tax base disparities and concentrations of poor people.

C. Vertical Imbalance

General revenue sharing, instituted in 1972, was a response to the perception that the federal level had captured the high ground in revenue-raising powers with its income tax and its then-perceived immunity from fear that redistributive taxes would drive down the tax base or the economy. The federal tax system, furthermore, was judged to be more equitable (i.e., progressive) and administratively efficient than state and local systems.

Confidence in these propositions and predictions of sustained economic growth created the forecast of future federal fiscal dividends that could be shared with states and localities. Subnational governments were otherwise expected to suffer from revenue systems that were not responsive to income growth. The federal fiscal dividends of the 1960s and 1970s were created not just by a healthy economy but also by a cutback in the share of the budget going to defense, the existence of social security surpluses that covered deficits elsewhere, and increased resort to deficit financing.

Now these conditions and prospects appear to have been sharply reversed. The guidelines of the past now work against the case for across-the-board federal assistance on the basis of general "vertical imbalance." The budget projections for the federal government look as deficit-ridden or more so than those for state and local governments. The state government portion of the GRS program was eliminated in 1980 when state budgets were perceived to be in surplus. The New Federalism proposal would turn back more responsibility than revenues to the states.

Any case for federal general purpose aid to local governments now must address the conservative challenge that permitting the pleasure of spending without the pain of taxing encourages the unnecessary growth of government. Balanced attention is needed not only to factors like tax competition that constrain spending but also to potentially expansionary biases from opportunities to export state and local taxes. In this atmosphere, a creditable argument based on vertical imbalance would require more than a comparison of deficit and surplus projections among the levels of government. The case would have to be made that services—at least some particular services—carried out by local governments would be chronically undernourished in the absence of intergovernmental aid. One example might be compensatory education and other services which are somewhat redistributive in nature. In order to succeed, the argument must focus both on the local governments that are constrained most strongly and on the particular services likely to be undernourished.

D. Spillovers

Federal assistance for state or local services whose benefits spill over to residents of other jurisdictions has been justified on the grounds that otherwise local governments would provide less than the socially desirable level of those services. Examples include functions such as transportation and pollution control which are regional in scope, often crossing state boundaries.

The spillover rationale for grants is seemingly embodied in the matching grants that govern the flow of a heavy portion of federal grant dollars. Yet the matching rates in some nonwelfare areas seem inexplicably high in relation to spillovers of benefits, at the margin, beyond the recipient jurisdiction. Federal matching rates for intrastate highway programs, for example, are 70% or more.

Federal grants have served as an alternative to forging difficult multijurisdictional collective decisions at the substate and interstate levels. While federal involvement was encouraged as a way to overcome political obstacles to cooperative action, it may be more appropriate fundamentally to rely on subnational solutions, though admittedly they are not always easy to find. There is room in this area for greater use of subnational mechanisms for sharing costs and service provision among governments and less federal grant assistance.

The spillover rationale has on occasion been a veneer over the more basic objective of simply delivering dollars to jurisdictions otherwise felt in need or wanting back their "fair share" of federal taxes. The terrain of grants loosely tied to the spillover rationale deserves some scouting for excesses that could be curbed at a time when priorities will require sharpening. Lowering the matching rates could help control total program costs, though it will not necessarily help target funds to the cases of most serious need.

E. Public Investment

There is sometimes a presumption that potentially productive public investments would go unmade by states or localities in the absence of federal assistance. State and local governments are criticized for having a myopic view in not undertaking public investment projects that could be expected to prove worthwhile in the long run. When the costs of "collective decision making" and capital financing can be minimized by doing once in Washington what would otherwise have to be done in 50 state capitals or thousands of city halls, and when the federal treasury is not under strain, Congress is susceptible to calls to override inaction by lower levels of government.

Federal budget strain, on the other hand, should force some careful appraisal of these appeals for federal aid. Even if aid might finance a worthwhile investment, federal aid transfers from other parts of the country that do not benefit need not be made when the beneficiary's self-interest in the investment is substantial and evident. In a time of austerity, the federal government must attend first to nationally needed programs that are not within the geographic or traditional span of state or local government control. Akin to the argument regarding spillover activities, greater effort could be put forth by jurisdictions that benefit from the investment, particularly when the area's overall economic capacity is not an issue.

Criticisms that eligibility criteria for federal aid programs are too lax deserve attention. According to the criteria used by the Economic Development Administration, for example, as of FY82, 80% of the nation's population lived in areas that had been designated as distressed and eligible for assistance (though not all of those areas received assistance awards). For programs billed as dealing with distress, stricter targeting may be required for credibility, despite political pressures from constituents to broaden eligibility.

Temporary federal support for experimental local or state programs of "public investment" are not suspect per se. They can serve an important demonstration role. But commitments to long-term capital financing and operating subsidies deserve serious question.

F. State or Local Governments as Federal Agents

In the 1960s and 1970s, when Congress wanted to be responsive but did not want the burden of full federal financial or administrative responsibility, it was prone to create a grant. The grant was intended to leverage state or local responses in pursuit of an adjudged national interest. The tests for the presence of a national interest were weaker than if more direct federal action had been required.

In order to increase the flow of fedderal aid, many self-interested state or local governments may have encouraged this process of extending grants in the name of national interest, especially when activities already underway for reasons of home interest could thereby be financed. The CETA (Comprehensive Employment Training Act) program in its early years is a favorite example of how cities used federal funds to pay workers to carry out standard municipal services. In the more austere 1980s, programs which would pass fungible funds along to states and localities in the name of general themes like national defense, technological development, or international competitiveness deserve to be evaluated more strictly for their relevance and effectiveness.

V. CONCLUSIONS

President Reagan's New Federalism proposal to dismantle much of the system of federal intergovernmental assistance poses a challenge to those who feel that there are areas of legitimate federal involvement in local affairs. What would a convincing counterproposal be? An approach of "challenging other constituencies" rejects the forecasted need for domestic spending constraints in the 1980s. The "disorderly retreat" approach may prevail if it is too difficult to muster the necessary political leadership to unscramble what has now become a jam-up from the political logrolling of the past 20 years.

The approach of "setting priorities" is not, however, without its limitations. Their strong district orientation and weak political party discipline make members of Congress reluctant to appear to deny their constituents a portion of the federal pie. Furthermore, citizens speak with different political voices on what public programs there should be, depending upon whether they speak as a locality, a state, or a nation. The setting-priorities approach does not tell us clearly when citizens should speak with one national voice rather than many regional voices. Is one voice needed on the subject of aid to the poor, while many are appropriate on the subject of economic development strategies or public transportation? Should urban policies be set by the cities themselves, states, or the federal government?

Nonetheless, a review of past criteria for intergovernmental involvement can offer some guidelines for setting priorities among federal urban programs when budget and political pressures call for spending cutbacks. Our review suggests a continued federal commitment to aid for the poor and some attention, through block or unrestricted grants, to the problems of horizontal fiscal imbalance affecting communities with a large number and heavy concentration of their residents in poverty. Failing a more coherent national consensus on the subject of public assistance, grants for welfare programs may merit strong support, although a reallocation of dollars from matching grants to direct transfers to individuals should be considered. The implications for urban areas of low-cost welfare reform proposals deserve more consideration when policy choices are being made.

Our analysis also suggests some paring down of commitments otherwise made in the name of horizontal imbalance or vertical imbalance. Assitance could be targeted more selectively to places with low fiscal resources and a large number and high concentration of poor people.

For the categories of spillovers, public investment, and state and local governments as federal agents, our evaluation finds an important federal role in testing innovations and supporting pilot programs but resists a federal commitment to widespread and long-term operating or capital subsidies. Federal matching rates could be reduced and eligibility criteria could be tightened. Greater efforts could be made to encourage subnational solutions for the financing and provision of services, especially in places with adequate fiscal capacity.

In sum, the criticisms of overextensions and low effectiveness in federal urban aid programs implicit in the New Federalism proposals are not without substance. Combined with the constraints of fiscal austerity, these criticisms are a challenge to urban advocates to reevaluate which federal programs are most worth fighting to maintain and which could reasonably be eliminated or turned over to states, local governments, or even the private sector.

ACKNOWLEDGMENT

The views expressed here are those of the authors and do not necessarily represent the position of the members or staff at large of the Advisory Commission on Intergovernmental Relations or of the Congressional Research Service of the Library of Congress.

NOTES

1. Some loan and grant programs did survive in the FY83 budget proposal because they conformed to the operating principles of the Reagan administration's economic development strategy. HUD's Urban Development Action Grant (UDAG) program was touted for its success in leveraging private capital, and HUD's Community Development Block Grant program (CDBG) was found consistent with the policy of giving decision-making authority to state and local governments. The Small Business Administration's (SBA) loan guarantee program was cited for its role in addressing imperfections in the capital market, although its direct loan program was slated for elimination. The CDBG program, however, was later proposed for future termination as part of the New Federalism plan to shift responsibilities for cities toward state governments.

2. Anthony Downs, "Urban Policy," in Joseph A. Pechman (ed.), *Setting National Priorities: The 1979 Budget* (Washington, D.C.: The Brookings Institution, 1978), p. 181.

3. From the *Baseline Budget Projections for Fiscal Years 1983-1987*, Congressional Budget Office, Washington, D.C., February 1982. The baseline concept, as used in this 1982 report, produces estimates on the basis of law as of the end of 1981, budget policy set by the Congress, and economic forecasts. Note that the baseline defense projections provide only about 3.5% per year annual real growth in defense outlays, far short of Reagan requests for future fiscal years.

4. U.S. Congress, Senate, *Conference Report to Accompany H.R. 4961*, Senate Report No. 97-530, August 17, 1982, Table 2, p. 691.

5. Advisory Commission on Intergovernmental Relations, *Significant Features of Fiscal Federalism*, 1979/80 Edition, Table 103, p. 161; 1980/81 Edition, Table 10, p. 19; Table 40, p. 60; Table 42, p. 62.

6. ACIR, *Significant Features of Fiscal Federalism*, 1980/81 Edition, Table 38, p. 58; Table 39, p. 59.

7. Computed by the authors from past annual editions of U.S. Bureau of the Census, *City Government Finances* (Washington, D.C.: U.S. Government Printing Office).

8. For preliminary evidence see Richard Nathan, Philip Dearborn, Clifford Goldman, and associates, ''Initial Effects of the Fiscal Year 1982 Reductions in Federal Domestic Spending,'' in John Ellwood (ed.), *Reductions in U.S. Domestic Spending: How They Affect State and Local Governments* (New Brunsick, N.J.: Transaction Books, 1982).

THE STRUCTURAL CHARACTER
OF FEDERAL AID:
AN EXAMINATION OF FISCAL IMPACT

Robert M. Stein

I. INTRODUCTION

President Reagan's call for another New Federalism underscores the tenuous
nature with which the national government has viewed its relationship with states
and local governments. Since the 1930s we have experienced no less than four
major redefinitions of American federalism (Wright, 1982), beginning with FDR's
New Deal and culminating full circle with Reagan's "new" New Federalism.
Each of these periods has been characterized by specific changes in the character,
scope, and direction of federal-state and federal-local relations. During these
periods the level of federal aid allocations has changed, as well as the mechanisms
for distributing the federal largess to state and local governments. Moreover,
the conditions and regulations associated with this fiscal exchange have varied
between stringency and leniency on the part of the federal donor (see Wright,
1982). Throughout each of these periods of Federalism, federal assistance to

Research in Urban Economics, Volume 4, pages 167-185.
Copyright © 1984 JAI Press Inc.
All rights or reproduction in any form reserved.
ISBN: 0-89232-423-6

state and local governments has grown, often overshadowing other changes in the character of American intergovernmental relations. Since the creation of the New Deal's social welfare programs, the flow of federal funds to subnational units of government has risen steadily with intermittent periods of accelerated growth (i.e., the Great Society programs of 1964-1968). It is this growth in fiscal federalism, and current attempts to curb this growth, that has captured the attention of the popular press and research community. Overlooked have been structural and substantive changes in the way the national government defines its fiscal relations with state and local governments.

A popular misconception is that all federal aid programs are structurally similar and that important differences arise only in funding levels and the substantive content of the aid program. In fact there are myriad program requirements and related traits which are applicable, in varying degrees, to all of the 1,074 federal aid programs currently listed in the U.S. Catalog of Federal Domestic Assistance. There are significant differences in content of federal grant programs which affect the impact of federal aid policies (U.S. Advisory Commission on Intergovernmental Relations, 1977a, b; Whitman and Cline, 1978). The FY82–83 federal budget calls for the consolidation of 59 urban categorical aid programs into five block grants to be allocated directly to state governments. This shift in the structure of federal aid offerings represents a major change in the direction of American federalism and requires more careful examination. Though much has been written on the fiscal impact of different delivery mechanisms (Gramlich, 1977), there is a paucity of empirical work which examines a host of other grant traits, ranging from eligibility to program requirements, and their impact on the implementation of aid policies.

The purpose of this study is to examine the literature on the fiscal and programmatic impact of federal aid programs. In this regard we will endeavor to show that some of the ambiguity in the literature arises from an incomplete definition of the structural attributes of federal aid programs. An expanded definition of the structural character of federal aid programs will be presented and examined in light of existing aid legislation. Drawing on this expanded definition of federal aid programs, we will present a theory of grant utilization that can in part explain the ambiguity in the findings of the grant impact literature. Finally an empirical test of this alternative explanation will be presented.

II. PREVIOUS RESEARCH

The flow of federal monies to subnational recipients is designed with specific goals and purposes in mind (e.g., fiscal stimulation, redress of inequality, and national standards). Often more than one goal is associated with a single aid program. As a means of fulfilling some or all of these program goals Congress has incorporated into the enabling legislation of each grant program traits and mechanisms that presumably maximize the probability of success. These traits define the character of the grant offering and may condition the implementation of aid programs independent of funding levels. Gramlich (1977) in his review of the grant impact literature identifies three methods for distributing federal assistance which he labels A, B, and C type grants.

Type A grants (e.g., Medicare, Medicaid, and AFDC) are intended to adjust benefit spillovers by reducing the price associated with the production of a good or service from which the producing community is unable to recoup all costs. By matching state and/or local expenditures on the specific good or service, the federal government enables the producing community to recover its costs. The open-ended nature of the matching grant allows the producing community to continue production until optimality is reached. Type A grants are normally distributed on a formula basis. Type B grants (e.g., general revenue sharing and some block grants) address the income and fiscal inequality problem by providing a lump-sum nonrestrictive grant to recipient governments. The purpose here is merely one of income redistribution by the most direct means available. Type C grants, the most widely employed aid mechanism, are intended to extract some form of compliant policy behavior from the recipient. These closed-ended conditional grants enable the federal government to stimulate programmatic expenditures, innovations, or the achievement of minimum service levels. Hicks (1968) and Schultz (1974) note that the proper way of viewing these grants is as a "device by which local governments are acting as the agents or contractors for the central government in carrying out specific tasks" (Gramlich, 1977:222).

Presumably Congress and/or its agents employ one of these aid mechanisms in order to maximize the achievement of specific programmatic goals. Gramlich's review of the aid impact literature suggests that this effect is not always achieved. Though there is ample evidence that each mechanism is associated with a specific fiscal and policy impact, it is not altogether clear which mechanisms are best at achieving the desired policy impact. Gramlich notes that the fiscal impact of grants (i.e., their ability to increase or decrease recipient spending) should be greatest for type A grants, next greatest for type C, and least effective for B grants. The empirical findings, however, do not fully confirm this hypothesis. In the case of type A grants recipient spending is somewhat "less than the size of the grant, indicating that the price elasticity of demand for most services is probably less than unity" (Gramlich, 1977:234). Moreover, type B grants stimulate much more recipient spending than would be expected from the rather generous and lenient conditions associated with this delivery mechanism. Finally, type C grants actually stimulate higher levels of recipient spending than either type B or A grants, usually equal to the size of the grant. Probably the most significant finding in Gramlich's review is the absence of a significant degree of fiscal stimulation. When discounting those studies which are either methodologically or substantively flawed, Gramlich finds a surprisingly low level of fiscal stimulation attributable to federal aid offerings.

This condition does not go unexplained by Gramlich and other researchers

(Miller, 1974). The greater stimulative effect of type C grants relative to A and B grants may be due to the fact that demand is more price elastic for those goods and services funded by type C grants. Thus the functional character (i.e., price elasticity, economies of scale, etc.) and not the closed-ended nature of type C grants may account for the strong stimulative effect on the expenditures of recipient governments. The fact that type B grants actually stimulate recipient expenditures suggests a need for some revision in theories that assume a harmony of interests between city officials and voters. The median voter thesis suggests that lump-sum conditional grants are used to either reduce local tax burdens or do the same indirectly by substituting federal monies for own-source revenues. The empirical findings suggest that local officials let federal monies "stick where it hits." This would of course imply a disharmony between the interests of the public and those within government. Moreover, it might suggest a sharing of values between local and federal officials concerning the utilization of federal aid monies. The more puzzling question is why this condition is not more pronounced for type A and C grants.

To resolve these ambiguities in the literature Gramlich recommends a move away from the underlying theory of grants as promulgated by economists and an examination of "questions more relevant for specific legislation:"

> Each existing or prospective grant program is obviously unique and the response of local governments to it will depend on underlying elasticities, the size of the grant, the homogeneity of local expenditures, restrictions on the grant and any other political factors .... If econometric research pretends to be relevant it must extend beyond the broad and general and get into these more specific questions of individual programs (Gramlich, 1977:234).

Essentially Gramlich is suggesting that there are other dimensions to the grant system which have yet to be examined. Besides the delivery mechanism, there are a host of program-specific and nonprogram-specific traits associated with federal grants. Each of these traits can enhance or weaken the attainment of specific program goals. The potential recipient of a grant approaches participation in the federal aid system with an awareness of these traits and their potential impact. Empirically, the relationships between different delivery mechanisms and other traits represent constraints on the operation of the delivery mechanism and thus might account for some of the indeterminancy in the grant impact literature.

III. THE RECIPIENT PERSPECTIVE ON GRANT IMPACTS

Previous explanations of aid impacts have centered on the price and income effects of different delivery mechanisms. These models may be empirically flawed to the extent that other conditions of the grant distort the income or price effect of the delivery mechanism. For instance, requiring recipients of open-ended matching grants to fulfill National Environmental Protection Act standards imposes a direct cost on the aid recipient which increases rather than decreases the price of the aided function. These costs need not always be fiscal in nature. Many aid programs impose significant political costs on aid recipients. The grant notification and clearinghouse function (A-95) and mandated state plans require aid recipients at one level of government (e.g., cities) to obtain approval and/or conform to state and/or regional plans in order to qualify for federal funding. These conditions do more than distort the fiscal decisions of aid recipients. They also transfer a significant portion of local autonomy to other levels of government. The policy consequences of these traits are extensive and in no way limited to only fiscal impacts.

The impacts of these "other traits" operate through two specific stages of the grant process; the application and implementation stages. The forces that shape the nature and scope of participation in the federal aid system directly impact on the fiscal response of participants to different aid mechanisms. From the perspective of the potential aid recipient, each grant mechanism and trait may increase the costs associated with seeking and receiving a grant award.

A number of researchers have suggested that not all potential recipients are equally capable of seeking and receiving federal assistance. Porter, Warner, and Porter (1973), Saltzstein (1977), Reed and Green (1978), and Stein (1979, 1981) have shown that there are significant obstacles to grant seeking which indirectly structure the allocation and programmatic impact of federal assistance. Certain nontransferable costs (i.e., application, implementation, and opportunity costs) confront each applicant for federal assistance. Each of these costs adversely affects the grant-seeking activities of communities who are either less able to bear the costs, or fail to perceive significant benefits that would accrue from participation. The resulting condition is one in which only those recipients capable and/or willing to bear the costs of seeking federal assistance apply and receive federal aid monies.

The structure of a federal aid package has an important impact on the potential recipient's decision to seek, receive, and eventually comply with the conditions of federal assistance. Certain aid packages stimulate grant seeking while other aid programs have either a neutral or a negative effect on grantsmanship. Type C grants require formal applications and are competitively awarded by administrative officials. In varying degrees matching expenditures and restrictive compliant policy behavior are required of all recipients of type C grants. Consequently, some communities find these grants difficult to apply for and politically undesirable to accept. Those communities who seek type C grants, in spite of these obstacles to participation, presumably do so because they concur with the purposes and goals of the aid program. The uniformly high stimulative effect of type C grants might be explained by the implicit consensus that exists between aid participants and the federal government over the goals and purposes of the grant. Those communities who find type C grants too restrictive and costly select themselves out of the universe of project grant recipients, effectively increasing compliance with federal guidelines.

Aid programs with minimal entry costs and broad eligibility attract a larger and more diverse population of applicants and participants. This population will not be uniformly committed to the goals and purposes of the individual aid program and may seek to avoid total compliance. If the conditions of the grant are sufficiently loose to allow for noncompliance (i.e., substitution or reduced levels of fiscal stimulation), recipients might express their cost/benefit calculations at the implementation rather than the application stage of the grant process.

Implicit in this explanation of the fiscal effect of type C grants is a cohesiveness to the structure of this grant type. Program, application, and matching requirements are assumed to be either uniform or significantly invariant among type C grants. The absence of this structural cohesiveness will produce a set of inconsistent cues for potential aid participants which would in turn produce variation in the fiscal response to these aid programs.

The limited stimulative effect of type A grants may be due to a set of inconsistent and variable program traits associated with this grant mechanism. Consistently broad eligibility requirements and variable program requirements may produce a set of highly variable fiscal effects for type A grants. The effect of this condition may neutralize the stimulative effect of an open-ended matching grant.

Two sets of grant traits are relevant to this explanation of the fiscal impact of federal aid. Factors associated with the application process serve to screen out certain eligible recipients from participation in the aid program. Those remaining participants are either more willing or capable of complying with federal aid initiatives. The second set of grant traits relate to the implementation of the grant program. The extent of program requirements, recipient funding obligations, and the scope of program beneficiaries directly affect the fiscal and programmatic response of aid recipients. These latter traits operationally define the degree to which a grant is conditional.

Empirically we are interested in: (1) the extent to which grant traits can discriminate between types of grant delivery mechanisms; and (2) whether these grant traits influence the fiscal response of the aid recipient, independent of the delivery mechanism. The fiscal impact of these traits is expected to vary with the delivery mechanism. The fiscal impact of delivery mechanisms exhibiting cohesive structures (i.e., traits are intercorrelated within the delivery mechanism) is less likely to be influenced by these nominal legal characteristics than are delivery mechanisms with less cohesive structures. Consequently, type C grants are not expected to vary in their fiscal impact across the different categories of grant traits. Conversely, the fiscal impact of type A and B grants is likely to be influenced by these grant traits.

IV. OPERATIONAL MEASURES AND DATA

The following grant-specific traits are identified as relevant to the fiscal impact of different delivery mechanisms:

Program Content. Gramlich notes that the functional content of certain aid programs may exert a significant and independent influence on the fiscal response of aid recipients. Certain functions are known to be associated with significant diseconomies of scale (Fox et al., 1977; Hirsch, 1964) and as such are prone to higher per-unit costs as production increases. Consequently, federal aid is expected to be more stimulative of recipient spending for diseconomies rather than for economies of scale goods and services. As federal aid increases the recipient's production of the aided diseconomy, the level of stimulation has the effect of increasing outlays by an additional factor associated with higher costs of increased production.

Normally economies of scale accrue for capital-intensive goods and services with fixed costs across production levels (e.g., water services). Diseconomies of scale are associated with labor-intensive goods and services (e.g., education). Using a capital versus service-intensive dichotomy and the work of other researchers as a guide (Fox et al., 1977), grant programs were grouped according to whether they were capital-intensive economies of scale or labor-intensive diseconomies of scale goods or services.

A-95 Grant Review. Applicants for certain federal assistance programs must submit their applications to regional planning commissions whose function is to determine whether the proposed use of aid monies conform to regional plans. Advisory only, the recommendations of these review agencies can structure both the decision of the grantor agency and the content of the applicant's application. Others have found that A-95 reviews tend to increase programmatic compliance with both federal and regional plans (Bombardier, 1975; Steinman, 1979).

State Planning Requirement. As part of the same administrative circular as A-95, state governments are required to submit a comprehensive plan for the implementation of grant programs. These state plans are implicit contractual agreements between the recipient and federal grantor, and as such can limit the options of recipient governments when implementing the awarded grant. It is expected that the submittal of a state plan, as a condition for seeking and receiving a federal grant, will increase the stimulative effect of federal assistance on local spending.

Eligibility. The number of different governmental units eligible for a specific federal grant decreases the aggregate stimulative effect of the grant. As noted earlier, broad eligibility standards allow for a more diverse set of aid recipients to enter the aid system who are unlikely to subscribe to federal goals and standards. This in turn is likely to lead to wider variation in compliance with federal aid guidelines and thus decrease the overall stimulative effect of a grant. Aid programs with narrow eligibility standards are likely to be targeted to a smaller and more homogeneous constituency. Unless the thrust and content of the aid program are completely at variance with the preferences of eligible recipients, it is expected that a broader consensus about program goals and requirements will exist between aid recipients and federal authorities for programs with narrow eligibility standards.[1]

Recipient Matching Requirements. One of the most difficult traits of a federal grant to define is the scope of programmatic requirements. The most widely recognized measure of programmatic requirements is the level of recipient matching expenditures.[2] Researchers have found that matching requirements are positively related to recipient expenditures for the aided function (Whitman and Cline, 1978). Matching ratios, however, do not fully capture the extent to which federal grants constrain the content and policy direction of the recipient's response to federal aid initiatives. In fact, Chernick (1979) has found that federal administrators reduce matching requirements as a means of obtaining greater program compliance in the awarding of federal grants. Another useful indicator of program requirements is the degree to which aid is to be targeted to recipients within the recipient jurisdiction.

Program Beneficiaries. The number or scope of intended beneficiaries of a federal aid program provides a means of assessing the extent to which federal officials intend to target the allocation of federal aid monies within the recipient's jurisdiction. The greater the specificity of aid beneficiaries in the grant legislation, the less discretion aid recipients will have to divert aid monies from their intended use. Greater specificity of aid beneficiaries should correspond to higher levels of fiscal stimulation, since opportunities for substitution of aid monies should (assuming adequate enforcement) be limited.[3]

Environmental Impact Statement. Many grant programs are burdened by legislatively mandated crosscutting aid requirements. These regulatory features require that the recipient become:

> responsible not only for fulfilling the directly enacted purpose of the grant, but also for assuring that those funds are administered in such a manner so as to redress past discrimination, protect and enhance the environment. . .(ACIR, 1977b: 233).

One of the most costly of these crosscutting requirements is the environmental impact statement (EIS). Aid recipients are required to assess and if necessary correct (at their own expense) any environmental damage that may result from implementation of the awarded grant. The costs of just preparing an EIS are significant. The U.S. Advisory Commission on Intergovernmental Relations (ACIR)(1977b) estimated that the average EIS cost for highway construction grants was $23,900. Add to this cost the requirement to correct environmental damage caused by the grant program and recipients could easily face costs well in excess of those intended.

Two different data bases are used in this study. Data on specific grant programs were obtained from the U.S. Catalog of Federal Domestic Assistance (CFDA). Published by the Office of Management and Budget, the CFDA provides a compendium of all federal aid programs which provide assistance and/or benefits to subnational units of government, individuals, private and nonprofit organizations. The catalog, published annually, provides detailed information on each assistance program's characteristics as well as data on current and past levels of appropriations.

Data on the allocation of grant awards is analyzed at the state level using the Community Services Administration's Federal Outlays reports. The Outlays reports provide information on all federal expenditures including grant awards by CFDA number. Merging data from the CFDA and the Outlays reports allows us to measure the fiscal impact of individual aid programs and their associated traits on aggregated state and local expenditures for 1977.

Only federal aid programs providing fiscal assistance to state and local governments (including school boards and other special districts) are studied. Thus loans, guaranteed loans, equipment transfers, and direct assistance to individuals are excluded from our analysis. All fiscal transfers to general or special purpose governments were classified into one of Gramlich' three types of grant delivery mechanism. A total of 569 grant programs are studied, representing 38% of total federal domestic outlays for FY77.[4]

V. ANALYSIS

The analysis is divided into two sections. First we analyze the structure associated with each grant delivery mechanism. Having established the degree of structural cohesiveness associated with each delivery mechanism, we estimate the fiscal impact of each delivery mechanism and its associated traits on state and local spending.

Discriminant function analysis is employed as a means of assessing the structure associated with each aid mechanism. Discriminant analysis is designed to find the optimal combination of independent variables (e.g., grant traits) that will discriminate between two or more groups of cases. This combination is used to classify cases into one of the three types of federal aid programs. The resulting classification schema is then compared to the observed distribution of cases in order to assess the predictive power of the model and is thus analogous to R^2 in regression analysis. Three components of discriminant function analysis are presented: (a) the centroid group means in reduced space (these figures represent the location of the three group means in reduced two dimensional space; the greater the distance between means, the more the groups are differentiated on that dimension); (b) the discriminant coefficient (which provides a means of comparing the relative strength of each trait to discriminate between categories of the dependent variable); and (c) the percentage of cases correctly predicted by grant type.

Table 1 reports the results of the discriminant function analysis. Though the overall classification of grant mechanisms from individual program traits is quite high (87.8%), there is considerable variation in the percentage of cases correctly classified by delivery mechanism. Slightly less than half (45.3%) of type A grants and 56.3% of type B grants are misclassified. Errant type A and B grants were most frequently classified as type C grants. Misclassification of type C grants was negligible and evenly divided between type A and B grants. The results of the discriminant classification partially confirm our earlier hypothesis. Though there is a modest degree of coherence to the structure of federal aid programs, this structure is limited to type C project grants. Both type A and B grants fail to exhibit a cohesive structure, distinguishable from each other and type C grants.

Table 1. Discriminant Function Classification of Federal Aid Programs By Type (Controlling for Prior Probabilities)

Actual Group	Predicted Group Membership[a]		
	Type A	Type B	Type C
Type A	29	2	22
(N = 53)	(54.7)	(3.7)	(41.5)
Type B	0	19	25
(N = 44)	(0)	(43.1)	(56.8)
Type C	11	9	452
(N = 472)	(2.4)	(1.9)	(95.7)

Note: [a]Percent of cases correctly predicted = 87.8.

Table 2 reports the discriminant function coefficients and centroid means in reduced space. When we combine the directional sign (+ , −) for the group means with the sign of each discriminant coefficient we have a measure of both the relative contribution of each variable to the observed function and the direction of this impact on the classification of each aid program.

The centeroid means for function 1 most discriminate between type A (− 1.45) and type C grants (.297). A secondary discrimination occurs between type B (.01) and type C grants. Narrow eligibility, required state plans and A-95 review are associated with type C grants. The level of mandated recipient matching expenditures is the only trait which significantly distinguishes type A grants from type C. The second function distinguishes between type B grants (2.02) and both type A and C grants. Two traits clearly define and thus distinguish type B grants from the other two categories of federal assistance: service content and

Table 2.   Discriminant Function Analysis of Federal Aid Delivery Mechanisms

	Discriminant Function Coefficient	
Variable	Function 1	Function 2
State Plan	.830*	−.043
A-95	.678*	−.207
Matching Require. (%)	−.401	−.563*
Eligibility	.479*	−.297*
Content	.247	.455*
Beneficiaries	.099	.370*
Envir. Impact	−.044	−.121
Centroid group means in reduced space		
Type A	−1.45	−.07
Type B	.01	2.02
Type C	.29	−.09

Note: *Important variables are at least half as large as the absolute value of the largest coefficient.

the scope of program beneficiaries. Type B grants are generally service oriented and have a narrowly defined set of program beneficiaries. The negative loadings for matching rates, A-95 and eligible governments suggest that on these traits, type A and C grants are relatively indistinguishable, accounting in part for the high number of misclassified type A grants. The findings in Tables 1 and 2 provide strong support for the thesis that federal aid programs which employ different delivery mechanisms are in fact quite similar when compared on other structural attributes. Whether these nominal legal provisions and the variation in their occurrence across delivery mechanisms are important in terms of fiscal effects remains to be demonstrated.

Tables 3–6 report the estimated spending elasticities for nominal grant traits. Aid outlays by CFDA program number were grouped by delivery mechanism and categories of nominal grant traits (e.g., service versus capital-oriented type A grant outlays). Because we have limited our analysis to only those federal outlays that involve cash transfers to general and special purpose governments we have included in the regression model the per capita amount of federal assistance received by each state (and its localities) not included in our definition of federal assistance. Finally, the level of per capita personal income was included in the regression model to control for the main within-state influence on state–local spending.

Table 1 reports the estimated spending elasticities for all 569 federal aid programs and their associated grant traits. The spending elasticities for each of the nominal grant traits is significant and always in the predicted direction. In the case of program content and environmental impact requirements the fiscal impact is quite pronounced. A 1% increase in service-oriented grant outlays is

Table 3. Estimated Elasticities Between Total State and Local Spending Per Capita and Selected Variables and Grant Traits: FY 1977 (T-Values)[a]

Equation No.	P.C. Income	Other Aid	Ser.	Cap.	A95	Non-A95	Eis	Non-Eis	High Match	Low Match	St. Pl.	Non-St. Pl.	Brd Ben.	Nrw Ben.	Brd El.	Nrw El.	R²
1	.923 (8.4)	.516 (5.7)															.760
2	.914 (8.1)	.425 (4.6)	.169 (3.0)	-.074 (2.2)													.881
3	.921 (7.6)	.435 (5.1)			.112 (2.7)	.035 (1.2)											.780
4	.938 (9.4)	.378 (5.7)					.194 (2.6)	-.014 (1.0)									.775
5	.938 (8.4)	.435 (5.4)							.026 (.4)	-.018 (.6)							.757
6	.929 (8.5)	.406 (4.6)									.062 (1.1)	-.003 (.1)					.760
7	.897 (8.5)	.350 (3.7)											.106 (2.2)	.039 (.3)			.757
8	.914 (8.1)	.425 (4.6)													-.117 (2.7)	.166 (3.0)	.762

[a] T ≥ 2.05; P ≤ .05.

associated with a .168% increase in total per capita state–local spending. Interestingly, capital-oriented aid programs have a mild substitutive effect on state–local spending, with a spending elasticity of − .074. A similar trend is found for aid programs requiring environmental impact statements. The imposition of this requirement is associated with a spending elasticity of .194, while the absence of this requirement has an insignificant but negative effect on state–local spending (− .014).

Eligibility and beneficiary standards have expected effects on state spending levels. Greater specificity of intended beneficiaries is associated with a spending elasticity of .106. Grant programs with broad eligibility standards have a substitutive effect on state–local spending (− .117), while narrow eligibility produced a significant and positive spending elasticity of .166. Required state plans and matching levels were not associated with significant spending elasticities. The latter finding is particularly surprising given previous research (ACIR, 1977; Cline and Whitman, 1978) which has found that programs with high matching requirements are signficantly more stimulative of recipient spending than those with low matching requirements. Our nominalization of this variable may account for the absence of a strong stimulative effect on state–local spending. A more plausible explanation seems to be the fact that matching ratios are generally too low to have a significant effect on state–local spending, independent of delivery mechanism and other grant traits. Only 41% of the 569 programs studied require recipient matching expenditures, and among these programs the average matching rate is only 21.6%, a rate which other researchers (Miller, 1974; Chernick, 1979) have found to be too low to effect significant fiscal stimulation.

Tables 4–6 report the estimated spending elasticities for grant outlays by nominal grant category and delivery mechanism. The first equation in each table reports the spending elasticity for all outlays of a given delivery mechanism. The remaining equations estimate spending effects for outlays by nominal grant categories for each delivery mechanism.

The spending effects of each grant type are consistent with those identified by Gramlich and others. Type C grants have the largest spending elasticity, followed by type B and A grants. When controlling for the effect of different categorical traits (Table 4) type A grants exhibit a moderate stimulative effect on state–local spending. In fact, controlling for six of the seven categorical traits produces spending elasticities which are larger than the spending effect for all type A grant outlays.

Service-oriented type A grants and those requiring environmental impact statements have the strongest stimulative effect among type A grants. A 1% increase in outlays for these programs produces between a .10% and .11% increase in per capita state–local spending. Interestingly, narrow eligibility standards, though associated with a larger spending elasticity than narrow eligibility grants, do not have a significant effect on state–local spending. High matching ratios for type A grants do make a modest difference in their stimulation of state–local spending.

Table 4. Estimated Elasticities Between Total State and Local Spending Per Capita and Selected Variables and Type A Grant Traits: FY 1977 (T-Values)[a]

Equation No.	P.C. Income	Other Aid	Total A Aid	Ser.	Cap.	A95	Non-A95	Eis	Non-Eis	High Match	Low Match	St. Pl.	Non-St. Pl.	Brd Ben.	Nrw Ben.	Brd El.	Nrw El.	R^2
1	.923 (8.4)	.412 (4.7)	.025 (1.7)															.749
2	.910 (9.4)	.297 (3.6)		.108 (2.4)	.054 (2.0)													.780
3	.909 (9.3)	.303 (3.7)				.101 (2.3)	.054 (2.0)											.778
4	.912 (9.5)	.291 (3.6)						.115 (2.5)	.055 (2.1)									.783
5	.902 (8.9)	.330 (3.9)								.066 (1.7)	.048 (1.4)							.766
6	.859 (9.1)	.232 (3.2)										.069 (2.7)	.020 (1.2)					.800
7	.894 (9.1)	.311 (3.7)												.087 (2.5)	.050 (1.7)			.773
8	.859 (8.1)	.343 (3.9)														.039 (1.0)	.078 (2.0)	.770

[a] T ≥ 2.05; P ≤ .05.

Table 5. Estimated Elasticities Between Total State and Local Spending Per Capita and Selected Variables and Type B Grant Traits: FY 1977 (T-Values)[a]

Equation No.	P.C. Income	Other Aid	Total B Aid	Ser.	Cap.	A95	Non A95	Eis	Non-Eis	St. Pl.	Non St. Pl.	Brd. Ben	Nrw. Ben	Brd. Elig.	Nrw. Elig.	R^2
1	.951 (9.4)	.392 (5.9)	.045 (.2)													.757
2	.940 (8.9)	.401 (6.0)		.125 (2.6)	.028 (.8)											.784
3	.961 (9.2)	.391 (5.8)				.017 (.6)	.056 (1.7)									.757
4	.936 (8.6)	.414 (6.2)						.014 (.4)	.023 (.5)							.752
5	.951 (9.2)	.404 (6.1)								.038 (.8)	.015 (.3)					.756
6	.953 (9.2)	.400 (6.0)										.119 (2.4)	.038 (.9)			.805
7	.971 (8.2)	.388 (5.6)												.027 (.6)	.051 (.15)	.758
8																

[a] T ≥ 2.05; P ≤ .05.

Table 6.   Estimated Elasticities Between Total State and Local Spending Per Capita and Selected Variables and Type C Grant Traits: FY 1977 (T-Values)[a]

Equation No.	P.C. Income	Other Aid	Total C Aid	Ser.	Cap.	A95	Non-A95	Eis	Non-Eis	High Match	Low Match	St. Pl.	Non-St. Pl.	Brd Ben.	Nrw Ben.	Brd El.	Nrw El.	R²
1	.946 (9.0)	.430 (7.1)	.065 (2.4)															.750
2	.991 (7.7)	.457 (6.2)		.024 (.6)	.009 (.3)													.752
3	1.01 (8.6)	.469 (6.9)				.035 (2.2)	.010 (.4)											.758
4	.942 (8.9)	.434 (5.9)						.008 (.3)	.007 (.1)									.749
5	.946 (9.0)	.405 (6.1)								.037 (2.8)	-.010 (.3)							.754
6	1.01 (8.6)	.469 (6.9)										.035 (1.2)	.010 (.4)					.758
7	.921 (7.1)	.429 (7.0)												.008 (.3)	.015 (.3)			.750
8	.961 (8.8)	.438 (7.1)														-.002 (.1)	.022 (.7)	.752

[a] T ≥ 2.05; P ≤ .05.

182

A spending elasticity of .066 is associated with high matching type A grants, a significant increase over the .025 spending elasticity for all type A grant outlays. These findings confirm our earlier hypothesis that the stimulative effect of type A grants is masked by nominal legal provisions associated with each type A grant. When controlling for the influence of these categorical traits, we observe a significant stimulative effect for type A grants.

The fiscal impact of type B grants is only marginally affected by controls for categorical traits. Only service-oriented grants and grants with highly targeted beneficiaries are associated with significant spending elasticities. The spending elasticities for both these categories of type B grants (.125 and .119, respectively) are larger than the spending elasticity for all type B grant outlays. It would appear that the unexpectedly high stimulative effect of type B grants is due largely to their service orientation and the highly targeted specification of grant beneficiaries. Both these characteristics are widely associated with type B grants, as confirmed by the discriminant function analysis in Table 2. The impact of nominal grant traits on the stimulative effect of type C grants is negligible. The effect of the delivery mechanism overshadows any impact the nominal legal provisions of each grant have on the delivery mechanism's stimulative effect. The direction and relative size of these spending elasticities are consistent with earlier hypotheses; however, in only two instances were the spending elasticities statistically significant. Type C grants with high matching rates and A-95 reviews both have significant but modest stimulative effects on state–local spending. Moreover, these elasticities are smaller than the total effect of type C grants on state–local spending. Given the rather cohesive structure of type C grants, it is not surprising to find that the fiscal impact of these aid programs is largely unaffected by the nominal legal provisions of each grant program. This is due largely to the fact that associated grant traits complement the categorical character of type C grants.

VI. DISCUSSION

The evidence presented suggests that the nominal legal provisions of different grant programs have a significant impact on the fiscal response of aid recipients, independent of the program's delivery mechanism (i.e., type A, B, or C grants). Moreover, these nominal grant traits reduce some of the indeterminancy in the fiscal impact literature. When controlling for the effect of various nominal grant traits, type A and B grants exhibited the expected level of fiscal stimulation.

These findings suggest that greater attention needs to be paid to the legal provisions of federal aid programs. More importantly, our findings suggest that Reagan's shift to type B block grants and revenue sharing may not achieve the desired effect, greater decentralization. If the nominal legal provisions of these block grants are not consistent with the goals of decentralization and greater discretion for recipient jurisdictions, it is unlikely that Reagan's new federalism will fulfill its goals. It is uncertain at this moment what the effect of these nominal traits will be on the implementation of the new block grants. The enabling legislation for these new block grants is silent on the question of A-95, state planning, and other crosscutting requirements. In some instances the question of coverage by these nominal aid provisions is an administrative decision. Thus the U.S. Advisory Commission on Intergovernmental Relations (ACIR) has noted:

> The federal government needs to clarify which cross-cutting requirements apply to block grants and how their implementation is to be shared between the federal government and recipient jurisdictions (1982).

In part the fight for the New Federalism is likely to continue not only in Congress but also in the agencies responsible for administering it.

NOTES

1.   The CFDA identifies 13 different governmental units eligible to receive assistance from among 569 aid programs. An eligibility score was constructed for each aid program by summing the number of governmental units eligible to receive assistance under each program. For the regression analysis the score was nominalized, using the median eligibility score to differentiate between programs with narrow and broad eligibility requirements.

2.   Matching requirements were nominalized for the regression analysis using a cut-off of 25% or below for low matching requirements and 26% and above for high matching requirements. For a more detailed discussion of this procedure see ACIR (1977a).

3.   The CFDA identifies 67 different categories of aid beneficiaries. A beneficiary score was constructed for each aid program by summing the number of program beneficiaries for each aid package. The score was nominalized in the regression analysis by using the median beneficiary score to differentiate between programs with narrow and broad beneficiaries.

4.   Some liberties were taken in classifying grant programs. Programs which employed a matching formula allocation device were classified as type A grants. Not all of these programs, however, are open-ended, as stipulated by Gramlich's definition. Gramlich's definition of type B grants identifies general revenue sharing as the only unconditional lump-sum grant. Our own definition relaxes the absolute unconditional nature of the delivery mechanism and identifies nonmatching lump-sum grants as type B grants. Type C grants are identified by the CFDA and pose no definitional problems.

REFERENCES

Bombardier, Gary (1975). "The Managerial Function of OMB: Intergovernmental Relations as a Test Case." *Public Policy* p. 23: 317-354.

Chernick, Howard (1979). "An Economic Model of the Distribution of Project Grants." in Peter Mieszkowski and William Oakland (eds.) *Fiscal Federalism and Grants-in-aid*. Washington, D.C.: Urban Institute, pp. 81-102.

Fox, William et al. (1977). *Economies of Size in Local Government: An Annotated Bibliography*, Washington, D.C.: U.S. Dept. of Agriculture.

Gramlich, Edward (1977). "Intergovernmental Grants: A Review of the Empirical Literature." in Wallace Oates (ed.) *The Political Economy of Fiscal Federalism*, Lexington: D.C. Heath. pp. 219-241.

Hicks, U.K. (1968). *Public Finance*, 3rd Edition, Cambridge: Cambridge University Press.

Hirsch, Werner (1964). "Local Versus Areawide Government Services." *National Tax Journal*, 34:331-339.

Miller, E. (1974). "The Economics of Matching Grants: The ABC Highway Program." *National Tax Journal*, 44:221-230.

Porter, David with David Warner and Teddie Porter (1979). *The Politics of Budgeting Federal Aid: Resource Mobilization by Local School Districts*, Beverly Hills, Ca.: Sage.

Reed, B.J. and Roy Green (1978). "City Management and Perceptions on Grant Administration in Small Cities: A Preliminary Examination of two National Surveys." Presented at the annual meeting of the Southern Political Science Association.

Saltzstein, Allan (1977). "Federal Categorial Aid to Cities: Who Needs it Versus Who Wants it." *Western Political Quarterly*, 30:371-383.

Schultz, C.L. (1974). "Sorting Out the Social Grant Programs: An Economists Criteria." *American Economic Review*, Supplement, pp. 181-189.

Stein, Robert (1981). "The Allocation of Federal Aid Monies: The Synthesis of Demand-Side and Supply-Side Explanations." *American Political Science Review*, 72:334-343.

——— (1979). "Federal Categorical Aid: Equalization and the Application Process." *Western Political Quarterly*, 32:396-409.

Steinman, Michael (1979). "The A-95 Review Process: Putting it in Prespective." A paper presented at the annual meeting of the American Political Science Association.

Whitman, Ray and Cline, Robert (1978). *The Fiscal Impact of Revenue Sharing in Comparison with Other Federal Aid: An Evaluation of Recent Empirical Findings*, Washington, D.C.: Urban Institute.

Wright, Deil (1982). *Understanding Intergovernmental Relations*, Monterey: Brooks/Cole.

U.S. Advisory Commission on Intergovernmental Relations (ACIR). (1977a). *Federal Grants: Their Effects on State–Local Expenditures, Employment Levels and Wage Rates*. Washington, D.C.: U.S. Government Printing Office.

——— (1977b). *Categorical Grants: Their Role and Design*, Washington, D.C.: U.S. Government Printing Office.

——— 1982. "Cross-Cutting Aid Requirements," Mimeo, Washington, D.C.

AMERICA'S INTERGOVERNMENTAL SYSTEM:

AN EXPANDED ROLE FOR THE STATES?

Henry A. Coleman and Colin L. Wood

I. INTRODUCTION

The future of urban areas is a subject of much concern and debate. The movement of individuals to, among, and within these urban areas suggests that they will play an important, diverse, and ever-changing role in the years ahead. Much of the fate of urban areas will be determined by their relationship with other levels of government, both federal and state, and the changes experienced by those levels of government. This is particularly true of state government. Localities are created by their parent state, and their activities and powers are governed by state law. Thus, local units of government are particularly sensitive to program or policy changes at the state level. State policies influence the revenues, expenditures, boundaries, and functions of localities.

Since the early 1960s, the authority of the states with respect to their local governments has been somewhat obscured or overshadowed by the policies and

Research in Urban Economics, Volume 4, pages 187-204
Copyright © 1984 JAI Press Inc.
All rights or reproduction in any form reserved.
ISBN: 0-89232-423-6

187

actions of the federal government. Primarily through its grants-in-aid policies, and the concomitant mandates and regulations, the federal government has exerted its influence over the policies, programs, and actions of both state and local government. On the surface, it appears that both state and local governments were at least passively involved in this usurpation of state authority by the federal government. Localities, especially urban local governments, willingly and sometimes eagerly responded to federal incentives to provide an expanded number and level of services. State governments were also the recipients of significant amounts of federal largess. Perhaps more importantly, states helped to undermine their own authority, especially with respect to urban areas, by being unable and/ or unwilling to respond to the sometimes unique set of problems confronting urban localities.[1]

The ability of state government to respond to local urban areas was influenced by a variety of factors including, most importantly, the ability of the state to provide (fiscal and nonfiscal) assistance to their urban jurisdictions. The willingness of the state to aid its urban areas was often a function of how well state legislatures reflected the importance of urban populations within the state.

In recent years, a number of steps have been taken that seek directly or indirectly to restore states to a place of prominence within the American federal system. These steps have been both internal, initiated at the state level, and external, initiated by actions taken by the federal government. The actions in question impact on both the ability and the willingness of state government to deal with the problems of their local jurisdictions. Unfortunately, neither the internal or the external steps have produced unambiguous results. Moreover, due to the recent nature of some of the actions taken, only preliminary or qualitative results are available.

In this paper, we examine some recent actions initiated at both the state and federal levels aimed in part at restoring states to a more prominent position within the American federal system. The list of actions examined is not meant to be exhaustive but instead to represent those actions that in our view have been most significant. Before examining these actions, we briefly review the role of state government within America's federal system, specifically with respect to localities. In the second section, we consider state and federal policy changes affecting the ability of states.[2] The next section examines evidence indicating the extent to which states are willing to assist their urban areas. Finally, the outlook for urban areas is reviewed in the context of the earlier discussion.

II. THE ROLE OF STATES

Within the American federal system, states play a multidimensional role. According to the U.S. Advisory Commission on Intergovernmental Relations (ACIR), states serve as direct service providers, regulators of private activities, agents on federal grants, public policy laboratories, and overseers of local government activities (ACIR, 1982b). These various dimensions of the state role are not assumed to be mutually exclusive and conceivably may even be in conflict from time to time.

As overseer of local government activities, state government exerts perhaps its greatest influence on urban areas. As summarized in *The President's National Urban Policy Report* (1982: 57):

> State governments have the authority to correct the imbalances in the fiscal capabilities of local governments within a state resulting from inappropriate boundaries, inequitable allocations of functions, and inadequate tax bases. It is the State governments that are in the best position to encourage metropolitanwide solutions to problems that spill over political boundaries, and to allow the creation of suitable neighborhood units of governance, where appropriate. And it is State governments that are capable of mobilizing the broad bases of support to tackle the economic, financial, and social problems that affect the well-being of the State as a whole as it competes with others to attract and retain residents and businesses.

Thus, both ACIR and the framers of the President's urban policy foresee broad and substantial powers and functions for state government. However, some debate continues to surround the role of states with respect to poor people (see Guzzardi, 1982) and poor localities. Moreover, within a particular state, questions remain as to whether the state should play a similar role for large and small cities, growing and declining cities, or cities otherwise experiencing disparate circumstances. This last set of issues will be considered in more detail during our later discussion of targeting.

III. LIMITS ON STATE GOVERNMENT ABILITIES TO AID LOCALITIES

States can best aid their localities by either decreasing the need for local expenditures or increasing local access to revenues. The former strategy would include situations in which the state government either directly assumed the responsibility for providing a service that was previously the responsibility of localities or where the state assumed a significant portion of the financial burden of providing a service.[3] The latter strategy, increasing local access to revenue, is manifested in state actions to finance local circuit breakers, establish special districts, increase local access to nonproperty taxes and other nontax revenues such as user fees, and finally, and perhaps most importantly, state fiscal transfers to localities. In each instance, urban areas in general and large urban areas in particular are believed to be the principal beneficiaries of the state strategies.

The ability of a state to pursue these strategies is primarily a function of its ability to generate revenue. The three principal sources of state revenue are taxes, federal aid, and debt.[4] The impact of recent public policy changes on each of these components of state aid will be considered in turn.

A. State Debt

State government issued debt has grown from $16.9 billion, and 3.6% of gross national product (GNP), in 1959 to $122.0 billion, and 4.8% of GNP, in 1980. Within the aggregate public sector, state debt has more than doubled, from 4.8% to 9.8%, as a percentage of all government debt over the same period. The cost of servicing state-issued debt has also increased significantly, from $453 million, or 0.1% of GNP, in 1959 to $6,763 million, or 0.3% of GNP, in 1980. As a percentage of state general revenue, debt service has increased from 2.5% in 1959 to 4.0% in 1980 (ACIR, 1981b).

Recent policies at the federal and state levels may impact significantly on the market for state debt. Most obvious is the impact of recent monetary policy. The tight money policy pursued by the Federal Reserve System has produced higher interest rates. These higher interest rates increase the costs of servicing state debt. Recent estimates suggest that each percentage point increase in interest rates will result in an additional $500 million per year in debt servicing charges for state and local governments (see Evans, 1982).

The market for state debt is affected by other recent changes in federal policies, although these impacts may be more subtle. The Economic Recovery and Tax Act of 1981(ERTA) has affected state-issued debt in two ways. First, ERTA introduced All-Savers Certificates, a tax-exempt debt instrument issued by financial intermediaries, and extended the features of Individual Retirement Accounts (IRAs). These competing tax-exempt debt instruments will drain off funds previously used to purchase state (and local) government tax-exempt securities. The increased competition for limited amount of funds available for investment in tax-exempt debt will put upward pressure on the rate of return that issuers must offer to attract new investors to this market and to induce existing investors to hold one type of debt rather than another.

The ERTA affects the market for state debt also through the reductions in (marginal) tax rates that it provides. These tax rate reductions change the incentives, at the margin, for individuals to seek tax-exempt securities and other forms of tax shelters in their attempts at tax avoidance. Again, to overcome this effect, state debt obligations must be made more attractive in terms of offering higher risk-adjusted rates of return, greater liquidity, etc. Any of these modifications will result in higher costs to states in issuing debt.

Policies initiated at the state level also contribute to the problems states encounter in issuing debt. Motivated in part by the desire to circumvent referenda requirements, restrictions on taxing policies for servicing debt, and other constitutional and statutory restrictions pertaining to full faith and credit debt obligations, the percentage of long-term, nonguaranteed, state-issued debt has increased significantly in recent years, from 49% of state gross long-term debt in 1973 to 56% in 1979. With nonguaranteed debt, the repayment of both the principal and interest is not backed by the taxing authority of the issuing jurisdiction but, instead, is contingent upon the successful operation of the sponsored project. In order to induce bondholders to accept these riskier forms of debt, risk premiums are generally required. This raises the overall costs of the debt issue.

B. Federal Aid to States

Federal aid to state governments grew substantially between 1960 and 1980. In 1960, federal aid to state governments totaled $6,382 million, 31% of state general revenue from own sources, and grew to $64,326 million, 38% of state own-source general revenue, by 1980. In addition to the dollar amount of federal aid to states, there was also a rapid increase in the number of aid programs, from 132 in 1960 to over 500 in 1980 (ACIR, 1981b). Much of the federal aid to states is routinely passed on to their localities, although the amount of state pass-through funds to localities is still very much an open question. Stephens and Olsen have estimated that over 31% of all federal aid received by states in 1977 was passed through directly to local jurisdictions and another 12% was passed through indirectly (Stephens and Olson, 1979). Estimates by ACIR suggest that the amount of pass-through funds is on the increase, from just over $7.3 billion in 1972 to $12 billion in 1980 (ACIR, 1981c). Concomitant with the growing importance of passed-through federal funds has been the growth of direct federal-to-local aid. Although direct federal aid to localities is only about one-fourth the size of state aid to localities, it has grown far more rapidly as a percentage of local government own-source general revenue since 1960 and, unlike state aid which is heavily concentrated in education, tends to support a broader range of local activities.

A second aspect of federal aid has been the associated growth of federal mandates and regulations. Between 1960 and 1970, over 160 mandates were imposed on states or their localities, either as direct orders or conditions for receiving aid. Between 1971 and 1978, the number of new mandates ballooned to over 1079 (Stanfield, 1980). The federal regulations on subnational jurisdictions are generally categorized as direct orders, crosscutting requirements, crossover sanctions, or partial preemptions (Beam, 1981). These various rules of behavior are generally considered to have significantly reduced the autonomy of states and added to their costs in that states pay, for example, 100% of the cost of crosscutting mandates (President's Urban Policy Report, 1982).

Recent changes in federal policies will potentially have a significant impact on the amount and type of federal aid to states, thus affecting a primary source of state revenues and therefore the ability of states to aid their localities. In the Omnibus Budget Reconciliation Act of 1981 (OBRA), an attempt was made to reduce both state government reliance on federal aid and the amount of influence exerted on state and local activities by the federal government as either direct orders or conditions for aid. OBRA significantly reduced federal aid to state and local governments below the FY81 level of $95 billion.[5] For FY82, state and local aid absorbed a third of total federal budget reductions even though such aid comprised only about 15% of the federal budget (Lawson and Stenberg, 1982).

To offset some of the impacts of the reduced federal aid, OBRA also changed the form of some of the remaining aid. Some 57 categorical aid programs were converted into nine block grants. Block grants presumably increase the amount of discretion exercised by the states over the grants. OBRA also reduced the amount of aid going directly from the federal to local governments.

The amount of discretion exerted by the states as a result of OBRA remains unclear for a number of reasons (see Coleman and Wood, 1981; Stanfield, 1981a). First, the number of programs consolidated (57) and their level of funding are small relative to the total number of federal programs and the total amount of federal aid. This suggests that the impact of OBRA on the entire federal grant-in-aid system is likely to be quite modest due to the small scale of the program. In addition, the changes contained in OBRA are to be phased in over a number of years. Thus, while all but three states moved immediately to take over the maternal and child care block grant, 11 states chose to defer assuming responsibility for the community services block grant and three states decided not to accept any of the new block grants that they were not required to accept (Stanfield, 1981a, 1982a, 1982b).

Second, many of the block grants were not stripped of the strings or conditions that had characterized the old categorical programs. Thus, the alcohol, drug abuse, and mental health block grant required states to allocate funds to those services in essentially the same proportions that had prevailed under the categorical programs. For some programs (e.g., community services and primary care), the amount of program funds that states may devote to program administration is restricted. In fact, new strings were attached where previously none had existed as in the case of the maternal and child health care block grant where states are prohibited from charging low-income people for services (Stanfield, 1981a).

Greater state flexibility is further questionable in that only a few federal aid programs (e.g., general revenue sharing, community development block grants, etc.) are truly considered as flexible by state and local officials. The percentage of total federal aid in the form of general purpose or broad-based grants peaked at 27% in 1978 and has declined steadily to 17.8% in 1981 (OMB, 1982). By this measure, grant flexibility for states and localities seems to be decreasing rather than increasing.

One final measure further supports the conclusion that state (and local) government discretion over grants is decreasing rather than increasing. Much of federal aid is channeled through subnational units of governments to individuals. With these programs, such as medicaid and AFDC (Aid to Families With Dependent Children), individuals, and not the state or local government, are the ultimate recipient and exercise the greater influence over the allocation of funds. Under OBRA, grants to individuals were reduced by about 4.5% versus 13.4% for grants to governments, relative to their 1981 level. As a percentage of total federal grants, grants to individuals have increased from less than 36% in 1960 to an (estimated) 45% in 1982 (ACIR, 1981b).

Finally, a variety of sorting out or New Federalism plans have been proposed or discussed. While each plan varies with respect to details, all attempt to redefine functional responsibilities and suggest how revenue sources are to be shared among levels of government (ACIR, 1982a). At this point, the implications for state revenue levels or discretionary authority under these proposals remain unclear.

C. State Taxes

State tax revenues have increased sharply over the years since 1960. In that year, state per capita taxes collected equaled $101.35 compared to $571.78 in 1979. However, over that same period, taxes per capita as a proportion of revenues per capita have declined, indicating the growing importance of nontax sources of revenues among the states. Within state tax systems, a number of other notable changes have also taken place. Among the most significant developments has been the number of states adopting growth-responsive or elastic revenue systems. In 1960, 34 states employed general sales taxes and 31 used income taxes. By 1981, the corresponding figures were 45 and 40, respectively. Perhaps more important, in 1981 only two states employed neither an income nor a general sales tax, whereas 36 states used both (ACIR, 1981b). The advantage of having a more elastic tax system is that tax revenues increase with real or inflation-induced income growth and without resort to politically sensitive tax rate increases or adoption or expansion of tax bases. This furthers the ability of states to generate tax revenue and renders the states better able to provide aid to their respective localities as well as to assume direct responsibility for the provision of more services.

As states began to rely more and more on income-elastic types of taxes, other types (e.g., motor vehicle fuel, tobacco products, alcoholic beverages, and property taxes) assumed relatively less importance. These other forms of taxes generally produce revenues that are far more stable or reliable than income or sales taxes.

However, actions by an individual state to modernize its tax system often do not produce benefits (or costs) for any (and certainly not for all) other states (see Walker, 1980) beyond perhaps a demonstration effect. Thus, even after updating efforts, considerable variations in individual state tax capacity and tax effort may produce wide divergences among states in terms of their ability to aid their localities. Recent work by ACIR (1982c) measuring state total tax bases shows that, in 1979, tax bases varied from 71% of the national average in Mississippi to 215% in Alaska. Similarly, tax effort ranged from a low of 63% of the national average in Texas to 172% in New York.

Again, recent actions at the state and federal government levels impact on state efforts to collect tax revenues, their principal source of revenues. In response to real or perceived threats of voter-imposed tax limitations, many states began to impose constraints on their own fiscal behavior. States adopted constitutional and statutory provisions indexing their tax systems, thereby at least partially offsetting some of the advantage gained by moving to a more elastic revenue system. In 1981, 18 states faced such restrictions, 14 of which were enacted after 1977 (ACIR, 1981b). In 1982, when states found it necessary to raise taxes, most states did not raise their major (e.g., income or sales) taxes. Instead, 13 states raised cigarette taxes, 18 raised taxes on alcoholic beverages, and 27 increased motor fuel taxes (Stanfield, 1982c). For a handful of energy-producing states, severance taxes produced sizable increases in revenues.

Recent federal policies have had their most dramatic impact on state tax collections. Passage of ERTA also reduced state tax revenues since many state tax systems are coupled to the federal tax system. Twenty-five states have tax laws that, for example, are automatically connected to the liberalized business depreciation provisions contained in ERTA. Citizens for Tax Justice has estimated that the loss to these states, unless offset by an explicit tax increase, would total $1.6 billion in 1982 and $15 billion through 1986. If the new laws governing business depreciation are adopted by the remaining states, state treasuries stand to lose $27.5 through 1986.[6]

The recession that began around the second quarter of 1981 may be the single most debilitating factor facing state tax revenue collections. Recession-induced revenue shortfalls have been significant, and they have affected nearly every state, although the problems posed by the shortfalls vary depending upon the fiscal strength of the state prior to the recession (see Gold, 1982; Gold et al., 1982). Hardest hit have been the states of the Northwest, ravaged by the impact of the housing industry slowdown on timber and wood production, and the Midwest, where manufacturing, durable goods, and the automobile industry have been particularly hard pressed. Michigan has seen its "rainy day fund," funds set aside during good times to help out during bad times, run dry to the point that further retrenchment may jeopardize essential services (Hoffman, 1982). Collectively, states have seen their surpluses, totaling 9% of expenditures in 1980, fall to 1.5% in 1982. In 1982, six states actually experienced year-end deficits despite the fact that all but one state, Vermont, have constitutions requiring balanced budgets (Gold et al., 1982). The recession points out one of the major disadvantages of modernized state tax systems. That is, unless growth (real or inflation-induced) continues to occur, revenues from elastic state tax systems will level off and may decline. States then face declining tax revenues, reduced budget surpluses, and stepped-up demand for services as, for example, AFDC and medicaid eligible individuals grow in number.

Thus, despite efforts to circumvent archaic restrictions on indebtedness, to streamline the federal grant system, and to modernize state tax systems, each of the major sources of state revenue is threatened by recent policy changes at the federal and state levels of government. The potential escalations in cost or disruptions in the flow of state revenues may seriously jeopardize a state's ability to provide assistance to its localities, especially the more troubled urban areas.

IV. STATE WILLINGNESS TO AID URBAN AREAS

Problems in evaluating the capacity of states to aid their localities, especially urban areas, often tend to obscure equally important concerns about the willingness of states to take such actions. The problems of state capacity to perform relative to willingness to perform are interdependent. Indeed, default by the states with respect to aiding their urban areas is one reason often cited for the initial federal involvement in the problems of urban areas (see Buckwalter, 1982; Elazar, 1974; Guzzardi, 1982; Stanfield, 1981b). This initial federal involvement has, as the previous section has shown, contributed in part to greater uncertainties concerning overall state capacity to aid urban areas.

State urban strategies have been the subject of a good deal of recent attention. In general, the actions of states show much diversity and few generalities. These state actions influence and are influenced by federal actions. Two key indicators of state desire to aid localities are how representative state governing bodies are of urban areas and the extent to which available state aid is targeted to urban areas.

A. Representative State Governments

Prior to 1960, the legislatures of state governments were alleged to be dominated by representatives from rural or nonurban areas. In addition, these legislatures were made up of representatives from geographical districts designed to contain widely varying numbers of individuals. Specifically, rural legislators represented districts containing fewer residences than their urban counterparts, thus violating the principle of "one man, one vote" (ACIR, 1981c). The result was that urban areas within states, and particular population elements concentrated within those areas such as blacks, were underrepresented in state houses across the nation.

In 1962, with the *Baker* v. *Carr* decision, and again in 1964, with the *Reynolds* v. *Sims* decision, the U.S. Supreme Court rendered landmark decisions that reapportioned state legislatures, furthered the "one man, one vote" principle, and increased the representativeness of state houses as state districts were changed to create more equitable geographical representation. That the state governing bodies have become more representative as a result is indicated in part by the fact that much of the post–World War II growth in state expenditures has been channeled into urban areas (Elazar, 1974). Where debate within state legislatures continues, it more often reflects intraurban rather than rural–urban conflicts.

Similarly, *Baker* v. *Carr* subsequent Supreme court decisions, and the Voting Rights Act of 1965 have resulted in greater minority representation at each level of government, including the state level. The number of black elected officials at the state level grew from 169 in 1970 to 323 in 1980 and blacks constituted 4.4 percent of state legislatures in 1982 (as compared, for example, to 3.9 percent of the U.S. Congress (Guzzardi, 1982).

While these gains in urban areas and minority representation have been important, severe problems still remain. State legislatures are characterized in many cases by favoritism toward well-to-do individuals. One measure of this pro-rich or anti-poor bias is given by a state's welfare contribution relative to its level of per capita income. The state share of welfare payments as a percentage of per capita income ranges from a low of 4% in Mississippi to a high of 26% in New York. Moreover, a type of regional bias in favor of the rich seems to exist, as the 11 states showing the lowest percentage are all part of the Deep South (Guzzardi, 1982).

B. Targeted State Assistance

A key indicator of state willingness to assist its urban areas is the extent to which state aid is targeted. Targeting refers to the process of channeling limited available resources in an effort to alleviate local needs that are seen as being most critical. In determining how well resources are targeted, a great deal depends on the concept of need adopted. The concept of local need may have many dimensions (e.g., social, economic, or fiscal) and can vary among localities, among states, and between the federal and state governments.

1. Targeting Objectives

Federal aid programs are directed primarily at alleviating problems of (social, economic, or fiscal) distress resulting largely from the loss of population and employment in urban areas. These programs fail to consider fully the difficulties encountered by localities undergoing rapid development or those in need of growth. At the state level, the interdependence of these problem areas receives greater consideration. Thus small town development will moderate pressures due to rural-to-urban migration, and containment of suburban sprawl will retard the general decline of urban centers. North Carolina, for example, follows a balanced-growth policy that emphasizes designated growth centers and regional balance through state placement of public services to achieve dispersed growth across substate regions. North Carolina, along with other states such as Oregon and Florida, pursues strategies designed to avoid future distress among localities rather than to address problems due to past decline (Warren, 1980).

While the above discussion suggests that the targeting objectives may differ among states and between the federal and state governments, with some states often focusing less on distress as a criterion for aid, there is, however, some evidence to suggest that states target assistance to distressed localities on a par with national government. Using 55 hardship cities as determined by the Nathan–Adams Hardship (Nathan and Adams, 1976) Index, Warren (1981) found that, while the majority of the cities received more federal than state aid, 60% of the 15 most distressed cities received more help from their state than from the federal government.

Other evidence of state fiscal transfers is less encouraging. In 1980, general purpose local governments in 49 states received general support assistance from 235 state revenue sharing programs. Less than half of his general support aid was directed at equalizing local disparities in taxing ability or need (ACIR, 1980).

In evaluating the extent to which states target assistance to urban areas, other forms of state aid, beyond direct fiscal transfers, must also be considered. These alternative forms of aid may be fiscal or nonfiscal, direct or indirect. The extent of targeting among alternative aid devices and whether the collective forms of state aid to localities are better targeted to measures of distress, relative to federal aid, are unresolved issues to date.[7]

The ACIR outlined five areas where state aid to distressed communities could produce significant impacts (ACIR and NAPA, 1981). The areas were housing, economic development, community development, fiscal reform, and local self-help. Within these areas, specific state actions were viewed as significant indicators of state willingness to aid urban areas. Housing indicators, for example, show state efforts at improving housing conditions for low- and moderate-income individuals. Similarly, fiscal reform indicators would indicate state efforts to equalize fiscal disparities among localities. Indicators for other areas were similarly defined.[8] ACIR findings show that, while states have made considerable strides in improving their efforts to assist their localities, few states have fully exploited the avenues for assistance available to them (Roberts, 1981). While these "deficiencies" in state performance toward their urban areas may be consistent with taste or preference for reduced or low levels of certain activities among residents of a state, they may also imply unwillingness on the part of the state to expand its activities.

2. Federal Disincentives

A number of disincentives are, however, implicit in federal policies and actions and may deter states from pursuing more constructive strategies for aiding their urban areas. The General Revenue Sharing (GRS) program operated by the federal government provides unrestricted funds to over 38,000 local units of government. By providing aid directly to local governments and restricting that aid to particular types of local governments, the federal government has propped up some of these general purpose local governments, provided incentives for them to remain in existence and at a level of operation beyond that that would have existed in the absence of the federal GRS aid, and changed the composition of local governments (Coleman, 1981a). Many of these "propped up" local governments are very small, perform few functions, and often employ less than one full-time worker (Stephens, 1979). Moreover, the disincentives provided by the GRS programs mean that states are less willing to establish limited-purpose local governments, such as special districts, where such jurisdictions may offer clear advantages over their general purpose counterparts.[9] In a similar vein, state incentives to improve local government efficiency through annexation, consolidation, and other boundary reorganizations may be thwarted if the reduced number of local governments reduces the number of such units eligible for federal aid (Warren, 1981).

Federal policies may also adversely affect state government incentives to grant localities greater access to nontax sources of revenue or to encourage the use of these alternative sources. The "tax effort" factor in the GRS formula discourages local use of user charges and fees, special assessments, and short- and long-term borrowing, even where these methods of generating local revenue may be more appropriate. Similarly, the federal tax code allows taxpayers to offset local tax payments against their federal tax liability. Similar offsets for user charges are not allowed.

3. Federal Incentives

Federal government policies and actions impact significantly on the willingness as well as the capacity of states to assist their localities. Although all of the states have not moved to assume responsibility for the new block grants to be phased in as a result of the OBRA, the overwhelming majority of the states have. Moreover, in a 13-state study recently completed, the General Accounting Office (GAO) found that, during the first 6 months after the takeover, the states were managing well despite the many adjustment problems remaining to be resolved (Fitzgerald, 1982). Efforts made by the National Governors' Association, the National Association of State Legislators, and other similar organizations to work with the Reagan administration in fashioning an acceptable "New Federalism" plan are further indications of increased incentives on the part of state governments resulting from federal policies.

Three other federal actions are generally agreed to have had positive impacts in improving state incentives in aiding localities (ACIR, 1979). First, the White House Conference on Balanced National Growth and Economic Development in 1978 attempted to increase the awareness and channel the efforts of state officials in the area of local economic development. Second, the first urban policy report issued by President Carter in 1978 identified a formal and useful role for the states in local community development and preservation. This report also served as something of a model for many of the state urban strategies that followed. Finally, federal grant funds, made available primarily through the Department of Housing and Urban Development's 701 Planning Assistance Program and the Economic Development Administration's 302 Program, were used to subsidize the development of urban strategies in many states (Warren, 1980).

V. THE OUTLOOK FOR URBAN AREAS

As stated at the outset, our ultimate concern in examining issues surrounding any expanded role for state government is the impact of that changed role on the present and future plight of urban areas in general and cities in particular. In our attempt to take a balanced approach, we have presented arguments implying that either expansion or contraction in the role of state government may result from recent changes in public policy. This ambiguity remains largely because of continuing debate over the role to be played by the states, greater volatility in the ability of states to assume whatever role, and conflicting signals regarding the willingness of states to become more active within America's federal system.

One of the basic unresolved issues is that of which level of government should have responsibility for providing for poor individuals. The timeliness of the issue was evident most recently during the discussions and negotiations surrounding President Reagan's New Federalism proposal (see Demkovich, 1981; Pierce, 1982). On the one hand, state legislators and governors argued that the federal government should be (financially) responsible for such individuals and that the major income-redistributive programs (e.g., medicare, medicaid, food stamps, and AFDC) should be financed totally by the national government. The Reagan administration, on the other hand, contended initially that food stamps and AFDC should be state responsibilities. State policymakers hold that if these services are made the responsibility of the states, individuals will have the incentive to relocate among states in pursuit of higher benefits. This will either depress benefit levels in all states or result in situations where the poor are left concentrated in a relatively few states. Moreover, it is argued that the ability to meet the true needs of the poor should not be limited to the resources of a particular state, which may vary considerably from the resources at the disposable of other states. Reagan officials counter that the needs of the poor and the attitudes toward assisting the poor vary widely across the states and that benefit levels should reflect these widely varying needs and attitudes. Resolution of these issues will impact significantly on the nature and size of the state role.

Also unresolved are the questions relating to the state role with respect to localities particularly disadvantaged by federal policies. This would include situations such as the impact of federal trade policies (e.g., automobile imports on Michigan localities, textile imports on southern cities, etc.), federal refugee resettlement policies (e.g., the impact of Cuban and Haitian refugees on localities in Florida, the impact of refugees from Indochina on localities in Washington and Arkansas, and the impact of Mexican immigrants on localities in Texas and California), and the impact of federal macromanagement policies that disproportionately burden certain localities. Since the impact of these federal policies are not shared equally by all states (and their localities), some responsibility for reducing or eliminating these local burdens may reasonably be said to rest with the federal government. Whether the federal government recognizes and accepts any responsibility in these areas will affect both the size and direction of change for the role assumed by the states. If the state role is defined to include the provision of income-redistributive services, they may be both less able and less willing to engage in other activities of importance to urban areas.

Urban areas are unlikely to benefit significantly from increased ability of states to offer assistance. State revenue systems now show greater cyclical sensitivity as a result of greater reliance on income and sales taxation. Moreover, secular growth in tax revenues may be reduced due to constitutional and statutory controls. The OBRA will offer only limited changes because of continued federal strings, the small scale of the programs involved, and the fact that most of the programs involved were already administered by the states, which suggests at least the possibility of only very modest changes in the overall flow of aid and administrative conditions as viewed by localities.

Perhaps the most difficult area to conjecture about involves the future willingness of states to come to the aid of their urban localities. Here, the signals are quite mixed. Coleman and Wood (1981) estimate that the reduction in general revenues experienced by localities as a result of OBRA ranged from 2% to 6%. Since the overall reduction in federal aid to subnational jurisdictions was larger than the decline in general revenues of localities, state governments apparently absorbed a disproportionate share of the reductions, thus reducing the amount of disruptions imposed on localities. A disproportionate amount of the federal aid cuts occurred in programs primarily benefiting urban areas, especially central cities.

States are also moving more to aid the borrowing efforts of their localities. The creation of special districts with borrowing ability, state bond guarantees, and state bond banks are all examples of recent initiatives taken by states to increase local government access to private capital markets (Peterson and Miller, 1981).

On the other hand, the desire of states to assist urban areas, particularly the central cities within urban areas, remains suspect. The study by ACIR and NAPA showed that, while states have taken significant strides in developing urban strategies and designing programs to aid urban areas, the strategies and programs currently available are vastly underutilized by most states. Moreover, despite landmark Supreme Court decisions, state legislatures still are not representative of the poor and minority residents within their total population. State legislatures have a higher percentage of black lawmakers relative to the U.S. Congress but the percentage (4.4%) is far less than the percentage of blacks in the U.S. population (11.7%; see O'Hare et al., 1982).Moreover, the pace at which the gap closes will likely slow as the annual rate of increase for black elected officials (at all levels of government) decelerated from about 27% in 1971 to less than 3% in 1981 (Cavanagh and Stockton, 1982). Within state houses, recent reapportionments will allocate a greater number of legislators to noncentral city areas to reflect continuing suburbanization and accelerating nonurban movements by the total population. This will occur as blacks are becoming more concentrated in central cities (O'Hare et al., 1982).

To fashion a general conclusion from these many diverse, disparate, and sometimes conflicting bits of evidence and observations is necessarily a risky undertaking. Much will depend on the outcome of the New Federalism proposal debates and the strength and duration of the expected economic recovery. At this point, however, it seems unlikely that the states will experience a significant increase in their role within the American federal system and, for central cities and urban areas, that might prove to be quite fortunate.[10]

ACKNOWLEDGMENTS

We wish to thank Stephen Barro and Helen Ladd for helpful comments on an earlier draft of this paper. The views expressed are our own and do not necessarily reflect those of the U.S. Department of Housing and Urban Development or the Scottish Development Department.

NOTES

1. In the discussion to follow, the ability and willingness of states to respond to the needs of their localities are treated as separate and distinct. We realize that this distinction is somewhat artificial and that the ability and willingness of states to respond may be inextricably linked or at least similarly affected by any given policy or policy change. Nevertheless, this distinction is conceptually possible and, in our view, quite useful in isolating the issues and impacts to be examined.

2. Federal policy may influence service needs as well as the capacity and willingness of states to address those needs. See ACIR (1981a).

3. For a general discussion of alternative forms of state aid to localities, see Coleman (1981b) and Sidor (1982).

4. States also receive revenue from user changes, licensing activities, and local-to-state fiscal transfers. These revenues are, on average, relatively modest and will be ignored hereafter.

5. The size of the aid reduction varies depending on whether one considers actual outlays or budget authority. Budget authority, funds available immediately or for future use, was reduced by 20%–25%; whereas outlays, or actual spending, for federal aid decreased only about 4% relative to 1981 levels.

6. The estimates are reported in Evans (1981).

7. A number of papers exploring these issues can be found in Marando and Zimmerman (1981).

8. A sampling of state indicators would include: (1) single and multifamily home construction; (2) customized job training and the use of industrial revenue bonds; (3) state revenue sharing, reimbursement for mandated programs, and education finance reform; (4) tax increment financing

and the creation of local development authorities; and (5) capital improvements. See ACIR and NAPA (1981).

9. In general, special districts are not limited by state debt controls, they offer greater flexibility with respect to the imposition of user fees, and they are less constrained by existing political boundaries. See ACIR (1981c) and Coleman (1981b).

10. For a somewhat different assessment of the situation and conclusion, see Warren (1980; 1981) and Teitelbaum et al. (1981).

REFERENCES

ACIR (1982a). Changing the Federal Aid System: An Analysis of Alternative Resource/Responsibility Turnbacks and Program Tradeoffs. A Staff Working Paper. Washington, DC (January).
――――― (1981a). The Federal Influence on State and Local Roles in the Federal System. A Commission Report A-89, Washington, DC: U.S. Government Printing Office (November).
――――― (1981b). Significant Features of Fiscal Federalism: 1980-81 Edition. Washington, DC: U.S. Government Printing Office (December).
――――― (1982b). State and Local Roles in the Federal System. Washington, DC: U.S. Government Printing Office (April).
――――― (1981c). State and Local Roles in the Federal System. In Brief. Washington, DC: U.S. Government Printing Office (November).
――――― (1979). State Community Assistance Initiatives: Innovations of the Late 70s. An Information Report. Washington, DC: U.S. Government Printing Office (May).
――――― (1980). The State of State-Local Revenue Sharing. An Information Report, M-121. Washington, DC: U.S. Government Printing Office (December).
――――― (1982c). Tax Capacity of the Fifty States: Methodology and Estimates An Information Report, M-134. Washington, DC: U.S. Government Printing Office (March).
ACIR and NAPA (1981). The States and Distressed Communities: The 1980 Annual Report. Washington, DC: U.S. Government Printing Office.
Beam, D.R. (1981). "Washington's Regulation of States and Localities: Origins and Issues." Intergovernmental Perspective, Volume 7, Number 3. Washington, DC: U.S. Government Printing Office (Summer) pp. 8-18.
Buckwalter, D.W. (1982). "Dillon's Rule in the 1980s: Who's in Charge of Local Affairs?" National Civic Review, Volume 71, Number 8. New York, NY: National Municipal League (September) pp. 399-406.
Cavanagh, T.E. and D. Stockton (1982). "The Characteristics of Black Elected Officials," A Working Paper. Washington, DC: Joint Center for Political Studies.
Coleman, H.A. (1981a). "An Evaluation of Financial Strategies." A Background Paper for the OECD, Ad Hoc Group on Urban Problems, Policy Project Group on Urban Public Finance Policies. Washington, DC: Mimeo
Coleman, H.A. (1981b). "State Targeting of Assistance to Localities." The Urban Interest, Volume 3 (Special Issue) pp. 83-96.
Coleman, H.A. and C. Wood (1981). "The Impact of Changes in Federal Grant-In-Aid Policy on Local Government Finances." Washington, D.C.: Mimeo.
Demkovich. L.E. (1981). "Political, Budget Pressures Sidetrack Plan for Turning AFDC Over to States." National Journal (September 19) pp. 1671-1673.
Elazar, D.J. (1974). "The New Federalism: Can the States Be Trusted?" The Public Interest. (Spring) pp. 89-102.
Evans. R. (1981). "State, Local Officials Assess Void Left by Budget Cuts: Ask Program Swap, Tax Turnback." Congressional Quarterly (Special Report: Federalism). (October 24) pp. 2047-2051.
Fitzgerald, S. (1982). "First Six Months of Takeover." Washington Post (August 27) p. A17.

Gold, S.D. (1982). "Federal Aid and State Finances." Legislative Finance Paper 17. Denver, Colorado: National Conference of State Legislatures, Fiscal Affairs Programs.

Gold, S.D., K.M. Benker, and G.E. Peterson (1982). "State Budget Actions in 1982." Legislative Finance Papers. Denver, Colorado: National Conference of State Legislatures, Fiscal Affairs Program.

Guzzardi, Jr., W. (1982). "Who Will Care for the Poor?" *Fortune* (June 28) pp. 34-42.

Hoffman, D. (1982). "Michigan, in Fiscal Crisis, Cuts and Cuts and. . ." *Washington Post* (September 7) p. A1 & A5.

Lawson, J. and C.W. Stenberg (1982). ""Rebalanced Federalism:" The States' Role and Response." Intergovernmental Perspective, Volume 8, Number One. Washington, D.C.: U.S. Government Printing Office (Winter) pp. 30-41.

Marando, V.L. and U. Zimmerman (eds.) (1981). *The Urban Interest* (Special Issue, Volume 3).

Nathan, R.P. and C. Adams (1976). "Understanding Central City Hardship." *Political Science Quarterly*, 91. (Spring) pp. 47-62.

Office of Management and Budget (1982). Federal Aid to State and Local Governments. Special Analysis H. The Budget of the U.S. Government, 1983. Washington, D.C.: U.S. Government Printing Office.

O'Hare, W.P. et al. (1982). Blacks on the Move: A Decade of Demographic Change. Washington, D.C.: Joint Center for Political Studies.

Peterson, G.E. and M.J. Miller (1981). "Financing Options for Urban Infrastructure." Final Report. Washington, D.C.: The Urban Institute.

Pierce, N.R. (1982). "Snelling: Both Sides Have Much to Lose if New Federalism Talks Don't Succeed." *National Journal* (March 6) pp. 420-421.

The President's Urban Policy Report (1982). Washington, D.C.: U.S. Government Printing Office.

Roberts, J.F. (1981). "Fiscal Issues Dominate As States Meet The Eighties." Intergovernmental Perspective, Volume 7, Number One. Washington, D.C.: U.S. Government Printing Office (Winter) pp. 19-29.

Sidor, J. (1982). "State Support for Local Actions: The Performance is Uneven." National Civic Review (June) pp. 298-302.

Stanfield, R.L. (1982a). "Block Grants Trickle Down." *Planning*, Volume 48, (February) pp. 10-14.

———(1981a). "For the States, It's Time to Put Up or Shut Up on Federal Block Grants." *National Journal* (October 10) pp. 1800-1805.

———(1980). "If You Want the Federal Dollars, You Have to Accept Federal Controls." *National Journal* (January 19) pp. 105-109.

———(1982b). "Picking Up Block Grants - Where There's A Will, There's Not Always a Way." *National Journal* (April 10) pp. 616-620.

———(1981b). "Reagan's Policies Bring Cities, States Together in a Marriage of Convenience." *National Journal* (December 19) pp. 2224-2228.

———(1982c). "States Find Fiscal Modernization Has Ironic Outcome - Empty Coffers." *National Journal* (August 7) pp. 1379-1381.

Stephens, G.R. (1979). "The Great Reform in Federal Grant Policy or What Ever Happened to General Revenue Sharing" in L.K. Hubbell (ed.), *Fiscal Crisis in American Cities: The Federal Response*. Cambridge: Ballinger Publishing Company.

Stephens, G.R. and G.W. Olson (1979). *Pass-Through Federal Aid and Interlevel Finance in the American Federal System 1957-1977*. Kansas City; NSF.

Teitelbaum, F., D.D. Arnold, and D. Lyttle (1981). "State Assistance to Distressed Cities." *Urban Interest*, Volume 3 (Special Issue) pp. 60-72.

Walker, D.B. (1980). "The States and the System: Changes and Choices." Intergovernmental Perspective, Volume 6, Number 4. Washington, D.C.: U.S. Government Printing Office (Fall) pp. 6-12.

Warren, C.R. (1980). The States and Urban Strategies: A Comparative Analysis. Washington, D.C.: U.S. Government Printing Office (September).

———(1981). ''Targeting of State Assistance: Opportunities and Realities.'' *The Urban Interest* (Special Issue) Volume 3, pp. 21-32.

LOCAL GOVERNMENT REVENUE:
TAX RELIANCE, REVENUE DIVERSIFICATION, AND METROPOLITAN FINANCE

Ronald C. Fisher and Janet E. Kohlhase

I. INTRODUCTION

The 1980s promise to be a period of change and uncertainty for local government finances.due to changes in demographic structure the age-old problem of how to maintain city revenues so as to provide adequate services to its constituents has intensified. Changing roles in federal-state-local relations may call for revamping, or at least a reevaluation, of revenue producing strategies at the local level. The final outcome of the continuing tax revolt is also unknown.

The central city vs. suburban exploitation hypothesis may have evolved into a more complex issue. The distinction between the central city and suburbs in terms of their economic role is no longer so clear. Suburbs now compete among themselves as well as with the older central city for residents, investment, and jobs. There may now be more substantial fiscal flows between all jurisdictions

Research in Urban Economics, Volume 4, pages 205-227.
Copyright © 1984 JAI Press Inc.
ISBN: 0-89232-423-6

in a metropolitan area. The time may be ripe for the reconsideration of local tax sharing schemes.

This paper examines the revenue prospects for one type of local government, municipalities, for the decade of the 1980s. This is accomplished by first reviewing past trends in municipal revenues. The prospects for local government revenues in the 1980s are discussed with an emphasis on what we feel will be the emerging issues for the 1980s. Finally we take an in-depth look at one possible solution to the problem of equitable sharing of local resources by simulating a Metropolitan Area Revenue Sharing (MARS) program for Detroit and Cleveland. Under the program, increased tax reliance on a local sales or income tax may be equitably shared among the jurisdictions within an SMSA.

II. LOCAL GOVERNMENT REVENUE SOURCES: PAST TRENDS

In order to analyze municipal fiscal prospects for the 1980s, past trends must be analyzed in their political, economic and demographic milieu. Cities exist in a federal system. As such they are subject to pressures from above, including declining federal or state aid, and pressures from below, such as the tax revolt.

A. Overview of Local Government Finances Since World War II

Spending by the total public sector has grown from more than one-quarter of GNP in 1954 to about one-third in 1981. Over the same period the share of state and local expenditures grew by almost a factor of two, from 8% to 13% of GNP. The most interesting occurrence in government spending is not the increase in share of GNP, but the turnaround in the trend of growth. State and local spending rose dramatically after World War II until it peaked at 15% of GNP in 1975, but over the next 6 years the share declined to 13%. This stands in sharp contrast to the recent rise in federal spending relative to GNP (which had been declining since 1975), from 21% in 1978 to over 23% in 1981.[1]

The turnaround in state-local spending can only be understood in context of the social milieu in which it occurred, the result of the interaction of four shocks to the state-local system and three long-range changes in American society and institutions.[2] The shocks to the state-local system were the 1974-1975 recession, the 1975 fiscal crisis of New York City, the taxpayer revolt against inflation-induced tax hikes and shifts in tax burdens, and the 1980 election. The effects of these shocks were deepened by long-term changes in demographic structure from a young, growing population to an aging one, a post-Watergate loss of confidence in the ability of government to solve domestic problems and to spend money efficiently, and a macroeconomy that changed from being characterized by high real growth to one with low real growth.

Moreover, the location decisions of residences and businesses have continued to affect the revenue generating ability of local jurisdictions and influence the demands for local services. Within SMSAs of more than 100,000 people, both population and employment have been decentralizing since 1960. In 1960, 63% of SMSA jobs were located within the boundaries of the central city; by 1970, the share had dropped by one-sixth to 54%.[3] For the same time period, commuting patterns also changed. The number of people living and working in the central city actually fell, whereas those living in the central city and working in the suburban ring and those living in the ring and working outside the SMSA rose dramatically.[4] Moreover, the historic trend since 1920 toward increasing urbanization came to a rather unexpected halt. From 1970 to 1978 the nonmetropolitan population grew 10.3% while metropolitan areas gained only 6.2%.[5] The increasing decentralization of economic activity places some suburbs in a position to integrate the activities of entire metropolitan areas and take on characteristics of the core cities of the past. These suburbs may also be equipped to integrate the areas beyond their metropolitan boundaries that have recently emerged as residential nuclei during the urban-rural turnaround.[6]

B. City Revenues Since 1960

All the above factors influence the revenue and spending of local governments. Table 1 illustrates how municipalities' reliance on different sources for general revenue has changed over the decade from 1970 to 1980. There is an abrupt turnaround in reliance on aid compared to own-source revenue over the decade. Reliance on intergovernmental aid grew and reliance on own-source revenue declined from 1970 to 1976, but thereafter the story switches to one of increasing dependency on own-source revenue.

Turning to the composition of own-source revenues, one finds ample evidence of tax diversification. Reliance on property taxes steadily declined over the decade, while local income taxes and local sales taxes comprised larger and larger shares of municipal general revenue. The reliance on user charges only increased significantly after 1975.

City reliance on all intergovernmental aid and state aid peaked in 1976, while reliance on federal aid peaked in 1978. In general, all cities receive more aid from their state governments than the federal government. About one-quarter of own-source revenue comes from state aid.

C. Local Sales and Income Taxes

In 1934 New York City instituted the first local sales tax to finance the welfare costs of the Depression. Data provided by the U.S. Advisory Commission on Intergovernmental Relations show that in 1980 over 5600 cities and counties in 26 states used some form of sales tax.[7] The growth in the use of sales taxes has been tremendous, but over 16,000 counties and municipalities could potentially adopt the tax if their states approved.

Table 1.   Sources of Municipal Government General Revenue,
1970-1980[a] (as percent of general revenue)

	1970	1972	1974	1976	1978	1980
A. Own Source Revenue	70.3	67.3	62.4	59.8	60.6	62.8
Taxes	51.3	48.8	44.0	42.2	42.5	41.1
Property	34.3	31.5	27.7	25.6	24.9	22.2
General Sales and Gross Receipts	5.6	5.3	5.4	5.6	6.1	6.7
Selective Sales and Gross Receipts	3.5	3.8	3.5	3.7	3.8	4.1
Income[b]	—	—	—	—	5.1	5.3
Other[b]	7.9	8.3	7.4	7.3	2.6	2.8
User Charges	11.7	11.3	11.2	11.1	11.7	13.0
Interest Earnings	2.3	2.0	2.9	2.6	2.2	4.1
Other	5.0	5.2	5.3	4.0	4.2	4.7
B. Intergovernmental Aid	29.7	32.7	37.6	40.2	39.4	37.2
Federal	5.0	7.2	12.4	13.4	15.6	14.3
State	23.2	24.0	23.7	24.9	22.1	21.0
Other Local Units	1.5	1.6	1.6	1.8	1.7	1.9
Total General Revenue	100.0	100.0	100.0	100.0	100.0	100.0

Notes:
[a] For fiscal years ending with the indicated digits.
[b] Income tax collections are included in the "other" category until FY 77-78.
Sources: U.S. Department of Commerce, Bureau of the Census, *City Government Finances*, Table 1, various
   years.

These local sales taxes are almost always administered by the state government and thus conform to the state sales tax base. Local sales tax rates vary from .5% to 7%. On average, cities that employ a local sales tax receive about 22% of all tax revenue from local sales taxes. The share of tax revenue generated by local sales taxes for municipalities is as much as 40% (in Denver, New Orleans, Oklahoma City, Tulsa, and Phoenix).

In 1932, Philadelphia was authorized to collect city income taxes, but it did not exercise its authority until 1940. By 1981, local income taxes were levied by about 4500 cities, counties, and school districts in 13 states, although most of the use occurred in just 4 states—Indiana, Maryland, Ohio, and Pennsylvania. The local income tax is not necessarily a large-city phenomenon. Of over 4000 cities taxing local income in 1980, only 52 of the cities had 1970 populations over 50,000.

The naure of the tax base and rate structure vary greatly from state to state, although uniform rates are most common. In most cases, nonresidents pay local income tax on their earnings where they work, although local income taxes are based entirely on place of residence in Maryland and Iowa.[8] In 1980, local income taxes provided from 21% (Baltimore) to 77% (Youngstown, Ohio) of tax revenue for those cities employing an income tax, with a substantial portion coming from nonresidents.

Like local sales taxes, the potential application of local income taxes is as yet unrealized. Only 13 states authorize local income taxes and only about one-fifth of counties and municipalities use it. States must authorize the taxation before muncipalities can take advantage of this significant revenue source.

To examine the potential for local sales and income taxes, retail sales and money income bases for 15 large cities and their SMSAs are shown in Table 2. The growth in per capita retail sales and per capita money income from 1972 to 1977 in these large metropolitan areas illustrates the trends in urban tax bases.

Over the 5-year period 1972 to 1977 the GNP state and local deflator rose by 46% and the CPI rose by 44.8%. Comparing the growth in tax bases with these figures allows one to assess the tax bases' flexibility with respect to inflation. The evidence shows that most growth rates of the per capita tax bases in these cities are about equal to or greater than the growth in the indices. The central cities are more likely than the suburbs to have lower growth rates of both income and retail sales than indices' growth rates. The difference in growth rates of retail sales between the central city and suburbs is greater than the difference in growth rates of income between those two areas. These findings are as expected since the newer suburban malls captured larger and larger shares of SMSA sales over the decade. Moreover, the pull of the suburbs for higher-income people continued over the decade of the 1970s.

The findings in Table 2 indicate that instituting a local tax on an income base may cause fewer fiscal disparities than a tax on retail sales (at least for center cities vs. suburbs). What is not included in Table 2 is an analysis of the disparities between *all* cities in a municipal area. Peterson (1976) finds that many of the older suburban cities close to the central city face the same problems of slowing rates of growth of tax bases as does the central city. This view is confirmed by the Fisher and Kohlhase study of Detroit (1982).

D. Tax Limitations, Circuit Breakers, and Homestead Exemptions

Concomitant with increased reliance on other sources of revenue has been a dramatic downturn in property tax reliance. These changes occurred amid a decade of property tax relief and reform. Included in this reform effort are circuit breakers and homestead exemptions and credit programs to aid the poor and the elderly, assessment by property class, and revenue diversification.[9]

Moreover, in the 1970s, as housing values grew faster than inflation with assessment increases not far behind, owners of residential property saw their effective property tax bill climb. Thus, voters increased the fervor of their call to revamp the property tax system. One form the public outcry took was embodied in the tax limitations movement most vividly exemplified by California's Proposition 13, passed in 1978. If representative democracy was unable to ensure

Table 2. Local Tax Bases, 1972 and 1977, Per Capita Retail Sales and Per Capita Money Income

	Retail Sales		Money Income	
	77	%Δ 72-77	77	%Δ 72-77
Baltimore SMSA	$3198	45.6%	$6255	51.4
Baltimore	2637	27.8	5242	45.5
Balance	3527	53.9	6855	52.3
Boston NECMA	3370*	38.6	6079	44.3
Boston	3160	16.5	5088	38.2
Balance	3426	45.5	6258	45.1
Chicago SMSA	3586	45.7	6795	50.1
Chicago	2938	24.4	5797	45.0
Balance	4081	60.5	7559	52.2
Cleveland SMSA	3448	54.4	6510	54.0
Cleveland	2757	34.0	4917	50.7
Balance	3754	61.7	7217	52.9
Detroit SMSA	3613	53.4	6805	54.7
Detroit	2360	20.2	5689	49.7
Balance	4117	62.6	7267	55.6
Houston SMSA	4043	65.6	6829	67.9
Houston	4545	59.5	6848	66.0
Balance	3269	81.1	6800	70.8
Los Angeles SMSA	3657	47.5	6612	48.4
Los Angeles	3691	47.1	6661	47.9
Long Beach	3535	50.6	7031	49.6
Balance	3642	47.5	6436	46.3
Milwaukee SMSA	3381	55.2	6535	56.4
Milwaukee	3097	50.1	5826	51.1
Balance	3610	57.8	7107	58.5

	Retail Sales		Money Income	
	77	%Δ 72-77	77	%Δ 72-77
New York SMSA	$3381	55.2	$6535	56.4
NYC	2409	22.7	5787	36.0
Balance	3660	42.1	7836	42.8
Philadelphia SMSA	3100	41.2	6075	47.6
Philadelphia	2466	28.4	5335	45.3
Balance	3469	46.4	6507	48.0
Pittsburgh SMSA	3306	59.6	6035	57.6
Pittsburgh	3500	47.7	5789	56.3
Balance	3260	63.3	6093	57.7
San Francisco-Oakland SMSA	3812	45.8	7650	56.3
San Francisco	4291	51.2	7676	54.7
Oakland	3368	37.8	6397	51.5
Balance	3708	60.2	7831	57.2
St. Louis SMSA	3345	54.1	6124	54.8
St. Louis	2797	30.1	5049	52.7
Balance	3492	60.4	6412	54.4
Seattle SMSA	3996	66.4	7224	67.0
Seattle	4636	63.4	7655	63.6
Balance	3630	71.0	7011	70.0
Washington, D.C.	3783	54.4	7994	49.5
District of Columbia	3093	26.3	7074	47.1
Balance	3981	58.2	8259	49.6
U.S.	3314	51.5	5751	51.7

Note: *Retail Sales are for Boston SMSA

Sources: 1. Retail sales (1972) Bureau of the Census, County and City Data Book 1977, Tables 3 and 4. (1977) Bureau of the Census, 1977 Census of Retail Trade, Vol. 11, Pt. 1, U.S. Summary, Tables 5 and 7.

2. Money Income and Population Bureau of the Census, Current Population Reports, Series P-25, No. 546-595, 645-699, 873 and 882-886.

210

that local officials would be sensitive to voters' demands,, then voters may have perceived that more stringent control over the workings of the tax would ensure that the acts of government might more closely approximate their desires. Whether the measures achieve this or make matters worse is open to debate. By June 1981, 45 states had imposed some sorts of limits on the use of local government property taxes. The phenomenon of limits is not new, but the pace was particularly rapid in the late 1970s. Of the restrictions in force in 1981, about one-third were enacted before 1970, one-third from 1970 to 1977, and one-third after 1978.[10] Moreover, during the 1970s several new methods for restriction emerged. The trend has been to diversify away from the traditional specific rate limit to limits on tax levies, and toward reform of the assessment process.

Other trends in property tax relief during the 1970s focused on attempts to make the property tax more progressive. In 1970, 28 states had some type of property tax relief for the elderly, and by 1981 every state had instituted some form of a circuit breaker, homestead exemption, or homestead credit scheme.[11] The impact of circuit breakers and exemption/credit schemes on property tax revenues is significant. Courant (1982:476) reports that Michigan property tax receipts in 1977 were reduced by 9% when adjusted for circuit breaker activity. The effects in other states are likely to be smaller since the Michigan circuit breaker program is one of the largest.

III EMERGING MUNICIPAL REVENUE ISSUES IN THE 1980s

These changes that occurred in the last several years herald the prospects for the 1980s. Not only is federal and state intergovernmental aid not expected to increase at anywhere near the rates prevalent in the mid-1970s, but nominal decreases in aid are expected. Significant increases in property taxes also do not seem likely. In the most recent ACIR poll on public attitudes toward taxes and expenditures, the property tax was picked as the worst tax by 33% of the respondents.[12] In addition the property tax bases of many older central cities are growing slowly or even declining. When these grim prospects for intergovernmental aid and property taxes are combined with a potential increase in fiscal responsibility for local governments as part of the emerging philosophy of the "New Federalism," it seems likely that cities and other local governments will be forced to look closely at other own-source revenues and innovative revenue options.

Among the city revenue options often discussed are (1) the use of local sales and income taxes, (2) greater use of charges, (3) property tax base sharing, and (4) regional tax schemes. It is expected that many new adoptions of local sales taxes and income taxes will occur in counties, cities, and school districts. Increases in rates for existing taxes are also likely. Already in 1981, Detroit and Cleveland raised their income tax on residents to 2% (for Cleveland, the second increase since it defaulted on its short-term notes in 1978). Also likely are more adoptions of special charges, such as licenses and fees, as municipalities strive to become more self-reliant. Another important revenue source, particularly for capital financing, is state and local government borrowing. Finally, the attractiveness of each of these revenue options, and the subsequent use of them by local governments, will be influenced by the significant changes that have already taken place in and that are planned for the federal income tax. In short, the relationship between federal taxes and state-local revenues may become very significant in the 1980s. Because the issue of benefit financing is considered in the chapter by Pascal in this volume, we shall concentrate on the others.

A. Local Sales and Income Taxes

In 1980, U.S. municipalities received, on average, about 19% of total general revenue from local nonproperty taxes, while all governments together depended on all local nonproperty taxes for about 9% of general revenue. These averages are somewhat deceiving both because they include various local excise taxes and because so many jurisdictions received no revenue from sales or income taxes. There are also wide variations of use of nonproperty taxes within states.

A more detailed discussion of the nature and use of local sales and income taxes is unnecessary here because of the existence of a well-known and substantial literature on this subject.[13] Rather, drawing on this literature, we turn now to a short discussion of the advantages and disadvantages of local sales and income taxes.

Four major advantages are usually noted: (1) these taxes have the potential to provide a substantial amount of revenue to local governments; (2) these taxes may be administered at relatively low cost if they can be collected in combination with the corresponding state tax; (3) either the income or sales base may be a relatively stronger tax base, particularly in terms of growth, than the property tax base in many older, central cities; and (4) these taxes can be a way for cities to tax nonresidents who consume city services or, with local income taxes, at least the commuter component of nonresident users.

On the other hand, a number of disadvantages have also been identified, including: (1) these local taxes, on top of similar state or federal taxes, may raise tax rates to high enough levels to create severe disincentive effects; (2) use of local sales or income taxes by only some jurisdictions in a metropolitan area, or by all jurisdictions but at different rates, can create new sources of inefficiency by influencing residential or firm location or shopping patterns; (3) there is evidence that in many metropolitan areas there is greater disparity between jurisdictions in local sales or income bases than in property bases; (4) moreover, those jurisdictions that have relatively strong income or sales bases may also be the jurisdictions with relatively strong property bases; (5) the distribution of retail sales in metropolitan areas is determined by the location of retail centers and thus may be essentially arbitrary and have little relation to expenditure benefits.

These advantages and disadvantages imply an important quandary for the use of local sales or income taxes to aid fiscally distressed cities in metropolitan areas. The problem has been noted with particular clarity by Stocker (1976:319):

> It appears that local sales taxes pose the same dilemma noted earlier for income taxes. They have a significant revenue potential for central cities. But unless they are confined to the largest cities, they result in egregious and indefensive fiscal disparities. On the other hand, if they are imposed only by large central cities they tend to accelerate the movement out of downtown.

One solution to this problem is to have widespread use of the local tax in metropolitan areas and then use an equalizing formula to allocate the revenue among jurisdictions. If the local tax is adopted across a metropolitan area, then any incentive to change the location of business or residence or purchases is reduced. The revenue can be distributed among municipalities on a per capita basis, thereby reducing fiscal disparities.

To some degree, this technique is already used in several states. In Kansas, Nevada, New York, North Carolina, and Tennessee, the revenue from countywide sales taxes is at least partially distributed to local jurisdictions in the county. Similarly, in Indiana, counties have authority to levy local income taxes with the revenue shared among counties, cities, towns, and school districts.

Of course, revenue sharing is not necessarily mandatory or done on an equalizing basis in all of these states. In Tennessee, for example, the local sales tax revenue is shared between the county and cities *only if* a city also levies a local tax, the shares determined by sales location.[14] In New York, the counties *may* enter into agreements with cities to share the county sales tax revenue, but are not required to. Nor are the features of any sharing agreement imposed. In 12 of the 45 counties (excluding New York City) the county government retains 100% of the sales tax revenue, while the others share revenue using such allocation factors as population, property value, and average daily attendance in schools. The sharing formula varies from county to county.[15] There is also an element of local choice in the county sales tax system in North Carolina, where the county commissioners can choose two alternative methods for sharing the sales tax revenue; either according to population *or* property taxes levied. At present, 65 counties use per capita sharing while the remainder allocate by property tax.[16] In Kansas, the county sales tax revenue is shared among counties, cities, and junior college districts according to *both* population and property tax levy, while in Nevada sharing is done on a per capita basis.

Although many states allow local sales or income taxes, only these six follow the prescribed policy of widespread use of the tax coupled with interjurisdictional sharing. As we have shown, when sharing exists it is not always on an equalizing basis. It is important to note also that the local sales or income tax sharing system often varies within states, allowing for specific local government situations or characteristics. In other words, these countywide sales and income taxes with intergovernmental sharing are, in a very important way, different from uniform state revenue sharing programs.

B. Capital Financing and Borrowing Costs

The fundamental changes in the nature of local government borrowing and the municipal bond market in the 1970s, combined with an expected increase in capital financing requirements of local governments during the 1980s, pose some serious potential problems. The borrowing costs of local governments have recently been and are expected to continue to be high, not only in historical terms but also relative to the costs of similar taxable issues. There has been a substantial narrowing of the traditional interest rate differential between similar taxable and municipal bonds and notes.

There are four primary reasons for this change in relative borrowing costs, three of which relate to recent changes in federal income tax law. First, the reduction in personal income tax rates—both that have occurred and that may yet occur—makes the purchase of income tax exempt securities less attractive. The reduction in the maximum personal income tax rate from 70% to 50% is likely to be the most significant rate change in this regard. Second, the new liberalized treatment of depreciation and the allowed transfer of depreciation deductions among corporations may be a way for some firms who might otherwise purchase municipal securities to eliminate federal tax liability. Third, the recent tax laws made available to many individuals new nontaxable savings options— All-Savers Certificates and Individual Retirement Accounts—that directly compete with municipal bonds and notes, particularly through tax-exempt mutual funds. All of these changes in federal income tax law are expected to reduce the supply of loanable funds to the municipal market and lead to higher municipal interest rates.

The fourth reason for the rise in municipal interest rates is the increase in the municipal market largely resulting from the proliferation of state and local government borrowing for nontraditional purposes. This fundamental change in the nature of municipal borrowing has been chronicled by Petersen (1981). In 1970, two-thirds of all new long-term municipal issues were so-called general obligation bonds backed by the general taxing authority of the subnational governments, while the remaining one-third of new issues were non-tax supported revenue bonds. By 1980, this relationship was exactly reversed, with revenue bonds comprising about 70% of new issues and general obligation bonds only about 30%. Similarly, the functions for which subnational governments borrowed also underwent substantial change in the 1970s. Petersen reports, for example, that in 1980 about 25% of tax-exempt borrowing was for housing purposes and 17% for industrial aid, compared to less than 1% for both functions in 1970. Borrowing for the traditional functions of education and transportation declined in importance during these years, from 29% to 9% for education and 18% to 4% for transportation. As Petersen puts it, "The traditional borrowing purposes and financing vehicles of state and local governments have been supplanted by a rapidly growing array of new uses of proceeds and new borrowing devices. . . . The rapidly growing areas of tax exempt financing are those that support essentially private sector investments" (1981:2 and 4).

Some researchers believe that the 1980s will be a period when many state and local governments face rising capital financing requirements as many older cities face massive costs of repair and maintenance just to maintain the existing capital stock. Many newer, growing cities, on the other hand, face large costs to create an infrastructure that either does not now exist or to improve the structure that is inadequate for the growing number of people living in those areas. Traditionally about half of the financing for subnational government capital projects comes from borrowing, with another large chunk from federal aid. With federal aid reductions, then, there may be a great demand for tax-exempt loanable funds in the 1980s that may either exacerbate the interest rate problems of municipalities or pose problems for selling these bonds.

For these reasons, during the 1980s attention may turn (or return) to two potential policy issues. There is expected to be continued debate about federal government restrictions on the use of industrial development bonds and housing mortgage bonds by state and local governments or their development entities. Under the current system, there is little incentive for any individual subnational government to restrict their use of these devices although it may be in the interest of *all* subnational governments to do so. Second, the old idea of a taxable municipal bond option with direct federal government subsidy of borrowing costs may be resurrected as a means of making more loanable funds available to subnational governments.

C. Relationship Between Federal and Subnational Government Taxes

Many of the taxes utilized by state and local governments in the United States are structurally linked to the federal income taxes both because many subnational governments have regularly adopted federal income tax base definitions and because many subnational government taxes are deductible expenses for individuals who itemize deductions against the federal personal income tax.

In 33 of the 41 states with broad-based personal income taxes, changes in federal exclusions or additions to income have automatic effects on state personal income tax revenues (ACIR, 1980).[17] In addition, in 12 or about 30% of these states changes in federal personal exemptions or deductions also automatically affect the state tax. Nor is this issue of common income tax base definitions limited to the personal income tax. It has been historically true that most all states adopt the federal Internal Revenue Code rules for asset depreciation for their state corporate income taxes.

A period of substantial structural change in the federal income taxes, then, can also be a period of automatic change in subnational government tax revenue. For example, changes in the holding period necessary for a capital gain to be deemed long-term, in the fraction of long-term capital gains excluded from taxation, in depreciation rules, and in special income exclusions are all in this category.

Because of many recent changes in the federal tax law, which represented some fundamental structural revisions, many states and localities have begun to uncouple their own tax laws from the Internal Revenue Code to reduce the subnational repercussions from federal tax changes. If the 1980s are a period of continuing structural change in federal income taxation, as some have proposed, then the issue of the relationship between taxes of different levels of government in the federal system will continue to be important. In that case, there may be reconsideration of many older public finance questions about the relative merits of tax coordination and tax autonomy and more explicit discussion about the appropriate structure (rather than level) of subnational government taxes.

The second way that the federal and subnational government tax systems are related is through intergovernmental tax deductibility. Both federal personal and corporate income taxes effectively allow deductions for state and local property, sales, and income taxes. In addition, 6 states allow deduction of federal corporate income taxes in determining state corporate income taxes while 16 states allow deduction of federal personal income taxes against the state personal income tax.

Our major concern here is with the federal personal income tax deductibility of subnational taxes, which reduces the individual cost in terms of foregone consumption from these state and local taxes. Federal deductibility of subnational taxes is not neutral between states nor between taxes within states. This occurs because the value of deductibility depends both on the distribution of taxes *and* income.

It follows that if there are reductions in federal income tax *rates*, then the net individual marginal cost of local taxation rises, with differential effects by tax and by region. This could be a major issue in the 1980s because of the tax rate reductions included as part of the 1981 Tax Act and because additional major changes may occur. For example, the 1981 reduction in the highest personal income tax rate from 70% to 50% substantially increased the net marginal cost of local taxes to taxpayers in that bracket.

One area of public finance where research is lacking is about the choice of tax mix by governments. Although there is some survey evidence and some recent econometric work (Inman, 1979; Fisher, 1981), the issue of the actual effect of these intergovernmental tax incentives on the choice of taxes by subnational governments has not been resolved. The early results suggest that exportability—including through tax deductions—has *some* effect on tax choice, although the magnitude of the effect is not certain. This seems to be a fruitful area for additional research in the 1980s.

D. Regional Taxation and Base Sharing

One possible solution for addressing the growing concern of urban fiscal disparities in the 1980s is the regional taxation concept of metropolitan area revenue sharing or MARS, a method by which specific tax receipts in a region are allocated to member localities by a formula that takes into account the characteristics of the local jurisdictions.

In many cases such a MARS program can provide the advantages associated with local sales or income taxes while at the same time avoiding many of the potential problems. That is, a single MARS program can provide substantial revenue to all jurisdictions in a metropolitan area at low cost. In addition, the entire metropolitan area tax base applies for each jurisdiction so that each is guranteed a strong base. Because the tax is levied throughout the metropolitan area, there are no location incentive effects, and because the revenue is allocated by formula fiscal disparities need not be created.

One potential advantage of MARS is as a means of compensating large cities for the cost of services consumed by nonresidents. Research by Neenan (1972) and Green, Neenan, and Scott (1974) has shown that there are substantial benefit spillovers in metropolitan areas, particularly when the financial responsibility for caring for the region's poor is taken into account. If the MARS program redistributes revenue to those cities that effectively provide services to residents throughout the metropolitan area, then it will reduce the inequities, and perhaps the inefficiencies, resulting from these externalities.

Moreover, MARS may be preferable to alternatives often proposed and used to compensate for these externalities. If local income taxes are used by some cities to tax commuters, then only a portion of the other residents in the SMSA are contributing toward financing city services in this way. But, Greene et al. find that commuters often already pay the cost of city services they consume as commuters, without this local income tax. Therefore, to ensure that it is all noncity residents who contribute to these city service externalities, a regional tax is preferred to a commuter tax.

In addition, a regional tax with formula allocation may be preferred to a combination of increased state taxation and increased state aid for the opposite reason. Many of the local government services that generate external benefits, such as police services, city libraries and museums, city transportation facilities, and city redistributive services, provide those benefits almost exclusively within the metropolitan area. One is hard pressed to justify, therefore, on equity grounds, *state* subsidies for these regional services. As we have already seen, the mechanism for sharing countywide sales tax revenue in New York, North Carolina, and Tennessee varies among counties in each state. These three states have explicitly recognized that a common statewide aid program does not allow for regional differences in fiscal structure to the extent regional programs can.

A traditional argument for metropolitan taxation is as a way for the older cities in a metropolitan area to capture part of the tax base growth in the other, perhaps newer sections of the SMSA. But there are other SMSA advantages to sharing tax base growth besides aiding the older central cities. If the tax is levied throughout the metropolitan area, then the tax itself will not distort location decisions by either consumers or firms within that area. Moreover, if if all jurisdictions share equally (for example in per capita terms) from tax base growth in the SMSA, then potentially damaging tax competition between local jurisdictions may be reduced. MARS may therefore be a way to improve not only the relative fiscal position of central cities but also the allocation of resources within the metropolitan area.

When public finance specialists consider regional tax sharing plans, what is usually thought of is a property tax base sharing plan similar to the one used in the Minneapolis-St. Paul metropolitan area. Under that program, increases in the commercial or industrial property tax base anywhere in the metropolitan area are shared among *all* jurisdictions in the region according to formula. This type of tax sharing differs in several important ways from the MARS program we propose. First, only a portion of the tax base is shared in the Minnesota program, and, second, local governments retain the right to levy different property tax rates on that shared base.

A number of criticisms have been levied at the idea of metropolitan sharing programs, some of these criticisms arising from the specific form of tax base sharing used in Minnesota. For example, Bahl and Puryear (1976) argue that regional tax schemes may not achieve all their potential advantages. First, regional taxes applied countywide may not be very redistributive or advantageous to the older central cities because often many of the local jurisdictions in central counties share the fiscal problems of the larger cities. Greater redistribution is possible with metropolitan area taxes, although the implementation of those taxes may be less likely. Second, there is concern that likely allocation factors—population, income, or property value—usually work to the disadvantage of those fiscally distressed localities that the tax sharing program may be partly designed to assist. A third concern is that the adoption of a regional tax may increase the regressivity of the overall local tax system. For example, substitution of a regional sales tax for local property taxes may increase regressivity partly because these taxes are "exported" at different rates. Finally there is concern about intrajurisdictional redistribution. Most local jurisdictions are not perfectly homogeneous, and certainly large central cities are quite heterogeneous. Equalizing jurisdictional resources is not equivalent to equalizing the tax burdens of all individuals with equal income.

In summary, Bahl and Puryear argue that "the most likely forms of regional taxation are those least likely to reduce metropolitan fiscal disparities'' (Bahl and Puryear, 1976:333). Implicit in this notion of likelihood are the numerous political constraints that some believe will prevent truly significant change by regional taxation.

Another potential difficulty with regional taxation, one that has been emphasized by those evaluating the Minnesota property tax base sharing program, is the reduced incentive for local governments to accept or attract tax base that will be shared. In the Minnesota program, 40% of increases in the commercial and industrial base is shared, leaving 60% of any project to provide property tax revenue to the jurisdiction of location. It is clear that, with less revenue going to a jurisdiction, there may be less incentive for that jurisdiction to attempt to attract or retain new investment.[18] Sometimes it is possible for the public service costs associated with a specific commercial or industrial project to be even larger than the property tax revenue generated to the host jurisdiction. In such a situation, all jurisdictions have an incentive to encourage capital investment in the metropolitan area but not in their specific jurisdictions.

A MARS program based on a metropolitan area sales or income tax may not discourage localities from attracting investment, however. Unless the MARS revenue is intended to substitute for a large fraction of current property tax revenue (rather than for existing local sales or income taxes), then property tax revenue from a capital investment will go to the host jurisdiction to compensate for the service costs of the project. The attendant income or sales tax revenue will be shared.

It is impossible to evaluate these questions about the relative advantages and disadvantages of regional tax programs, including MARS programs, without specific empirical evidence. Because we believe it is possible that regional taxation may be an important policy issue in the 1980s, we begin the process of presenting this empirical evidence in this paper.

III. METROPOLITAN AREA REVENUE SHARING (MARS)[19]

The objective of this section is to clarify three issues about tax base sharing: (1) the potential redistributive effects of simple allocation formulas (population, income, etc.); (2) the relative redistributive effects of countywide compared to metropolitan areawide taxation; and (3) the nature of the revenue distribution and changes over time in that distribution from both sales and income tax based MARS programs.

We selected the Detroit and Cleveland areas for study because both are large, fragmented urban areas with older major central cities that have recently experienced serious fiscal problems. Local income taxes are used by cities in both SMSAs in addition to local property taxes. The Detroit SMSA covers 6 counties with a total 1980 population of about 4.4 million. The 15 cities in the SMSA with population of at least 50,000 in 1980 serve as the basis for our comparison of regional revenue sharing to local taxation. In population, they vary from 1.2 million residents in Detroit to 54,000 in Roseville. The Cleveland SMSA consists of 4 counties, with 80% of the SMSA population in the central county of Cuyahoga and 30% in the city of Cleveland. The 15 cities in the Cleveland SMSA with a 1980 population of at least 25,000 are included in the analysis.

A. Tax Sharing Formula

In selecting a formula to allocate local sales or income tax revenue among local jurisdictions, it is desirable to maintain simplicity. Much of the knowledge gained from research on U.S. general revenue sharing can be applied so that errors are not repeated. Particularly, one should avoid unnecessary and harmful incentives. Thus allocation on the basis of population or income or property value is probably acceptable because the data are usually available and because no strong incentives to change allocation variables would result (assuming there is already an effective mechanism to prevent underassessment). On the other hand, allocation according to property tax collections, all tax collections, or tax effort should probably be avoided because of the obvious incentives involved.

If metropolitan area tax revenue is shared on a per capita basis, then all jurisdictions in the SMSA receive *equal* per capita shared revenue and the growth of per capita shared revenue in every jurisdiction depends only on the growth of SMSA-wide variables and not on any jurisdiction specific variables. Each jurisdiction receives per capita shared revenue equal to the SMSA per capita amount. If follows that the *per capita shared revenue* to each jurisdiction rises or falls equally over time as the SMSA per capita tax base rises or falls. Specifically, if the SMSA per capita tax base increases, then the *per capita* shared revenue to a central city would increase even if the population of the central city declines.

B. Metropolitan Area Revenue Sharing in Detroit

We first examine the potential economic effects of a retail sales tax across the Detroit SMSA with the revenue allocated to cities and townships in the SMSA according to population. We assume a 1% tax rate applied to a retail sales tax base excluding sales of food, medicines, and most services. This 1% retail sales tax in 1977 would have generated per capita revenue of about $26.70 per resident. Such a MARS program would have generated a substantial amoung of revenue for these cities, including $33.5 million for the city of Detroit. Among these cities the MARS revenue would have varied from a low of 4% of the general revenue to a high of 16%.

C. Metropolitan Area Revenue Sharing in Cleveland

The MARS program in the Cleveland SMSA is also based on a 1% sales tax levied across the SMSA, although in this case on a base consisting of total retail sales. This base probably overstates any likely sales tax base, while the base excluding sales of food and drug stores used for Detroit probably understates potential revenue. This 1% retail sales tax in 1977 would have generated per capita revenue of about $34.29. As before, if the total sales tax revenue were allocated by population, each municipality would have received $34.29 per resident. This MARS program would have generated nearly $21 million for the city of Cleveland in 1977.

D. Distributional Effects of MARS

A summary of the distributional effects of these MARS programs among the 15 cities examined in both the Detroit and Cleveland SMSAs is given in Table 3. In each panel of the table, the per capita tax base provided by the sales tax based MARS program is compared to the per capita tax bases from separate local government use of sales, property, and income taxes. For various ranges of the ratio of the per capita MARS base to the per capita total tax base, the entries in each case show the number of cities whose population is growing or declining, whose per capita income is greater or less than the SMSA average per capita income, and whose per capita property value is greater or less than the SMSA average, as is appropriate for each tax comparison.

First, one can compare the per capita shared base received with MARS to each city's per capita retail sales tax base. If the MARS base is greater than the per capita retail sales in a city, that city gains from MARS compared to separate city sales taxation. From the data at the top of Table 3, it is apparent that the distributional pattern of MARS compared to separate local sales taxes is not clear. While some low income or property value cities do better with MARS, others would have done better with separate local taxation, at least in 1977. Of course, if one of these cities' per capita retail sales grew slower than the SMSA per capita retail sales since 1977, that situation could have changed.

Separate local sales taxes are not necessary, or even likely, to be the alternative to MARS. Thus the comparison of the MARS base to both local property and income tax bases is also reported in Table 3. The ratio of the per capita MARS base to the per capita property tax base is strongly negatively correlated with per capita income in Detroit. (− .75), but less strongly correlated with income in Cleveland (− .28). From Table 3, the MARS base to property base ratio is less than average in 7 cities in the Detroit SMSA, 6 of which have above-average per capita income, while of the 11 cities in the Cleveland area that lose with MARS compared to the local property tax, 7 have above-average income. In the Detroit case, those cities that would gain most from a metropolitan wide sales tax shared on a per capita basis compared to the property tax tend to be

Table 3. Distributional Effects of Sales Tax Based MARS Compared to Local Taxes, for 15 Cities in the Detroit and Cleveland SMSAS, 1977[a]

MARS vs. Sales Tax

MARS BASE PER CAPITA RETAIL SALES	POPULATION GROWTH > 0	POPULATION GROWTH < 0	PER CAPITA INCOME > SMSA AVE	PER CAPITA INCOME < SMSA AVE	PER CAPITA PROPERTY VALUE > SMSA AVE	PER CAPITA PROPERTY VALUE < SMSA AVE
Greater Than 1.0	1 2	3 7	3 4	1 5	1 3	3 6
Less Than 1.0	5 2	5 4	6 5	5 1	6 2	5 4

MARS vs. Property Tax

MARS BASE PER CAPITA PROPERTY VALUE	POPULATION GROWTH > 0	POPULATION GROWTH < 0	PER CAPITA INCOME > SMSA AVE	PER CAPITA INCOME < SMSA AVE
Greater Than SMSA AVE	1 1	6 3	3 2	5 1
Less than SMSA Ave	5 3	2 8	6 7	1 4

MARS vs. Income Tax

MARS BASE PER CAPITA INCOME	POPULATION GROWTH > 0	POPULATION GROWTH < 0	PER CAPITA PROPERTY VALUE > SMSA AVE	PER CAPITA PROPERTY VALUE < SMSA AVE
Greater Than SMSA AVE	2 1	3 5	1 1	5 5
Less than SMSA Ave	4 3	5 6	6 4	3 5

Note: [a] Top entry is number of sample cities in Detroit SMSA with those characteristics. bottom entry is number of sample cities in Cleveland SMSA.

222

the cities with lower per capita income and those whose property values are growing more slowly. The trend, although weaker, is similar in Cleveland.

Compared to separate local income taxes, this MARS program clearly favors cities with below average per capita property values and is roughly neutral with respect to growing or declining cities. Similar to the above case, the ratio of the MARS base to the local income tax base is very strongly and negatively correlated with per capita property value in Detroit ($-.84$) and still negatively correlated in Cleveland ($-.25$). In these cases, then, those cities that would benefit from a metropolitan area sales tax shared on a per capita basis compared to local income taxes are those cities with lower per capita property values and, obviously, lower per capita incomes.

One misconception about allocation by population should be cleared up. Even if a city's population declines, its *total* shared revenue from this type of MARS scheme could increase. For example, although Detroit's population fell by 10.5% from 1972 to 1977, its total shared revenue from this MARS program would have risen by 35.2% because per capita SMSA retail sales rose by 51%.

E. County vs. Metropolitan Area Tax Sharing

One can also investigate the redistributive effects of a *countywide* sales tax with the revenue allocated to cities in the county on a per capita basis and compare those results to the MARS programs above. It is not immediately obvious whether fiscally distressed cities would have been better off with a metropolitan or countywide revenue sharing program. For example, with the MARS program, Detroit receives $26.71 per capita but only $24.85 per capita from county revenue sharing. On the other hand, Pontiac, a city whose fiscal problems are at least as bad as Detroit's, would have received $26.71 per capita from MARS but $36.37 per capita from county sharing. In the Cleveland area, 1977 per capita retail sales in the older central county of Cuyahoga were slightly greater than the per capita sales in the entire SMSA. It is true that, from 1972 to 1977, retail sales grew more slowly in the central counties of both SMSAs than in any other part of the SMSAs. Although even countywide sales tax based revenue sharing would have provided substantial redistribution in 1977, the growth of retail sales suggests that the degree of benefit to cities in the older central part of the SMSA would have declined over time.

In sum, it is not possible, based on this evidence, to determine whether countywide tax sharing programs would be preferred on distributive grounds to metropolitan areawide tax sharing. Clearly, nonwealthy cities in wealthy counties prefer countywide sharing while even wealthy cities in nonwealthy counties may prefer SMSA-wide sharing.

F. Constraints and Conclusions

Some conclusions about the sales tax based MARS program in these metropolitan areas are possible.

1. These MARS programs have *no revenue disparities* because every municipality receives equal per capita revenue. Also, per capita revenue grows equally in all municipalities.
2. Allocating the metropolitan areawide sales tax revenue on a *per capita* basis serves to *equalize* the distribution of resources among municipalities in the metropolitan area, both compared to the local property and income taxes. The degree to which this is so is expected to vary substantially for different metropolitan areas.
3. The metropolitan area sales tax can be administered at relatively low cost by piggybacking on the existing state sales tax.
4. The MARS program can be easily administered because population data are readily available on a timely basis.

It seems clear that the main constraint to enactment of such a MARS program is political opposition by those municipalities whose local sales tax base is very strong or opposition by individuals who believe that the implicit tax substitution would not be to their advantage. The first reason for opposition is easier to deal with. In the Detroit SMSA there is no prospect of separate local sales taxes, so the MARS program would not remove existing taxing authority from any jurisdiction. In addition, all jurisdictions have the option of reducing other local taxes and substituting the shared sales tax revenue. In times of dissatisfaction with the property tax, the opportunity for property tax rate reductions of 5%-15%, which would be afforded by these sales tax based MARS programs, may be attractive to many cities. This may even be true for cities that lose from MARS compared to separate local taxes, if MARS is the only viable means of providing property tax relief by tax substitution.

It remains to inquire whether uniform per capita distribution of regional tax revenue is realistic or politically viable and whether statutory action by state legislatures, which might be required to enact MARS, can be expected. On the first point, as previously noted, per capita distribution of countywide taxes is already used in several states. Moreover, as we have shown, per capita distribution has the characteristic of being perceived as fair while at the same time redistributing revenue compared to current local taxes. The second question is more problematic. It does seem likely that state legislatures will be forced by some of the issues discussed in this paper to make some changes in existing revenue sources or use new revenue sources during the 1980s. One can only speculate about whether metropolitan area tax schemes, or MARS in particular, will be adopted.

In the end, of course, the rationale for any regional tax program, including a MARS scheme, must rest on a desire of the residents of the metropolitan area to support public services throughout the SMSA, an inherently redistributive effort. Moreover, these residents must be convinced that it is necessary to accomplish this objective locally rather than through a state or federal aid program.

ACKNOWLEDGMENTS

We thank John Bowman, Robert Ebel, and Michael Wasylenko for helpful comments and Lynn Farris for analyzing revenue sharing in Cleveland.

NOTES

1. Shannon and Calkins (1982) p. 24, Table 1. The change in relative shares is due to the greater growth rate of federal expenditures. See *The Economic Report of the President*, 1982, Table B-75.

2. *Ibid*, p. 24.

3. *U.S. Census of Population 1960*, Table 302, and *U.S. Census of Population 1970*. At the time of this writing the 1980 data are not yet available; however, the trend toward increasing decentralization is expected to continue.

4. Between 1960 and 1970 the number of people living in a central city of an SMSA and working in the ring increased by 70% while the number living in the ring and working outside the SMSA increased by 96%.

5. *Current Population Reports*, Series p. 25, no. 873, February 1980, Tables 5, 6, 7. Chalmers and Greenwood (1980:534) discuss five cumulative causes and consequences of the urban-rural turnaround.

6. The increased taxes of ring area cities could contribute to the increased urban-rural migration. Citizens may perceive lower tax burdens even further from the core than the suburban ring. See also Chalmers and Greenwood (1980).

7. See ACIR, *Significant Features of Fiscal Federalism*, 1979-1980 edition, Tables 77-79.

8. See ibid., Table 88.

9. These are just a few of the attempted relief measures. Others include business tax abatement, user charges, exemption of certain property classes, and phase-out of personal property tax. See Gold (1979) for a thorough discussion.

10. ACIR (1981), Table 20.

11. See Gold (1979), Chs. 3 and 4, for descriptions of the various types of programs.

12. Acir (1981), p. 4.

13. See, for example, Mikesell (1971), ACIR (1974), Stocker (1976), Bowman and Mikesell (1977), Gold (1979), and Rodgers (1981). The 1974 ACIR report on local revenue diversification remains perhaps the most comprehensive statement on the topic, although valuable insights and more current data are provided by all the other articles.

14. This information about county sales taxes in Tennessee was provided by the Tennessee County Services Association.

15. New York county sales tax information was provided by the New York State Association of Counties and Sales Tax Distribution Office, New York State Department of Treasury.

16. This North Carolina County sales informaltion was provided by the North Carolina Association of County Commissioners.

17. The effects of federal tax changes on subnational government revenues are *automatic* in the sense that they occur with no legislative action by subnational government. Obviously, by changing the state or local tax law these revenue losses can be avoided.

18. This problem does not always accompany tax base sharing. In fact, many jurisdictions use

tax abatement as a device to attract firms, suggesting that removal of *some* of the tax base does not discourage local jurisdictions from seeking more investment.

19. The analysis of MARS in the Cleveland SMSA was prepared by Lynn Farris.

REFERENCES

Advisory Commission on Intergovernmental Relations (1974). *Local Revenue Diversification: Income, Sales Taxes, and User Changes.* Report A-47, Washington, D.C.: (October).

Advisory Commission on Intergovernmental Relations (1980-81). *Significant Features of Fiscal Federalism, 1979-80 Edition.* Edition, Washington, D.C.:

Advisory Commission on Intergovernmental Relations (1981). *Changing Public Attitudes on Governments and Taxes, 1981,* Report S-10, Washington, D.C.

Bahl, R. W. and D. Puryear (1976). "Regional Tax Base Sharing: Possibilities and Implications." *National Tax Journal,* Vol. 24, (September), pp. 328-335.

Bowman, John H. (1981). "Urban Revenue Structures: An Overview of Patterns Trends and Issues." *Public Administration Review,* Vol. 41, January, pp. 131-143.

Bowman, J.H. and J.L. Mikesell (1977). "Fiscal Disparities and Major Local Non-Property Taxes: Evidence From Revenue Diversification in Indiana, Maryland, Ohio, and Virginia." *NTA-TIA, Proceedings of the Seventieth Annual Conference,* pp. 412-422.

Bowman, J.H. and J.L. Mikesell (1978). "Revenue Diversification Within Metropolitan Areas: Effects on Disparities and Central City—Suburban Fiscal Relationship." *The Review of Regional Studies,* (Winter), pp. 66:78.

Chalmers, James A. and Michael J. Greenwood (1980). "The Economics of the Rural to Urban Migration Turnaround." *Social Science Quarterly,* Vol. 61, (December) pp. 524-544.

Courant, Paul N. (1982). "The Property Tax." In Harvey E. Brazer (ed.), *Michigan's Fiscal and Economic Structure,* Ann Arbor, University of Michigan Press.

Fisher, R.C. (1981). "Local Government Demand Studies With Intergovernmental Tax Incentives." Presented at the Eastern Economics Association Meetings, Philadelphia, (April).

Fisher, R.C., and Janet E. Kohlhase (1982). "Fiscal Problems and Policies of the Cities." In *Michigan's Fiscal and Economic Structure,* H. Braxer, (ed.), The University of Michigan Press, Ann Arbor, pp. 854-892.

Fisher, R.C., J.E., Kohlhase, and L. Farris (1982). "Metropolitan Area Revenue Sharing: Evidence from Detroit and Cleveland." Michigan State University.

Gold, S.D. (1979). *Property Tax Relief,* Lexington, Mass.: Lexington Books.

Greene, K.V., W.B. Neenan, and C.D. Scott (1974). *Fiscal Interactions in a Metropolitan Area,* Lexington, Mass.: Heath Publishing.

Inman, R.P. (1979) "The Fiscal Performance of Local Governments: An Interprelative Review." In *Current Issues in Urban Economics,* P. Mieszkowski and M. Straszheim, (eds.), The Johns Hopkins University Press, pp. 270-321.

Lauson, Jean and Carl W. Stenberg (1982). "Rebalanced Federalism: The States Role and Response," *Intergovernmental Perspective,* (Winter) Vol. 8, pp. 30-41.

Michigan Statistical Abstract (1980). D. Verway, (ed.), Graduate School of Business Administration, Michigan State University, (September).

Mikesell, J.L. (1971). "Local Government Sales Taxes." Chapter 10 in J.F. Due, *State and Local Sales Taxation,* Public Administration Service, Chicago.

Neenan, W.B. (1972). *Political Economy of Urban Areas,* Chicago: Markum Press.

Petersen, John E. (1981). "The Municipal Bond Market: Recent Changes and Future Prospects." Washington, D.C. Government Finance Research Center, Municipal Finance Officer's Association.

Peterson, George (1976). "Finance." In *The Urban Predicament,* W. Gorham and N. Glazer (eds.), Washington, D.C.: The Urban Institute.

Reschovsky, A. (1977). "New Strategies for Metropolitan Area Cooperation: Sharing Rather than

Competing for Business Tax Base.'' *NTA-TIA, Proceedings of the Seventieth Annual Conference*, pp. 155-162.

Shannon, John and Susannah Calkins (1982). "The New Formula for Fiscal Federalism Austerity Equals Decentralization." *Intergovernmental Perspective*, Vol. 8, (Winter), pp. 23-29.

Stocker, F.D. (1976). "Diversification of the Local Revenue System: Income and Sales Taxes, User Charges, Federal Grants." *National Tax Journal*, Vol. 24, (September) pp. 312-321.

U.S. Bureau of the Census (1970). *Census of Population 1960*, Washington. D.C.

U.S. Bureau of the Census (1977). *Census of Retail Trade*, Geographic Area Services, Washington, D.C. 1972.

U.S. Bureau of the Census (various). *City Government Finances*, Washington, D.C., 1969-1980.

U.S. Bureau of The Census (1980). *Statistical Abstract of the United States: 1980* (101st edition), Washington, D.C.

U.S. Bureau of the Census (1980). *Current Population Reports*, series p-25, no. 873, (February).

U.S. Congress, Joint Committee on Taxation (1981). "The Economic Recovery Tax Act of 1981." Washington, D.C.: U.S. Government Printing Office.

THE POST MUNICIPAL CITY

Anthony H. Pascal

I. INTRODUCTION

The financing of local government is becoming increasingly problematical as the American federal system begins to negotiate the final decades of the twentieth century. New ways to pay for, produce, and deliver the services traditionally provided by municipal government are being sought.

This paper attempts to sketch the rudiments of a new approach to local public finance. In searching for solutions it stresses the stripping away of nonessentials, the employment of market-oriented mechanisms, and the imposition of direct charges to beneficiaries. At the same time the paper seeks to deal with the equity issues posed by the suggested reforms. The ideas contained here are offered in order to stimulate a wide-ranging exchange on possible futures for the local public sector.

As a shift from the predominance of manufacturing to the primacy of service-

Research in Urban Economics, Volume 4, pages 229-241
Copyright © 1984 JAI Press Inc.
All rights of reproduction in any form reserved.
ISBN: 0-89232-432-6

based economic activities marks the passage from the industrial to the postin-
dustrial society, so the impending alteration in the nature of local government
might be referred to as the arrival of the postmunicipal city. The city of the
future will look much more like a private sector firm and much less like the
municipal bureaucracy we are used to seeing.

The Fiscal Pressures on Local Government

An era of fiscal restraint is upon us. Resistance to tax increases, formal fiscal
controls, tax base erosion, and the decline in grants from federal and state
government have all contributed. The retrenchment now visible comes after a
long period of growth in the prominence of subnational government.

In 1965, the average American spent about one-seventh of personal income
on state and local taxes. By 1979, that figure was almost one-fifth, an increase
of more than 25%. Taxpayers noticed the difference. Opinion polls document
the increasing disenchantment with the amount of taxes levied and the way in
which they are being spent. The public registered its displeasure directly in the
voting booth; by 1975, almost three-quarters of local bond and tax override
elections were failing (Pascal and Menchik, 1980).

Even more dramatic was the epidemic of fiscal limitations measures that swept
the country in recent years. Notable is the speedup in the adoption of financial
controls on state and local government during the 1970s; 25 states joined the
movement during that decade. Only 16 states remain without any limitation
measure. The measures naturally vary in scope and effectiveness. Some merely
constrain growth, but others such as in California, Idaho, and Massachusetts
significantly reduce customary levies (Pascal and Menchik, 1979).

Many factors help explain the containment of government. The rapid postwar
rise in tax burdens, the shift in government spending away from universalistic
and toward redistributive programs, rapid inflation combined with stagnant real
incomes, and rising distrust of politicians and governmental institutions have all
alienated large fractions of taxpayers. The result has been a resistance to further
tax increases and a tendency to vote for candidates and ballot initiatives which
promise to reduce the scale of government.

The tax and expenditure limitation measures and the outflow of jobs and people
from the nation's larger old cities have recently constrained some sources of
state and local revenue. Local own-source revenues (adjusted for inflation and
changes in population but excluding federal grants) grew steadily during the
1960s. Their progress was much more volatile in the following decade, and
since 1974 they have declined when measured in real per capita dollars to a
point where they now stand below the 1969 figure. State own-source revenues
peaked in 1976.

Federal grants in the last half of the 1970s accounted for about a quarter of
all state and local spending. Compared to previous years, federal transfers flowed

freely from 1960 to 1978. The Carter administration cut grants sharply, and under Reagan federal aid to state and local governments has dropped even further. Federal aid reached its peak (real per capita dollars) in 1978; since then it has fallen to about the 1974 level. Local governments have also gotten accustomed to a growing level of grants from state capitals. Between 1965 and 1975 subventions from the states supported a growing fraction of spending by cities. But as limitation measures increasingly constrain the states' own financial freedom— between 1977 and 1980, 38 states reduced taxes or adopted lids on their own taxes or expenditures—this form of assistance will dwindle. Grants from states dropped from over two-fifths of municipal own-source revenue in 1975 to about one-third in 1980 (ACIR, 1981:59).

A reduced local tax base, due to social and economic changes in the city, increasingly widespread legal limits on taxes and spending, and the downward trend of grants from higher levels of government combine to present the local policymaker with a serious dilemma. On one hand the city's diminished ability to finance services forces retrenchment. On the other there is the need to satisfy the vociferous demands of urban inhabitants. The citizens remaining in town are increasingly those most in need of public services: the old and the poor. Cities also face growing unfunded pension obligations, particularly for the uniformed services. Moreover, municipal infrastructure—roads, bridges, sewers, and fire and police stations—need constant repair and renovation.

II. REFORMING THE SERVICE FINANCE AND DELIVERY SYSTEM IN MUNICIPAL GOVERNMENT

A potential comprehensive solution, which combines a system of market-like mechanisms, is gaining increasing attention. For example public officials are awakening to the promise of pricing/rationing devices for rationalizing the provision of services with a high private good content. Recommended reforms often feature charges directly on the beneficiaries of the services cities provide. A decided advantage of user charges stems from the fact that they may be imposed on all users, even nonresidents. Instead of assuming that tax and grant shortfalls should dictate reduction in scale of operations, cities are beginning to approach their citizens as potential consumers to whom they offer public services on a fee basis. But appropriate reforms go beyond the application of user charges. Below I indicate how special assessments and neighborhood-specific taxes might be employed. I also discuss departures in procedures for allocating labor and capital across service agencies and the prospects for interjurisdiction sales of services based on a network of jurisdictional specializations. I present some ideas for a multipurpose public service voucher as a means of maintaining vertical equity.

A. Utilizing Benefit-Based Financing

User charges, fees-for-service, and special assessments are examples of benefit-based financing; they hardly constitute new ideas in local finance. But some critical facts are becoming clear. First, local government people are sometimes unaware of the myriad possible applications of benefit-based financing, including those applications which have proven successful in practice. Second, many officials worry about the inequitable effects of benefit-based financing because they fear the switching from taxes to charges will inevitably shift the financial burden of government toward lower income groups. Third, cities often lack technical expertise to design fee schedules which reflect the often shifting cost and demand conditions that particular services operate under.

That is, officials recognize the potential of the benefit-based approach for raising revenues. They are open to the argument that this approach would make government more efficient since it would encourage people to consume only as much service as they are willing to pay for. What they often fail to realize is that many applications are technically feasible and that equity protections can be built into benefit-based financing so as to safeguard the welfare of lower income groups.

Requiring the public to pay directly for services promises to reduce waste in consumption. In theory consumers will purchase increments to the point where marginal gains to them equal additional costs. Thus, collaterally, an important criterion governing the employment of user charges is the ability to identify benefits and beneficiaries (ACIR 1974:63-77). If the benefits are not visible to and largely appropriable by the potential consumer of the services, few will volunteer to pay. Trash collection then is highly amenable to financing through user charges while traffic control is not.[1]

A second choice criterion for the employment of charges as against taxes is based on the prospect for economizing behavior in the use of public resources. Services in which consumption levels are sensitive to price differentials are good candidates for the application of user charges. From this perspective parking fees may be more appropriate than sewer service charges. Ease of administration constitutes an additional selection criterion (ACIR, 1974:63-66). The costs of monitoring production and consumption also affect the feasibility of switching to benefit-based financing. Additional obstacles to the extension of the user charge mechanism lie in the difficulty cities have in calculating price elasticities, marginal costs, and the distribution of benefits (Stocker, 1976:320).

Municipalities derived one-third of their own-source revenues from charges and fees in 1980, whereas in the early 1970s less than a quarter of own-source revenue was raised in this fashion. Although three-quarters of all cities claim to be making increasing use of charges and fees, those under fiscal limits have been the most avid in adopting beneficiary charges (Shannon, 1982). A majority of the public feels it is the single best way for government to raise more revenues (Shannon, 1982).

Opportunities for the establishment of user charges at the local government level occur in water distribution, education, hospitals, solid and liquid waste disposal, some aspects of fire protection, parking and road usage, recreation, and for licenses and permits. User charges can often be imposed for specific components of services which in general have a high public good content. For example, crowd control at public events or special patrols at shopping centers may be financed through user charges, while other more general aspects of police protection are financed through taxes (Mushkin and Bird, 1972:24-25).

Many capital-intensive municipal services could be funded through special assessments. These are charges made by a government against a landowner for a public improvement adjacent to his property which, while generally beneficial to the community, is especially beneficial to the landowner assessed. They differ from taxes in that there is a direct relationship between the value of the benefit received and the amount of the assessment. Also, unlike most taxes they are usually one-time payments. Equity protections can be integrated into special assessment financing. For example, the collection of assessments that finance improvements redounding to the benefit of property owners (e.g., street lighting and repairs, sewer projects, etc.) could be deferred until the sale of the individual parcels so affected (Shoup, 1980). Low income property owners could then vote for special assessments that generate net gains to the value of the property, but would be relieved of cash flow problems. Except in the smallest jurisdictions a steady state would soon evolve in which revenues from deferred assessments would be equal to what they would have been without the deferral feature.

Generally, the adoption of benefit-based approaches need not imply the abandonment of redistributive objectives. For example, rights to consume basic levels of certain services (e.g., library privileges, emergency medical care, etc.) could be guaranteed to the poor—say by the issuance of vouchers—while other consumers would pay fees based on cost of production. Adjusting the price of a service to the characteristics of its consumers has become more feasible with newly available technologies. The Washington (D.C.) subway system collects lower fares in certain low income neighborhoods and from senior citizens and handicapped persons, for example. Or, prices for particular services (e.g., parking charges at local parks, adult education, etc.) might vary along with the average income level of the neighborhood. To extend the applications, standard amounts of some services might be provided free of charge while consumption of additional increments would require a fee (e.g., trash collection, some social services).

Systematic thinking on this subject will generate many other promising applications for the principle. Police, fire, health, and education services are the big ticket items in local government. Paramedic services provided by the fire department would seem particularly suited to benefit-based financing since consumption of this good has minimal spillover on other persons. On the other hand, it is sometimes argued that emergency medical service is a truly "free" good, at least at currently demanded levels, since it is usually provided by a corps of firefighters who need to stand by anyway. Police protection for certain properties such as warehouses, industrial parks, and shopping centers could also give rise to special charges. The technical feasibility is suggested by the frequency with which these facilities hire their own private security guards. It may even prove feasible to impose charges for emergency services on those at fault in auto and other accidents. Some jurisdictions have begun to impose fees for responding to false alarms in home and business security systems.

B. The "Essential City" vs. the "Responsive City"

The ideas contained in the market-oriented approach need to be integrated into new structures for local finance. Required is a fiscal plan for the postmunicipal city. Even in the age of austerity cities will have to provide public goods to be financed out of tax revenues and whatever higher level subventions remain. But for services above the basic, bare-bones level, fees, charges, assessments, and sales of services comprise the best method of financing city activities. Below is laid out in a step-by-step fashion a series of reforms for the consideration of those who preside over the future of cities faced with inadequate revenues.[2] The reforms emerge from a comparison of the "essential city" and the "responsive city."

1. Projecting Available Revenues

The first task for a city contemplating fiscal shortfalls is to decide how far it can go under traditional tax financing. Forecasts of future population and pace of economic activity will permit an estimate of returns from the property tax, sales tax, and other local sources. A straightforward projection of current fees would be appropriate at this juncture. Assumptions will be necessary to project future levels of grants-in-aid from higher levels of government. Complications will arise to the extent that maintenance of effort provisions affect the magnitude of categorical grants, since the coming austerity promises to reduce local tax collections. However, as the relative importance of categorical grants diminishes, this particular problem recedes over time.

2. Identifying Essential Services

The resources available from the projected revenues are not all usable for the production of services. There are in most cities fixed charges which make first claim. Some are contractual, such as for pensions or for interest on accumulated debt. Others are constitutional, as for elections. These charges may absorb 30-40% of city revenues.

The next step involves the determination of what can be supported with the projected revenues minus the fixed charges. Local priorities need to be identified so as to be able to screen the traditional services for inclusion in what might be called the essential city budget. Cost for all activities so identified must then be adjusted for the effects of future inflation.

In most cities the essential budget will need to ensure:

- The continuation of central administrative functions such as mayor and council, city attorney and clerk, land use control and the like.
- The protection of life and property, including such services as fire suppression, building inspection, and police response to emergencies. (Snow removal is often considered part of emergency services because it is necessary to provide access for emergency vehicles.)
- the maintenance of core infrastructure. Although opinions will differ on the degree of need, some actions must be taken to sustain the continuing usability of public capital facilities.

In general, the essential services have a high content of pure public good, or are goods for which it is relatively costly to exclude those who do not pay charges. Depending on local sensibilities, the list of essentials might also include some minimum redistributive functions as well.[3] Inevitably, the list of services to be included in the essential city will be determined in part by political factors.

C. Financing the Essential City

The first necessary comparison is to ascertain whether foreseeable revenues will cover the budget necessary to support the chosen list of essential services. To the extent that the revenue forecast exceeds the essential service budget, additional services could be added to the essential core.

The above calculations combine to delimit what we might call the "essential city," the basket of services which can be supported out of currently predictable taxes and grants. Beyond the levels anticipated, attempts to increase taxes are likely to lead to taxpayer resistance—as when tax overrides are defeated—or to taxpayer revolts—as when Proposition 13 or Proposition 2 1/2 is adopted. And grant levels above what are currently scheduled—perhaps even in nominal terms— do not seem likely given current attitudes in Washington and in most state capitals. For many American cities foreseeable revenues will support little more than fixed costs, stripped down central administration, hard-core protection, and low level of maintenance on roads, sewers, and vital public facilities.

D. Organizing the Responsive City

All of the other agreeable things cities tend to do, i.e., those services with a high merit good content, will likely have to find other sources of finance. They must become part of the responsive city and cease to be part of the essential city. Parks, swimming pools, golf courses, zoos, arts and crafts classes, after-school recreation, libraries, street sweeping, refuse collection, health clinics (except for inoculation against communicable diseases) can be financed by some combination of benefit-based financing and sales to other jurisdictions.

The responsive city is to be manifested through a new public management entity, the "revenue center." For the responsive services city agencies should behave as do private providers, selling the services they produce at prices based on long-term costs of production and the strength of local demand. The agency should be cut free of as many bureaucratic restrictions as possible so that it

- Determines its own product line
- Retains some of the net revenues (i.e., over and above cost of doing business) with which to pursue expansion or to reward particularly productive employees
- Arranges to secure inputs efficiently by hiring employees or services from the central administration or from private suppliers through contracting out.

1. Load Shedding

The failure to encounter sufficient effective demand for a particular service would imply that the revenue center ought not to produce that service. Marginal revenues should cover marginal cost at a scale where long-run average costs are minimized. When these conditions do not occur, the revenue center must shed the load. The service may then be offered by a lower cost provider (private firm, voluntary organization, another jurisdiction) or may simply cease to be offered.

2. Contracting Out

Revenue centers will often be able to increase their efficiency by buying rather than producing certain inputs. The term contracting out refers to the purchase of inputs by government from private sources in the process of producing a public service. The purchase typically encompasses only a component part of the whole of the service delivered to the public. Some cities, for example, contract for tree trimming in public parks or for forensic laboratory examinations in producing, respectively, recreation and police services for their residents.

Competition for city business, for which bids are often taken, is chiefly responsible for the lower cost of contracted services. Minneapolis has 50 companies competing for trash collection contracts; Wichita has 80. The cost savings can be substantial. In the early 1970s in the borough of Queens, New York publicly provided refuse collection cost $207 per household per year, while three miles away in Bellerose, Long Island, the private costs for the same service were $72 (*U.S. News and World Report*, 1975). Savas (1974:109) alleges that street resurfacing under municipal auspices cost $57 per ton of asphalt laid, while private contractors did the same job for $20 in New York City.

Ahlbrandt (1974), in discussing contracting out, argues that "the most significant long run benefits are with respect to research and development, the adoption of new technology, and the satisfaction of consumer preferences." Scottsdale, Arizona's Rural Metropolitan Fire Protection Company, for example, makes substantial use of light trucks (as compared to the heavy engines typical of municipal fire departments) and has adopted innovative deployment strategies. Other services appropriate for contracting out include emergency ambulances, building security, street cleaning, snow removal, and school lunches.

3. Special Assessments and Neighborhood Special Taxes

Some of the new revenue centers will rely primarily on special assessments voted by inhabitants of circumscribed subareas within the city limits. These assessments would be calibrated to reflect the increase in the value of the property attributed to the existence of the public facility or service. Thus, for a park the size of the assessment might be a function of the value of the property and its distance from the park. To protect low income property owners against cash flow problems, the collection of the assessment might be deferred until the sale or transfer of the property.

For other services neighborhood-specific taxes might be an effective mechanism. For the privilege of retaining a branch library reading room, residents might adopt a neighborhood head tax while circulation services could still be financed through fees. Generally, pieces of public capital which generate substantial local benefits (e.g., police station, playground, clinic) but have little effect on property values are good candidates for financing through the neighborhood head tax.

4. Centrally Provided Capital and Labor Services

No matter what the source of revenue the new "revenue centers" could rent or lease capital—police cars, fire stations, parks lands—from the central administration to preserve central control of debt obligations and to give elected officials some influence over the plans of the revenue centers.

Just as the desire for accountability may work to retain the centrality of capital acquisition and control, the legal status of civil service arrangements may lead to a centralization in human resources. If revenue centers could compete for workers who hold citywide (sometimes referred to as "wall-to-wall") rather than departmental seniority, an internal labor market would be created. Those workers not hired away by the centers but who remain in the pool provide flexibility for peak demand periods (Hirsch, this volume); they also call attention to what potential supervisors perceive as their low productivity. Such a scheme may increase the longer term chances of selective terminations for low productivity workers insofar as taxpayers will not long countenance the employment of persons not deemed worth putting to work in the revenue centers.

5. Interjurisdictional Service Provision

The revenue centers would not be limited to individual consumers in defining their markets. Sales of services could also be arranged with neighboring juris-dictions, special-purpose jurisdictions, or higher level jurisdictions. For example,

- A central city fire agency might sell fire suppression services to surrounding suburbs
- A recreation agency might sell leisure-time activities to the local school district
- A zoo agency might bill the state for part support of a cultural amenity whose benefits extend well beyond the confines of its city

In these ways are economies of scale exploited to the benefit of all the taxpayers. In addition particular jurisdictions may find they have a comparative advantage in providing particular services for reasons other than scale economies, e.g., as a result of historical factors, demography, location, etc. Encouraging interjur-isdictional sales of services will encourage specialization and greater overall efficiency.

E. Equity Protection in the Responsive City

How fare low income groups in the responsive city? Without special protection they will find burdens rising as they begin to pay for the services they once received "free," i.e., those which were financed by taxes.[4] But protection devices are available. One mechanism that is particularly appealing from a philosophic standpoint—but perhaps complex administratively—is the multi-purpose public service voucher administered by a central municipal redistribution office. In this arrangement a qualified household receives the right to spend a specified sum on a wide range of public services or to pay special assessments or neighborhood taxes. The sum accorded to a particular household would be a function of its income, its size, and its nature (i.e., the presence of children, disabled, elderly, etc.). If the sum were determined to be $1,000 per year for a household with an income below $10,000, then spending $200 for paramedics would leave $800 for swimming pool admissions, library privileges, special taxes to support parks, and all the other things it might like to secure from public revenue centers. The household could be issued a credit card with an upper limit. The revenue center could collect from the redistribution office.

The funds to support the redistribution office come from the tax-supported general fund. In this way citizens and their elected representatives can make a deliberate choice of the level of redistribution they prefer and of the forms they would like to see it take. The service-producing entities are relieved of the concern about fair access to their products; they treat all consumers equally.

Note that the above recommendations are aimed at maintaining some measure of *vertical* equity, i.e., equity defined in income or ability-to-pay terms. Public finance writers also discuss horizontal equity in which burdens are a function of benefits received. From the standpoint of that latter definition the shift from taxes to charges would be movement toward great equity, prima facie.

F. Transition to the Responsive City

Distinguishing the essential from the responsive city and organizing the latter by means of revenue centers is a less radical notion that it might at first appear. The use of fee financing is growing apace. In California, where property taxes have been severely constrained, the use of special assessments has been expanding rapidly (Misczynski, 1982). Special funds budgeting—a halfway house to revenue centers which was stimulated by the plethora of categorical grants during the 1970s—is more and more familiar to city management. Many cities already sell services to other jurisdictions. The organization of cities into ward or councilmanic districts facilitates neighborhood level organization of service provision.

Another advantage is that the responsive city can be built gradually and deliberately. Revenue centers can be established one by one and the level of general fund tax support each receives can be reduced slowly so as to minimize disruption. Thus, low demand services will not vanish overnight but will wither away as subsidies decline. In general, user fees provide information on the demand for public services that is not available under conventional financing arrangements.

Converting city finances to benefit-based, market-oriented, responsive modes is not without problems. As well as the equity complications described above there are a number of additional considerations which may prevent the easy adoption of these approaches.

Fees and charges are not deductible against federal and state income taxes as are the property or other taxes they replace. Thus, there is likely to be a noticeable opposition to charges by sophisticated taxpayers. Some state constitutions and city charters constrain the use of fee mechanisms. Grant formulas by which federal and state revenues are distributed to local governments often do not include fees and charges, as they do tax-supported expenditures, in the definition of local effort. New legislation would be required to deal with problems of deductibility and maintenance of effort.

Privatization and contracting out are sometimes attacked on the grounds that a shift from public to private provision means the replacement of the civil service by big business. In reality, however, the employees of the contract-securing private organizations are likely to be more modestly compensated than the civil servants they supplant. Differential employee costs in fact constitute a chief explanation of the cost reductions promised by competitive provision. The result will be more job opportunities for lower paid workers and fewer for the higher paid, which is certainly not inequitable, however anti-union it may appear.

The organization of revenue centers as discussed in this paper will necessitate basic changes in the civil service system. Lifetime tenure within particular agencies may no longer be viable. A switch to private provision of public goods may also threaten to reverse affirmative action gains. The public sector has in the last 15 years been considerably more hospitable to minorities, employing in many large cities twice the fraction of such workers as does the general economy (see Pascal and Menchik, 1980). Although equal opportunity regulations may serve to protect the jobs of minorities (and women) already on public payrolls, new opportunities would be severely squeezed, with resultant deleterious effects on oncoming cohorts of minority workers. On the other hand, it should be possible to require appropriate equal opportunity policies among private service providers as a precondition to bidding on government contracts.

CONCLUSIONS

The essential/responsive distinction and the employment of market-like mechanisms are growing increasingly attractive as solutions to the local fiscal crisis. The emerging fiscal plight of local government makes the timing right. The inherent philosophy appears to accord with current preferences for local self-help and private sector-style solutions to public problems. Technical assistance in implementing the concept promises something to the leaders of troubled cities at a time when direct federal financial assistance is shrinking. Obviously, instituting it will require some ingenuity and some boldness. All in all, however, a hearty welcome for the postmunicipal city seems in order.

NOTES

1.   All true public goods have spillover benefits. In the case of trash collection, for example, these would involve neighborhood sanitation and amenity. In general, the higher the externalities and the less the appropriability by the direct consumer, the less amenable is the service for financing and delivery by means of user charges. (For the general theory of user charges and a review of the pre-1972 literature on this topic, see Milliman, 1972).

2.   A debt of gratitude is owed to Rand colleague Kevin Neels, who participated in the development of many of the ideas presented here.

3.   Methods for realizing income distribution objectives are discussed below.

4.   To the extent fees replace taxes which were themselves a heavy burden on the poor, such as the property tax (see De Tray et al., 1981), the net rise in burden will be diminished. Low income families tend not to use the property tax deduction privilege in calculating income tax obligations and so would feel less pain on that score in the switch from taxes to fees.

REFERENCES

Advisory Commission on Intergovernmental Relations (1974). *Local Revenue Diversification: Income Taxes, Sales Taxes and User Charges.* Washington, D.C.

———(1981). *Significant Features of Fiscal Federalism, 1980-81 Edition,* Washington, D.C.

Ahlbrandt, R. S., Jr. (1974). "Implications of Contracting for a Public Service." *Urban Affairs Quarterly* (March):337-359.

Ballabon, M. B. (1972). "The Self-Service Group in the Urban Economy." *Journal of the American Institute of Planners* (January):33-42.

De Tray D., et al. (1981). *Fiscal Restraints and the Burden of Local and State Taxes.* Santa Monica: The Rand Corporation.

Hirsch, W. Z. (1983). "Towards a More Productive Municipal Government." In R. D. Ebel (ed.), *Research in Urban Economics,* 4. Greenwich, Conn.: JAI Press.

Legislative Analyst (1979). "An Analysis of the Effect of Proposition 13 on Local Governments." State of California.

Levin, D. J. (1978). "Receipts and Expenditures of State and Local Governments, 1959-76." *Survey of Current Business* (May):15-21.

Milliman, J. M. (1972). "Beneficiary Charges—Toward a Unified Theory." In S. J. Mushkin (ed.), *Public Prices for Public Products.* Washington, D.C.: The Urban Institute.

Misczynski, D. J. (1982). "California's Nonplunge into Benefit Levydom." Conference on Special Assessments, Los Angeles, UCLA (January 22-23).

Mushkin, S. J. and R. M. Bird (1972). "Public Prices: An Overview." In S. J. Mushkin (ed.) *Public Prices for Public Products.* Washington, D.C.: The Urban Institute: 3-25.

Pascal, A. H., et al. (1979). *Fiscal Containment of Local and State Government.* Santa Monica: The Rand Corporation.

Pascal, A. H. and M. Menchik (1979), *Fiscal Containment: Who Gains? Who Loses?* Santa Monica: The Rand Corporation.

———(1980). *Restraints on Taxing and Spending: Trends, Portents, Consequences.* Santa Monica: The Rand Corporation.

Paul, E. S. (1972). "Pricing Rules and Efficiency." In S. J. Mushkin (ed.), *Public Prices for Public Products.* Washington, D.C.: The Urban Institute.

Savas, E. S. (1974). "Municipal Monopolies vs. Competition in Delivering Urban Services." *Urban Analysis,* 2:93-116.

Shannon, J. (1982). "The 1975-81 Shift in Local Finance to Benefit-Based Taxes, User Charges and Exactions." Conference on Special Assessments, Los Angeles, UCLA, (January 22-23).

Shoup. D. C. (1980). "Financing Public Investment by Deferred Special Assessment." *National Tax Journal,* 33(4).

Sloan, H. J. and A. J. Zurcher (1970). *Dictionary of Economics.* New York: Barnes and Noble.

Sonenblum, S., et al. (1975), "Selecting Structures for Providing Municipal Services." Institute of Government and Public Affairs: Los Angeles.

Stocker, F. D. (1974). "User Charges: Their Role in Local Government Finance. *Proceedings of the 67th Annual Conference, National Tax Association,* Tax Institute of America.

———(1976). "Diversification of the Local Revenue System: Income and Sales Taxes. User Charges, Federal Grants. *National Tax Journal,* (September):312-321.

Vickery, W. S. (1972). "Economic Efficiency and Pricing." In S. J. Mushkin (ed.), *Public Prices for Public Products.* Washington, D.C.: The Urban Institute.

"Ways Private Firms Can Save Money for Burdened Cities" (Interview with John Diebold) (1975). *U. S. News and World Report* (November):79:82.

"When the Government Lets Somebody Else Do Its Job" (1977). *National Journal* (October):1410-1414.

Wilcox, M. C. and S. J. Mushkin (1972). "Public Pricing and Family Income: Problems of Eligibility Standards." In S. J. Mushkin (ed.), *Public Prices for Public Products.* Washington, D.C.: The Urban Institute.

URBAN GOVERNMENT EXPENDITURES IN THE 1980s

David L. Puryear and John P. Ross

I. INTRODUCTION

This paper examines the prospects for urban government expenditures in the 1980s along with a number of important factors that influence these prospects. The 1980s will present urban local governments with a new set of problems, challenges, and opportunities. The quality of future urban life will be significantly affected by the way urban governments respond to these new demands. For example, focusing more attention on efficient service delivery—doing more with less—while at the same time reducing in-kind income redistribution at the local level is likely to have a considerable consequence for urban areas. Furthermore, reassigning government responsibilities and at the same time readjusting taxing powers to approximate expenditure requirements more closely is also likely to yield a substantially different set of urban outcomes than the current allocation

Research in Urban Economics, Volume 4, pages 243-255.
Copyright © 1984 JAI Press Inc.
ISBN: 0-89232-423-6

of responsibilities. Since all of these policy changes are probable, it is worth a careful look at the prospects for urban public services in the 1980s.

Local governments can be expected to respond to these new demands in a variety of ways. For example, some public services that are now considered essential will not be a part of local government by the 1990s.[1] Other services that are presently produced by the local public sector will be placed in the hands of private contractors. At a somewhat less dramatic level, changing patterns of demand will generate changes in both the level and composition of the expenditures of urban local governments. Finally, the level of urban tax revenues and other receipts will play a major role in determining urban spending levels because virtually all state and local governments have statutory if not constitutional prohibitions against deficit spending and in the 1980s local governments will not be able to simply increase revenues to meet the demand for public services as was done in the 1970s. Thus, the revenue constraint will be a much more serious one.[2]

The ideal approach to urban spending prospects for the 1980s might be to estimate a formal model, but that is not feasible because even the most successful forecasts of state or local government spending are valid only for two or three years into the future.[3] Furthermore, the underlying structure of intergovernmental fiscal relations is in such flux that even short-term forecasts are nearly impossible. What were formerly taken as parameters of such formal models are changing in the 1980s. Therefore, instead of a forecasting model, this paper examines three kinds of evidence regarding urban spending to see what we can infer about urban expenditures for the decade ahead. Specifically, this paper looks at recent trends in spending, at other changes in the economic environment likely to influence spending, and at the potential impacts of the Reagan administration's initiatives for a ''new federalism.''

This paper is divided into three additional sections. The first of these will review past trends in the pattern and composition of expenditures. The next section will examine influences on urban spending patterns that lie outside the realm of intergovernmental relations, but that cannot be ignored in assessing the urban public spending that will occur during the 1980s. These include taxing and spending limits and changes in financial markets.

The final section of the paper will summarize the various trends influencing urban government spending and identify several key research issues arising as a result of these changes. Real urban government expenditures are expected to continue to fall or at least flatten out over the course of the next decade. As a result, urban areas throughout the nation can expect substantial budget changes in the 1980s. Unless research is undertaken to identify these changes and possible strategies to address them, important opportunities for improving urban conditions may be overlooked or lost.

II. THE PATTERN AND COMPOSITION
OF MUNICIPAL SPENDING

During the 1960s and for at least part of the 1970s, state and local governments were a major growth industry. As the nation's economy grew, the subnational public sector took on new functions, increased the quality of some of their publicly provided goods, and in many cases provided more services for each of their residents. The result of this increased activity was a rapidly expanding urban public sector.[4]

This pattern underwent a dramatic turnaround in the mid- and later 1970s. Real federal aid to state and local governments also began to decline, ending several decades of rapid growth. The following tables indicate the differences in growth of expenditures by type of government and show the dramatic shifts that occurred in the 1970s. The tables look successively at state and local spending, in the aggregate, on a per capita basis, and on a real per capita basis. They then turn to the relative size of federal, state, and local spending and to the mix of spending by type of local government activity.

A. Local Government Spending Levels

State, local, municipal, and county government spending has steadily increased in *current* dollars since 1955 (Table 1). The annual percentage changes have

Table 1. Total Direct General Expenditures of State and Local Government,
(in millions)

Fiscal Year	Total State Local	Percent Change	Total* Local	Percent Change	Municipal	Percent Change	County	Percent Change
1955	$ 33,724	—	$ 22,534	—	$ 7,870	—	$ 4,629	—
1960	51,876	10.8%	33,931	10.1%	11,700	9.7%	6,600	8.5%
1965	74,546	8.7	48,405	8.5	15,758	6.9	10,000	10.3
1970	131,332	15.2	82,582	14.1	27,249	14.6	17,036	14.1
1971	150,674	14.7	94,196	14.1	31,507	15.6	19,827	16.4
1972	166,873	10.8	104,822	11.3	35,187	11.7	22,339	12.7
1973	181,086	8.5	113,822	8.6	38,409	9.2	24,612	10.2
1974	198,618	9.7	124,668	9.5	41,920	9.1	27,083	10.0
1975	229,474	15.5	143,148	14.8	47,964	14.4	30,903	14.1
1976	255,561	11.4	159,720	11.6	52,855	10.2	35,383	14.5
1977	273,002	6.8	169,467	6.1	54,576	3.3	38,768	9.6
1978	295,510	8.3	182,995	8.0	59,034	8.2	42,041	8.4
1979	326,024	10.3	201,470	10.1	63,846	8.2	46,422	10.4
1980	367,339	12.7	223,621	11.0	70,426	10.3	51,383	10.7

Note:
*Includes all local governments.
Source: Advisory Commission on Intergovernmental Relations, *Significant Features of Fiscal Federalism, 1980-81 Edition,* Table 10, Washington, D.C., December 1981, page 19.

ranged from about 7% to more than 15% for total state-local spending. For cities by themselves the range has been even greater—from about 3% to more than 15% per year. As might be expected given the aggregate economic situation, much of the extreme fluctuation in these percentage changes in public expenditure came during the 1970s.

One of the reasons for these increasing expenditures was the increase in population both in the aggregate and in cities. Thus, it is interesting to note that per capita spending exhibits the same pattern of increases as aggregate spending (Table 2). Per capital spending in current dollars has consistently increased over the last 10 years. The average annual change in per capita spending has not been stable; rather it has fluctuated over almost as wide range as total spending.

Table 2.   Per Capita Direct General Expenditure of State and Local Governments

Fiscal Year	Total State Local	Percent Change	Total* Local	Percent Change	Municipal	Percent Change	County	Percent Change
1970	$ 641.03	—	$ 403.08	—	$206.43	—	$ 83.15	—
1971	727.71	13.5%	454.94	12.9%	237.08	14.8%	95.76	15.2%
1972	799.02	9.8	501.94	10.3	262.99	10.9	106.96	11.7
1973	858.63	7.5	539.69	7.5	285.17	8.4	116.70	9.1
1974	937.32	9.2	588.33	9.0	309.18	8.4	127.81	9.5
1975	1974.52	14.6	670.30	13.9	351.43	13.7	144.71	13.2
1976	1187.77	10.5	742.36	10.7	384.75	9.5	164.46	13.7
1977	1258.77	6.0	781.39	5.3	394.70	2.6	178.75	8.7
1978	1351.11	7.3	836.68	7.1	424.20	7.5	192.22	7.5
1979	1478.00	9.4	913.35	9.2	455.84	7.5	210.45	9.5
1980	1648.69	11.5	1003.65	9.9	499.62	8.8	226.34	7.6

Note:
*Includes all local governments
Source: Advisory Commission on Intergovernmental Relations, *Significant Features of Fiscal Federalism, 1980-81 Edition* and *Economic Report of the President, 1982*, various tables.

It should be noted that average municipal per capita expenditure data mask larger variations in spending per person among different places. For example, in fiscal year 1980, cities with over 1 million residents spent on average about $1,101 per person while those with less than 50,000 residents spent on average only slightly more than $307.

The rates of expenditure growth in cities of various sizes have also differed substantially over the last 10 years. Per capita expenditures for cities of over 1 million have grown by about 90% while those of cities with less than 50,000 residents have grown by over 150% for this 10-year period.

Data from the 1980 census indicate that a number of large cities, particularly those in the Northeast and Midwest, have stopped growing in population size. In some cases entire SMSAs have started to lose population. This loss of population does not mean that we can expect a reduction in municipal public spending, however. Because the households remaining in declining areas often have lower incomes, they require more in support services than was required by those that have moved elsewhere. Thus, the result of such population changes is not necessarily a reduction in overall state and local public sector spending. It may mean that per capita and, in some cases, total municipal spending actually increases.

A second reason often given for the increase in local government spending, both in the aggregate and on a per capita basis, is the rapid increase in federal aid that has gone to subnational units of government. Real federal aid per capita to state and local governments increased rapidly from the mid-1950s to the mid-1970s (Table 3). Since 1978, however, real federal aid to state and local government per capita has declined.

Table 3.   Own Source Real Per Capita Expenditures and Federal Aid

Fiscal Year	State	Total Local	Municipal	County	Federal Aid
1955	$106.70	$204.83	$127.39	$35.33	$ 37.98
1960	113.27	233.31	143.10	41.29	67.59
1965	129.00	263.59	151.89	51.59	86.44
1970	162.49	292.29	165.38	53.69	124.50
1971	172.00	304.58	173.29	57.81	136.67
1972	168.83	311.85	176.83	59.29	156.40
1973	159.65	293.23	164.68	57.24	179.61
1974	170.10	281.04	158.92	53.93	167.49
1975	183.13	296.25	161.70	58.93	176.64
1976	182.58	305.24	162.70	63.45	195.07
1977	181.90	292.18	150.77	63.10	209.78
1978	181.58	288.32	152.05	61.67	217.67
1979	186.91	284.85	152.00	60.15	211.18
1980	192.92	294.50	161.92	64.77	210.88

Source: U.S. Department of Commerce, Bureau of the Census, *Governmental Finances* (Washington, D.C.: U.S. Government Printing Office, various years).

In the years prior to 1978, the rapid increase in federal aid had two principal effects on municipal spending. First, through the use of matching requirements and other prohibitions on expenditure reductions, these grants-in-aid increased the pressure on local governments to spend more on their residents. Even the shift in emphasis from categorical to block and general purpose grants that took place during the 1970s only slightly reduced this pressure for greater local government spending. While some matching requirements were removed, with the growth of block and general purpose grants, more governmental units were brought into the system and as a result total local spending grew.

In addition to the pressure to increase spending, the growth in grants-in-aid forced local groverments into functional areas which, if left to their own devices, they might not have taken on. The federal government used local governments as a delivery mechanism for a number of otherwise federal public services. Good examples of this behavior are contained in recent federal government counter-cyclical policy that included the Comprehensive Employment and Training Act (CETA) grants, the Local Public Works programs, and other countercyclical grant programs. Countercyclical policy is almost universally considered to be the province of the federal government. These programs were a departure from earlier intergovernmental arrangements and through matching and maintaince of effort requirements increased the pressure on own-source local expenditures. Thus, the grants system, even when used simply as an alternative service delivery mechanism, has increased the pressure on local governments to spend.

A final important pressure on local government expenditures has been inflation. Inflation has increased both the revenues available to local governments and the cost of providing public services. Therefore, inflation has induced increases in local government expenditures.[5]

In order to understand what is likely to occur in the 1980s, it is necessary to see what has happened to local government spending in the recent past. Table 3 adjusts local government spending for inflation and for grants-in-aid and demonstrates that real per capita own-source spending peaked in the mid-1970s (several years prior to the passage of California's Proposition 13) and has been stable or falling even since. For cities, the peak in their own-source spending may have come as early as 1972/73 and has been fairly flat since. Even real federal aid peaked in 1978, the middle of the Carter administration, and it has been falling for the past four years.

Local Government Spending Composition

Along with the level of local government spending, composition is also quite important in determining what local spending will look like in the 1980s. The most striking feature of spending composition by level of government is the consistency of the shares over time (Table 4). The federal government accounted for 65% of direct public sector spending in 1955 (excluding intergovernmental aid). Its share declined continually until 1976 when it reached a low of 46.3% of total public sector spending. Since 1976, the federal share of total spending has increased to about 49.2% of the total.

The municipal share of total public spending ranged from 8.1% to 11.1% peaking in 1975 and 1976 at 11.1%. The municipal share of total public sector spending has declined steadily since 1976.

The biggest change in the way municipalities spend their money is in the reduction in importance of capital spending relative to current spending (Table 5). In 1970/71 the ratio of current to capital spending was about four to one; by 1979/80, that ratio had increased to about five to one.[6]

This review of the level and composition of local public sector spending suggests two points. First, municipal spending has begun to fall for the first time since World War II. This decline is occurring in both absolute terms and relative

Table 4. Spending Shares by Level of Government

Fiscal Year	Federal	State	Total Local	Municipal	County
1955	65.2%	11.6%	23.3%	8.1%	4.8%
1960	59.7	14.0	26.4	9.1	5.1
1965	57.1	15.1	27.9	9.1	5.8
1970	52.2	17.7	30.0	9.9	6.2
1971	50.0	18.8	31.3	10.5	6.6
1972	48.1	19.3	32.6	10.9	7.0
1973	47.4	19.5	33.1	11.2	7.1
1974	47.6	19.5	32.9	11.1	7.1
1975	46.9	20.0	33.1	11.1	7.1
1976	46.3	20.1	33.5	11.1	7.4
1977	46.9	20.1	33.0	10.6	7.5
1978	47.6	19.9	32.4	10.5	7.4
1979	48.3	19.7	31.9	10.1	7.4
1980	49.2	19.9	30.9	9.7	7.1

Source: Advisory Commission on Intergovernmental Relations, *Significant Features of Fiscal Federalism 1980-81 Edition*, Washington, D.C., December 1981, p. 19.

Table 5. Per Capita Municipal Spending by Category, 1970 and 1979

	1970	Percent of total 1970	1979	Percent of total 1979
All Functions	$242.02	100.0%	$513.95	100.0%
Capital	48.05	19.9	86.75	16.9
Other	193.96	80.1	427.20	83.1
Education	39.71	16.4	65.86	12.8
Highways	20.18	8.3	42.40	8.2
Public Welfare	20.36	8.4	26.97	5.2
Hospital	13.48	5.6	23.52	4.6
Health	4.12	1.7	8.09	1.6
Police	26.29	10.9	58.17	11.3
Fire	15.12	6.2	32.17	6.3
Sewerage	13.39	5.5	37.61	7.3
Sanitation	9.42	3.9	18.53	3.6
Parks	10.90	4.5	24.35	4.7
Housing	10.92	4.5	24.54	4.8
General Government	17.53	7.2	35.10	6.8
Interest on Debt	9.91	4.1	21.67	4.2
Other	30.66	12.7	69.08	13.4

Source: U.S. Department of Commerce, Bureau of the Census, *City Finances* (Washington, D.C.: U.S. Government Printing Office, various years).

to other levels of government. Second, real federal aid to state and local governments has also begun to decline. Both of these trends began prior to the Reagan administration and have continued into this administration.

III. OTHER SPENDING INFLUENCES

Four other factors will have a major potential impact on urban spending in the 1980s: the cost of public services, statutory and constitutional limitations, financial markets, and the new federalism. Each of these factors complicates the task of forecasting future urban spending patterns to a considerable degree.

A. Service Costs

Urban governments face inflation just like other consumers in the economy. Changes in the cost of purchasing the materials and labor necessary to provide public services can make a significant difference in the level and the composition of spending. Obviously, if the rate of inflation continues to decline, urban governments will be able to maintain service levels with less spending than otherwise. More important in terms of real spending levels is whether the cost of public service inputs rises faster or slower than the general price level. Labor inputs in particular may exhibit differential rates of increase in compensation. Although it is difficult to determine the true cost of public sector labor in the absence of reliable, precise measures of output or productivity, both nominal and real wages in the urban public sector have grown more slowly in recent years than in the 1960s and early 1970s.[7] The period of rapid catch-up with the private sector appears to be over. Furthermore, the increased sophistication of public sector managers in the area of fringe benefits may have helped to slow their growth. The fiscal stress experienced in many urban areas in recent years has also contributed to slower compensation growth if only because many cities simply could not afford large wage increases.[8]

B. Statutory and Constitutional Limitations

State and local governments have operated under various statutory and constitutional limitations on taxing and spending since the republic began. Since California's Proposition 13 was passed by public referendum in June 1978, however, considerably more attention has been focused on such limits and a number of them (such as Michigan's Headley Amendment, Massachusetts's Proposition 2 1/2 and TRIM in Prince Georges' County, Md.) have imposed restrictions on governments' ability to raise or spend money for public services. Whether these legal limits precede or follow declines in spending, they clearly reflect public preferences for slower growth in the public sector during the 1980s.

Limits such as these also tend to have some side effects that frequently work to reduce the resources available to local governments in the long run. For example, a frequently proposed form of limitation is a cap on the *rate* of spending growth. It is tied to the growth rate of state or local income in the most recent year for which reliable data are available. This imposes a downward ratchet effect on spending because the typical lag between the year for which income data are available and the budget year affected is two years, resulting in stringent budget limits in years of revenue prosperity and vice versa. Because nearly all state and local governments are prohibited from enacting deficit budgets, the revenue constraint will hold budget growth below the limit level in some years and the limit will hold budget growth below revenue capacity in other years. The long-term result of such a system is a *shrinking* public sector rather than a stable one.

Among the other side effects of these limits with implications for urban government spending in the 1980s are competition between entitlement programs and nonentitlement programs. State and local budgets, like the national budget, consist of "controllable" items that can be cut at will, such as highway maintenance and economic development; and "uncontrollable" items such as unemployment compensation, pension obligations, interest on outstanding debt, and matching funds in federal programs. While most of the literature on uncontrollable expenditures is concerned with federal countercyclical programs, the problem is in some respects more severe for state and local governments because they cannot engage in deficit spending. An overall cap on expenditures requires cuts in the controllable items, while the uncontrollable expenditures eat up the budget. In the long run, this can make sensible public management much more difficult.

Furthermore, a spending cap drives expenditures underground. It will shift substantial amounts of spending into off-budget channels such as special authorities and managed funds. This trend is already clear in the federal budget in such agencies as FNMA, whose independent budget is larger than that of its parent agency, the U.S. Department of Housing and Urban Development (HUD), but does not appear in the federal budget. It not only places large expenditures outside the budget, it places management responsibility beyond easy scrutiny by the taxpayer.

Finally, a number of these limitations break the linkage between the actual value of the tax base and the taxable value. Proposition 13, for example, limits growth in assessments to 2% per year, regardless of market value. In the long run this is likely to cause slower growth in tax receipts than in the general level of economic activity because the underlying level of economic activity will often exceed the 2% limit. In the absence of other revenue sources, local public spending in California would have to shrink relative to the overall level of economic activity.

C. Financial Markets

Several recent trends in the financial markets indicate greater difficulty for urban borrowing in the 1980s. One important, even if inefficient, federal subsidy for state and local government borrowing is the tax-exempt status of these bonds. In equating after-tax yields at the margin, the bond market translates this tax exemption into a lower interest rate on state and local government bonds because the after-tax yield is higher than for a taxable bond at the same interest rate. Several recent trends have narrowed this differential, however, and have reduced the benefit of the tax exemption.

Because the rate differential depends on the relative supply and demand for tax-exempt and nonexempt bonds (which in turn depends on the rate differential), factors affecting these supplies and demands will influence the differential and affect the savings enjoyed by state and local government borrowers. The dramatic increase in the use of industrial revenue bonds in recent years, for example, has added to the supply of tax-exempt issues and, other things equal, it has reduced the advantage of tax-exempt bonds.

Recent changes in the federal tax law have also reduced the advantage enjoyed by tax-exempt bonds. Lower marginal income tax rates reduce the benefits of tax exemptions. Faster depreciation may make some "taxable" investments a more attractive investment alternative than state and local government bonds. Finally, the new IRA options offer many taxpayers a tax benefit (deferral) without the need to settle for lower tax-exempt rates of return.

D. The New Federalism

All of the Reagan administration proposals for revising the functional responsibilities of federal and state governments appear to reflect a philosophical assumption that most nondefense federal programs have no significant spillover benefits across state boundaries and should therefore be carried out by the states. This is a political definition of spillovers and reflects the political nature of all collective decisions. Whether this definition is accepted or not, implementing it will clearly lead to reduced levels of public spending on many functions shifted to the states. This is true for several reasons. First, the states could spend more now but choose not to and there is some evidence that their responses to recent reductions in federal aid have been minimal.[9] Second, state and local tax bases are less income elastic than that of the federal government so revenue constraints are tighter. Third, as noted above, many state and local governments operate under restrictive limitations which may work to reduce the size of the state and local public sector in the long run.

IV. WHERE DO WE GO FROM HERE?

Two basic conclusions emerge from this paper. First, the trend toward slower growth in urban public spending appears to be here to stay. It is neither a short-term phenomenon of recession nor an aberration caused by policies of the Reagan administration. It began in the mid-1970s and has persisted through economic upswings as well as recessions and through Democratic as well as Republican administration. A variety of pressures have combined to achieve this trend and they are not likely to disappear. Thus, the 1980s will see a continued slowdown in real urban public spending, with consequences as yet unknown.

The second message is that the proposed changes in intergovernmental responsibilities—the New Federalism—could alter the urban public sector almost beyond recognition. Because the changes proposed by the Reagan administration would be so substantial, they raise a host of questions about the future of urban areas.

A declining urban public sector suggests that greater emphasis will be placed on managing existing (or shrinking) resources. This has already begun at the state/local level, e.g., particularly with respect to managing intergovernmental aid. Thus, one set of research questions is related to how much room there is for productivity improvement in the public sector. If new federal programs cannot be afforded, what self-help solutions exist for urban areas? This search for greater productivity will stimulate greater innovation and experimentation in service delivery and may well generate some significant improvements.

The New Federalism also raises interesting issues. Even if only a part of the proposed New Federalism is implemented it will strongly reinforce the decline in urban spending on existing urban programs. The competition for limited state and local tax revenues will intensify as responsibilities increase. In general, because they cannot deficit finance, state and local governments must be more conservative than the federal government in their fiscal behavior, so as programs are shifted to state and local governments, they are very likely to shrink in size. This trend is further exacerbated by the competition among subnational jurisdictions for economic development because low tax rates are seen by many jurisdictions as important incentives for attracting economic growth despite some significant evidence to the contrary.[10]

The New Federalism also raises questions about the long-run revenue elasticities of the tax bases proposed by the Reagan administration for "turnback" to the states, about the feasibility of maintaining current real spending levels with these tax bases, and about the long-run future for the shifted programs: will they be effectively shifted to the states or will they in fact virtually disappear?

The next impact of these broad trends as well as of the policy changes involved in the New Federalism is not neutral with respect to all groups in the population. They are tilted against lower income households and toward those with more income and less need for local public services or transfer programs. Because redistributive issues are often sensitive ones, it is important to note that the overall trend in urban spending since the mid-1970s is more accurately described as a leveling off after a period of growth than as a decline from a peak. As Table 3 indicates, real municipal spending per capita did peak in 1972, but the 1980 level was only slightly lower. What the future will bring as federal aid continues to decline is uncertain, but it is not at all clear that there is a trend toward, or a popular preference for, severe cuts in urban service levels. What is certain is that both the restructuring of the urban public sector caused by the federal aid cuts already accomplished and the potential changes implicit in the proposed New Federalism require careful research if the nation's urban areas are to make the difficult transition to a smaller public sector without unnecessary hardship.

ACKNOWLEDGMENT

*The views and opinions expressed in this paper are those of the authors and do not necessarily reflect the views of the U.S. Department of Housing and Urban Development.

NOTES

1. The future of urban governments is discussed in some detail by Anthony H. Pascal. In this volume.

2. The prospects for urban revenues are examined in some detail elsewhere in this volume. See, R.C. Fisher and J. Kohlase, "Local Government Revenue: Tax Reliance, Revenue Diversification, and Metropolitan Finance."

3. For a summary and discussion of these kinds of models, see R.W. Bahl and L. Schroeder, *Projecting and Planning State and Local Government Fiscal Activity in a Declining Region: A Budgetary Forecasting Model for New York*, Metropolitan Studies Program, Syracuse University, Syracuse, New York, 1980.

4. These trends have been documented in a number of different sources. For example, for an excellent statistical description, see, Advisory Commission on Intergovernmental Relations, *Significant Features of Fiscal Federalism, 1980-81 Edition* (Washington, DC: U.S. Government Printing Office, 1982).

5. For a detailed discussion of the impact of inflation on State and Local Government Expenditures, see Advisory Commission on Intergovernmental Relations, *State-Local Finances in Recession and Inflation: An Economic Analysis*, A-70 (Washington, DC: U.S. Government Printing Office, May 1979).

6. Much work has been done in the areas of local government capital financing. For some of the best, see George E. Peterson, ed., *America's Urban Capital Stock*, Vol. I-VI (Washington, DC: The Urban Institute, 1979).

7. For a detailed discussion of the cost of public sector labor, see, Roy Bahl, Jesse Burkhead, and Bernard Jump, Jr., eds., *Public Employment and State and Local Government Finance* (Cambridge, Mass.: Ballinger Publishing Company, 1980).

8. These factors are discussed in Hearings before the Joint Economic Committee, *Local Distress, State Surpluses, Proposition 13: Prelude to Fiscal Crisis or New Opportunities?* 95th Congress, 2nd Session (Washington, DC: U.S. Government Printing Office, 1978).

9 This discussion is extended in John L. Palmer and Isabel V. Sawhill, eds., *The Reagan Experiment* (Washington, DC: The Urban Institute, 1982).

10. For a discussion that disputes this point, see, Roger W. Schmenner, *The Location Decisions of Large, Multiplant Companies*. (Cambridge, Mass.: Joint Center for Urban Studies of the Massachusetts Institute of Technology and Harvard University, 1981).

REFERENCES

Advisory Commission on Intergovernmental Relations (1982). *Significant Features of Fiscal Federalism, 1980-81 Edition* M-132. Washington, D.C.: U.S. Government Printing Office.

Advisory Commission on Intergovernmental Relations (1979). *State-Local Finances in Recession and Inflation: An Economic Analysis*, A-70. Washington, DC: U.S. Government Printing Office.

Bahl, R.W., Burkhead, Jesse, and Jump, Bernard, (eds.) (1980). *Public Employment and State and Local Government Finances*. Cambridge, Mass.: Ballinger Publishing Company.

Bahl, R.W., and L. Schroeder (1980). *Projecting and Planning State and Local Government Fiscal Activity in a Declining Region: A Budgetary Forecasting Model for New York*. Syracuse, N.Y. Metropolitan Studies Program, Syracuse University.

Council of Economic Advisors (1982). *Economic Report of the President*. Washington, D.C.: U.S. Government Printing Office.

Fisher, R.C. and J. Kohlase (1984). "Local Government Revenue: Tax Reliance, Revenue Diversification, and Metropolitan Finance." in R.D. Ebel (ed.), *Research in Urban Economics*, Vol. 4, Greenwich, Conn.: JAI Press.

Palmer, John L. and Sawhill, Isabell V. (1982). *The Reagan Experiment*. Washington, D.C.: The Urban Institute.

Pascal, Anthony H. (1984). "The Post-Municipal City." In R.D. Ebel (ed.), *Research in Urban Economics*, Vol. 4. Greenwich, Conn.: JAI Press.

Peterson, George E. (ed.) (1979). *America's Urban Capital Stock*, Vol. I-VI. Washington, D.C.: The Urban Institute.

Schmenner, R.W. (1980). *The Location Decisions of Large, Multiplant Companies*. Cambridge, Mass.: Joint Center for Urban Studies of the Massachusetts Institute of Technology and Harvard University.

U.S. Congress, Joint Economic Committee (1978). *Local Distress, State Surpluses, Proposition 13: Prelude to Fiscal Crisis or New Opportunities?* 95th Congress, 2nd Session. Washington, D.C.: U.S. Government Printing Office.

HOUSE PRICES AND LOCAL GOVERNMENT ACTIVITY

Michael J. Lea and Michael S. Johnson

I. INTRODUCTION

Only recently has the importance of the interrelationship between housing markets and the local public sector become widely recognized. Factors that influence house prices influence the revenue base of local governments. If tax rate and service differentials are capitalized into house value, the provision and financing of public services by local governments can affect house prices. Further, regulatory activities of local governments, such as development controls and condominium conversion ordinances, affect the supply of housing characteristics available in a jurisdiction and therefore house prices. In turn, changes in house prices affect the tax prices for local service provision and local public sector decision making.

While these interrelationships have been generally recognized, the research in this area has tended to be fragmentary. In order to systematically analyze

Research in Urban Economics, Volume 4, pages 257-271.
Copyright © 1984 JAI Press Inc.
All rights or reproduction in any form reserved.
ISBN: 0-89232-423-6

potential changes in housing markets, urban development, and the local public sector, it is necessary to construct a general framework that takes into account the many interrelationships between housing markets and the local public sector. In this paper, we offer the base for such a framework with the intent to provide directions in which research is needed. In Section II we outline a model of the house value determination process. The model developed in this section takes into account the effects of changes in the financing arrangements and tax advantages for housing on house prices (particularly owner-occupied housing). In addition, the effects of the local public sector on house prices, through its influence on the composition of housing bundles, are highlighted. In Section III we explore local decision making through the voting mechanism, emphasizing the key role of housing market influences on the perceived benefits and costs of voting decisions. Section IV offers a research agenda of key issues and questions raised by the framework developed in the preceding sections and speculates on several potential developments in the decade ahead.

II. HOUSING MARKETS AND HOUSE PRICE DETERMINATION

In order to forcast changes in the local public sector, it is necessary to have an understanding of the housing market and the factors that affect house prices. The general level of house prices depends heavily upon several macroeconomic variables, such as inflation, interest rates and financing terms, and federal income tax provisions. In addition, local house prices vary with the individual characteristics of the housing bundle, including those characteristics influenced or controlled by local governments.

As a long-lived asset, the market value of housing is determined by a process analogous to the determination of other asset prices. Under this approach, the nominal value (V) of housing can be viewed as the capitalized value of the stream of income generated by the asset. In general terms,

$$V = \frac{P(Z_i)}{(1 - \theta) [i (1 - \lambda) + m\lambda + p] - a + d}, \qquad (1)$$

where   P is gross market rent;
    a is the expected rate of house price appreciation;
    d is the depreciation rate;
    p is the property tax rate;
    m is the mortgage interest rate;
    λ is the mortgage balance-to-value ratio;
    θ is the marginal tax rate of the market
        clearing buyer; and
    i is the before-tax nominal discount rate.[1]

The numerator is the gross rental flow of the dwelling unit, determined by the characteristics (Z_i) of the unit, while the denominator is the cost of capital of the market-clearing purchaser.

House prices are strongly affected by the components of the cost of capital. Table 1 contains elasticities of house value with respect to changes in the individual components. These entries give the percentage change in house value implied by a 1% change in the given component, all other variables held constant.[2]

There are two interesting aspects of Table 1. First, note the current trends in several of the parameters are working in the same direction. Increases in financing rates and property tax rates and reductions in marginal tax rates and expected appreciation all lead to reductions in house price. Second, note that the elasticities rise with the income tax bracket of the homeowner. The value of housing-related deductions and exclusions rises with the income tax bracket of the homeowner, which, holding other factors constant, lowers the cost of capital. Thus, for given changes in the cost of capital, house price changes may be larger in upper income areas.

Table 1 shows a potentially large impact of reductions in marginal tax rates, such as those contained in the Economic Recovery Tax Act of 1981, on house value. Households in initially high tax brackets with a low cost of capital may bid less for a unit with a given gross market rent after the tax rate reduction, leading to large decreases in house value (e.g., the 2.2 elasticity in the Table 1 implies a 2.2% fall in house values due to a 1% cut in marginal tax rates). In addition, if the "new federalism" policies require substituting property taxes for income taxes in order to maintain local service levels, the resulting combination of rising property tax rates and declining income tax rates could create severe price declines in housing markets, particularly in higher income areas. The large capital losses to existing homeowners will undoubtedly have political repercussions. More attention needs to be focused on the house price implications of realigning Federal and local finance.

The elasticities in Table 1 also show that rising nominal interest rates and falling expected future house price appreciation each exhibit a strong negative influence on nominal house prices. Again, the result is more powerful the higher

Table 1. Elasticity of House Value to Changes in the Cost of Capital*

Variable	$\theta = .20$	$\theta = .30$	$\theta = .40$
θ	0.5	1.1	2.2
p	−0.3	−0.4	−0.6
i	−0.4	−0.5	−0.7
m	−1.3	−1.5	−2.0
a	1.3	1.8	2.7

* The parameter values used in these calculations are as follows: $\lambda = .75$; $a = .06$; $i = .10$; $m = .10$; $d = .01$; $p = .02$.

the marginal tax rate of the price-setting mover. It is apparent that high real mortgage interest rates were responsible in part for weak housing demand and a softening of house prices in the early 1980s. In addition, alternative mortgage instruments, which pass interest rate risk to the borrower, reduce the attractiveness of housing as an investment. Coupled with enforcement of due-on-sale clauses, which remove the possibility of mortgage-related capital gains on fixed rate mortgages, the changing financial environment may lead to falling house prices. Creative financing (referring to widespread use of unique buyer-seller financing arrangements such as short-term balloon notes and mortgage buy downs) may have temporarily supported owner-occupied housing markets during the last two years and allowed some sellers to avoid explicity reducing nominal house price. Such arrangements are likely to be a temporary reprieve from reality and may even lead to higher rates of mortgage default in the next few years if house prices do not rise.

If house prices rise at a slower rate than at the end of the 1970s or even begin falling in the 1980s, consumers will revise their expectations of appreciation downward. Such a revision tends to have a snowballing effect because it raises the cost of capital, further depressing house prices. The magnitude of this effect on the housing market depends in part on the timing of the changes in appreciation expectations. If these changes happen all at once, the impact on house prices could be quite large. If distributed over a reasonable time interval, the effect on house prices may be less abrupt.

The formulation in equation (1) can also be applied to rental housing. The cost of capital expression (for the landlord) will be different than that for owner-occupied housing due to the differences in tax treatment of the two types of housing. Holding gross rents constant, the 1981 tax law will change the relative valuations of rental and owner-occupied units.[3] While the reduction in marginal tax rates also applies to landlords, it is more than offset by the changes in depreciation allowances reducing the cost of capital for rental units relative to owner-occupied units. Simulation research by Hendershott and Shilling (1982b) indicates that the 1981 tax law changes may result in a significant shift of capital from owner-occupied to rental housing.

In addition, the composition of the housing bundle contributes to cross-sectional variation in house prices. Local governments are able to exert significant influence over house prices through their control of various characteristics of the housing bundle. Changes in the supply of various characteristics influence bids for individual properties and therefore house prices.

The effect of local government actions on house prices can be highlighted by rewriting the numerator of equation (1). Gross rents (imputed for homeowners) are determined by the interaction of buyers and sellers for the many attributes which are in the housing bundle. In the short run, moving households bid for an essentially fixed stock of available units. The market outcome is often modeled as a hedonic price function, where the coefficients represent the implicit market-clearing prices or characteristic valuations.[4] To emphasize local government-housing interactions, attributes have been divided into three types according to the local government's ability to influence them:

$$P = f(\Sigma p_j z_j + \Sigma p_k z_k + \Sigma p_l z_l). \tag{2}$$

The z_j's represent attributes largely beyond the scope of local government (e.g., many structural features and some neighborhood factors); the z_k's are determined by local government service provision (e.g., the level and mix of local government expenditures); and the z_l's represent attributes affected by local decisions but not the result of direct expenditures. Examples of the latter include square footage of the unit if it is constrained by zoning minimums, attributes subject to planning board approval, and the location of facilities, (e.g., public tennis courts or neighborhood schools).

With a fixed stock of available units, the coefficients on the hedonic price function are determined by the marginal valuation of the characteristics by moving households and the fixed supply of the characteristics in the market. Therefore, in order to predict where house prices are most likely to change in response to changes in housing costs, one must estimate the underlying structural demand equations for individual characteristics. In practice, this task has proven to be extremely difficult. Past studies of house price determination have failed to separate the various demand and supply factors that determine house prices. Without reliable estimates of characteristic demand functions, it is impossible to predict precisely where local house prices are most likely to change. All we can say at this point is that moving households will respond to rising house costs by changing their demands for particular housing characteristics. Resident households may respond to such housing market changes in their capacity as voters within local jurisdictions by changing those characteristics under their control (Z_k, Z_l). Such a response will engender further changes in house prices as movers respond to changing supplies of housing characteristics. In order to understand these interactions between housing and local public sector characteristics, it is important to model how local communities make their decisions, a subject to which we now turn.

III. LOCAL PUBLIC SECTOR DECISION MAKING AND HOUSE PRICES

The previous section has outlined a framework for analyzing the factors that influence house prices. As shown in equation (2), local governments can affect house prices through their ability to control various attributes in the housing bundle. Local public services such as education, fire-fighting and police services, water and sewer facilities, and streets are provided directly by local governments for their residents. In addition, a majority of local public services are funded through the property tax. Voting actions by residents, either through referenda or the election of local government officials, determine absolute service levels, the mix of services provided, and property tax rates in different jurisdictions.

Local public sector actions also indirectly affect the supplies of housing and neighborhood characteristics available to moving households. Zoning laws and other development controls affect the supply of land available for development and therefore the amount of new construction that can take place. These laws can also affect the structure-to-land ratio for new housing, the mix of structure types, the density of housing development, and the minimum price necessary to locate in a particular community. Control over these attributes can influence the neighborhood quality of housing and the socioeconomic composition of the population in an area. Other forms of land use and structure regulation, such as housing codes and condominium conversion regulation, can also influence the composition of the housing stock.

Resident households in local political jurisdictions are most likely cognizant of these relationships. They were once mover households who evaluated housing bundles in terms of the quantities of the various characteristics they contained. Assuming that homeowners are motivated by the investment potential of their homes, they are likely to support local government actions which maintain or increase the value of their properties. Several authors (Edelson, 1976; Lea 1979; Yinger, 1979) have suggested that the appropriate model for examining local public service and tax decisions is one in which voters attempt to maximize own property value. This formulation implies that homeowners will vote for service-tax packages for which movers would bid the most. Under this view, it is the potential capitalization of services and taxes into property values which determines local government activity. Voters will vote for a level of public services (or other property value enhancing actions) that equates the capitalized benefits of the service into their property value with the household share of the marginal cost of service provision.[5]

Voting decisions can depend not only on the individual voter's property value and tax share but also on the distribution of property value changes throughout the community that result from local expenditure and tax changes. Differential or intrajurisdictional capitalization, which occurs if local public goods are not pure, can lead to over- or underspending as compared with efficient levels due to the distribution of benefits (as well as taxes) within the community.[6] This situation is especially likely with geographically fixed local government activities. For example, school services may be valued more highly if the housing unit is located near a school. Other examples include the placement of group homes for the handicapped, the location of recreation facilities, and the determination of mass-transit routes. Other intrajurisdictional effects may not be locationally determined but still significant. For example, the valuation of school services may vary with the size of the house or number of bedrooms. In such cases, the benefits from local public services are not uniform within a jurisdiction but accrue differentially to certain households or housing units. Therefore, it is not just average house price and tax base differences between communities that lead to spending differentials. The distribution of public services within a community can also have house price effects and thus influence voting behavior.

The source of funding for local public services may also significantly affect house prices. For example, if capitalization of local public service differentials occurs, a shift away from property tax financing to nonlocal sources of revenue may affect both house prices and the efficiency of local public service provision. In the standard analysis, block grants and revenue sharing have only an income effect; that is, they expand total expenditures in the community but do not affect voting behavior because they do not affect the relative prices of service delivery. In a capitalization model, this result no longer necessarily holds. Intergovernmental aid, which may raise local spending levels without raising local tax rates, may raise the bids for housing in the area and give rise to capital gains for existing residents. If intrajurisdictional capitalization occurs, intergovernmental aid can affect house prices and therefore voting behavior.

During the last two decades, there has been a significant shift away from reliance on local property taxes and an increase in nonlocal funding (a large portion of which is in the form of block grants and revenue sharing). As reported by Break (1980), intergovernmental aid as a percentage of municipal own-source revenue rose from 29% in 1962 to 66% in 1977. The shift was even larger for large cities as municipalities with population over 500,000 received intergovernmental aid in an amount greater than 74% of own-source revenues in 1977. The shift away from property tax financing may have contributed to the increase in the level of house prices during the 1970s.[7] This shift may also have income distributional implications, depending on the variation in the use of nonlocal revenue. In communities that rely more heavily on revenue sharing or block grants, residents are receiving the benefits of locally provided services while shifting part of the cost to federal income taxpayers in general.

Property value maximization motives may also affect the nonexpenditure activities of local governments. Local voters influence zoning policy, either directly through referenda or indirectly through election of zoning board officials. Zoning decisions can be seen as reactions to market forces that establish property values in the housing market. During the 1970s, inflation, coupled with the tax treatment of owner-occupied housing, reduced the after-tax real costs of homeownership, thereby contributing to an increase in the demand for housing. Local residents in certain areas (particularly those with desirable public service or neighborhood amenities) may have responded to the increased housing demand by reducing the supply of land available for development or imposing constraints on the characteristics of new houses in order to perpetuate these gains. More restrictive zoning ordinances may be both property value enhancing and reduce an existing homeowner's tax share if the value of the new houses allowed in the community is greater than own property value. The incentives for restrictive zoning may act in the opposite direction in the future. With rising real after-tax homeownership costs, moving households may demand less space. Thus, property values may be enhanced if less restrictive zoning ordinances are adopted, allowing single-family homes to be split into two-family units or allowing rental apartments in such homes.

The property value maximization model provides but one way of looking at local public sector decision making. It is also important to consider other explanations of voting behavior or at least to question the quality of owner-voters' perceptions of what is property enhancing. As Edelson (1976) points out, the property value maximization approach is equivalent to a utility maximization model if the occupant's evaluation function is the same as the market's evaluation function. However, if these evaluations differ, activities of local communities such as opposition to zoning changes permitting conversion of single-family dwellings into two-family dwellings may be better understood.

A basic assumption of the property value maximization model is that residents have the same valuation function as the market. This is not likely to be the case except in income- and taste-homogeneous communities. Thus, the capitalization model is more relevant to new, low-density, high-income suburbs but is of less use in older areas, heterogeneous areas, and areas where movers differ markedly from existing residents. For example, the extreme mortgage interest rate increases of the past few years have clearly led to circumstances where many existing households are locked in by low-rate nonassumable mortgages. The value of the residences to existing owners may far exceed their value to potential purchasers.[8] The owners' voting decisions may be based on their perceptions of house value that may differ from those of the market.[9]

The growing divergence between valuations by existing residents and those by price-setting movers can explain the apparent paradox of opposition to zoning and conversion changes that are value enhancing. If existing residents intend to remain in the community for any length of time, it is their (unobserved) valuation of their housing bundle which affects their voting decisions, not observable market values. Therefore, support for restrictive zoning decisions may be more consumption enhancing than value enhancing if the desire to maintain neighborhood homogeneity dominates the incentive to allow value-enhancing changes in the existing housing stock.

The effect of differences between residents and movers can be incorporated into the house price model presented in Section II. The value of a particular property can be viewed as an *individual's* bid or offer function if the values on the right-hand side of equation (2) are viewed as the individual's gross rent and the individual's cost of capital. In fact, the value of housing to the jth individual can be expressed as

$$V_j = \frac{P_m + (P_j - P_m)}{K_m + (K_j - K_m)}, \tag{3}$$

where the subscript m refers to the market-clearing value, and K is the cost of capital as expressed in the denominator of (1). Hence, value to a bidder or to an existing household is expressed as market value plus the individual's deviation from the market-clearing value.

A few overlooked aspects of housing market and voting behavior can be understood from this simple expression. Consider first those households who move to a community. To those households, housing attributes are essentially fixed, including those endogenous to the local government. At the time of the move, the household is willing to pay a price for housing that equals the market price, $V_j = V_m$. In other words, the individual responds to the overall price of housing and balances his or her marginal valuations for attributes so that

$$\frac{P_j}{K_j} = \frac{P_m}{K_m} \,. \tag{4}$$

Note that the equality of market and mover marginal valuations of the *housing bundle* need not imply equality of marginal valuations for *each attribute*. Given a less-than-infinite number of available housing bundles, it may be erroneous to conclude that movers are voting with their feet for local governments; instead they may be voting for another attribute for which they have a higher than average marginal valuation (e.g., a house with a view) and accepting the price of good schools as an unavoidable part of the joint purchase. As long as tastes vary and some attributes are relatively scarce, the market-clearing attribute prices tell us very little about the individual demand for local services and amenities. The implications of bundling of housing characteristics need to be incorporated into the analysis of mobility and local government efficiency.

Over time, the equality in equation (4) may vanish, due to either deviations between individual homeowner's and the market-clearing bidder's valuation of attributes or deviations between their cost of capital. Such deviations can affect voting behavior because it is the *perceived* tax price, rather than the actual tax price, that influences voting decisions. The potential for deviation between actual and perceived tax prices needs to be explored in the modeling of local public sector decision making.

IV. RESEARCH NEEDS FOR THE DECADE AHEAD

The discussion to this point has offered a framework for analyzing housing markets and local government interactions. However, very little research has been carried out in some of the areas discussed. Several potentially key parameters and variables have been identified, but sound policy decisions require that the magnitude of their importance be assessed.

The house value formulation presented in equation (1) points out the crucial role of the cost of capital in overall house price determination. There is little doubt in the minds of most analysts that the cost of capital for housing, particularly owner-occupied housing, will rise in the 1980s. Reductions in marginal tax rates and increases in real financing costs are likely to be the primary factors driving this increase. If increases in homeownership costs lead to a reduction in the attractiveness of housing as an investment, households may reduce their housing demand with resultant decreases in house price appreciation. At the same time, higher homeownership costs may reduce the proportion of households that either choose or can afford homeownership. In this event, rental housing demand may increase (in the short run), increasing the value of rental units relative to owner-occupied units.

The cost of capital, however, is not constant across households and regions. The market-clearing household may have vastly different characteristics from housing submarket to submarket, even within the same metropolitan area. Differences in bids for housing bundles may be the result of differences in income tax rates and financing arrangements available to movers as well as differences in the marginal valuations of the housing bundle. In other words, units with similar characteristic bundles may differ in value because the cost of capital of the market-clearing bidder is different. More research is needed as to the impact of variations in the cost of capital on housing prices across spatial areas, between movers and nonmovers, and also between rental and owner-occupied units. In particular, it is essential to identify the characteristics of the market-clearing household, or "median mover," for different areas or bundle types. House price variation may reflect not only income differences but also differences in financing arrangements and expectations.

Another area of research interest in examining house prices is the specification of expected appreciation. The cost of capital and therefore house price is likely to be very sensitive to the specification of this term. More research is needed on how households form expectations of future appreciation. In particular, house price expectations may be a function of the characteristics of the housing bundle, leading to differences in the cost of capital by region, city or suburban location or type of unit.

There are significant implications of these trends for local governments. The most obvious implication is that the major local tax base for many local governments will not be growing very fast and may very well begin to shrink. In that event, local governments would have to raise property tax rates to maintain a constant level of services or seek alternative revenue sources. The former solution is likely to run into substantial opposition from local voters who either suffer from tax rate illusion or have already constrained the use of property taxes through constitutional ceilings on property tax rates. In addition, higher property taxes would exacerbate the problems of a stagnating property tax base. If the alternative to raising property tax rates is a greater use of nonlocal sources of revenue, local residents may find that they have less control over budgetary decisions.[10]

A particularly interesting potential interaction between housing markets and the local public sector may occur if local governments attempt to reduce high financing costs through the provision of below-market financing for new residents through the sale of mortgage revenue bonds. While the future tax exempt status of these bonds may be in doubt, local governments could float nonexempt issues to buy down interest rates for incoming home buyers.[11] Activity by local governments to maintain property values by lowering the homeowner's cost of capital would be most likely in high-income communities and in jurisdictions with binding property tax rate ceilings. If this trend does develop, it would mark the ultimate acknowledgement of the local government-housing market nexus emphasized throughout this paper.

In terms of examining the demand for housing attributes, current research utilizing hedonic price estimation is far from satisfactory. While reduced form estimation provides useful insights into housing market conditions, what is really needed is the ability to disentangle the demand and supply effects that are determining prices. Identification and estimation of characteristic demand functions is an area of particular research importance in order to predict the effects of increasing housing costs or changing demographic patterns on housing markets. In addition, more sophisticated econometric analysis is necessary to infer the demand for local public services from property markets.

While it is hard to speculate about future demands for characteristics because little is known about characteristic demand functions, a couple of observations are in order. The increase in housing costs and continuing presence of a larger proportion of smaller households in the housing market almost certainly implies a decreased demand for space. While household size and household formation will adjust to some degree to rising housing costs, continued low rates of fertility and the aging of the population will exert a downward force on household size.[12] These demographic shifts will also affect the demands for various local public services. In particular, school services may be much less in demand if moving households have fewer children. These trends have serious implications for suburban communities. A decreased demand for space and the traditional suburban public services may make many large single-family houses white elephants in housing markets. Communities that refuse to allow conversions of such units to multiple occupancy could be seriously affected. If the demand for schools falls at the same time as the demand for large houses, the resultant fall in the price of such houses may be quite large. The decreased demand for housing in many suburban areas, coupled with the budgetary problems noted above, may make the 1980s the decade of the crisis of the suburbs.

The potential for significant changes in house prices in the 1980s suggests that more research is needed on capitalization effects. It seems fruitless to continue work under the assumption of no capitalization effects; long-run equilibrium conditions are little more than a pipe dream in housing markets. When the endogeneity of property values and local government activities is taken into account, housing market research becomes intimately tied to local public finance analysis. Do households actually take into account potential capitalization in their voting decisions? What feedback effects exist as a result of local fiscal decisions? Should we seek to separate the analysis of property-value enhancing activities of local governments such as capital infrastructure development from individual specific activities such as social welfare programs? What role does the housing market play in determining the level of provision of such activities? Does the source of funding lead to different house price effects? If so, will the new federalism alter the demand for local public services?

Land use regulation is a area of particular research interest in terms of the impact of potential capitalization on local decision making. Most of the literature in this area has attempted to relate property values to proportions of land zoned for various purposes. However, if communities make their zoning decisions in response to market forces, it suggests that the causality may run in the opposite direction. That is, zoning ordinance changes (either more or less restrictive) may be a function of changes in relative fiscal capacity and demographic characteristics of communities. More research is needed in the area of the timing of zoning decisions and into the factors influencing the restrictiveness of both residential and nonresidential zoning. A time series approach linking zoning changes and property value changes over time would be an important addition to our understanding of the relationships between local regulation and property markets.

Our earlier analysis suggests the importance of identification of the median mover and the median voter in a community. As the discussion in Section III shows, if existing resident voters have different valuations of housing attributes than do market-price setting movers, the property value maximization model may be insufficient to describe housing market and local government interactions. One possible formulation for a model of local public sector decision making is to divide motives for voting into property-value-enhancing and consumption-enhancing votes. An empirical implementation of this approach may involve examination of the extent of differences between the characteristics of long-term residents and newcomers in the community. The larger the differences in income or demographic characteristics, the greater the possible divergence between market values and individual values and the larger the role for consumption-enhancing voting.

Consumption-enhancing voting could be particularly relevant in analyzing the behavior of renters. To our knowledge, no economic studies of local decision making have systematically treated the role of renter households. Renters may attempt to minimize rents, which would explain community decisions to adopt rent control (if renters constituted a majority of voting households) but this model would not do as well in explaining public service decisions. (For example, would renters always oppose rent-enhancing services?) If the market accurately reflects the valuations of the characteristics of the housing bundle, then renter households may have an objective function similar to property-value-maximizing homeowners. The difference in the decisions by the two household types would then revolve around the degree of perceived property tax shifting to renters. Integration of a decision-making model for renter households in the analysis of local public sector actions is an important research consideration for the near future.

How will local residents react to these housing market changes? The property-value-maximization model, which provides the most direct link between housing markets and the local public sector, suggests that local residents will undertake actions to maintain property value. This framework suggests that they will vote to reorient the mix of local public services to correspond to movers' demand for characteristics. An example of this reorientation would be closing down schools and converting them to entirely new uses, such as housing or community centers. Another possible reaction would be to relax zoning ordinances to allow the splitting up of large single-family homes into two-family or multiple-family homes. If such changes are property value enhancing, zoning restrictiveness will be relaxed to the point where the property value effects are balanced by the increased cost of public service provision to incoming households. Local regulations on the conversion of owner-occupied to rental property could also be relaxed. In addition, zoning could be modified to allow the construction of multifamily housing in traditional single-family areas. The latter action may be necessitated by budgetary problems confronted by communities with predominantly single-family houses.

The outlook for the 1980s suggests that the consumption vs. property value motives for voting will lead to conflict in public sector decision making. During the 1970s, these two rationales influencing voting decisions (particularly for exclusive zoning ordinances) often worked in the same direction. In the 1980s, the desire to maintain property values at the same time as excluding less desirable households (from the individual voter's viewpoint) may be at odds. It may be good for the local budget and individual property values to allow more renter households into the community. But the potential increase in heterogeneity may be undesirable for existing residents. The conflict over condominium (and other types of unit) conversions will continue as the demand for smaller, cheaper housing units becomes more intense. Finally, there will be extreme interest taken by existing residents in the closing of existing facilities (schools, social service centers, hospitals, transit stops) and the location of new facilities. If differential capitalization of local public service provision does indeed occur, the property value effects of these decisions may be more visible and therefore more subject to debate and argument in the decade ahead. It is the growing divergence between existing community residents and newly formed households which gives urgency to the research agenda we have outlined.

ACKNOWLEDGMENTS

Helpful comments were provided by Robert Ebel, Patric Hendershott, Wilhelmina Leigh, and Charles Leven.

NOTES

1. For a discussion of the proper specification of equation (1) see Hendershott and Shilling (1982a) and Villani (1982).

2. The calculations in Table 1 are point elasticities, calculated by differentiating equation (1) with respect to different variables and using the parameter values shown at the bottom of the table. The values selected for the parameters are arbitrary, but quite reasonable in the current environment. Nevertheless, they are only suggestive, not predictive, and are sensitive to the values of the parameters of the cost of capital.

3. See Brueggeman et al. (1982).

4. See Johnson and Lea (1982) and Diamond and Smith (1981) for an analysis of the underlying structure of hedonic price equations. It should be noted that this formulation suggests the use of gross rents, not house values, as the dependent variable in capitalization studies. To our knowledge, only Sonstelie and Portney (1980) have empirically used gross rents. However, given a constant cost of capital, the use of house values is perfectly appropriate and probably preferred since imputing an unobserved rent for owner-occupied houses is no simple task.

5. This model is derived explicitly in Lea (1982).

6. See Johnson and Lea (1982) and Li and Brown (1980) for empirical evidence of differential capitalization. Bloom et al. (1980) provide a thorough discussion and investigation of intrajurisdictional property tax capitalization.

7. This point is discussed in greater detail by Robert M. Buckley, Lily Ann Marden, and John C. Simonson, "Federal Grants to Local Governments and Changes in the Property Tax," in this volume.

8. See Hendershott and Hu (1982) and Lea (1982) for a discussion of the potential magnitude of these effects.

9. This implies that empirical estimation of expenditure determinants using actual property values as part of the tax price may lead to biased estimates.

10. For one possible scenario, see Anthony H. Pascal, "The Postmunicipal City," in this volume.

11. Note that this activity already occurs with tax exempt issues. The negative capitalization of property tax rate increases into property value partially offsets the positive capitalization of interest rate reductions. The elasticity calculations in Table 1 indicate that house values are likely to be more sensitive to interest rate changes than to property tax rate changes, though the resultant effect depends on the magnitude of the parameter changes as well as their direction.

12. See Joint Center for Urban Studies (1981). This statement is true even if baby boom births raise the aggregate birth rate. Data clearly show trend away from large families.

REFERENCES

Akin, John and Douglas Young Day (1976). The Efficiency of Local School Finance. *Review of Economics and Statistics* (May): 255-258.

Bloom, Howard S., Helen F. Ladd, and John M. Yinger (1980). Draft Report: Intrajurisdictional Property Capitalization. Department of City and Regional Planning, Harvard University (July).

Break, George (1980). *Financing Government in a Federal System.* The Brookings Institution.

Brueggeman, William, Jeff Fisher and Jerrold Stern (1982). Rental Housing and the Economic Recovery Act of 1981. *Public Finance Quarterly* 10, 2 (April):222-241.

Brueggeman, William and Richard Peiser (1979). Housing Choice and Relative Tenure Prices. *Journal of Financial and Quantitative Analysis* 14 (November): 735-751.

Diamond, Douglas (1980). Taxes, Inflation, Speculation and the Cost of Homeownership. *AREUEA Journal* (Fall): 281-298.

Diamond, Douglas and Barton Smith (1981). Housing as an Implicit Good, unpublished manuscript (November).

Dougherty, Ann and Robert Van Order (1982). Inflation, Housing Costs and the Consumer Price Index. *American Economic Review* 82 (March): 154-164.

Edelson, Noel (1976). Voting Equilibria with Market Based Assessments. *Journal of Public Economics* 5: 269-284.

Hamilton, Bruce (1978). Zoning and the Exercise of Monopoly Power. *Journal of Urban Economics* (January): 116-130.

Hendershott Patric (1980) Real User Costs and the Demand for Single Family Housing. *Brookings Papers on Economic Activity* 2:401-444.

Hendershott, Patric and Sheng Hu (1982). Accelerating Inflation annd Nonassumable Fixed Rate Mortgages: Effects on Consumer Choice and Welfare. *Public Finance Quarterly*, 10, 2 (April): 158:184.

Hendershott, Patric and James Shilling (1982a). The Economics of Tenure Choice: 1955-79. In C. F. Sirmans, (ed.), *Research in Real Estate*, Greenwich, Ct.: JAI Press, Vol. I.

Hendershott, Patric and James Shilling (1982b). Capital Allocation and the Economic Recovery Tax Act of 1981. *Public Finance Quarterly*, 10, 2 (April:242-273.

Johnson, Michael and Michael Lea (1982). Differential Capitalization of Local Public Service Characteristics. *Land Economics* 58 (May): 189-202.

Joint Center for Urban Studies of MIT and Harvard University (1981). Trends on Housing and Demographic Factors: An Interim Report to the President's Commission on Housing (December).

Lea, Michael J. (1979). Local Public Expenditure Determination: A Simultaneous Equations Approach. *National Tax Association-Tax Institute of America, Proceedings of the Seventy-First Annual Conference*: 131-136.

Lea, Michael J. (1982). Local Tax and Expenditure Capitalization: Integrating Evidence from the Market and Political Processes. *Public Finance Quarterly* 10 (January): 95-117.

Lea, Michael J. (1982). Housing Demand and the Standard Mortgage Instrument: Comment. *Public Finance Quarterly* 10, 2 (April: 185-192.

Li, Mingche M. and H. James Brown (1980). Micro-Neighborhood Externalities and Hedonic Housing Prices. *Land Economics* 56 (May): 125-141.

Mills, Edwin (1979). Economic Analysis of Urban Land Use Controls. In Peter Mieszkowski and Mahlon Straszheim, (ed.), *Current Issues in Urban Economics*. The Johns Hopkins University Press: 511-541.

Rosen, Sherwin (1974). Hedonic Prices and Implicit Markets: Product Differentiation in Pure Competition. *The Journal of Political Economy* 82 (January-February): 34-55.

Sonstelie, Jon L. and Paul R. Portney (1980). Gross Rents and Market Values: Testing the Implications of Tiebout's Hypothesis. *Journal of Urban Economics* 7 (January): 112-118.

Tiebout, C. (1956). A Pure Theory of Local Expenditures. *Journal of Political Economy* 64: 416-424.

Villani, Kevin (1982). The Tax Subsidy to Housing in an Inflationary Environment. In C. F. Sirmans, ed., *Research in Real Estate*, Greenwich, Ct.: JAI Press, Vol. 1.

White, Michelle (1978). Self-Interest in the Suburbs: The Trend Toward No-Growth Zoning. *Policy Analysis* 4 (Spring): 185-203.

Yinger, John M. (1979). Capitalization, the Theory of Local Public Finance, and the Design of Intergovernmental Grants. Department of City and Regional Planning, Harvard University (September).

Yinger, John M. (1981). Capitalization and the Median Voter. *American Economic Review* 71 (May): 99-103.

FEDERAL GRANTS TO LOCAL GOVERNMENTS AND CHANGES IN THE PROPERTY TAX

Robert M. Buckley, Lily Ann Marden and
John C. Simonson

I. OVERVIEW

Our analysis focuses on what appears to have been one of the most fundamental changes in local government in the past 15 years—a new means of financing almost one-sixth of local expenditures. Between 1964 and 1980, as Table 1 shows, federal grants have substituted for the property tax almost point-for-point as a percentage of local expenditure. This paper investigates the implications of that substitution and speculates about the effects of recent policy changes that will almost certainly reverse the shift from property taxes to federal grants.

Although we are particularly interested in how these changes may have affected the housing market, we first review recent analyses of federal grants to local governments. The point of this discussion is to suggest, first, that the incidence of such a shift in revenue sources depends upon the nature of the real resource constraints on local governments and, second, that the nominal constraints im-

Research in Urban Economics, Volume 4, pages 273-287.

Table 1. Sources of Local Expenditures, 1964 and 1980

1964	Revenue as-percent of local Expenditures		1980	Revenue as per-cent of local Expenditures
\$43.2 bill.		Local expenditures	\$212.1 bill.	
12.4	29%	Federal and state grant-in-aid	93.3	44%
20.5	48	Property tax	65.6	31
3.0	7	Other taxes	20.8	10
6.9	16	Debt financed plus user charges	31.8	15
6.8%		Expenditures as a share of GNP	8.1%	

Source: Significant Features of Fiscal Federalism 1981-1982 Edition (Washington, D.C.: Advisory Commission on Intergovernmental Relations, 1983), Tables 1, 2, 17.

posed by granting authorities may be quite different from the real resource constraints on local expenditures. We then show why these considerations are important in analyzing the housing market effects of changes in local revenue sources. Finally, we consider some of the public finance issues likely to be associated with shifts in federal-local financing arrangements.

To summarize our findings for the housing market, in the late 1970s the apparent substitution of federal grants for the property tax as a local revenue source significantly decreased the cost of capital for homeownership; not surprisingly, it also contributed to the notable tenure shift toward homeownership. In retrospect, these results may seem to be relatively straightforward. However, the property tax component of the change in the homeownership subsidy generally has been either overlooked or underestimated by the literature on the after-tax cost of homeownership. Consequently, the relative costs of owning vs. renting have been higher than has been estimated and, correspondingly, the large tax-induced tenure shift toward homeownership has probably been overestimated.

Our results suggest that the after-tax cost of homeownership followed the decline described in previous studies, but it was from a substantially higher level. During the late 1960s and early 1970s increases in the property tax partially offset decreases in other components of the homeownership cost of capital. Then, after 1971, and particularly after 1974, decreases in the property tax rate reinforced the interaction of inflation and the federal tax code in decreasing the homeownership cost of capital.

The property tax burden on owner-occupied housing appears historically to have been higher than is commonly thought to be the case; hence, at least with regard to the property tax, owner-occupied housing tends to be taxed more heavily than is other capital.[1] However, due to changes in revenue sources, the property tax is now financing a diminished share of local government expenditures. As a result, the cost of capital for homeownership has been significantly affected by shifting sources of local government finance.

With respect to public finance effects, our findings are: (1) Reduced reliance on the local property tax has very likely improved not only the economic efficiency of local governments but also the overall economic efficiency of resource allocation. The likely reversal in this trend associated with the New Federalism and the budget cuts to local governments can be expected to reduce the efficiency of resource allocation. (2) According to the "new view" of the property tax, the incidence of the shifts in revenue sources has been regressive. This implies that the New Federalism's shifting of costs back to local governments is likely to be progressive. However, in a broader fiscal analysis the regressivity of the substitution of grants for the property tax seems much less likely, particularly when interjurisdictional tax differences are considered. (3) Substitution of federal grants for property tax revenue has probably been a significant factor in the growth in the government share of the economy. (4) Seemingly minor changes in the federal tax code have increased the homeownership cost of capital by a greater amount in less rapidly growing cities, particularly during a period like the present when refinancing costs are substantial.

In what follows we briefly discuss recent analyses of grants to local governments and present an analytical framework. We then present estimates of the effect on the housing market and tenure choice. Finally, we discuss the more general public finance issues and qualify our results.

II. ANALYTICAL FRAMEWORK

Our analytical framework takes as given the increased volume of federal grants to local governments, giving no consideration to why the federal government chose this course of action. We do, however, offer a theoretical explanation for why local governments have opted to substitute federal grants for property tax revenue on an almost dollar-for-dollar basis.

We also offer a rationale for why nonmatching federal grants appear to have a more stimulative effect on local spending than do increases in community income. Our analysis relies upon neither Mieszkowski and Oakland's (1979) "flypaper effect" (money sticks where it hits), or Courant, Gramlich, and Rubinfeld's (1979) appeal to fiscal illusion from voters' confusion of marginal and average costs. Nevertheless, we do not offer this view as the only plausible explanation of why local governments have substituted grants for the property tax. Our point is much simpler: when real rather than the nominal resource constraints upon local governments are considered, local government behavior is readily understandable in terms of conventional economic decision making. There is no need to invoke fiscal illusion, lack of fungibility, or bureaucratic maximization frameworks as others have done. When real constraints are identified, seemingly noneconomic behavior (associated with nominal resource constraints) is clearly perceivable as economically rational behavior.

In brief, our explanation of local governments' substituting federal grants for property tax revenue follows, first, from our viewing the property tax as a tax on capital rather than as a user price, and second, from voters' realization that, in the long run, federal grants to localities must be paid for by higher federal taxes. The result is the observed substitution between revenue sources, the greater stimulus associated with grants vis-à-vis community income, and the increased share of GNP accounted for by local governments.

Following Mieszkowski (1967) and Aaron (1975), we view the property tax as being, in effect, two kinds of taxes. First, it is a tax on capital. Second, the many interjurisdictional differences in property taxation make it similar to an excise tax, to the extent that these differences do not reflect varying levels of local services.

If local government officials try to maximize community wealth, and individuals believe that grants to communities must be financed out of increased federal taxes in the long run, grants/taxes will tend to have exactly offsetting income effects. A grant shifts the household's budget constraint out by the same amount that the anticipated increased income tax to finance the grant shifts it back. Instead of viewing a grant to the community as a simple resource transfer from the rest of the economy to their community, households realize that their community's ability to qualify for a grant is not unique. Similar grants to other communities will have to be financed through federal tax payments. Hence, grants are not perceived as being equivalent to a resource transfer and, therefore, do not have an income effect.

Grants do have a price effect, however, If the property tax is a tax on capital rather than a user fee, then the individual owner of capital benefits to the extent the grant is substituted for the property tax. In addition, because the property tax is a deductible expense in calculating federal income tax liability, increases in the federal income tax rate have served to lower the after-tax burden associated with a given property tax.

We assume that the marginal property tax burden on owner-occupied housing exceeds the marginal benefits of local services to the housing unit; therefore, at least part of the property tax can be assumed to be a true tax rather than a fee for local services. Substituting the federal income tax for this excise-like tax on property changes the relative prices of local public goods so that more public goods are demanded for a given level of real income. Thus, grants financed through the federal income tax can increase the demand for local public goods directly. It is the change in relative prices rather than confusion between marginal and average costs, or the lack fungibility presumed by the aforementioned "money sticks" proposition, that induces a change in demand for public goods.

Our perspective on the property tax is also consistent with the conventional notion that the burden of this tax is on the owners of capital at the time the tax was imposed. This suggests that the incidence of the property tax depends upon household tenure. Renters do not pay the property tax; owners do. Hence, we expect more revenue substitution in communities with higher homeownership rates, other things being the same.

III. HOMEOWNERSHIP COST OF CAPITAL

To track the effect of the property tax on the cost of homeownership and how it may have changed over time we must first estimate the property tax rate on housing. Previous estimates of this rate have assumed it to be constant—Hendershott (1980), Hendershott and Hu (1981) and Hendershott and Shilling (1982)—that it equals the property tax rate on other capital—Rosen and Rosen (1980) and Ladd (1973)—or that it is less than the rate on other forms of capital—Aaron (1975). We take issue with these assumptions.

Besides ignoring the potential effects of changing sources of local revenues, studies based upon such assumptions overlook the effects of: (1) tax concessions that local governments frequently give to corporationss to induce them to locate in their communities; (2) difficulties associated with appraising corporate properties which are infrequently sold, and not readily marketable; and (3) the fact that government owns about 20% of the economy's net capital stock which is not taxed, and that other exempted properties may comprise as much as an additional 10% of the capital stock which is also not taxed.

Biases in estimating property tax rates on housing can be reduced substantially by utilizing National Income Product Accounts (NIPA) estimates of the property tax on owner-occupied nonfarm housing vis-à-vis the rest of the capital stock. These estimates indicate that the approximately 25% of the capital stock comprising owner-occupied housing has provided about 40% of total property tax revenue, the remaining 75% of the capital stock providing about 60% of the property tax revenue. On average, therefore, the property tax on owner-occupied housing has been about twice the rate on other capital (40/25 vs. 60/75). The Commerce Department surveyed the rates of tax on various forms of taxable capital stock in 1967 and 1971. From these surveys, along with Rosenberg's (1969) analysis, we can infer that the property tax rate on owner-occupied housing exceeded that on other forms of taxable capital by about 11% in each year for which there are data.

The first column of Table 2 presents estimates of property tax rates during the period 1964-1979. Four things seem noteworthy about these estimates:

First, they are initially higher than those presented by Hendershott's work which assumes a constant property tax of 1.8%, and they increase until 1971. As a result, a significant share of the fall of the relative cost of capital for homeownership between the 1960s and early 1970s is illusory. For example, between 1964 and 1970 Hendershott and Hu estimate that the cost of homeownership fell by 158 basis points or 24%. But during the same time period the after-federal-income-tax property tax rate on owner-occupied housing increased

Table 2.   Relative Revenue and Expenditure Trends, 1964-1980

	Property Tax Rate	Federal Expend./ GNP	Local Expend./ GNP	Federal Grant-in Aid/ GNP	Federal Marginal Tax Rate
1964	1.80	18.5	6.8	1.6	.18
1965	1.86	17.9	7.0	1.8	.19
1966	1.86	19.0	7.2	1.8	.19
1967	1.96	20.5	7.4	1.9	.19
1968	1.97	20.7	7.6	2.2	.19
1969	1.95	20.0	7.8	2.1	.19
1970	2.16	20.6	8.0	2.4	.19
1971	2.16	20.5	8.1	2.5	.19
1972	2.05	20.6	8.4	2.9	.22
1973	1.90	19.9	8.6	3.2	.22
1974	1.77	20.9	8.8	3.0	.22
1975	1.77	23.0	9.2	3.0	.22
1976	1.73	22.4	8.7	3.3	.22
1977	1.63	22.0	8.5	3.5	.22
1978	1.40	21.3	8.4	3.6	.25
1979	1.27	21.1	8.1	3.6	.24
1980		22.9	8.1	3.6	.25

Source: Various tables from the *Economic Report of the President,* 1982, and *Significant Features of Fiscal Federalism,* 1980-81. Marginal Tax rates from Diamond (1980).

The property tax rate is equal to the indirect business tax and non tax liability of residential owner-occupied dwellings divided by the net capital stock of residential owner-occupied housing inflated by the residential property site/value ratio.

For further discussion of the estimates see Buckley and Simonson, "Estimating The Property Tax on Owner-Occupied Housing," unpublished staff paper, HUD.

by 30 basis points. That is, almost 20% of Hendershott and Hu's estimated reduction in the cost of homeownership over this period was offset by the increase in the property tax rate. Furthermore, if the difference between the property tax rate on owner-occupied housing and other forms of property capital was constant, then the property tax rate on owner-occupied housing exceeded the rate on other capital by an average of roughly 100 basis points. This differential has an excise-tax-like effect on homeownership, offsetting another 60% of the estimated reduction in housing's cost of capital. Taken together, these changes offset 80% of the presumed fall in the estimated homeownership cost during the last half of the 1960s, although the rate of decline is very similar.

Second, when estimates of the real after-tax cost of homeownership are considered, it is clear that the size of the discrepancy between the rates presented here and previous estimates is sizable. While there is a good deal of difficulty in estimating the after-tax inflation-adjusted homeownership cost of capital (hcc), Dougherty and Van Order (1982) estimate that between 1968 and 1980 the average rate was about 1.5% for households in the 25% marginal income tax bracket. In Hendershott's analyses, hcc is estimated at approximately 4% for a household in the 30% bracket. The difference between our estimates of the property tax, 2.16% to 1.27%, and Hendershott's assumption of a constant rate of 1.8% are plus 0.36% and minus 0.53%, respectively. In terms of overall costs, this difference is as much as one-third of Dougherty and Van Order's estimates of the total effective cost of capital for homeownership, and one-eighth of Hendershott's.

Third, the relevant tax rate on housing services vis-à-vis other capital taxes appears to be higher than previously estimated. Ladd, for example, calculates that a property tax rate of 1.8% in 1969 translated into a 26% tax on the imputed income from housing. Assuming a real rate of return of 5%, she calculates

$$\frac{\text{property tax}}{R + \text{property tax}} = 26\% \qquad (1)$$

But, if R = 4% as Hendershott estimates or 1.5% as Dougherty and Van Order estimate, then, for our estimates of the property tax rate the imputed income tax is as high as 35% to 59%, respectively.

Fourth, after peaking in 1971 property tax rates have declined by over 40%. This trend, taken together with the increased share of GNP spent by local governments, suggests that changed property taxes are only part of the story. Higher federal taxes were needed to pay for the increased federal grants which enabled a reduced reliance on local revenue.

Moreover, the method of paying for these higher federal expenditures was through inflation-related tax bracket creep which, in turn, further increased the subsidy to homeownership. For example, the median income household in 1964 was in the 19% cumulative marginal federal and state income tax bracket. By 1979 this household was in the 29% cumulative bracket.[2] The amount that the increase in marginal tax rates increases the relative subsidy to homeownership depends upon the expected inflation rate. To take an illustrative example, interpolating between Hendershott and Shilling's calculations of the homeownership cost of capital for households in the 15% and 30% marginal brackets, we calculate that in 1979 the increase in marginal tax brackets reduced hcc by almost 40% for the median income household.

Now consider, albeit crudely, how much of that bracket creep was attributable to increased federal grants to local governments. In 1964 federal grants to localities accounted for 1.6% of Gross National Product; in 1980 the share was 3.6%, a 2 percentage point increase. Overall government expenditures as a share of GNP rose from 18.5% to 22.9% during this period, a 4 percentage point increase (see Table 2). Federal transfers to individuals also increased by about 4% of GNP. In sum, then, the federal share of GNP increased by about 8 percentage points. If grants had been maintained at their 1964 share of GNP, the government share of GNP would have increased by 25% less, other things remaining the same. If we assume that 25% of the bracket creep experienced by the median income household from 1964 to 1980 financed the expanded use of grants, then, instead of increasing from 19% to 29%, the median income household would have been in a 26% cumulative marginal tax bracket at the end of the period. Thus, according to our earlier interpolations, the bracket creep associated with financing the reduced property tax rates may have reduced home-ownership costs for the median income household by an additional 10%. Thus, it seems likely that the indirect effects associated with financing the reduction in property taxes reduced hcc by a greater amount than did the direct reduction in property taxes.[3]

IV. TENURE CHOICE

To examine how these changes may have affected tenure choice decisions we must make some critical assumptions about the incidence of the tax. In what follows we consider the incidence of only that part of the property tax that can be viewed as a tax on capital; we ignore any interjurisdictional differences in property tax reduction. We assume as did Mieszkowski (1967) that:

> A renter who does not own any wealth will not bear any of the burden of the property tax. An individual who owns a $20,000 house and another individual who owns $20,000 worth of manufacturing equipment will both bear the same tax burden.

Figure 1 standardizes Hendershott and Shilling's estimates of the capital cost of owning a home for a household in the 30% marginal tax bracket, with 1964 equal to 100. We then make two adjustments.

The first adjustment, immediately above the solid line, accounts for year-to-year changes in the property tax rate as well as the higher property tax rate on owner-occupied housing relative to other forms of capital. It indicates that, over the entire period considered, the cost of owning declined more rapidly than Hendershott and Shilling estimated due to the reduction in property taxes. It also indicates that, prior to 1978, the cost of owning was about 12% higher than they estimate.

Of course, this is only the direct effect. As noted above, the bracket creep associated with increased reliance on grants caused the subsidy to homeownership to increase significantly. The "marginal" homebuyer should not be characterized as having had a constant marginal tax bracket over this time period as Hendershott and Shilling have done. In 1964 a household in the 30% marginal tax bracket was in the top income quintile and had a homeownership rate in excess of 75%, whereas by 1979 such a household approximated the median income family. The dotted line in Figure 1 indicates that, prior to 1978, the homeownership

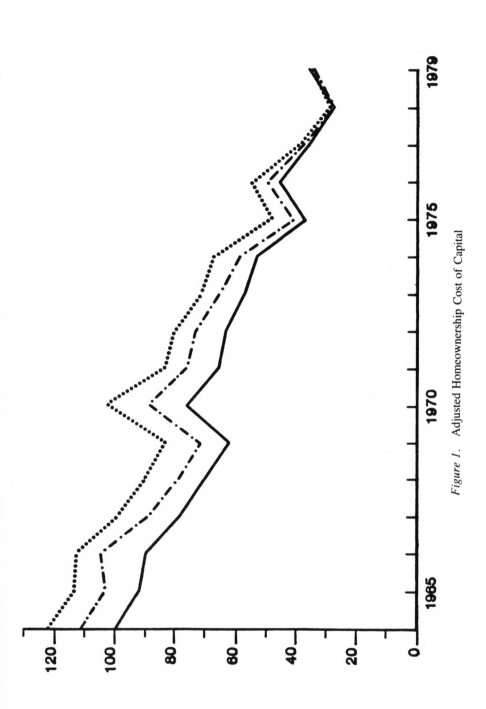

Figure 1. Adjusted Homeownership Cost of Capital

281

cost of capital averaged 19% higher than Hendershott and Shilling estimate, as long as we consider the median-income household to be the marginal homebuyer.[4]

In summary, our analysis suggests that the homeownership cost of capital may have been significantly different than estimated by Hendershott and colleagues. To determine the effect of this difference on tenure choice and housing demand requires an explicit model, which is beyond the scope of this paper. However, Hendershott's (1980) work provides some support for the view that the effects are not trivial.

In his model hcc affects tenure choice with a long lag. Given our adjustments to hcc, one would expect housing demand to increase greatly very late in the 1970s. This is precisely what happened. Hendershott's out-of-sample simulations between 1978:1 and 1980:2 significantly underpredicted the number and quality of housing starts. Although other factors may also be involved, this result is consistent with what our estimates would tend to imply.

V. PUBLIC FINANCE EFFECTS

As noted earlier, we view the property tax as a tax on capital and, therefore, characterized by inefficiencies inherent in local government revenue generation. This suggests that, to the extent increased federal grants substitute for property taxes, resource allocation would be improved, provided, of course, that inefficiencies associated with financing grants are less than those associated with property taxation. However, we analyzed neither the costs of the inefficiencies nor the structures of the grants designed to overcome them. We cannot comment directly, therefore, on whether displacement of property taxation by federal grants did or did not improve resource allocation. Nevertheless, we can argue by inference that the displacement led to greater efficiency for local governments.

The almost percentage-point-for-percentage-point substitution of grants for property taxes as well as the only slightly larger share of GNP accounted for by local government expenditures are both consistent with the supposition that increased use of grants has improved efficiency of resource allocation by local governments. Indeed, one could suggest that the extent to which grants have been substituted for the property tax provides a measure of the grants' price as opposed to income effect on communities' resource constraints. From this perspective it appears that increased used of federal grants entailed almost exclusively price effects; therefore, ignoring the possible distorting price effect that matching grants might have had, increased use of federal grants would seem to have resulted in substantially improved allocative efficiency. This view undoubtedly overstates the improvement in economic efficiency of local government finance attributable to increased federal grants, but it also implies how difficult it would be to argue that local government efficiency was not at all improved by the increased use of federal grants.

The issue of how this substitution of grants for the property tax affects the efficiency of resource allocation is especially critical given recent macroeconomic policy changes. For example, indexation of the federal income tax implies that bracket creep will not continue to finance an increased share of GNP in grants to local governments. Furthermore, if this "no growth" in grants constraint is combined with: (1) the implicit premise of the New Federalism that localities should finance local public services, and (2) the increased demands on federal revenues by planned defense spending, it is clear, as Gramlich and Laren (1982) show, that the substitution of federal grants for property taxes is not only at an end, it has been reversed.

Unless there are significant changes in the current thrust of macroeconomic policy, local governments can be expected to finance more of their expenditures through the property tax, and households' tax brackets will not increase with inflation. Substituting property taxation for federal income taxation of households will reduce efficiency. For instance, suppose that in 1971 the tax code was indexed in such a way that the property tax rate stayed at the 1971 level rather than fell to the 1979 level. According to our earlier calculations (see Section III), this would result in an increase in the tax on capital from 24% to 35% (at a 4% rate of return).

To estimate how much this increased tax on capital reduces the tax on labor, we need to identify factor shares for capital and labor. If capital's share is 30% of income, then, ignoring price effects, the same level of tax revenue can be attained by reducing the average tax on labor by about 5% $(.3 \times .11)/.7 = .05$.

While the calculation of the deadweight loss, associated with this kind of shift, is complicated by a number of factors, it is relatively straightforward to argue that there is a loss in economic efficiency when the tax on the factor with the greater elasticity, capital (almost three times greater, according to estimates by Boskin, 1978, and Hausman, 1980), is increased by more than twice the rate that the tax on the less elastic factor is reduced. Because capital's factor share is so much smaller than labor's, this effect is increased further still.

The new conventional wisdom suggests that it is an easy step to comment on how reducing the property tax affects income distribution. However, our analysis of recent shifts in local government revenue sources indicated that an understanding of income distribution effects requires a broad fiscal analysis which identifies local governments' real resource constraints. One cannot determine the incidence of a particular shift in revenue sources, for example, solely by examining the distribution of tenure groups by income class.

Nevertheless, such data do provide a useful starting point. Table 3 shows the distribution of renters and owners by income quintile in 1970 and 1978, showing that homeownership rates have increased sharply both by income quintile and over time.

To the extent that it is borne by landowners, the property tax is, as Aaron (1975) has noted, a progressive tax. Federal income tax, on the other hand, is generally thought to be a proportional tax (Pechman and Okner, 1974). It follows,

Table 3.   Homeownership and Rental Rates by Income Quintile, 1970 and 1978

	Homeownership		Rental	
	1970	*1978*	*1970*	*1978*
Lowest Income Quintile	49.84%	45.25%	50.16%	54.71%
Next to Lowest Quintile	51.15	60.00	48.85	40.00
Median Quintile	60.74	73.14	39.26	26.86
Next to Highest Quintile	72.43	81.55	27.57	18.45
Highest Income Quintile	80.17	88.11	19.83	11.89
TOTAL	62.87	65.2	37.13	34.8

Source: 1970 Data from 1970 Census of Housing. 1978 Data from 1978 Annual Housing Survey Part A.

then, that substituting federal income taxes for property taxes results in a more regressive overall distribution of tax burden. However, the reason why the property tax is relied upon so heavily by local government is an important consideration in assessing its overall fiscal incidence.

For example, suppose the property tax is relied upon too heavily by communities because of an inability to finance capital expenditures efficiently, e.g., because of some capital market imperfection. If local government capital stock is distributed more progressively than is the rest of the capital stock, it may well be the case that the property tax is regressive. In a more general fiscal context such as this, the property tax is seen as shifting the incidence of the burden associated with a borrowing inefficiency from the owners of local public goods to the owners of other capital. The distribution of this tax may be regressive, progressive, or proportional depending upon the progressivity of the distribution of local public capital relative to the distribution of private capital. To the extent that differences in local property taxes are positive excise taxes, regressivity is more likely.

We should further qualify the view that the growing use of grants has been regressive by noting that this is an aggregate effect. It assumes that grants were indeed substituted for the property tax. In many areas of the country this substitution simply was not possible, and it may well be the case that our reliance on aggregate figures masks serious differences existing among localities, including those which were unable to, or which simply chose not to, substitute federal grants for the property tax. Olsen (1971), for example, has demonstrated how individuals eligible for a tied federal grant can be categorized into three mutually exclusive groups. The optimal response to such a government subsidy is very different for individuals in each of these groups. There may be a similar categorization scheme for local government response, depending upon, as we noted earlier, the distribution of voters over tenures. If so, the excise tax aspects of the property tax will be more important.

The excise tax effects are particularly important in areas of the country where the housing stock turns over much less rapidly and bears a relatively high property tax rate. In such areas it is much more difficult for local government to substitute grants for the property tax. For many of these communities their higher-than-average property tax rates already act as a positive excise tax on housing. Not only is there a lack of an expanding tax base, because property is appreciating slowly, but liberalizations in the standard deduction have reduced the likelihood that property tax payments are deducted from federal income taxes.[5]

Finally, it is interesting to speculate on how the increased use of grants affected the government's role in the economy. In Table 2 we showed that between 1964 and 1980 the increase in the share of GNP spent by local governments was about 20%, or 1.3% of GNP. Another perspective on the influence of grants is gained were we to assume that the respective shares of local expenditures financed by federal grants and by the property tax remained at their 1964 rates (e.g., that in 1980 the property tax had to finance 48% of the $212 billion in local expenditures in that year), and then estimate the property tax rate on owner-occupied housing that would have been needed to finance these expenditures. The property tax would have had to yield $36 billion more, with owner-occupied housing having to contribute about $14-15 billion of this increase. This would have required about a 50% higher property tax rate on owner-occupied housing than actually existed in 1979. Given household resistance to the current declining property tax rate, it seems highly unlikely that taxpayers would have accepted such increases. In sum, it seems reasonable to conclude that the shift in sources of local government finance has played a nontrivial role in the growth of the government share of the economy.

ACKNOWLEDGMENTS

We would like to thank Douglas Diamond, Helen Ladd, Kathy Bradbury, and Robert Van Order for helpful comments without implicating them in any errors. The views expressed here are those of the authors and not those of the U. S. Department of Housing and Urban Development.

NOTES

1. Among the previous studies which have assumed owner-occupied housing to be taxed at the same or even lower rate than other capital are those by Hendershott (1980), Ladd (1973), Hendershott and Hu (1980), Rosen and Rosen (1980), and Aaron (1975).

2. Our estimate of the marginal state income tax rate assumes that the same relationship between the average tax rate and the marginal tax rate for the median income household exists between state rates as is the case with federal rates. We then applied this ratio to average state tax rates which are published. The marginal rate for state income tax ranged from 1% to 4%.

3. Using equation (1) we can estimate that the property tax reduction between 1964 and 1979 was 7%.

4. This estimate uses our estimates of cumulative marginal tax rates which include state income taxes as well as federal. We use the marginal tax bracket of the median-income household and then

interpolate hcc from Hendershott and Shilling's cost of capital for households in the 30% and 15% brackets.

5. Consider the case of a median-income household that purchased a home in Massachusetts during the mid-1960s and a household with the same income and nonhousing tax deductions that purchased a comparable housing unit in California three years ago. If the housing/capital stock ratios in both states are the same, then the average property tax rate on the former unit is almost two and one-half times the rate on the California house. In Massachusetts, in 1964/65, 41.0% of local expenditures were financed by the property tax. California local expenditures had a similar share (44.0%). In Massachusetts the share actually increased by 4 percentage points by 1980, while in California the property tax share dropped by over 60% to 16.8% of local expenditure. In addition, because of the increase in the standard deduction the Massachusetts household cannot deduct property tax payments. The result is that the property tax component of the after-tax housing cost of capital for the Massachusetts household is the same as the before-tax rate. Consequently, it is four rather than two and a half times higher than the California rate. In 1964, on the other hand, before grants were substituted for the property tax, and before the liberalization in the standard deduction, these households would have paid virtually the same property tax (see Column 3). Clearly the federal government's sharing of the property tax burden favors more rapidly growing areas of the country.

REFERENCES

Aaron, H. J. (1975). *Who pays the Property Tax?* Studies of Government Finance. Washington, D.C.: The Brookings Institution.

Boskin, M. (1978). "Taxation, Saving, and Investment." *Journal of Political Economy.*

Courant, P. N., E. M. Gramlich, and D. L. Rubinfeld (1979). "The Stimulative Effects of Intergovernmental Grants: Or Why Money Sticks Where It Hits." *Coupe Papers on Public Economics*, edited by Peter Mieszkowski and William H. Oakland. Washington, D.C.: The Urban Institution.

Diamond, D. B. (1980). "Taxes, Inflation, Speculation, and the Cost of Homeownership." *American Real Estate and Urban Economics Association Journal* (Fall): 281-298.

Dougherty, A. J. and R. A. Van Order (1982). "Inflation, Housing Costs, and the Consumer Price Index." *American Economic Review* (March): 154-164.

Gramlich, E. and D. Laren (1982). "The New Federalism," in Joseph Pechman (ed.), *Setting National Priorities The 1983 Budget*. Washington, D.C.: The Brookings Institution.

Hausman, J. (1980). "Income and Payroll Tax Policy and Labor Supply," in *The Supply-Side Effects of Economics Policy*, Proceedings of the 1980 Economic Policy Conference, St. Louis Federal Reserve Bank.

Hendershott, P. and S. Hu, (1980). "The Relative Impacts of Various Proposals to Stimulate Business Investments." *The Government and Capital Formation, in Capital Investment and Savings*, George M. Von Furstenberg (Ed.). Cambridge, MA, Ballinger Publishing Company,

Hendershott, P. (1980). "Real User Costs and The Demand for Single-Family Housing." *Brookings Papers on Economic Activity.*

Hendershott, P. and S. Hu (1980). "Government-Induced Biases in the Allocation of the stock of Fixed Capital in the United States." *Capital, Efficiency and Growth in Capital Investment and Savings*, Vol. 3, edited by George W. Von Furstenberg, Cambridge MA. Ballinger Publishing Company.

Hendershott, P. and J. S. Shilling (1982). "The Economics of Tenure Choice, 1955-1979." *Research in Real Estate*, Greenwich, Ct.: JAI Press 105-133.

Ladd, Helen F. (1973), "The Role of the Property Tax: A Reassessment." In R. Musgrave (ed.), *Broad Based Taxes: New Options and Services*, John Hopkins Press.

Mieszkowski, P. (1967). "On the Theory of Tax Incidence." *Journal of Political Economy*, (June), 250-262.

Okner, B. A. and J. A. Pechman (1974). *Who bears the Tax Burden?* Studies of Government Finance, Washington, D.C.: The Brookings Institution.

Olsen, E., (1971), "Some Theorems in the Theory of Efficient Transfers." *Journal of Political Economy*, (January/February): 166-176.

Rosen, H. S. (1979). "Housing Decisions and the U. S. Income Tax: An Econometric Analysis." *Journal of Public Economics* (February): 1-23.

Rosen, H. S. and K. T. Rosen (1980). "Federal Taxes and Homeownership: Evidence from Time Series." *Journal of Political Economy*, (February-June): 59-74.

Rosenberg, L. (1969), "Taxation of Income from Capital, by Industry Group." In A. C. Harberger and M. J. Bailey (eds.), *Taxation of Income from Capital*. Washington, D.C.: Brookings Institution.

MANAGING PROGRAM TRANSITION:
TAKING HOUSING VOUCHERS SERIOUSLY AS A NATIONAL PROGRAM

John M. Quigley

INTRODUCTION

By Executive Order, on June 16, 1981, the President's Commission on Housing was established to advise the executive branch on national housing policy and the appropriate federal role in housing markets. Among other tasks, the Commission was directed to "detail program options for basic reform of federally subsidized housing. . . ." An interim report was submitted by the Commission on October 30, 1981, and an outline of the Commission's recommendations was released on April 29, 1982.

The interim report recommended a fundamental change in the housing subsidy policies benefiting low-income households—the replacement of existing programs by vouchers, or housing allowances. In October 1981 the Commission recommended "that the primary federal program for helping low-income families achieve decent housing should be a consumer-oriented housing assistance grant.

Research in Urban Economics, Volume 4, pages 289-305
Copyright © 1984 JAI Press Inc.
ISBN: 0-89232-423-6

This grant system should replace future commitments to build additional units under Section 8, Section 202, and public housing.''[1] In the final report of the Commission, it proposed ''replacing Federal programs to construct subsidized new housing for low-income people with a program of direct payments to households to help them pay their rent.'' This ''Housing Payments Program'' would be modeled after the HUD Section 8 Existing Housing program and would include features of the housing allowance idea.[2]

The concept of a Housing Payments Program or a system of Consumer-Oriented Housing Assistance Grants is certainly not new. In fact, the concept of housing allowances was discussed extensively in the report of the *last* presidential housing commission (''The Kaiser Committee'')[3] in 1968, which concluded that the ''potential merits of the housing allowance approach are such that it should be tried promptly on [an] experimental basis. . . .''[4]

For the nonpoor, the concept of housing allowances was incorporated into an operational program more than 60 years ago by the Internal Revenue Code. These housing allowances are a combination of a ''housing-gap'' subsidy and a ''percent-of-rent'' subsidy and are provided only to a certain class of households, namely, homeowners who itemize deductions for their federal income taxes. The tax subsidy, arising from the treatment of imputed rent (or service flows) on owner-occupied housing, is equivalent to a voucher issued under a specific Housing Payments Program. The voucher entitles the recipient to a specified percentage reduction in the price of housing, with larger percentage reductions going to those with higher incomes. The administrative costs of the current Housing Payments Program are negligible. The subsidy is calculated annually when tax returns are filed, and vouchers are issued monthly in the form of reduced withholding taxes. The Congressional Budget Office has estimated that more than 40% of the vouchers issued under the existing housing payments program are redeemed by households in the top 15% of the income distribution.[5]

In any case, for low-income households the experiment recommended by the Kaiser Committee was adopted in Title V Section 504 of the 1970 Housing and Urban Development Act.

Support of housing allowances for the poor formed the basis for HUD Secretary James T. Lynn's testimony on housing and community development legislation in 1973,[6] and a series of experiments was implemented beginning in 1974 at a cost of more than $200 million.

In this discussion we assume that, at last, the policy question is no longer whether a program of housing allowances for the poor should be adopted. We do not recount the many arguments for or against some form of housing allowance program.[7] We accept the principle that some form of housing allowance of voucher program is to be adopted. We discuss instead the range of specific housing allowance programs, their implementation problems, and their costs.

Section II of the paper notes the five basic types of housing payments programs which have been the focus of the experiments. Together with the Appendix, which presents some simple economic and accounting models of housing allowances, Section II indicates how behavioral information and program design parameters can be used to estimate program costs and housing market effects.

II. PROTOTYPE VOUCHER PLANS: THE EXPERIMENTAL TREATMENTS

As noted before, during the past decade the federal government has spent some $200 million on experimental housing allowance programs. These experiments—the largest and most expensive social experiments in history—attempted by direct observation to determine the effects of five different Housing Payments Programs on household behavior and housing markets. The allowance formulas which have been tested using renter households in two metropolitan areas include a "percent-of-rent" program and three variants of a "housing-gap" program. A fourth housing gap program enrolled renters and owners in two other housing markets.

Under the first formula, eligible households of income y received a transfer payment θ which was some fraction x of its monthly rent R:

$$\theta(y_i) = xR_i, \qquad \text{for households with } y_i < y^*. \qquad (1)$$

Eligibility for this payment was based only upon verification that household income was below some cutoff level, y^*, which varied by family size. Eligible households thus received a payment of 100x "percent-of-rent," where x was varied experimentally from 0.2 to 0.6.

Under the second program, eligible households received a transfer payment ϕ which depended upon an estimate of the metropolitan wide cost of "minimum standard" housing, c, and household income:

$$\phi(y_i) = c - by_i, \qquad \text{for } y_i < y^*. \qquad (2)$$

The basic payment made to households of zero income, c, represents the average cost of "minimum standard" housing, which varied by family size (number of bedrooms) as well as metropolitan area; the tax rate on income, b, was varied experimentally between 0.15 and 0.35. Under this program, participating households received a payment representing the "gap" between the cost of minimally acceptable housing and 100b percent of household income.

The third and fourth programs used the same payment formula as (2) but imposed additional restrictions on eligibility. Under the third program, the so-called minimum-rent program, households received payments only if their rent exceeded some minimum, i.e., if $R_i > c$. Again c varied by family size; eligible households received payments only if their rental payments exceeded an estimate of the cost of minimum standard housing. Under the fourth program, the "minimum-standards" program, households received transfer payments only upon verification that they lived in dwellings that satisfied a specific list of 14 physical standards.

The fifth experiment was not really an experiment at all, but rather a "demonstration." This demonstration used a single payment formula, a "housing-gap" formula which compensated households for the difference between the estimated cost of standard housing and 25% of their incomes [i.e., b = 0.25 in equation (2)]. These payments were conditioned upon certification that households' dwellings satisfied a specific set of physical standards (similar but not identical to those of the fourth experiment). Owner-occupants as well as renters were eligible for transfers under this demonstration.

As noted in the Appendix, the effects of any of these allowance programs on recipients and on costs to the government depend upon only a few behavioral parameters. The elasticity of housing supply and the income and price elasticities of housing demand together determine the market effects and program costs of a policy using either of the first two types of formula. The latter three types of program all place earmarking restrictions on recipient behavior; it may therefore be perfectly rational for some eligible households to decline to participate in the program. Thus, to evaluate the market impacts and program costs of these three types of payment plan, it is necessary to know the effects of any plan's incentives upon the probability of household participation in the program.

Before considering the probable costs and effects of alternative programs, the incentives inherent in the first and the third experimental prototypes should be noted. In both cases, for any eligibility rule, the amount of the subsidy varies directly with the certified rent payment of the recipient regardless of the character of housing actually inhabited by that recipient household. Thus, under a national program modeled on the "percent-of-rent" or the "minimum-rent" experiment, there would be incentives for collusion between landlord and tenant—to inflate rent receipts above market rates and to share the additional subsidy.

It should be noted, first, that these incentives for collusion arise in a number of other programs as well. For example, merchants and food stamp recipients have common incentives to use food stamps for the trade of nonfood substances. Buyers and sellers of used cars have incentives to discount transaction prices and to share reduced state sales taxes.

It should also be noted that there is no experimental evidence that any landlords or tenants actually colluded to increase subsidy payments under the "percent-of-rent" or the "minimum-rent" formulas in either of the two metropolitan areas where the experiments were undertaken—at least no evidence that I have been able to uncover. Nevertheless, in a national Housing Payments Program, the potential gains to collusion between landlord and tenant are quite high; moreover, rental transactions are much more difficult and expensive to monitor than most others.[8] These grounds lead me to believe that a "percent-of-rent" housing payment plan or a voucher conditional upon minimum rental payments is unworkable administratively and unacceptable politically.

The choice between an unrestricted "housing-gap" payment and a "minimum-standards'' program, as well as the decision to include owner occupants among the class of eligible households, has both political and economic dimensions.

There are at least three aspects of this choice which affect program costs and housing market effects. First, the imposition of physical standards affects household participation rates (given any eligibility formula) and hence program costs. Second, the imposition of physical standards affects administrative costs by requiring inspections. Third, the eligibility formula, the level of payment, the inclusion or exclusion of owners, and the imposition of standards may not only affect program costs directly but may have indirect effects on costs and outcomes by increasing general housing prices.

III. DESIGNING A PAYMENT PLAN

A. Three Undesirable Program Features

There are three principal criticisms of current housing subsidy policies—criticisms that any housing payments play should be designed to avoid.

Table 1 illustrates graphically the first of these. It presents recent information on the distribution of household types by tenure, poverty status, and residence in subsidized housing. The table reports that about 8.15 million households, or about 30% of U. S. renter households, have incomes below 125% of the poverty level (or under about 50% of median income). In contrast, about 13% of owner households have incomes below 125% of the poverty level. As the table indicates, households of the same composition and income class are treated very unequally by current programs. For each low-income household served by current housing subsidies, about three others of similar circumstances are not served. Altogether, more than 6 million households with incomes below half of the median are unserved by low-income housing subsidies.

Table 2 illustrates the second major criticism of existing subsidy programs: the high cost to the government per household served. The table indicates that average subsidy costs per household served under the major programs currently providing low-income housing—public housing and Section 8 of the 1974 housing act. As noted, under new construction and substantial rehabilitation programs, government costs vary from about $200 to $300 per household per month. In fact, the average figures reported in Table 2 substantially underestimate the cost of subsidizing a marginal household under current programs. Estimates for marginal costs run as high as $3650 per year per household (averaged across programs).

By indicating the length of subsidy commitments, up to 40 years, Table 2 also hints at the third major criticism of existing programs: the long-term nature of federal obligations, and the uncontrollable nature of future outlays under existing contractual obligations.[9]

Clearly a housing payment program that overcomes these three objections—

Table 1. Distribution of Household Types by Tenure, Poverty Status and Residence in Publicly Subsidized Housing: 1980 (millions of households)

Type	Number of Households	Renter Households Total	Below 1.0 Poverty Total	Served*	Unserved	Below 1.25 Poverty Total	Served*	Unserved	Owner Households Total	Below 1.0 Poverty	Below 1.25 Poverty
All households	82.37	26.51	6.06	1.43	4.63	8.15	1.87	6.28	55.88	4.91	7.40
With children	34.33	10.04	3.13	0.79	2.34	3.95	0.92	3.03	24.29	1.80	2.66
Elderly	16.91	4.13	1.24	0.41	0.83	1.93	0.65	1.28	12.78	1.95	3.21
Inside SMSA's	56.07	19.96	4.26	1.08	3.18	5.80	1.41	4.39	36.11	2.48	3.83
Inside central cities	24.47	11.34	2.88	0.85	2.03	3.90	1.09	2.81	13.13	1.23	1.85
Female headed	9.08	4.53	2.11	0.67	3.47	2.49	0.77	1.72	4.55	0.86	1.17

Note: *Includes those "households residing in publicly owned or other subsidized housing."

Source: Department of Commerce, Bureau of Census, *Current Population Reports*, P60, No. 128, October 1981.

Table 2. Estimates of Program Costs per Household Served in
Selected HUD Programs in 1980

Program	Contractual Commitment	Range of Annual Costs
Section 8 Existing	15 Years	$1560–1750
Section 8 New Construction	20	2750–3300
Section 8 New Construction	30	2590–3390
Section 8 Rehabilitation	40	2490–3510
Public Housing	40	2200–2530

Source: Congressional Budget Office, *The Long-term Costs of Lower-income Housing Assistance Programs*, 1979, p. xiv.

horizontal inequity, high cost per household, and uncontrollable long-term commitments—must have three characteristics. First, it must be "universal" in the sense that households of the same circumstances (e.g., income, family size, or tenure) are treated identically in a given local area. Second, the payment formula must be designed so that payments to recipient households are "modest." Third, federal contributions to recipient households must be capped.

B. Standards, Eligibility, and Payment Schedules

Obviously decisions about eligibility rules and the payment schedules offered to those households deemed eligible are crucial to the determination of program costs. However, the nature and stringency of any minimum housing standards imposed is also an important determinant of costs. For given eligibility rules and payment schedules, the imposition of physical standards will change program costs directly by affecting the participation rate of eligible households and indirectly through the administrative cost of inspection and verification.

Should the housing payments program require recipient households to reside in dwellings certified as meeting physical standards? The answer to this question depends upon the relative importance attached to the housing adequacy of dwellings for low-income households vs. the affordability of these dwellings. It also depends upon the ease of identifying adequacy as compared to affordability.

Table 3 suggests the dimensions of the affordability program for low-income households. About 70% of renter households spend less than 30% of their incomes on rent. In contrast, almost two-thirds of very-low-income households spend more than 30% of their incomes on housing. Almost three in ten of these households spend half of their income on housing. This qualitative pattern is similar for owner occupants. Virtually any housing payment plan will help solve the affordability problem facing these low-income households (as long as demand is inelastic—even one in which the recipients do not use their transfers to buy more housing). If households are required to live in dwellings that meet certain

Table 3.   Distribution of Households by Tenure, Income Class, and
Housing-Income Ratio: 1977

	Percent of Income Spent on Housing		
	0-30	*31-50*	*51 +*
Renters			
All households	69.6%	19.3%	11.1%
Very low income[a]	37.4	34.2	28.5
Low income[b]	73.8	23.8	2.4
Owners			
All households	86.8	10.0	3.2
Very low income[a]	52.8	29.8	17.4
Low income[b]	80.0	17.5	2.6

Notes:

[a] Defined as households with incomes below 50% of median.

[b] Defined as households with incomes above 50% and less than 80% of median.

Source: Congressional Budget Office, *Federal Housing Assistance: Alternative Approaches*, May 1982, p. 10.

standards to qualify for assistance, then program participation rates will be lower. However, as both the housing allowance demand and supply experiments have shown, program participation rates are likely to be far lower for those households initially living in dwellings that do not pass housing standards.[10] These households, in turn, are likely to be of the lowest income and are more likely to be minority households. Thus, a program which imposes minimum standards is one which would provide fewer benefits, in terms of affordability, to those households with the greatest need for relief. It might be worth foregoing these benefits if we could be confident that the payment program really induced participating households to consume "better" housing by imposing standards. The experimental evidence suggests that this is not the case. In particular, by comparing housing consumed by participants in the "minimum-standards" housing allowance experiment, researchers discovered that the correlation between dwellings providing "minimally adequate" housing (according to other reasonable criteria) and those passing program standards (according to the checklist of specific items) was rather low.[11] Thus, on balance, it appears that a housing payment plan incorporating as few standards as possible is to be preferred. This, in turn, implies a higher participation rate among eligible households, and higher program costs, for a given set of eligibility rules and payment schedules.

What should be the income eligibility standards [y* in equation (2)] and payment schedules for a national program of housing vouchers? Here any choice among alternatives is based less on analytical issues and more on ethical views about appropriate levels of transfer and on a purely budgetary perspective. Table 4 illustrates the implications of alternative views about the "appropriate" share

Table 4. Alternative Income Limits for a Housing Payments Program: 1980

			Annual Income Limits			
				Assuming Tenant contribution of		
Size of Household	Number of Bedrooms	Estimated Fair Market Rent[a]	From Supply Experiment[b]	30%	35%	50% of Median[c]
1	0	$183	$ 8,760	$ 7,320	$ 6,274	$ 4,418
2	1	221	10,621	8,740	7,577	8,595
3	2	263	12,645	19,529	9,017	10,813
4	2	263	121,645	10,520	9,017	12,168
5	3	307	14,721	12,280	10,526	12,422
6+	4	346	16,613	13,840	11,863	14,449

Note:

[a] Estimated from samples of fair market rents for Section 8 existing housing and expressed in 1980 dollars. *Federal Register*, Vol 46, No. 52, pp. 17367-17511.

[b] Assuming, as in the housing allowance supply experiment, a tenant contribution of 25%

[c] U.S. Bureau of the Census, *Money Income and Poverty Status of Families and Persons: 1980*, Series P-60, No. 127, August 1981, Table 1.

of income spent on housing. The third column presents 1980 estimates of the monthly cost of standard housing [denoted by c in equation (2)] based upon random samples of HUD-established fair market rents drawn from the *Federal Register*. Column 4 presents estimates of the income limits [y* in equation (2)] for a housing payment program with the same eligibility rules as the housing allowance supply experiment, that is, adopting the norm that low-income households be "expected" to spend 25% of income [b in equation (2)] on housing. There is, of course, no normative significance to the 25% figure. Columns 5 and 6 present income limits consistent with 30% and 35% of income as the "expected" contribution of tenants for housing (that is, the incomes at which the subsidy is zero). For comparison, the last column presents a 1980 estimate of 50% of the median income for each family size. The table indicates that a program based on a 30% tenant contribution would result in income eligibility limits very similar to the limits if eligibility were confined to those households earning less than half of median income. Under such a program, the cap, or maximum government payment, would be about $2200 a year for a single person, $3600 for a family of five, and $4200 for the largest households.

IV. FINANCIAL ISSUES

A. What Would a Voucher Plan Cost?

Projections of the cost of an operational Housing Payments Program depend upon detailed information on the income and demographic composition of low-income households. In this section, we rely upon the most recent information available on the distribution of households by income, family size, tenure, and age to provide cost estimates of several operational programs.[12]

In addition to this body of data, however, any cost projections depend upon a number of highly specific behavioral assumptions as well. As far as possible, we rely upon the evidence amassed as a result of the allowance experiments for these behavioral assumptions. Where possible, we indicate the possible biases introduced by this procedure.

We consider six basic programs, differing by the income limit and tenant housing expenditure contribution and by the presence or absence of a minimum standards requirement similar to that adopted by the housing allowance supply experiment. The 30% tenant contribution refers to a program with the income eligibility limits presented in column 5 of Table 4. Eligible households receive a housing payment equal to the difference between the cost (market rent) of standard housing, which varies by family size, and 30% of their incomes. The 35% tenant contribution refers to a program with the eligibility limits presented in column 6 of the same table; payments under this program are equal to the difference between the cost of standard housing and 35% of income. Estimates are also presented for a 40% contribution rate. Given the cost of "minimum-standard" housing (fair market rents), the subsidy to any household can be computed from its income and family size; the average subsidy per household depends upon the distribution of household incomes by family size.

In a universal program that imposes no housing standards, participation rates are assumed to be 84% for both owners and renters (this represents the average of the observed participation rates for renters only in the unconstrained programs in the demand experiment).[13] In a universal program that imposes minimum housing standards, participation rates are assumed to be 30% for owners and 55% for renters, the average of the observed participation rates in the two metropolitan areas under the demonstration program.[14] This assumption may lead to an overestimate of the average cost per household served under a minimum standards housing payment plan.[15]

In a Housing Payments Program confined to the elderly, we use the more detailed participation rates calculated from the demonstration.[16]

The costs of administration, inspection, and monitoring are estimated to be 23% of transfers for programs imposing standards, due to inspection requirements, and 10% for programs that do not impose standards.[17]

Finally, we assume that the Housing Payments Program has no affect on housing prices.[18]

Table 5 presents estimates of the annual cost of alternative housing voucher plans. Each of the variants is a universal plan with eligibility varying by income, tenure, and elderly designation. For programs including all households, cost estimates range from $22.8 billion (for a tenant contribution rate of 30% with no standards imposed) to $9.3 billion (for a program imposing standards and requiring a 40% contribution rate).

Table 5. Estimates of Annual Cost of Alternative Housing Payment Plans[a] (billions of dollars: 1980)

Standards Enforced	*Yes*			*No*		
TenantContribution (% of income)	*30%*	*35%*	*40%*	*30%*	*35%*	*40%*
a. Costs						
All households	$13.4	$11.1	$ 9.3	$22.8	$19.0	$15.8
Renters only	9.2	7.7	6.5	13.2	12.3	8.8
Owners only	4.2	3.4	2.8	9.6	6.7	6.9
Elderly households	2.9	2.5	2.1	4.9	4.2	3.5
Renters only	2.0	1.7	1.4	3.1	2.6	2.1
Owners only	0.9	0.8	0.7	1.8	1.6	1.4
b. Householdds served (millions)						
All households	8.0	7.6	7.3	15.7	14.8	14.2
Renters only	5.3	5.1	4.9	8.1	7.8	7.5
Owners only	2.7	2.5	2.4	7.6	7.0	6.7

Note:
[a] See text for assumptions.

Programs confined to renters would cost $6.5-$9.2 billion if standards were imposed and $8.8-$13.2 billion without minimum standards. If eligibility were restricted to the elderly, programs requiring minimum standards would cost $2.1-$2.9 billion. Obviously, these estimates are subject to several sources of errors. An operational program based upon estimates of the rent for minimum standard housing varying by local market (such as the Section 8 program) would probably cost somewhat less than these projected figures.

B. Where Should the Money Come from?

Table 6 presents a comparison of federal housing outlays on the major programs of rental assistance and the modest (Section 236) homeowner program. A comparison of Tables 5 and 6 gives some perspective on whether a voucher program is at all feasible. It appears that all renter households could be eligible for a voucher plan with minimum standards and a 35% contribution rate for less than this year's federal outlay for other rental programs. Such a reallocation of resources would serve 5.1 million of the lowest-income households instead of the 3.9 million households currently served. Note that 1982 public housing expenditures, for debt service and operating subsidies, are about the same as annual expenditures for a voucher program covering all elderly households.

The most direct way to finance a Housing Payments Program would be through some combination of new appropriations and the transfer of unspent appropriations under existing programs. By transferring appropriations to the Housing

Table 6.   Distribution of Federal Housing Outlays by Program, 1979-1982
(in billions)

Program	1979	1980	1981	1982[a]
Section 8	$1.37	$2.10	$3.11	$3.91
Public Housing	1.16	1.36	1.47	2.84
Rent Supplements	0.27	0.27	0.28	0.28
Section 236	0.64	0.66	0.67	0.67
Section 235	0.10	0.11	0.20	0.29
	$3.54	$4.50	$5.73	$7.99

Note:
[a] Estimated.
[b] Including $1.6 billion for debt service expenses and $1.3 billion for operating subsidies.
Sources:
For 1982 estimate Congressional Budget Office, *Federal Housing Assistance: Alternative Approvals*, May 1982,
p. 17.
For 1979-1981   Office of Management and Budget, *Budget of the United States Government: Appendix* FY
1981 (p. 506), FY 1982 (p. 457), FY 1983 (p. 8-75)

Payments Program, more households can be served at the same cost. If the equivalent of about a third of this year's outlays under current rental programs could be diverted, a universal Housing Payments Program for the elderly could be financed. Such a program would be more equitable, would concentrate assistance on the neediest households, and would serve far more households for the same cost to the government.

APPENDIX:
SOME SIMPLE ECONOMIC AND ACCOUNTING
MODELS OF THE HOUSING PAYMENT PROGRAM

The logical benchmark for comparison or evaluation of allowance programs is the operation of the unsubsidized market. Equations (1a) through (4a) present a stylized example of the key market relationships:

$$h_i^d = A y_i^\alpha p_i^{d^\beta}; \tag{1a}$$

$$p_i^d = p_j^d = p^s; \tag{2a}$$

$$h_i^s = \sum_i h_i^d; \tag{3a}$$

$$h_i^s = B p^{s^\gamma}. \tag{4a}$$

Equation (1a) is a simple log linear demand curve for housing services. The quantity of housing services demanded by household i, h_i^d, depends on exogenous income, y_i, and the price of housing it faces, p_i^d, as well as the elasticity parameters, α and β, and an arbitrary constant. In equation (4a), the quantity of housing supplied in the market, h^s, depends upon the supply price, p^s, a supply elasticity γ, and an arbitrary constant. Competitive market equilibrium implies that supply equals market demand (3a) and that prices are equal for all suppliers and demanders (2a).

The simple model represented by (1a) through (4a) yields the equilibrium housing supply h^s, its distribution across consumers h_i^d, and the price p^s which clears the market.

Now consider the effect of housing allowances, "housing-gap" or "percent-of-rent" payments to selected households. Let $\phi(y_j) = \phi_j$ be a "housing-gap" allowance policy which increases the unrestricted income of households of income y_j by $100\phi(y_j)$ percent; let $\theta(y_j) = \theta_j$ be a "percent-of-rent" housing allowance policy which reduces the housing prices faced by households of income y_j by $100\theta(y_j)$ percent.

If the subsidy is "untied," in the sense that an individual qualifies for the program regardless of his choices in the market, the demand relationship for a qualified individual is

$$H_i^d = Ay_i^\alpha \, (1 + \phi_i)^\alpha P_i^{d^\beta}. \tag{1b}$$

Due to the subsidy, suppliers and demanders face different prices:

$$P_i^d = (1 - \theta_i)P^s. \tag{2b}$$

As before, however, housing supply is produced competitively, and supply and demand are equalized in equilibrium:

$$H^s = \sum_i H_i^d \tag{3b}$$

$$H^s = BP^s. \tag{4b}$$

Given the specification of a Housing Payments Program [i.e., $\phi(y_j)$ and/or $\theta(y_j)$], the model represented by equations (1b) through (4b) yields a new equilibrium housing supply H^s, its distribution across consumers H_i^d, and the price for housing which clears the market.

Under these simplified conditions, the aggregate effects of a specific housing payments program can be compared with the status quo. In general, the effects of the policy on housing markets and the costs of the policies to the government depend upon the price and income elasticities of demand, the supply elasticity, the specific housing allowance offer made to household i, its probability of accepting the offer, and the distribution of offers and acceptances throughout the market.

For example, the proportional increase in housing consumption by household i induced by this "untied" form of a housing payments program is

$$\frac{H_i^d - h_i^d}{h_i^d} = (1 + \phi_i)^\alpha (1 - \theta_i)^\beta \left[\frac{\Sigma_i y_i^\alpha (1 + \theta_i)^\alpha (1 - \theta_i)^\beta}{\Sigma_i y_i^\alpha} \right]^{\beta/\gamma - \beta} - 1. \qquad (5)$$

k

The proportionate change in the value of housing consumed by household i is

$$\frac{P^s H_i^d - p^s h_i^d}{p^s h_i^d} = (1 + \phi_i)(1 - \theta_i)^\beta [k]^{\beta + 1/(\alpha - \beta)} - 1. \qquad (6)$$

Finally, the proportionate change in the "rent burden" of household i, that is, housing payments as a fraction of income (call them R_i and r_i, respectively), is

$$\frac{R_i - r_i}{r_i} = (1 + \phi_i)(1 - \theta_i)^{\beta + 1}[k]^{\beta + 1/(\alpha - \beta)} - 1. \qquad (7)$$

Suppose, for example, the price elasticity of housing demand were minus one-half ($\beta = -0.5$) and the income elasticity were plus one-half ($\alpha = 0.5$). Under these conditions, if a small fraction of the households in the market received a 10% "housing-gap" allowance and a 10% "percent-of-rent" allowance subject to no restrictions ($\phi_i = 0.1$; $\theta_i = 0.1$), the policy would lead to an 11% increase in housing consumption by recipient households, to an equivalent increase in the value of housing consumed, and to a 6% decline in rent burdens regardless of the supply elasticity.[19] The subsidy S_i received by household i under the program is

$$S_i = y_i \phi_i + \theta_i A y_i^\alpha (1 + \phi_i)^\alpha \left[\frac{A}{B} k \right]^{\beta + 1/(\alpha - \beta)}, \qquad (8)$$

and the cost to the government is the sum of subsidies over the set of consumers.

It is instructive to consider the effects of one of the simplest forms of a housing allowance. Suppose housing supply is completely elastic ($\gamma = \infty$) and a uniform "percent-of-rent" policy is adopted ($\phi_j = 0$ for all j and $\theta_j = \theta$ for some class of eligible households).

The cost to the government for any household is

$$S_i = \theta(1 - \theta)^\beta A y_i^\alpha. \qquad (9)$$

This public subsidy produces two effects—generally effects which move in the opposite direction. First, the subsidy leads to an increase in the housing consumption of the recipient. The fraction f of the subsidy used to improve housing conditions is, from (1b) and (4b),

$$f = \frac{1}{\theta} [1 - (1 - \theta)^{-\beta}]. \tag{10}$$

Second, the subsidy leads to a reduction in the "rent burden" of the recipient. The proportionate reduction in the ratio of rental payments to income, g, is similarly

$$g = 1 - (1 - \theta)^{\beta + 1}. \tag{11}$$

As the price elasticity approaches 0, the fraction of the subsidy used to increase housing consumption approaches 0 and the fraction used to reduce rent burdens approaches 1. As the price elasticity approaches -1, the fraction of the subsidy used for housing increases and the effect upon rent burdens approaches 0.

At least for these simple stylized models, the costs of untied percent-of-rent or housing-gap policies can be forecast on the basis of three parameters α, β, and γ and the subsidy formulas themselves. The same behavioral and program parameters can also be used to forecast the effect of the policy upon the housing and nonhousing consumption of recipients. As α and β increase (in absolute magnitude), an unrestricted housing payments program looks more like a housing program; as α and β get closer to 0, any program looks more like a general income maintenance program. As γ is smaller, any housing payments program has less effect on the housing consumption of recipients.

These simple analytics become somewhat messier when "standards" are imposed, that is, when transfers are conditional upon the consumption of a certain amount or type of housing. In this case, eligible households may quite rationally decline to participate in a payments program if the value of the standards themselves is low relative to the value of the other components of housing and if the level of monetary payment is low.

The costs of this subsidy program to the government, z, vary with the probability of participation by eligible households, and for any individual this probability ρ_i, in turn, varies with the size of the subsidy offer s_i and the specifics of the restrictions on consumer choice:

$$z = \Sigma \, s_i \rho_i$$

and $\tag{12}$

$$\rho_i = \rho(s_i, \, \dots \,).$$

The costs of alternative national housing allowance programs estimated in Table 5 are derived from behavioral assumptions about consumer response consistent with the results of the housing allowance experiments. For example, for a program that imposes minimum standards, the participation rate for renter households is assumed to be 55% (i.e., $\rho = .55$). These behavioral assumptions are noted in the text. For a "housing-gap" subsidy formula [equation (2) in the text], the cost figures reported in Table 5 also depend upon the cost of standard housing c and the number of eligible households. The estimated cost of standard housing, which varies by family size, is reported in Table 4 for 1980. The number of eligible households is estimated from the Annual Housing Survey (AHS) for 1980. The AHS presents estimates of the distribution of households by tenure, income class, family size, and elderly status. These tabulations of raw data are presented below in Table A-1. The computations in Table 5 in the text further assume, where necessary for interpolation, that the density of households by income within any income class is uniform.

Table A-1. Distribution of Households By Tenure, Income, Family Size, and Elderly Status: 1980
(thousands)

	Household Income				
Family Size	$ –0– 2999	$3000 6999	$7000 9999	$10000 14999	$15000 +
a. Owners					
1	913	2739	1132	1183	1985
2	554	1955	2054	2964	9514
3	257	451	547	1213	7041
4	220	320	332	1007	8010
5	130	142	162	446	3951
6+	81	143	149	402	2524
b. Renters					
1	1351	3083	1323	1858	2169
2	675	1577	1136	1608	2984
3	363	830	624	911	1601
4	205	493	399	616	1240
5	88	249	200	313	507
6+	66	248	181	248	409

Source: U.S. Department of Commerce, Annual Housing Survey, *Characteristics of the Housing Inventory: 1980*, pp. i-vi.

NOTES

1. The President's Commission on Housing, *Interim Report* (mimeo), October 31, 1981, p. 6.
2. The President's Commission on Housing, *Highlights of Commission Recommendations* (mimeo), April 29, 1982, p. 1.
3. President's Commission on Urban Housing, *A Decent Home*, December 11, 1968, pp. 71-75.
4. *Ibid.*, p. 72.

5. U. S. Congressional Budget Office, *Federal Housing Policy: Current Programs and Recurring Issues* (Washington, D.C.: U. S. Government Printing Office, 1978), pp. 40-43.

6. U. S. House of Representatives, Committee on Banking and Currency Hearings before the Subcommittee on Housing, "Housing and Community Development Legislation," October 9-12, 1973, Part I, pp. 973ff.

7. For recent discussions of these issues, see Edgar O. Olsen, "Housing Programs and the Forgotten Taxpayer," *The Public Interest*, No. 66, Winter 1982, pp. 97-109, and Jill Khadduri and Raymond J. Struyk, "The Case for Housing Vouchers in a Time of Fiscal Restraint," *Journal of Policy Analysis and Management*, Vol. 1, No. 2, pp. 196-208.

8. For example, it is much easier to agree that a transaction on, say, a 1975 Volkswagen is at the "market rate" than it is for a particular two bedroom apartment in a metropolitan area.

9. Federal outlays on these programs are subject to little control, since tenant contributions are capped by law and any unanticipated cost increases are borne solely by the federal government. The long-term costs of commitments under existing housing assistance programs depend upon the rate of increase in housing expenditures and costs relative to recipient incomes over a long time horizon.

10. See Mahlon Straszheim, "Participation," in *Do Housing Allowances Work?*, Katherine L. Bradbury and Anthony Downs, eds. (Washington, D. C.: The Brookings Institution, 1982), pp. 113-146.

11. See David W. Budding, "Draft Report on Housing Deprivation Among Enrollees in the Housing Allowance Demand Experiment," Cambridge, Mass., Abt Associates, November 1978.

12. Basic data are taken from *The Annual Housing Survey: 1980 Financial Characteristics of the Housing Inventory*. The survey provides tabulations of income class, of tenure, and of family size for all households and a separate tabulation for elderly households (pp. 2-6).

13. See Stephen Kennedy and Jean MacMillan, *Draft Report on Participation Under Alternative Housing Allowance Programs*, Abt Associates, October 1979.

14. See Grace Carter and Steven L. Balch, *Measuring Eligibility and Participation in the Housing Assistance Supply Experiment*, Rand Corporation, 1981.

15. As discussed previously, if housing standards were imposed we would expect a lower participation rate among households with the lowest incomes and largest family sizes; that is, we would expect more of the most "expensive" households (and, arguably, most deserving) to drop out.

16. Under a program that does not impose minimum standards, we again assume an 84% participation rate. With standards, we follow Carter and Balch and assume: renter singles, 64%; renter couples, 31%; owner singles, 43%; owner couples, 24%. See Carter and Balch, *op. cit.*, pp. 76-78.

17. The 23% figure is consistent with the findings of the demonstration (see David B. Carlson and John D. Heinberg, *How Housing Allowances Work: Integrated Findings from the Experimental Housing Allowance Program*. The Urban Institute, 1978, pp. 40-47). The 10% figure is consistent with Aaron's observations about administrative costs under existing welfare programs (see Henry Aaron, "Policy Implications: A Progress Report," in Bradbury and Downs, *op. cit.*).

18. This is *consistent* with the experience reported from the two demonstrations where housing standards were imposed and thus participation rates lower. (See the Rand Corporation, *Fourth Annual Report of the Housing Assistance Supply Experiment*, May 1978.) This assumption is also consistent with the expected long-run effects of such a program.

19. If the fraction of households receiving subsidies is small, the term in square brackets, k, in equations (5), (6), and (7) is almost 1.

INDEX

Aaron, H.J., 276, 277, 283
Accelerated Cost Recovery System, 149
Adams, C., 197
Advisory Commission on Intergovernmental Relations (ACIR), 25, 134, 168, 174, 182, 184, 188-189, 190, 191, 193, 194, 195, 197, 198, 200, 207, 211, 215, 231, 232
Agglomeration economies, and business locational choice, 105, 107, 112
Age
  demographic change and, 2, 5
  migration patterns and, 40
  residential locational choice and, 93-94
Agriculture sector, and economic change, 13

Ahlbrandt, R.S., Jr., 237
Aid programs, see Federal aid programs
Aid to Familes with Dependent Children (AFDC), 169
  reduction in coverage under, 150, 156, 159, 199
  state government and, 192, 194
Alchian, Armen, 135
All-Savers Certificates, 214
Alonso, W., 98, 99
A-95 grant review, 173
Annual Housing Survey (AHS), 36, 84, 87, 304
Apilado, V.P., 107
Arizona, 107, 133

Bahl, R.W., 218-219
Baker v. Carr, 195, 196
Beam, D.R., 191

307

Beckmann, M.J., 98
Bergen County, New Jersey, 111
Birch, David L., 30, 117-131
Bird, R.M., 233
Birth rates
  demographic change and, 2, 3
  urban economic transformation
    and, 121, 122, 124
Blacks
  demographic change in cities and,
    54-55
  poverty in cities and, 36-38, 47
  state legislatures with, 200-201
  white migration from cities and,
    38, 39
Block grants, 192
Bombardier, Gary, 173
Bonds
  industrial aid, 107
  mortgage revenue, 267
Boskin, M., 283
Boston, 91, 92, 106
Boston Economic Development and
    Industry Commission, 106
Bradbury, K., 103, 104, 105, 110
Bradford, D., 100-101, 102, 104,
    113, 114
Break, George, 263
Buckley, Robert M., 273-285
Buckwalter, D.W., 195
Business locational choice, 105-113
  demand and, 107-110
  econometric evidence on, 107-113
  factors affecting, 70-71, 105
  financial obstacles to growth and,
    126-127
  local government revenue and,
    206-207
  match between companies and cit-
    ies in, 128-129
  physical attributes of cities and,
    126
  research methods for, 105-106

  supply and, 110-113
  variables in, 68-69

Cable television, 69-70, 74, 76
California, tax reform in, 133, 154,
    209, 230, 248, 250, 251-252
Carter administration, 198
  federal aid programs under, 151,
    248
  local government revenue under,
    231
Catalog of Federal Domestic Assist-
    ance (CFDA), 168, 175
Cavanagh, T.E., 201
Cellular radio, 69
Census
  1960, 84
  1970, 84
  1980, 52
Central business district (CBD)
  communications and data process-
    ing (CDP) and, 72-73
  industrial decentralization and, 27
  locational decisions and, 70-71,
    84, 91, 99, 100, 102, 113
Central cities
  black population changes in, 54-55
  business locational choice and, 106
  federal aid programs and, 150
  future prospects for, 44-47
  manufacturing jobs in, 55-56
  migration and, 38, 39, 44, 47
  population and household changes
    in, 53-54
  residential locational choice and,
    101, 102
  state and federal aid to, 56
Charney, A.H., 112-113
Chernick, Howard, 173, 182
Chicago, 99-100, 107-108
Chinitz, Benjamin, 67-77
Cincinnati, 107, 108-109
Circuit breakers, and local

government revenue, 211
Cities
  benefits of living in, 80
  black poverty in, 36-38
  central, *see* Central cities
  communications and data processing (CDP) and, 70-71, 76
  current economic transformation of, 120-124
  demographic change and, 2-6, 25-48, 52-56
  development of, and demographic change, 6-7
  economic change and, 1-48
  employment changes and, 26-32
  household formation rates and, 36, 53-54
  industrial restructuring and, 14-16, 26-27, 32
  locational decisions and, 70-71
  manufacturing job changes in, 55-56
  migration and, 4, 5, 6, 38-44
  population changes and, 32-38, 53-54
  poverty rates and, 36, 38
  public sector and jobs in, 117-131
  racial composition changes for, 54-55
  state willingness to aid, 195-199
  transformation of economies of, 118-120
  upper income residential revival of, 79-95
  white migration from, 38, 39, 40
Citizens for Tax Justice, 194
Civil service system
  privatization and contracting out and, 239-240
  productivity and, 142-143
  revenue centers and, 240
Clark, 12
Clay, Philip L., 51-64

Cleveland, 108-109, 111, 219, 220
Cline, Robert, 168, 174, 182
Coleman, Henry A., 187-201, 192, 198, 200
Communications and data processing (CDP), 67-77
  contradictory impacts of, 71-74
  labor force and, 75-76
  technology and applications of, 69-70
Community Services Administration, 175
Commuting, and residential locational choice, 81, 98, 99, 104, 113
Comprehensive Employment Training Act (CETA) programs, 150, 163, 248
Computers
  locational decisions and, 72
  productivity monitoring with, 138
  see also Communications and data processing (CDP); Personal computers
Construction sector, and demographic change, 6
Contracts for municipal services, 141, 236-237, 239-240
Cooke, T., 114
Courant, Paul N., 211, 275
Crime rates, and residential locational choice, 83, 102
Current Population Survey, 32

Data processing, *see* Communications and data processing (CDP)
Davis, Albert J., 147-164
DeAre, Diana, 32
Death rates
  population change and, 3
  urban economic tranformation and, 121, 122, 124

Demand, in business locational
    choice, 107-110
Demkovich, L.E., 199
Demographic change, 25-64
    advanced economies and, 2-6
    aging and, 5
    displacement issues in, 63
    household changes and, 5-6
    housing and residential investment
        and, 57-58
    industrial restructuring and, 14-16
    international migration and, 3-4
    labor force changes and, 5
    manufacturing jobs in cities and,
        55-56
    nature of, 2
    nonfamily households and, 54
    policy implications of, 59-63
    population change and, 53-54
    population size and, 2-3
    racial composition of cities and,
        54-55
    trends in, 52-56
    upper income residential location
        and, 82, 83
    urban development and, 6-7
Demsetz, Harold, 135
Department of Housing and Urban
        Development (HUD), 251
    section 8 housing program of, 159
    701 Planning Assistance Program
        of, 199
    Urban Development Action Grant
        (UDAG) Program of, 127,
        128
Detroit, 91, 92, 112-113, 209, 219-
        225
Development policies
    cities and, 61-62
    residential locational choice and,
        93
Diamond, D.B., 99-100, 113
Digital communications, 69

Division of labor, and urban eco-
        nomic changes, 118-119
Divorce rates, 3
Dougherty, A.J., 278, 279
Downs, Anthony, 103, 104, 105,
        110, 150
Downtown area, see Central business
        district (CBD)

Economic change, 25-48
    cities and, 7-21
    communications and data process-
        ing and, 67-68
    current urban transformation in,
        120-124
    energy costs and, 9-10
    industrial reorganization and, 9,
        14-16
    international division of labor and,
        8-10
    macroeconomic policies and, 14,
        16
    management and, 13-14
    per capita income levels by region
        and, 25, 26
    policy making and, 7-8, 16-21
    small firms and job growth and,
        121-124
    transformation of urban economies
        and, 118-120
    trends in sectors in, 10-13
Economic Development Administra-
        tion (EDA), 149, 162, 199
Economic Recovery Tax Act of 1981
        (ERTA), 149, 190, 194, 259
Edelson, Noel, 262, 264
Education
    business locational choice and,
        108, 109
    household patterns in cities and,
        54
    population changes and aid to, 59

residential locational choice and, 82, 101, 103-104

Elazar, D.J., 195, 196

Electronic mail, 70, 72

Eligibility requirements
federal aid programs and, 173-174, 182
housing vouchers and, 295-297

Employment
communications and data processing (CDP) and, 72-73, 75-76
core counties data on shifts in, 27-30
County Business Patterns (CBP) patterns in, 27, 28
current urban, by sector, 124
enterprise zone concept and, 128
financial obstacles to growth in, 126-127
future prospects for, 44-47
intraregional shifts in, 30, 31
match between companies and cities for growth in, 128-129
population changes and, 32, 33-34
public sector programs for, 127-129
regional shifts in, 26-32
residential locational choice and, 103, 104
suburban county gains in, 30-32
urban economic transformation and, 118-124
see also Labor force

Energy costs
economic change and, 9-10
service industries and, 11-12
suburban employment shifts and, 30-32

Energy industries, and economic change, 10, 14

Enterprise zones, 128, 149

Environmental impact statement (EIS), 174-175, 182

Environmental quality, and business locational choice, 110, 111

Equal opportunity regulations, 240

Erikson, R., 109, 112

Evans, R., 190

Family planning, 3

Family
migration and, 4-5
see also Households

Farmers Home Administration (FHA), 149

Federal aid programs
analysis of structure of, 175-183
A-95 grant review in, 173
Carter administration in, 151
change in strategy of, 147-150
decline in amount of, 133-134
discriminant function classification of, 176-177
education policies and, 59
eligibility for, 173-174, 182
environmental impact statements for, 174-175, 182
estimated spending elasticities for, 177-182
federal incentives in, 198-199
fiscal pressures on local government and, 230-231
General Revenue Sharing (GRS) disincentives in, 197-198
grant-specific traits and impact of, 173-175
horizontal imbalance in, 159-160
legal provisions of, 183
local government expenditures and, 245, 247-248, 273-274
local reliance on, 154-155
major redefinitions since 1930s of, 167-168
New Federalism and, 155-158
obstacles to seeking, 171

Omnibus Budget Reconciliation
Act of 1981 (OBRA) and,
191-192
outlook for urban areas in, 199-
201
poverty programs under, 158-159
previous research on, 168-170
program beneficiaries for, 174,
182
program content of, 173
property tax and, 282-285
public finance and, 56, 58-59
public investment in programs and,
162
recipient matching requirements
for, 174, 182-183
revenue sharing in, *see* General
revenue sharing (GRS)
setting priorities for programs under, 158
spillover rationale in, 161-162
state or local governments as
agents in, 162-163
state planning requirement in, 173
structural character of, 167-184
Types A, B, and C grants in, 169-
170
urban policies and, 18, 148-149
vertical imbalance in, 160-161
Federal government
budget constraints in, 251
cities and migration and, 47
economic change and urban policies of, 19
local and state governments and,
see Intergovernmental
relations
Federal Outlays reports (Community
Services Administration), 175
Federal Reserve System, 190
Fees-for-service, in public finance,
232-233, 234, 239
Female-headed households, and poverty in cities, 36-38, 47

Fiber-optic systems, 69
Finance, *see* Public finance
Fischel, W., 110, 111
Fisher, Ronald C., 205-225, 209,
216
Fitzgerald, S., 198
Fleetwood, Blake, 79
Food stamp programs, 150, 156,
159, 199
Fox, William, 110, 111, 112, 173
Frey, W.H., 101, 104, 105, 113

General Accounting Office (GAO),
198
General Revenue Sharing (GRS), 169
federal disincentives in, 197-198
local government revenue and,
213-214
vertical imbalance in federal pro-
grams and, 160-161
Gentrification, 57, 80
Gold, S.D., 194
Government, *see* Federal govern-
ment; Intergovernmental sys-
tem; Local government; State
government
Gramlich, Edward, 168, 169-170,
275, 283
Grants, *see* Federal aid programs
Great Society programs, 168
Green, Roy, 171
Greene, K.V., 217
Grubb, W.N., 102, 104, 110, 113
Guzzardi, W., Jr., 189, 195, 196

Hamer, A.M., 106
Hamilton, B.W., 100, 103
Harrison, Bennett, 27
Hausman, J., 283
Headley Amendment (Michigan),
250
Hendershott, P., 277, 279, 280-282
Hicks, U.K., 169

High technology industries, 11, 14
Hirsch, Werner Z., 133-145, 173, 237
Hoffman, D., 194
Homestead exemptions, and local government revenue, 211
Households
    demographic changes in cities and, 2, 5-6, 7
    future prospects for, 44
    growth rates for, 53-54
    housing and residential investment and, 57
    local government expenditures and, 246-247
    local government policy and changes in, 54
    median income by region and type of place and, 36, 37
    migration and, 40
    nonfamily, 54, 59
    population changes and formation rates for, 35-36
    residential location choice and, 85-86
House price
    capital costs and, 265-266, 277-280
    future research needs for, 265-269
    housing market and determination of, 258-261
    local government and, 257-269
    mortgage revenue bonds and, 267
    specification of expected appreciation in, 266
Housing
    demographic change and, 57-58
    displacement issues in, 63
    economic change and policies for, 18
    federal aid and programs for, 159
    future prospects for, 44
    gentrification and, 57

residential locational choice and, 83, 104
    tenure choice and, 280-282
Housing and Urban Development Act of 1970, 290
Housing Payments Program (housing vouchers), 289-304
    cost of, 297-299
    design of, 293-297
    economic and accounting models of, 300-304
    financial issues in, 297-300
    prototype plans for, 291-293
    source of money for, 299-300
    standards, eligibility, and payment schedules in, 295-297
    undesirable features in, 293-295
Hu, S., 277, 278
HUD, *see* Department of Housing and Urban Development (HUD)

Income
    household formation rates and, 36, 37, 44
    migration preferences and, 40, 43-44, 45-46
    per capita, by cities, 56
    per capita, by region, 25, 26
    poverty in cities and, 36-38
    rent-gradient location choice model and, 98-100, 113
    residential locational choice and, 100-101
Income redistribution policies, 47, 158-159
Income taxes
    fees-for-services and user charges and, 239
    local government use of, 208-209, 211, 212-214
    state government use of, 193

Individual Retirement Accounts
    (IRAs), 214
Industrial aid bonds, 107
Industries
    decentralization by, 26-27
    economic change and reorganiza-
        tion of, 9
    energy costs and growth of, 9-10
    future prospects for, 44-47
    locational choices of, *see* Business
        locational choice
    match between cities and, for job
        growth, 128-129
    small firms and job growth and,
        121-124
    urban and regional differentiation
        in, 14-16
    urban economic changes and, 118-
        119
Inman, R.P., 216
Intergovernmental system, 187-201
    federal aid program changes and,
        147-164
    horizontal imbalance in, 159-160
    limits on state government aid to
        localities in, 189-195
    Omnibus Budget Reconciliation
        Act of 1981 (OBRA) and,
        191-192
    public investment in programs and,
        162
    role of states in, 188-189
    spillover rationale in, 161-162
    state debt and, 190-191
    state or local governments as fed-
        eral agents in, 162-163
    state willingness to aid urban areas
        and, 195-199
    vertical imbalance in, 160-161
Internal Revenue Code, 216, 290
International migration, and demo-
        graphic changes, 3-4, 7
International trade, and urban eco-
        nomic change, 119

Jobs, *see* Employment
Johnson, Michael S., 257-269

Kaiser Committee, 290
Kansas City, 108-109
Kelejian, H., 100-101, 102, 104,
    113
Kern, Clifford R., 79-95
Kohlhase, Janet E., 205-225, 209

Labor force
    business locational choice and,
        110, 112, 113, 114, 126
    communications and data process-
        ing (CDB) and, 75-76
    demographic change and, 2, 5
    economic changes and interna-
        tional, 8-10
    industrial decentralization and, 26-
        27
    migration patterns and, 41
    see also Employment
Ladd, Helen F., 277
Land
    business locational choice and,
        105, 109, 112
    residential locational choice and,
        98, 99, 104, 113
Land use restrictions
    business locational choice and, 126
    house prices and, 262, 268
Laren, D., 283
Lawson, J., 192
Lea, Michael J., 257-269
Leibenstein, Harvey, 135
Local government
    advisory commissions on produc-
        tivity in, 144-145
    civil service provisions and, 142-
        143
    competitive environment for pro-
        ductivity in, 140-141
    contracting out or privatization of

services in, 141, 236-237, 239-240
decision making participation in, 61
demographic change and, 52, 60-61
economic change and policies of, 17-18, 20, 21
employee liability for failure to deliver and, 144
as federal agent in aid programs, 162-163
federal aid program reliance by, 154-155
federal aid program strategy changes and, 148, 149
federal and state governments and, *see* Intergovernmental system
finance and, *see* Public finance
fiscal pressures on, 230-231
household change and, 54
income redistribution programs and, 158-159
industrial aid bonds and, 107
legal changes for productivity in, 142-144
limits on state government aid to, 189-195
managers and productivity in, 139-140
managing population impacts in, 61-62
migration and, 63
mortgage revenue bonds from, 267
prevailing wage laws and, 143
productivity bargaining in, 139
productivity increases in, 133-145
public investment in programs and, 162
residency requirements for employment in, 143
shirking-monitoring framework for, 137-139

social forces and, 62-63
state willingness to aid, 195-199
tax reform movements and, 61
vertical integration of, for productivity, 141-142
Local government expenditures, 243-254
federal aid and, 273-274
financial markets and, 252
future directions in, 253-254
house prices and, 257-269
New Federalism and, 252, 253-254
pattern and composition of, 245-250
property tax and, 273-285
service costs and, 250
spending composition under, 248-250
spending levels in, 245-248
statutory and constitutional limitations on, 250-252
Local government revenue, 205-225
capital financing and borrowing costs and, 214-215
circuit breakers and, 211
emerging issues in, 211-219
homestead exemptions and, 211
local sales and income taxes and, 212-214
Metropolitan Area Revenue Sharing (MARS) and, 219-225
past trends in, 206-211
regional taxation and base sharing in, 217-219
relationship between federal and subnational government taxes in, 215-217
revenue sharing and, 213-214
state and federal aid and, 56, 58-59
tax limitations and, 209-211
Local Public Works programs, 248

Locational choice, *see* Business locational choice; Residential locational choice
Long, John, 30
Long, Larry, 32, 41
Los Angeles, 138-139
Lynn, James T., 290

McCarthy, Kevin, 48
MacCracken, Susan J., 117-131
Mail, electronic, 70, 72
Managers and management
  economic change and, 13-14
  horizontal movement in, 140
  productivity and, 139-140
  professionalization of, 139-140
  recognition programs in, 140
Manufacturing
  cities and changes in, 32, 55-56
  economic change and, 10-11, 14, 15
  employment shifts in, 27, 30, 32
  federal aid programs and, 147-148
  urban economic change and, 119-120, 124
Marden, Lily Ann, 273-285
Market factors, and business locational choice, 105
Marriage trends, 3
Massachusetts, tax reform in, 133, 230, 250
Medicaid, 156, 169, 192, 194
Medicare, 169
Menchik, M., 230, 240
Metropolitan Area Revenue Sharing (MARS) program, 206, 217, 219-225
  in Cleveland, 221
  constraints and conclusions on, 223-225
  county vs. metropolitan area, 223
  in Detroit, 220
  distributional effects of, 221-223

tax sharing formula in, 220
Michigan, 250
Microwave transmission, 69
Middle class, and locational decisions, 101
Mieszkowski, P., 275, 276, 280
Migration
  black poverty in cities and, 36-38
  cities and, 38-44
  demographic change and, 3-5, 6, 7
  future regional preferences in, 41-43
  household formation rates and, 36
  household type and, 40
  industrial restructuring and, 14
  internal, and demographic change, 4-5, 6
  international, and demographic change, 3-4, 7
  interregional, 41, 42
  local politics and, 63
  into nonmetropolitan areas, 40-41
  regional growth and, 52-53
  residential locational choice and, 101, 102-103
  size of place and, 43-44, 45-46
  suburbs and, 47, 86-87, 88-90, 101
  urban economic transformation and, 121, 122, 124
  white out-city, 38, 39, 40
Miller, E., 170, 182
Miller, M.J., 200
Mills, Edwin, 26, 98
Minneapolis-St. Paul metropolitan area, 102-103, 108-109, 141, 218, 219
Minority populations
  demographic changes in cities and, 54-55
  federal aid programs and, 147
  revenue centers in public financing and, 240

see also Blacks
Misczynski, D.J., 239
Monitoring local government productivity, 137, 138
Mortality rates, and population changes, 3
Mortgage revenue bonds, 267
Moses, L., 107
Municipal government, *see* Local government
Mushkin, S.J., 233
Muth, R., 98

Nathan, R.P., 197
National Association of State Legislators, 198
National Environmental Protection Act, 171
National Governors' Association, 156, 198
Neenan, W.B., 217
Nelson, Kathryn P., 25-48, 27, 38
New Deal, 168
New Federalism, 97, 198
    changes under, 155-156
    federal aid and, 167
    future prospects for, 183-184, 253-254
    house prices and, 268
    local government expenditures and, 244, 252, 253-254, 275
    local government revenue and, 211
    outlook for urban areas with, 199, 201
    responses to, 156-158
    setting priorities for programs under, 158
    state responsibility under, 161
New York City, 111, 206
    contracting out services in, 236-237
    local revenue sources in, 207, 213

residential locational choice study in, 84-91, 93
Noto, Nonna A., 147-164
Noyelle, T.V., 12
Nuclear energy, and economic changes, 10

Oakland, W.H., 110, 111, 112, 275
Oates, W.E., 100, 104
Office of Management and Budget (OMB), 192
O'Hare, W.P., 201
Oil crisis, 2, 8, 9
Okner, B.A., 283
Olsen, E., 284
Olson, G.W., 191
Omnibus Budget Reconciliation Act of 1981 (OBRA), 191-192, 193, 200

Pascal, Anthony H., 229-240
Patrick, Clifford, 27
Pechman, J.A., 283
Personal computers, 70
    labor force and, 76
    location decisions and, 72
Petersen, John E., 214-215
Peterson, G.E., 200
Peterson, George, 209
Philadelphia, 91, 92, 208-209
Pierce, N.R., 199
Policy, *see* Public policy
Pollakowski, H.O., 100
Population change
    annual rate of, 32-35
    cities and, 32-38, 47, 53-54
    demographic trends in, 2-3
    education policies and, 59
    employment shifts and, 32, 33-34, 47
    household formation changes and, 35-36
    impact of losses in, 35-36

local government expenditures and, 246-247
local policy implications of, 60-61
managing impact of, 61-62
residential locational choice and, 87, 93-95
social forces and, 62-63
state-aid formulas and, 59
urban economic change and, 119-120
Population density, and business locational choice, 108, 109, 113, 114
Porter, David, 171
Porter, Teddie, 171
Postlethwaite, A.J., 91, 92
Poverty
    blacks in cities and, 36-38, 47
    cities and rates for, 36, 38
    federal aid programs and, 147, 148, 149-150, 158-159
    migration into nonmetropolitan areas and, 40-41
    suburban, 48
President's Commission on Housing, 289-290
President's Urban Policy Report, 189, 191
Prevailing wage laws, 143
Prince Georges' County, Maryland, 250
Productivity
    advisory commissions on, 144-145
    civil service changes and, 142-143
    competitive environment for, 140-141
    contracting out of privatization of services and, 141
    employee liability for failure to deliver and, 144
    legal changes and, 142-144
    local government and, 133-145
    monitoring, 137, 138

municipal managers and, 139-140
prevailing wage laws and, 143
productivity bargaining in, 139
residency requirement laws for employment and, 143
shirking-monitoring framework and, 135-139
vertical integration of municipal government and, 141-142
X-efficiency and X-inefficiency in, 135
Professionalization of municipal managers, 139-140
Property tax
    business locational choice and, 106, 107, 108, 109, 110, 112-113
    circuit breakers and, 211
    city revenue from, 207
    demographic changes and, 57, 58
    excise tax effects of, 284-285
    homeownership cost of capital and, 277-280
    homestead exemptions and, 211
    house prices and, 263-264
    local government and, 273-285
    local revenue limitations and, 209-211
    reforms in, 133
    special assessments and, 239
    tenure choice and, 280-282
Proposition 2½, 58, 235
Proposition 13, 58, 154, 209, 235, 248, 250, 251-252
Public finance, 229-240
    benefit-based financing in, 232-234
    centrally provided capital and labor services in, 237-238
    civil service changes in, 239-240
    contracting out services in, 236-237, 239-240
    demographic change and, 56-59
    equity protection in, 238-239

fees-for-service in, 232-233, 239
financing essential city in, 235
fiscal pressures on local govern-
    ment and, 230-231
house prices and, 263
housing and residential investment
    and, 57-58
identifying essential services in,
    234-235
interjurisdictional service provi-
    sions in, 238
load sharing in, 236
nonfamily households and, 59
organizing responsive city in, 235-
    236
policy implications for, 59-63
projecting available revenue in,
    234
property tax and, 282-285
reforming, 231-240
revenue centers and, 239, 240
special assessments in, 232, 233,
    237, 239
tax base and, 58
transition to responsive city in,
    239-240
user charges in, 232-233
Public policy
    communications and data process-
        ing (CDP) and, 74, 75
    current urban transformation and,
        124-129
    development of cities and, 61-62
    economic change and, 7-8, 14, 16-
        21
    federal aid programs and, 148-149
    job creation and, 126
    match between industries and cities
        in, 128-129
    population changes and, 61-62
    residential locational choice and,
        91-95
Public sector, *see* Federal govern-

ment; Local government;
    State government
Puryear, David L., 218-219, 243-254

Quigley, John M., 289-304

Racial factors
    demographic changes in cities and,
        54-55
    poverty in cities and, 36-38
    residential locational choice and,
        104-105
    white migration from cities and,
        38, 39
Railroad access, in business loca-
    tional choice, 108, 109
Reagan administration
    federal aid programs and, 148,
        149, 150, 151, 231
    New Federalism and, 155-158,
        167, 198
    tax changes under, 149, 151-154
Recognition programs for managers,
    140
Reed, B.J., 171
Refuse collection, and productivity
    programs, 141
Regional areas
    employment and shifts in, 26-32
    industrial decentralization and, 26-
        27
    migration between, 41-43, 47, 52-
        53
    per capita income levels in, 25, 26
    taxation and base sharing in, 217-
        219
Rehabilitation Tax Credit, 149
Reigeluth, George A., 117-131
Renaud, Bertrand, 1-21
Rent-gradient location models, 98-
    100
Reschovsky, A., 102-103, 104, 113

Residency requirements, and municipal employment, 143
Residential locational choice, 81-82
   amenities and, 100-104
   changes in residential behavior
      and, 83-84
   demographic change and, 82, 83
   education and, 101, 103-104
   household changes and, 85-86
   income level and, 86-87, 100-101
   local government revenue and,
      206-207
   New York City study of, 84-91
   1960s patterns in, 84-87
   1970-1976 patterns in, 87-91
   population changes and, 87
   public policy and, 91-95
   racial prejudice and, 104-105
   rent-gradient models in, 98-100
   suburbs and, 86-87, 88-90
Retirement programs, 4-5, 138-139
Revenue centers, and municipal finance, 239, 240
Revenues, city, see Local government revenues
Revenue sharing, see General Reve-
   nue Sharing (GRS); Metropol-
   itan Area Revenue Sharing
   (MARS)
Reynolds v. Sims, 195
Roberts, J.F., 197
Rosen, H.S., 277
Rosen, K.T., 277
Rosenberg, L., 277
Ross, John P., 243-254
Rothenberg, Jerome, 93
Rural areas, and migration, 4, 7, 43,
   48

St. Louis, 91, 92
St. Paul, 102-103, 108-109, 218,
   219
Sales tax

local government use of, 207-208,
   209, 212-214
state government use of, 193
Saltzstein, Allan, 171
San Francisco, 91, 92, 99, 104
Satellites, communication, 69
Savas, E.S., 236
Schmenner, R.W., 107, 108, 109
Schultz, C.L., 169
Services sector
   communications and data process-
      ing (CDP) and, 75
   economic change and, 11-13
   employment shifts in, 27, 30, 32
   locational decisions and, 69
   urban economic changes and, 120,
      124
701 Planning Assistance Program,
   199
Shannon, J., 232, 233
Shilling, J.S., 277, 279, 280-282
Shirking-monitoring framework
      basis for, 135-137
   local government and, 137-139
Shoup, D.C., 233
Simonson, John C., 273-285
Smith, Adam, 134
Solid state electronics, 69
Special assessments, and public fi-
      nance, 232, 233, 237, 239
Stanfield, R.L., 191, 192, 194, 195
State government
   cities and migration and, 47
   debt and policies of, 190-191
   as federal agent in aid programs,
      162-163
   income redistribution programs
      and, 158-159
   limits on abilities to aid localities
      by, 189-195
   local and federal governments and,
      see Intergovernmental system
   New Federalism and, 156, 161

planning requirements for federal grants from, 173, 182
population trends and, 59
public finance and, 56, 58-59
public investment in programs and, 162
representatives of legislatures in, 195-196, 200
target assistance from, 196-199
tax reform movements in, 58
tax revenues to, 193-195
willingness to aid urban areas by, 195-199
Stein, Robert M., 167-184, 171
Steinman, Michael, 173
Steinnes, D., 114
Stenberg, C.W., 192
Stephens, G.R., 191, 198
Sternlieb, George, 93
Stigler, G., 106
Stocker, F.D., 213, 232
Stockton, D., 201
Subsidies, federal, *see* Federal aid programs
Suburbs
changes in residential behavior in, 83-84
communications and data processing (CDP) and, 70-71, 76
employment shifts in, 27, 28, 30-32, 48
factors affecting move to, 103-104
future prospects for, 48
local government finance and, 238
locational decisions and, 70-71
migration patterns and, 47, 48
racial prejudice and, 104-105
residential locational choice of, 81-82, 86-87, 88-90, 101, 103-104
tax base in, 58
Supply, in business locational choice, 110-113
Supreme Court, 195-196, 200

Tax Equity and Fiscal Responsibility Act of 1982 (TEFRA), 151
Taxes
business locational choice and, 105, 106, 107, 108, 109, 110, 113-114
economic change and planning for, 17
federal aid programs and, 159, 160
fees-for-service in local finance and, 232-233, 234, 239
housing market and, 259-260
local revenue limitations and, 209-211
manufacturing jobs in cities and, 55
neighborhood special, 237
New Federalism programs and, 155-158
public disenchantment with, 230
public finance and base in, 58
Reagan administration changes in, 149, 151-154
reform movement in, 58, 61, 133, 154, 206, 230, 235, 250-251
relationship between federal and subnational government, 215-217
residential locational choice and, 100, 101, 102, 103, 104, 105
special assessments in local finance and, 232, 233, 237, 239
state revenues from, 193-195
tax base sharing in, 217-225
user charges in local finance and, 232-233
Telecommunications, 74; *see also* Communications and data processing (CDP)
Teleconferencing, 70, 76
Telephone, and location decisions, 72
Television, cable, 69-70, 74, 76

302 Program (Economic Development Administration), 199
Tiebout, 100, 104
Trade
  labor changes and, 8
  urban economic changes and, 119
Transportation, and business locational choice, 105, 108, 109
TRIM, Prince Georges' County, Maryland, 250

Unemployment
  economic change and, 8
  population change and, 3
Upper income levels
  city residency and, 79-95
  demographic change and, 82, 83
  New York City study of, 84-91
  1970-1976 changes in, 88, 89
  rent-gradient choice model and, 98, 99
  residential locational choice and, 81-82
  suburbs and, 86-87
Urban areas, *see* Cities
Urban Development Action Grant (UDAG) Program, 127, 128
Urbanization, and demographic change, 2, 14
User charges, in public finance, 232-233

Van Order, R.A., 278, 279
Voting Rights Act of 1965, 196

Wage laws, and productivity, 143
Walker, D.B., 193
Warner, David, 171
Warren, C.R., 196, 197, 198, 199
Wasylenko, Michael J., 97-114, 109, 111, 112
Wheaton, W.C., 99, 100, 104, 113
White House Conference on Balanced National Growth and Economic Development, 198
Whites
  demographic change in cities and, 54-55
  migration from cities by, 38, 39, 40
  see also Racial factors
Whitman, Ray, 168, 174, 182
Williamson, H., Jr., 107
Wood, Colin L., 187-201, 192, 200
Wright, Deil, 167

X-efficiency and X-inefficiency, 135

Yinger, John M., 262

Zoning
  business locational choice and, 110-111, 126
  house prices and, 262, 263